T0351267

Varieties of Family Business

Hartmut Berghoff is an economic and business historian and the director of the Institute of Economic and Social History at the University of Göttingen in Germany. He has been the director of the German Historical Institute in Washington, D.C. from 2008 to 2015. He held various visiting positions at the Center of Advanced Study in Berlin, at Harvard Business School and Maison des sciences de l'homme in Paris, and the Henley Business School in the UK.

Ingo Köhler is an economic and business historian at the Humboldt University of Berlin. He has been Interim Professor for Economic History at the Universities of Goettingen (2013–15) and Bonn (2016), and Fellow of the German Historical Institute in Washington, D.C. in 2007.

Hartmut Berghoff, Ingo Köhler

Varieties of Family Business

Germany and the United States, Past and Present

Edited by the Foundation for Family Businesses
(Stiftung Familienunternehmen) in Munich

Campus Verlag
Frankfurt/New York

Foundation for
Family Businesses

ISBN 978-3-593-51246-4 Print
ISBN 978-3-593-44531-1 E-Book (PDF)
ISBN 978-3-593-44530-4 E-Book (EPUB)

Copyright © 2021 Campus Verlag GmbH, Frankfurt-on-Main
Cover design: Campus Verlag GmbH, Frankfurt-on-Main
Cover illustration: Cover picture of the magazine "Nation's Business: A General Magazine for Businessmen" (company name in picture has been changed), edited by the Chamber of Commerce of the United States (March 1933) © Courtesy of Hagley Museum and Library
Typesetting: publish4you, Engelskirchen
Printing office and bookbinder: Beltz Grafische Betriebe GmbH, Bad Langensalza
Printed in Germany

For further information:
www.campus.de
www.press.uchicago.edu

Contents

Acknowledgments

This book offers readers a comparative history of family businesses in the United States and Germany. Its findings are based on a research project conducted by the Institute for Economic and Social History at the University of Göttingen, a project that was initiated, in many ways supported and financed by the Foundation for Family Businesses (Stiftung Familienunternehmen) in Munich.

The foundation enabled us to develop a research concept that pursues new methodological approaches and perspectives. A review of the research landscape in the history of family businesses shows that case studies have been the primary approach used on both sides of the Atlantic. Most academic publications—and popular studies as well—have focused on individual companies and families. In contrast, we were less interested in individual cases. Instead, we approach the topic from a macro-perspective that allows us to observe the fundamental historic transformation processes that occurred in these two economic systems and cultures. Our guiding question is: To what extent did dissimilar institutional structures affect the existence, success and shape of family businesses in the United States and Germany over the long term? Our comparison of economic, socio-cultural and political conditions uncovers both distinctions and similarities in the historic development of family businesses. The common goal of the foundation and the authors is to outline a historical matrix that will allow future research to better place the individual company histories into the general development contexts. This serves two purposes: the much-debated differences between US shareholder and central European stakeholder capitalism can be seen in a new light, and the motives, path-dependencies and decision-making processes of companies and their owners become historically transparent.

In particular, we would like to express our gratitude to the Executive Board and Advisory Board of the Foundation for Family Businesses, which made this project possible. We would like to say a special word of thanks to Professor Rainer Kirchdörfer and Stefan Heidbreder, both of whom take a great interest in historical questions. We have pleasant memories of the stimulating discussions during our many meetings. Their knowledgeable notes and constructive questions contributed significantly to the quality of this study. We would also like to express our sincere gratitude to Dr. Bettina Wurster and Georg Blaha of the department of research and programs at the Foundation for Family Businesses. They supported us in many ways and patiently acquainted themselves with the work approaches that we apply as historians. Sibylle Gausing shouldered a number of rigorous editorial rounds. Her careful reviews of the manuscript, her valuable assistance with preparations for printing and the translation of the work into English lent the text the right form and gave it a finishing linguistic touch. We would also like to thank Charline Köhler of the foundation team for her tireless work in searching for historic photographs. Finally, the external proofreaders Jutta Pulter and Christel Schikora spotted many a linguistic or spelling mistake. Mary Tannert, Ph.D. skillfully translated the German version of this book into English with great professionalism and attention to detail.

Many people at the Göttingen Institute for Economic and Social History also contributed to the success of this project. Yassin Abou El Fadil worked very patiently and thoroughly to compile a large number of data and literature sources, generated statistics and offered insightful comments. Our student assistants made many trips to the library and tirelessly provided us with books, scans and copies. Sören Windeler did a tremendous job in preparing the index.

Finally, we would like to express our special thanks to Jürgen Hotz of the publishing company Campus Verlag GmbH, who turned our bare-bones study into two beautiful books published in German and English. He patiently assisted us with the selection of the design, title and illustrations, and drew on his design know-how and experience to make a valuable contribution to many details.

Family businesses embody history as no other form of company does. We hope that you enjoy our book and gain some new insights into the history and current state of family businesses from it.

Hartmut Berghoff and Ingo Köhler
Göttingen/Berlin, October 2020

Preview: The Key Results

Family businesses play an important economic role on both sides of the Atlantic. In addition to some parallels, there are also significant differences between Germany and America in terms of corporate and family cultures as well as the institutional environment for, and the lifespan of, family businesses.

This study investigates the differences and similarities between the development of family businesses in Germany and the United States from the mid-19th to the early 21st century. It analyses the causes and effects of the different corporate landscapes using a long-term, historical view. The focus is on the position of family companies in the two countries and the legal, structural, political and cultural environments that have emerged historically and influence the strategies of businesses and the families who own them. At a general level, the study concludes that the institutional fabric in Germany favored the development of multigenerational family businesses, while that of the United States tended to promote the dynamism of young companies, whose owners sold off all or parts of them after relatively short periods of ownership. German family businesses are, on average, much older than their US counterparts and more often focus on achieving intergenerational continuity.

Chapter A clarifies terminology and the statistical basis, while Chapter B provides a quantitative chronological overview. In Chapter C, the authors examine in detail the history of inheritance law, which for a long time was substantially less advantageous for family-business owners in the United States than for their German counterparts.

Chapter D compares the financing models of businesses in both countries. The German system of bank-based financing was diametrically opposed to America's capital-market-based system, which favored the rapid shift from family control to listed companies with a broad shareholder base. In Germany, on the other hand, long-lasting relationships between family businesses and their house banks were the order of the day, tending to promote continuity and a long-term mindset. Major differences in antitrust law pointed in the same direction. In the United States, there was a strong concentration of gigantic listed companies, whereas founder families continued to play a key role in some of Germany's biggest industrial companies for a very long time.

Politically, the German state played a role in ensuring the fortunes of the country's economy, especially the *Mittelstand* (small and medium-sized firms). This reflected Germany's economic model of cooperative capitalism. In the liberal market economy of the US, on the other hand, faith in market self-regulation remained strong. As Chapter E shows, state interventionism in this area did not start to increase until the second half of the 20th century and, in contrast to Germany, was relatively moderate and always controversial. Only after the crises of the 1970s did industrial policy in both countries tend to converge.

The differences in the two countries' corporate landscapes reach in part far back in history and are based on deep-rooted cultural characteristics— as Chapters F and G demonstrate. In Germany, the legacy of feudalism and the craft tradition left a lasting mark. A culture of continuity and quality, of balance and family associations, arose. In the US, individualism was much stronger, with the self-made man—not the preserver of family traditions— becoming the ideal. Uninterrupted immigration provided a steady flow of entrepreneurial talent: the US truly had no shortage of business founders. This energized the business community, but also made for cut-throat competition.

In Germany, a variety of factors—from the country's relative lack of raw materials to its multiple political upheavals—underscored the importance of solidarity within founding families, leading to a search for stable anchorage in the family in general and in family businesses in particular.

As multigenerational projects, family businesses were on the defensive in both countries throughout the 20th century—initially in the United States, where a modern consumer society arose much earlier than in Germany, offering potential successors options beyond traditional family roles and the world of family businesses. In general, however, since the last third of the 20th century, processes of convergence have been observable in a number of the areas examined here, processes that have worn down existing divergences without eliminating them altogether. The path dependencies attributable to the different types of capitalism in the two countries thus not only reach far into the past, they also have tremendous power to shape both the present and the future.

A. Introduction. Current Observations and Historical Questions

Across the globe, there are more family-owned enterprises than any other type of company. Regardless of their size or legal form, they are defined as companies under significant family control—usually through majority ownership of the company's capital, but occasionally also through multiple voting rights or pyramid structures. In the case of listed corporations, a blocking minority of 25 percent held by a single family or related families is often sufficient for the company to qualify as a family business. Owner-managed companies, i.e. those in which family members perform management duties, are a smaller sub-group within this broad definition of family businesses.

According to the Family Firm Institute of Boston, which largely follows this definition, in the second decade of the 21st century around two-thirds of all companies worldwide were family businesses, generating 70–90 percent of global gross national product (GNP) and providing 50–80 percent of jobs. These ratios are much higher in certain countries.[1] Figures like these initially reflect the enormous significance of small businesses and micro-enterprises: "Mom and pop stores [...] tend to be owned by mom and pop"[2] and—statistically speaking—make up the majority of family businesses.

Family businesses as such are no better or worse than companies constituted in other ways, and are strongly represented in both dynamic and stagnating economies. Family businesses are trust-based, highly innovative entities in which employees, owners and management alike exhibit exceptionally high levels of loyalty and intrinsic motivation. They benefit from low transaction costs, good reputations, the mobilization of family resources, the transfer of knowledge and skills within the family, and a long-term perspective. Researchers with a different perspective, on the other hand, emphasize the lack of both transparency and efficiency in family businesses, in which insiders are free to act without external control and nepotism crowds out the principle of merit. They say that oligarchs have a tendency towards political corruption and "rent-seeking". In their opinion, family businesses are conservative, averse to competition, and exhibit poor corporate governance.[3]

The advantages and disadvantages of family businesses certainly cannot be weighed up against each other wholesale, as they are visible only in individual cases. The objective of this study is thus not to pass judgement on the strengths and weaknesses of family businesses. Rather, it examines the hypothesis that the role of family businesses is a key distinguishing feature between the USA and UK on the one hand, and western and southern European countries on the other, between capital-market-driven Anglo-American capitalism and a model of capitalism in which not only social security schemes, but also family businesses play a bigger role.[4] This study focuses in particular on the United States and Germany, which are the most important exponents of these disparate systems, and uses a long-term historical comparison to investigate the extent and the causes of the contrasting status that family businesses enjoy in these two countries.

The first step is to thoroughly examine the key differences between the two economies today, taking that as a basis to look at their differing historical developments. If we compare the proportion of family businesses to the total number of companies in both countries, we initially see that they are closely matched.

Table 1: Quantitative significance of family businesses, 2014

	In percent of all companies	In percent of all employees	Revenue in percent of GDP
USA	80–90	57	57
Germany	95	56	63

Source: Economic Impact of Family Businesses and Family Firm Institute, Global Data Points.

The figures published by the Family Firm Institute (Table 1) show a similar presence of family businesses in Germany and the US in 2014. In the categories "in percent of all companies" and "revenues in percent of gross domestic product", Germany has a slight lead over the US and occupies the top position worldwide. When it comes to employees of family businesses as a share of all employees, the corresponding figures of 57 percent and 56 percent are virtually identical. On the basis of statistics published by the Mannheim Enterprise Panel (MUP) of the Centre for European Economic Research (ZEW) in 2014, the Foundation for Family Businesses calculated somewhat lower figures for Germany in 2013—91 percent (percentage of all companies) and 48 percent (revenue percentage)—while the employee percentage was the same, at 56 percent. The figure for owner-managed family businesses as a percentage of all companies in Germany was 87 percent.[5]

Table 2: Percentage shares of different forms of family businesses in the UK, France, Germany and the US, 2000–2003

	UK	France	Germany	USA
Family is largest shareholder	30%	32%	30%	10%
Family is largest shareholder, business is owner-managed	23%	22%	12%	7%
Family is largest shareholder, business is owner-managed plus primogeniture	15%	14%	3%	3%
Founder is largest shareholder	14%	18%	5%	18%
Founder is largest shareholder and CEO	12%	10%	2%	11%
Number of companies examined	152	137	156	290

Source: Bloom and Van Reenen, "Measuring", p. 58.

Consequently, family businesses are by no means a marginal phenomenon in the US. Indeed, they constitute a substantial share of the economy. Nonetheless, their significance differs considerably between the two countries—as a glance at medium-sized and large companies reveals. A representative sample of 735 selected medium-sized manufacturing companies in France, Germany, Great Britain and the US for the period 2000–2003 was, in the authors' opinion, "reasonably representative of medium-sized manufacturing firms" (50–10,000 employees). This sample makes it possible to compare the significance of family businesses in this segment (which, expressed more precisely, comprises medium-sized and small major companies). An analysis of these, more precisely, medium-sized and small major industrial enterprises with their differing legal forms and ownership structures (see Table 2) shows that the percentage of family businesses in this category was significantly lower in the US. The corresponding figures for European countries were, on the whole, quite comparable to each other and higher than in the US. This was the same for both family-controlled and family-managed companies. In both categories, German companies had a much higher percentage share than the US.[6]

It is notable, however, that the US had a substantially higher percentage of first-generation (= founder-generation) companies than Germany, meaning that founders played a much bigger role in the economy than family businesses of the second or later generations. There are comparatively many business founders in the US, but over successive generations, there is a pronounced movement away from family ownership—one not evident to the same extent in Germany. In other words, the lifespan of American family businesses appears to be shorter and the probability of their transformation into other types of company is higher.[7] One could also—and this is a key argument—speak of a comparatively strong start-up culture in the US and a relatively strong culture of multigenerational family businesses in Germany.

Table 3: Share of family businesses among the biggest companies in the US and Germany, 2013–2015 (in absolute and percentage terms)

	100 largest companies		200 largest companies	
	absolute	*in %*	*absolute*	*in %*
USA	7	7	13	6.5
Germany	21	21	42	21

Sources: Own survey on the basis of statistics from Fortune 500 (see Note 8), Top 500 Unternehmen (see Note 9) and the Global Family Business Index (see Note 10).

Striking differences are also observable if we leave the segment of medium-sized and small major enterprises, and turn to the family businesses among the very largest companies. The largest US and German companies by revenue in 2014 and 2015 respectively were recorded using the figures in the

Fortune 500 list[8] and the Top 500 Unternehmen (Top 500 Companies) list published by *Die Welt,* a German daily newspaper.[9] In order to calculate the share of family businesses among the top 100 and top 200 biggest companies in both countries, these two lists were then compared with the Global Family Business Index (GFBI)[10] published by the Center for Family Business of the University of St. Gallen.[11] The analysis revealed quite pronounced and stable differences.

Photo 1: Sam Walton's single-price business (5&10 store) in Bentonville, Arkansas—the origins of Walmart, the largest family business in the United States. The company museum is now located in this building.

In Germany, family businesses made up a good fifth of the top 100 companies by revenue during the survey period (2013–2015) and exactly the same share of the top 200 companies. In the US, family businesses accounted for only seven and 6.5 percent of these two groups. In other words, once US companies cross a certain growth threshold, they are much less likely to remain family-controlled. In both countries, only a minority of the very largest enterprises are family businesses. So, while there is a general correlation between size and the transition to external control, it is much more pronounced in the US. Conversely, large family businesses in Germany display much longer lifespans and greater continuity.

If we look at lists of the 25 largest family businesses in both countries, we mainly notice similarities, such as the wide variety of different industries covered (though retail is strongly represented). In both countries, a number of family businesses occupy positions at the very top of their economies. Tables 4 and 5 include global players and household names, strong automotive brands such as BMW and Ford as well as powerful media groups like Bertelsmann and 21st Century Fox. The biggest family businesses in the US are more likely to be active in the service sector and generally generate higher revenues than their German counterparts, which is why they usually outrank the latter.

The differences are even more pronounced when we shift our focus from the largest companies to the top performers in the medium-sized segment. The term "hidden champions",[12] coined by management consultant Hermann Simon in the 1990s, is used today to refer to companies with annual revenues of up to five billion euros that occupy one of the top three positions internationally in their segments (often niche markets). The majority of these companies are family-owned and many of them owner-managed.[13] They boast strong capital ratios, are extremely specialized, display a high degree of vertical integration and invest heavily in research and development. They are also highly protective of their independence, continuity and high quality standards, and maintain close relationships with their customers. They often have closely meshed distribution and service networks in many foreign markets, and are, in Germany, part of historically strong clusters. Due to their compact size and their restraint in the public sphere, the majority of these companies are not well known.

Of the 2,734 hidden champions across the globe that Simon identified in the latest edition of his book in 2012,[14] 1,307, or 48 percent, are from Germany. Other surveys conducted in 2015 even identify as many as 1,620 world market leaders among Germany's small and medium-sized enterprises (SMEs).[15] Figure 1 is based on Simon's figures and shows that, despite the sheer size of the US market, the absolute number of companies of this type in the USA is not even one-third that of Germany. Compared with other countries, the US still fares relatively well, with a clear lead over all other nations. Yet Germany boasts a uniquely high concentration of such companies.

Table 4: The 25 largest family businesses in Germany, 2013–2015 (by revenue)

Name	Position in global ranking	Founded in	Revenue (in USD billion)	Employees	Owner family	Family's share of capital
Volkswagen AG	2	1937	261.6	572,800	Porsche	32.2%
BMW AG	8	1916	101.0	110,351	Quandt	46.7%
Schwarz Group (Lidl, Kaufland)	9	1930	89.4	335,000	Schwarz	100%
Continental AG	24	1871	44.3	177,762	Schaeffler	49.9%
ALDI Group	32	1913	37.2	100,000	Albrecht	>50.0%
PHOENIX Pharmahandel GmbH & Co KG	45	1994	29.4	28,555	Merckle	100%
Heraeus Holding GmbH	59	1851	23.5	13,716	Heraeus	100%
Henkel AG & Co. KGaA	65	1876	21.7	46,800	Henkel	58.7%
Bertelsmann SE & Co. KGaA	66	1835	21.7	111,763	Mohn	100%
Marquard & Bahls AG	68	1947	21.1	9,281	Weisser	100%
C. H. Boehringer Sohn AG & Co. KG	79	1885	18.7	47,500	Boehringer	100%
Rethmann SE & Co. KG	97	1934	15.3	30,600	Rethmann	100%
Dr. August Oetker KG	100	1891	14.9	26,907	Oetker	>50%

Name	Position in global ranking	Founded in	Revenue (in USD billion)	Employees	Owner family	Family's share of capital
Schaeffler AG	101	1883	14.9	77,359	Schaeffler	100%
Porsche Automobil Holding SE	107	1931	14.3	19,456	Porsche-Piëch	98.4%
Merck KGaA	109	1668	14.2	38,154	Merck	70.3%
Adolf Würth GmbH & Co. KG	120	1945	12.9	63,571	Würth	100%
HELM AG	122	1900	12.8	1,431	Schnabel	100%
dm-drogerie markt GmbH + Co. KG	135	1973	11.5	52,062	Werner	98.8%
Tengelmann Warenhandelsgesell. KG	142	1867	10.7	83,437	Haub	100%
WISAG Dienstleistungsholding GmbH	151	1965	10.0	39,674	Wisser	100%
Droege International Group AG	156	1988	9.8	59,700	Droege	100%
C&A Mode AG	177	1841	8.8	35,672	Brenninkmeijer	>50%
Beiersdorf AG	188	1882	8.2	16,708	Herz	50.5%
Voith GmbH	200	1867	7.5	43,134	Voith	100%

Source: Global Family Business Index (see Note 10). The revenue data relates to 2013 or to the most recent status in 2015.

Table 5: The 25 largest family businesses in the United States, 2013–2015 (by revenue)

Name	Position in global ranking	Founded in	Revenue (in USD billion)	Employees	Owner family	Family's share of capital
Walmart Stores, Inc.	1	1962	476.3	2,200,000	Walton	50.9%
Berkshire Hathaway	3	1955	182.2	330,745	Buffett	34.5%
Ford Motor Comp.	5	1903	146.9	181,000	Ford	40%
Cargill, Inc.	6	1865	136.7	143,000	Cargill/Mac-Millan	90%
Koch Industries Inc.	7	1940	115	100,000	Koch	84%
Comcast Corp.	16	1963	64.7	136,000	Roberts	33.6%
The Long & Foster Companies, Inc.	20	1968	56	11,500	Long and Foster	>50%
Enterprise Products Partners LP	22	1968	47.7	6,600	Duncan	36.9%
Bechtel Group Inc.	31	1898	37.9	52,700	Bechtel	40–100%
Sears Holdings Corp.	33	1886	36.2	226,000	Lampert	48%
Tyson Foods, Inc.	36	1935	34.4	115,000	Tyson	27.1%
Mars, Inc.	38	1891	33	72,000	Mars	100%
Pilot Travel Centers LLC.	40	1958	32.1	21,000	Haslam	>50%

Name	Position in global ranking	Founded in	Revenue (in USD billion)	Employees	Owner family	Family's share of capital
21st Century Fox	41	1979	31.9	27,000	Murdoch	39.4%
Publix Super Markets, Inc.	47	1921	29.1	166,000	Jenkins	68.6%
Love's Travel Stops & Country Stores Inc.	50	1964	26	10,500	Love	100%
Reyes Holdings L.L.C.	64	1976	22	16,500	Reyes	100%
C & S Wholesale Grocers Inc.	67	1918	21.7	17,000	Cohen	100%
H.E. Butt Grocery Comp.	72	1905	20	76,000	Butt	100%
Penske Corp.	77	1969	19	39,000	Penske	>50%
Paccar Inc.	86	1905	17.1	21,800	Pigott	>50%
Enterprise Holdings Inc.	90	1957	26.4	83,000	Taylor	98%
The GAP	91	1969	16.1	137,000	Fischer	45.4%
Cox Enterprises Inc.	95	1898	15.3	500,000	Cox	99%
CBS Corp.	96	1986	15.3	19,490	Redstone	79%

Source: Global Family Business Index (see Note 10). The revenue figures relate to 2013 or to the most recent data from 2015.

A partial explanation for the lower number of family businesses among large and medium-sized enterprises in the US compared with Germany is that the latter's capital market has always been substantially smaller, both in absolute and relative terms, than in both the US and the UK—even though it has gained considerably in magnitude since the second half of the 1990s. In other words, going public was always much more difficult in Germany than in the US, making it less likely that family businesses would make the transformation to listed companies or be sold to investors from outside the founding family. Conversely, one could argue that in Germany, fewer companies wanted to go public and that the reason for the relatively low level of market capitalization was that family businesses were less interested in changing their status. In the US, by contrast, the sale of shares in a company forms part of a conscious strategy of asset diversification. The role of business owner is more often perceived to be a temporary phase in an entrepreneur's life and less often an obligation spanning generations.

Figure 1: International comparison of number of hidden champions, 2012

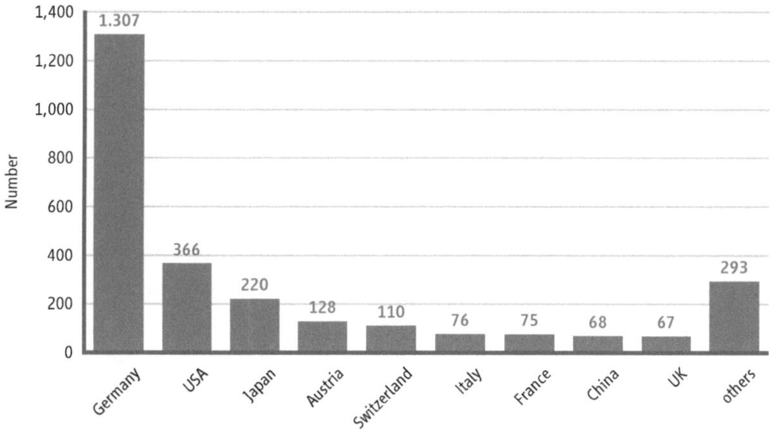

Source: BMWi, German Mittelstand, p. 8. Data for the USA from 2009.

The US capital market is liquid enough to accommodate a high number of company shares due to its size and maturity alone—not just in absolute figures (which reflect the sheer size of the country), but also relative to gross domestic product (GDP). The ratio of the value of all listed domestic companies to GDP is a good indicator of a capital market's liquidity (Table 6).[16]

Table 6: Market capitalization of domestic listed companies, 1975, 1990, 2000 and 2015 (as a percentage of GDP)

	1975	1990	2000	2015
USA	41.7%	51.7%	101.0%	140.0%
Germany	10.5%	20.1%	65.1%	51.1%
UK	35.5%	77.7%	106.0%	n.a.

Source: World Bank, http://data.worldbank.org/indicator/CM.MKT.LCAP.GD.ZS (accessed: August 12, 2018).

In Germany, founder families tend to retain control of their enterprises for longer and ensure that the family holds a relatively large share of the company's capital—even though family stakes definitely do decrease over time and as the company grows. A random sample of 592 German family businesses in the late 1990s revealed that founder families retained an average capital stake of 95 percent. Of these companies, 465 were even wholly owned by the family in question. The larger and older the companies, the lower the percentage of enterprises that were still wholly owned by their founding families. However, the ratio was still 60 percent of all the family businesses analyzed, even in the category of companies with annual revenues exceeding deutschmarks (DM) one billion.[17] Consequently, there is nothing inevitable about the transfer of company shares from founding families to external investors. As a rule, shares in family businesses in Germany—or at least the majority of those shares—are likelier to remain with the families than is the case in the United States, which is a country more strongly geared to the capital market.

The advanced state of financialization in the US[18] is associated with the much greater role of institutional investors, whether in the form of hedge funds, pension funds or private equity investors. On the lookout for worthwhile acquisitions, they can offer family business owners attractive conditions for the sale of their firms. The market for corporate control is thus larger and stronger in the US. This more advanced state of financialization in the US also triggered a shortening of time horizons at the expense of long-term strategies: in 1960, the average holding period for shares listed on the New York Stock Exchange was still around eight years; by 2015, it had fallen to eight months.[19]

A longevity comparison of the 80 largest German family businesses included in the St. Gallen index for 2013–2015 revealed an average age that was over one-fifth (22.4 percent) higher than in the US: the average age of the German companies was 107 years, as opposed to 83 years in the control group in the US.[20]

Even if we ignore large enterprises, the higher longevity of German family businesses compared with those in the US is obvious. Two regional case studies—which do not permit an exact comparison due to their differing methodologies and time frames—nevertheless indicate that medium-sized German family businesses are older on average than their US counterparts. John Ward chose a random sample of 200 family businesses in Illinois that had at least 20 employees in 1924 and had been in existence for a minimum of five years. By 1984, 80 percent of those businesses had disappeared. Only 13 percent were still in the ownership of the same family as in 1924. Seven percent had been sold.[21]

A German sample compiled by Christina Lubinski analyzed 161 family businesses based in Munich and Düsseldorf in 1960 with at least 250 employees each. Of this sample, 100 companies (62 percent) were more than 50 years old, while 29 (18 percent) were even more than 100 years old. In 2009, 41 of them were still independent family businesses with an average age of 130.[22] An analysis of 408 German family businesses with annual revenues of 50 million euros and more revealed an average age of 84 years in 2012, with the average age for industrial enterprises in this segment even reaching 91 years.[23]

In general, German companies have long lifespans, with family businesses being slightly older on average than other corporate forms. Of the 270,000 companies registered across Germany in 1995 with annual revenues of over DM two million, 28.5 percent were established prior to 1945, and the corresponding figure for family businesses was even higher at 31 percent. Of the 8,575 companies that existed before 1871, 6,388 were family businesses.[24] In general, the founding families hold very large capital shares in German family businesses, but with older companies, the share tends to be higher than with younger family businesses: a study of 1,014 family businesses with annual revenues of DM two to 50 million in 1995 revealed that 94–96 percent of the shares in companies established before 1959 were still in family ownership at the end of the 20th century, in some cases in the third or fourth generation. The figure for companies founded later was still between 90 and 94 percent.[25]

These statistics give rise to a number of key questions for the following historical analysis, which begins in the 19th century. What effective, long-term economic, sociocultural and legal factors explain the greater significance of family businesses in Germany, especially among medium-sized and large companies? Why do they have longer lifespans and remain family businesses for longer periods? Are there major national differences in the underlying conditions for family businesses in general and, in particular, for the transition between generations? Where are the parallels and similarities? We will also look at the political acceptance and/or promotion of family businesses in both countries, and consider similarities and differences in how the key challenges facing family-based companies (including financing, succession and innovative strength) are tackled.

Special attention must be paid to points of divergence in inheritance and competition law, in the training systems, the nature of the capital markets, demand structures as well as in the cultural and political appreciation of family businesses. A further point concerns the mindset and make-up of the founding families: What were their priorities and goals? What attitude did they have in dealing with their property?

Chapter B of this study begins by examining long-term trends as reflected in statistical findings. Despite many insoluble problems with regard to definitions and data, it attempts to describe historical trends, highlighting not only clear differences and points of divergence, but also similarities. Chapter C looks at the history of inheritance law. Here, clear national differences are apparent that have had a profound effect on the probability of intergenerational continuity. Chapter D analyses the growth of capital markets in both countries and explores how those market structures interact with the respective forms of corporate governance and modes of corporate financing. The focus here is on the size and composition of the capital market and its impact on family businesses.

Chapter E examines the extent to which the government's economic policy may potentially have promoted or hampered family businesses. The next two chapters deal with highly complex issues of cultural history. What corporate cultures became dominant and when? How did families perceive their roles? What written—and, above all, unwritten—rules existed? What are the origins of certain attitudes and mentalities? Chapter F looks at historical path dependencies that had a long-term impact. As a legacy of the 19th century they have shaped the cultural framework for family businesses and their owners to this day. Chapter G analyses the different historical paths taken by corporate culture in the US and Germany. It asks what general cultural factors influenced families and explain the average—though not necessarily individual—differences in behavior of business families on both sides of the Atlantic.

B. Long-term Trends. Structural and Institutional Change

Any statistical analysis of family businesses is fraught with difficulty since there is no agreed definition of a family business and the necessary data is not available or does not match the definitions. This problem manifests itself all the more in the case of a long-term historical study, because the official statistics it draws on have repeatedly changed their criteria over the decades.

Let's take a look at the plethora of definitions. The Witten Institute for Family Businesses (WIFU), one of a number of pioneers of academic research into family businesses, uses the following restrictive definition: "The transgenerational aspect is essential to a family business. For this reason, it is strictly speaking only correct to refer to a company as a family business if the family is planning to hand down the company to its next generation. Start-ups and owner-managed companies are therefore not yet family businesses in their own right." At the same time, another definition is presented which emphasizes the connection between ownership and management: "We use the term family business when an enterprise is owned wholly or partly by one family, several families or family associations and the latter have a determining influence on the development of the company based on entrepreneurial responsibility."[26]

Apart from the fact that the two definitions contradict each other, the first one eludes statistical analysis because plans and intentions cannot be reliably captured. The other definition published by the Witten Institute is similar to our own (Chapter A), but can also be operationalized only to a limited extent. Coalitions of families or business associations may be particularly opaque, and this is exacerbated by the fact that details of ownership are often kept strictly confidential.

Even today there are major problems in statistically capturing the significance of family businesses in the USA and Europe. According to Shanker and Astrachan, all empirical and quantitative attempts at doing so are based on fictitious accounts or street lore, more or less educated estimates, extrapolations based on small samples or facts on individual companies that are generalized.[27] In order to render such analyses more precise, they propose classifying family businesses into three groups based on the degree of family involvement in the business—from a broad definition (effective management control, significant ownership) through a middle-ground definition (founders or descendants run the company and have legal control of the majority of voting rights) to a narrow definition (multiple generations, family directly involved in running and owning the business, more than one member of owners' family has significant management responsibility). However, the available data remains problematic even for an analysis based on these criteria: depending on the definition you use the results will be completely different. If you sort the numerous studies conducted for the USA in the 1980s and 1990s on the basis of the broadest and the narrowest definition, you find that, depending on your choice, as many as 3.2 million (approximately 60 percent) of all partnerships and corporations could potentially be considered family businesses, or as few as 1.1 million (approximately 21 percent).[28] In comparison, a range of 78.5 percent to 15 percent for the proportion of family businesses in the United Kingdom has been determined by researchers in the UK using similar data records.[29]

Any attempt to contrast this—already heterogeneous—data from the Anglo-Saxon legal and economic system with the situation in Germany creates additional challenges for the task of finding a definition. Management analyst Sabine Klein has come up with another way of approaching the problem, which complicates the matter further. In her research, she expands the concept of family business yet again by also incorporating sole proprietorships and partnerships as potential multigenerational projects. Her definition is: "A family business is a company that is influenced by one or more families in a substantial way. A family is defined as a group of people who are descendants of one couple and their in-laws as well as the couple itself. Influence in a substantial way is considered if the family either owns the complete stock or, if not, the lack of influence in ownership is balanced through either influence through corporate governance (percentage of seats in the Aufsichtsrat [Supervisory Board], Beirat [Advisory Board], or others held by family members) or influence through management (percentage of family members in the top management team). For a business to be a family business, some shares must be held within the family."[30]

This approach can be attacked from several angles: even when looking at an individual entity, there are often only sketchy details of which groups of shareholders or owners have how much influence in the company. This applies specifically when, to determine whether family influence is relevant under the definition, the analyst must consider ownership interests that are so small that they can hardly be identified. What is more, it is impossible to capture companies that are established and owned as a collective by several (lines of) families. In general, there is controversy among researchers about the issue of whether founders or sole owners can consistently be attributed to the group of family business. Klein justifies their inclusion in the statistical-empirical analysis by introducing the status of "'potential family businesses' but clearly not non-family businesses". We agree with the finding that the term family business is a higher-level catch-all category for "family-owned, family-managed and family-controlled firms", which can occur in all sizes and legal constructs.[31] In reality, therefore, we are dealing with many over-lapping and grey areas. It seems more than vague, for example, to include all sole proprietorships and partnerships in the definition as future family businesses and to assume that anyone establishing a company will want to pass it on to future generations. However, since the statistics produced by government and industry associations as well as the accessible historical data series and registers documenting the corporate and industry landscape only distinguish companies according to basic criteria such as legal form or size, this approach is, for all its imprecision, the only feasible solution. The problems with the definition and the way data is collected are the reason that we can only provide rather crude statistical approximations and describe general trends.

The longevity of family businesses yields the most accurate comparison between the two countries. Successful family businesses that have established themselves at the top among the largest companies in their respective country tend to be significantly older in Germany than in the USA. For the German case, the Institute for SME research and entrepreneurship at the University of Mannheim conducted a study in 2015 in which it collated the years of establishment of the 500 largest family businesses by revenue and workforce size. It shows that 70.5 percent of family businesses were formed before 1950, and 31.7 percent of them before 1900. In 4.4 percent of the cases, the year of establishment was even before 1800. The average age of the German family business included in the study was therefore 101.8 years.[32]

Table 7: Comparison of average ages and founding periods of family businesses

	Est. before 1800	Est. in 1800–1899	Est. in 1900–1949	Est. in 1950–2009	Median	Average age
Germany	4.4%	27.3%	38.8%	29.5%	1923	101.8 years
USA	0.7%	15.5%	39.7%	44.0%	1939	74.5 years

Source: Own compilation based on Global Family Business Index (see Note 10) and the Forbes List of America's Largest Private Companies 2016, https://www.forbes.com/largest-private-companies/ list (accessed: September 2, 2018). For data on German family businesses, see Stiftung Familienunternehmen, Bedeutung, pp. 55 et seq. Details were kindly provided to the authors by Foundation for Family Businesses.

Legend: The data for Germany comprises the top 500 family businesses by revenue and workforce. For this reason, the country sample is based on a total of 587 companies. For the USA, the foundation dates of the 277 largest companies by revenue on the Forbes List were analyzed. The base data relates to the years 2013 to 2016.

Figure 2: Founding decades of German family businesses

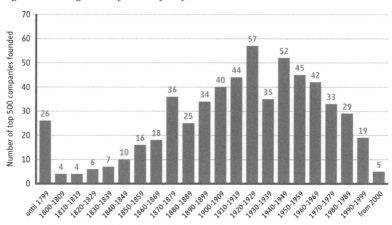

Source: own compilation, see information on Table 7.

The oldest large family firm is apparently the Coatinc Company, a surface finisher based in the northwestern German city of Siegen that employs about 1,500 employees at 22 locations. The company traces its roots back to 1502, the year in which a forge operated by Heylmann Dreseller, a master steel smith born in 1460, was first mentioned in records. The family has been active in the mining, iron and steel industries since that time. In 1945, ownership of the company passed to Werner Niederstein, the son of Alfred Niederstein and Luise, the daughter of Heinrich Adolf Dresler, and the Niedersteins have stood for family continuity ever since. Klaus (1936–2017) belonged to the 16th generation. His son Paul Niederstein (born in 1974) now heads the company in the 17th generation.

Photos 2 and 3: Family entrepreneurs in the 16th and 17th generations: Klaus (1936–2017) and Paul Niederstein (born in 1974), owners of the Coatinc Company, Siegen

With the exception of its extremely long history, Coatinc typifies many qualities of family businesses: the organic rise of a highly specialized industrial company from the craft sector; its role in helping shape technical progress over a long period of time from the pre-industrial production of iron to the creation of today's high-quality special steel; and its lasting roots in one of Germany's oldest mining regions, which have not prevented the internationalization of the company's activities since the 1970s. Today, the company has holdings in firms in Europe, Turkey, California and Mexico. The family is part of the local elite and has, in the past, exercised significant political influence: Family members from the 5th to 10th generations served as mayor of Siegen. The family's pride in its company is expressed in part by the way it fosters its own history. A "History of the Dresler Family" was published in 1918 as a gift to celebrate the 85th birthday of Heinrich Adolf Dresler. Even today, the company and family members express pride in a long tradition from which family members, according to their self-image, draw their values. As Paul Niederstein put it in 2019: The family has "a deep understanding of our history and of steel as a material" and "also of our down-to-earth region, which is unconventional and raw in a very special way. We find all of the values that guide us every day right here […]. Furthermore, our actions […] are shaped by our Christian values."[33]

Photo 4: Pride of the city. The entrepreneurial Dresler family of Siegen (undated)

William Prym GmbH & Co. KG of the North Rhine-Westphalian city of Stolberg is considered to be Germany's second-oldest company. Its predecessor was established in 1530 in Aachen as a guild member of the skilled trades that produced brass and copper. In 1642, during the Thirty Years' War, the family, which was Protestant, lost its guild rights in the Roman Catholic city of Aachen, joined the exodus of skilled trades from the city and set up operation in nearby Stolberg. The history of this company is characterized by its roots in the craft sector, by exceptional technological adaptability and innovativeness, by specialization and high-quality production. The company's internationalization already began in the late 19th century with direct investments in the Habsburg Empire.

Today, Prym produces haberdashery such as press fasteners and knitting needles as well as electronic components and contact elements. The company has a presence in Italy, France, England, Sri Lanka and China through acquisitions, investments and joint ventures. In 2016, the Prym Group employed 3,300 people at 32 locations around the world and generated revenue of € 380 million.[34] For 475 years until 2005, the company was exclusively owned and led by members of the Prym family, after which a minority stake was acquired by a group of unidentified entrepreneurial families and family offices. Today, the 19th generation of the family serves on the Advisory Board and is represented among the shareholders.

Moreover, the group of the most long-lived German companies counts a large number of pioneers in the manufacturing sector. They include Zollern GmbH & Co. KG in Laucherthal, a company in the metal industry established in 1708, Merck KGaA, which opened as a pharmacy in Darmstadt back in 1688 and now operates in the pharmaceutical and healthcare sector, the printing product and roller manufacturer Felix Böttcher GmbH & Co. KG in Cologne, which has been in business since the first third of the 18th century, or the Bielefeld-based plastics specialist Möller Group GmbH. These companies are rich in tradition and have in common that they have adapted their strategies to new fields of business and methods of production on several occasions, and have benefited from their stable local roots as family businesses when developing into global players. Other salient examples of particularly old family businesses are the gingerbread and chocolate manufacturer Aachener Printen- und Schokoladenfabrik Henry Lambertz GmbH (Aachen, 1688), Harry Brot GmbH (Hamburg, 1688) and Alois Dallmayr KG (Munich, 1700) in the food processing industry.[35] In the banking sector, they include two private banks, Joh. Berenberg, Gossler & Co. KG (Hamburg, 1590) and B. Metzler seel. Sohn & Co. Holding AG (Frankfurt a. M., 1674), which emerged as merchant banks from trading firms specializing in the exchange and lending business during the early years of industrialization. Especially in the banking business, a personal business style was beneficial for building relationships of trust with loan and industry customers. Families of bankers that were able to look back on several generations of financial stability were particularly adept at creating the necessary reputation and stable networks of business and private contacts.[36] Only when large modern joint-stock banks started to emerge at the end of the 19th century did their significance wane as the most important financiers of German industrialization. Today, both Berenberg and Metzler focus on investment banking and private wealth management.[37] Many entrepreneurial families continue to be customers of these family businesses in the banking sector.

Figure 3 shows a benchmark group of 277 US companies which were included by Forbes in 2016 in the list of America's Largest Private Companies on the basis of revenue and/or appeared in the Global Family Business Index for the USA of the University of St. Gallen for 2013 to 2015. An analysis reveals that 55.9 percent of the companies included here were founded before 1950, but only 16.2 percent of them before 1900. In only 0.7 percent of the cases was the company established prior to 1800. The two oldest companies are the brewery Molson, today Molson Coors Beverage Company (Colorado), established in 1786, and Sweet & Maxwell Legal Publishing, which was founded in 1799. After many intermediate changes, this company eventually became Thomson Reuters (New York/Toronto) in 2008. The average age of the US companies included in the study was 74.5 years, a significant 27.3 years less than in Germany.

Figure 3: Founding decades of US family businesses

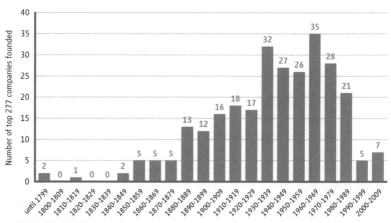

Source: own compilation, see information on Table 7.

A dominant pattern in the USA since the 19th century has been to establish spin-offs to accommodate children and create flexible network structures. This form stands for the fact that there was a marked preference for the establishment of new entities rather than continuing businesses across genera-tions.[38] A detailed case study of small and medium-sized enterprises (SMEs) in Poughkeepsie in the State of New York provides evidence that families are of major significance for the local economy, but also demonstrates a clearly discernible tendency towards diversified investments, instead of multi-gen-erational companies. In many cases, fathers gave their sons money to allow them to build new companies. According to the economic historian David Landes, this approach is typical of US "capitalism without a feudal past",[39] which he contrasts with European family capitalism that was dominated by pre-modern values such as the honor and dynastic obligation of families as well as the independence and longevity of family businesses. In the USA, by contrast, the focus was on individual achievement and independence.[40]

In Poughkeepsie, many of the mostly small family businesses were short-lived. The study refers to a "Darwinian jungle of small business in the Unit-ed States".[41] Unlike in Europe, bankruptcies were not dishonorable, but even took place with a certain amount of ease: failed entrepreneurs were given a second or third chance without being socially stigmatized. 60 percent of all companies disappeared between 1843 and 1873. In the minority of cases where sons joined the business of their fathers, around 20 percent left again after a certain period of time. Partnerships of brothers likewise did not last very long, with 53 percent of them dissolved within the first five years. Only 13 percent lasted 15 years or more. The same applied to larger companies: with only one exception, by 1900 all companies in the local manufacturing industry of the 1860s and 1870s were no longer owned by the founding fam-ily, i.e. they had been either sold or closed down.[42]

The family strategy consisted of the hope "that the sons would increase the family fortunes through diversification". This often applied to sons-in-law, too, who joined the existing family business less frequently than in Germany and instead, with the father-in-law's help, established their own companies in a different industry: "A son-in-law might reasonably hope to receive financial aid from his wife's family while remaining separate and independent in busi-ness."[43] This echoes the observation made by the sociologist Daniel Bell: "The son does not succeed the father but strikes out for himself." A cultural prefer-ence like this was naturally not observed in all families, but Bell attributes its popularity to the existence of vast areas of free land, and it prevented the USA, unlike Europe, from developing a "full system of family capitalism".[44]

This high rate of start-up activity persisted for a long time. A study of small companies entitled "Characteristics of Business Owners 1992" conducted on the basis of an official survey by the US Census Bureau concluded that over half of all entrepreneurs who had grown up in families of entrepreneurs had opted against working in their ancestors' companies. It was extremely rare that these businesses were passed on from one generation to the next by way of gifting, inheritance or other methods: only 8.2 percent of the companies surveyed changed hands this way. Nevertheless, socialization was an important factor in entrepreneurial families to create an interest among the descendants in looking for ways to achieve independence. The proportion of children of entrepreneurs in the USA who became entrepreneurs far exceeded the average for the population as a whole, although most of them did so outside their own family collective.[45]

Another factor that shaped the business landscape in the USA is the country's status as a land of immigrants. Prior to 1914, the massive influx of immigrants from Europe and all over the world ensured an endless supply of entrepreneurial talent. In the country's ascent to becoming the world's leading economic power, immigrants were an extremely positive resource.[46] On the other hand, the high levels of social mobility also hampered the creation of stable structures: fluctuation and competitive pressure were high and developed a sometimes destructive force, especially among SMEs. For example, in 1899 the rapidly expanding jewelry manufacturing industry in Providence/Rhode Island had around 200 companies with 7,000 employees. A mere ten years later, 290 companies employed 10,000 people. In 1914, the number of employees stood at around 18,000. Many individual companies were established. Some survived and prospered, while others were unable to withstand the competitive pressure in the new industrial district and vanished after a short time. A typical scenario was that some entrepreneurs failed repeatedly and tried their luck again with new companies.[47]

A typical representative of this fluid business community was Harry Cutler, who was born in Russia in 1875. His mother fled with him to the USA in 1885 to escape anti-Jewish pogroms. In 1890, when he was 15, Cutler began to work for a number of jewelry manufacturers. In 1899, at the age of 24, he struck out on his own, having mastered the technical skills required. With very little capital and two employees, he quickly rose to success, and within three years of establishing the business, he employed 75 to 100 people. In years that followed, Cutler became a local dignitary and was elected to his country's parliament. Although it was possible to climb the social ladder in a spectacular fashion in Germany, too, it could not be done at this speed or in such high numbers. In the USA, the prospect of starting one's own business quickly also led to a large drop in the significance of the traditional apprenticeship. It was also the reason that the Rhode Island School of Design, the vocational school specifically established for the jewelry district, only attracted few enrolments for its classes. For the workers, there was hardly any incentive to seek further training: they encountered an open labor market with high levels of demand, one that offered many employment opportunities even for those with little practical experience. Business owners did not encourage further qualification either. They quite rightly feared that well qualified specialists would quickly strike out on their own and increase the number of competitors.[48]

Low entry barriers and the constant influx from outside at times created a very dynamic environment, but also led to the medium-term demise of the jewelry industry in Providence, which critics compared to a "black hole in Calcutta". The industry there was marked by a cut-throat price war and atrocious working conditions; brand piracy and design theft were frequent occurrences. Everyone fought everyone else, and intermediaries drove prices to rock bottom levels. The industry association was unable to prevent these conditions and instead focused successfully on anti-union policies, resisting any kind of regulation of working conditions, such as the abolition of child labor or limits on working hours for women. Otherwise, its members believed in the blessings of unbridled competition and were "deeply wedded to the virtues of rugged individualism and free competition. Like many other small-scale producers, their brand of capitalism was robustly anti-trust and against price fixing."[49]

In Germany, the institutional framework that has emerged for SMEs since industrialization is completely different. During the monarchy, the attention of policy makers was attracted by constant complaints from the *Mittelstand* that they were at risk of being economically displaced by the growing industrial groups and wholesalers. Craft, industry and commercial sector enterprises, most of which were owner or family-managed, regarded themselves as the traditional backbone of the German economy and felt they were being marginalized in the competition and battle with the new anonymous corporations. Strong industry associations, trade guilds (Innungen) and chambers of commerce, trade and industry that had emerged from the guild tradition acted as their mouthpieces. In 1897, amendments to the Trade, Commerce and Industry Regulation Act (Gewerbeordnung) confirmed the chambers as institutions under public law, thus politically recognizing their demands for social protection and preservation of the status quo as being in the general interest and underpinning the self-regulatory interests of the *Mittelstand*.[50] The protection of the *Mittelstand* came, however, at the expense of a partial restriction of the freedom of enterprise. The state continued to meet their protectionist ambitions in the German Empire by imposing special taxes on department stores. The privilege of master craftsman training was retained, and this ultimately allowed the chambers and guilds to decide which new companies could enter the market. Industry associations thus retained a sustained influence over the regulatory shape of coordinated capitalism, with the priority of limiting price competition in order to ensure stable growth for small and medium-sized enterprises.[51]

As in the USA, cluster-like centers of new industries came into being in Germany in the 19th century. In the jewelry industry, Providence had its counterpart in the Golden City of Pforzheim. Mechanical engineering districts developed in Chemnitz just like in Cincinnati.[52] The cutlery industry concentrated around Solingen, the Märkisches Land around Wuppertal expanded its position as a location for the textile industry, Düsseldorf became the "Manchester of the Rhine" for the steel and metal construction industry, and industrial activity in Tuttlingen specialized in medical technology—to name but a few of the up-and-coming industrial and commercial regions. Yet even if similar synergies from sharing knowledge and creating joint support and training organizations were identifiable in business networks in the USA and Germany, they differed on one key point: in Germany, industry associations took on a far more influential role in coordinating the structural development of the clusters. Managed competition, fewer price wars, regulated market access and, not least, occupational qualification and training organized within the bounds of traditional instruction through chambers and guilds allowed greater continuity in both ownership and labor relations. The business landscape was significantly less fluid. Innovation was driven within the businesses, because major bureaucratic hurdles stood in the way of potential spin-offs. As a result, talented employees were less motivated to seek self-employment. This made it easier for companies to become multi-generational while pursuing a core workforce policy based on long-term employee loyalty. This trend was still being reinforced in the Weimar Republic, when the ideal of a social economy, moderated by the state or jointly by associations and trade unions, became the dominant regulatory concept. Here, too, protective measures intended to preserve the *Mittelstand* as well as their access to the training system continued and were even expanded in some cases.[53]

But what were the economic consequences of the multigenerational structures that were so widespread in Germany? Does it really matter whether a business is in its first or fifth generation of family ownership? To have more people starting new businesses, as happens in the USA, could well be an advantage over a large number of descendants inheriting one business. A general assessment is not possible, because the economic functionality of multigenerational structures depends decisively on the sector to which they belong. Continuity is a comparative advantage where experience and expertise for the manufacture of industrial quality products have been built from a skilled crafts base over extended periods and technical change is incremental. Examples can be found in mechanical engineering or instrument making, where German family businesses have a particularly strong presence. But where barriers to market entry are low, companies tend to be short-lived. And where disruptive innovation is the order of the day, such as in software development or other high-tech sectors, multigenerational structures can often be an impediment.

A study of 456 large German family businesses established before the First World War, with revenue in excess of 50 million euros in 2003, found that multigenerational structures produce additional motivational resources. The business owners interviewed emphasized the long-term perspective of their strategies, to which they attributed characteristics such as more restrictive dividend policies and lower risk appetite. "None of the family members surveyed considers the business to be a pure investment."[54] Although a continuous stream of income was very important, stability and a sustained increase in capital were more important still; they were the keys to ensuring family cohesion and building on the legacy of the ancestors by delivering business success. Responsibility to future generations was also named as a major issue. In addition, the company's long years of loyalty to its employees and its location played a major role. These factors gave the businesses and their workforces a specific identity and cohesion. The fact that employees identified with the company and enjoyed greater job security translated into higher productivity. Many of those interviewed indicated that, for them personally, these factors were great sources of strength and intrinsic motivation. Conversely, there was also something like a sociocultural or emotional dividend consisting of reputation and influence, especially in local and regional contexts. Direct access to holders of public office and recognition by the citizenry are some of the additional personal benefits.[55]

In the market, multigenerational businesses inspire confidence among business partners and customers and lay the foundation for strong brands. People know that to ensure their sustained existence, these businesses will continue to meet quality standards and keep promises such as warranties and customer service levels. In many cases, the success of German hidden champions is down to these kinds of reputational factors—even if it has not been possible so far to measure these symbolic and emotional effects. For one thing, family businesses exist in many shapes that cannot be distinguished clearly from one another, and ultimately there is simply not enough (historical) data to allow us to compare the economic performance of family and non-family businesses. Then, too, the effects that may help family-based networks of trust, business goodwill or corporate image to unfold depend on the respective systemic environment and the institutional framework applied to the economy. In the case of Germany, Ehrhardt, Nowak and Weber examined the financial performance of family businesses with a history of more than 100 years, and found that companies that have consistently retained the status of family business since 1903 have been financially more successful than those that transformed into corporations (with less than 50 percent of the shares held by the family) or even stock corporations with dispersed share ownership in the course of the 20th century. Especially in technology-based sectors, these family companies demonstrated greater persistence, higher innovative capabilities and better business performance. In addition, the authors speculate that lending banks tend to reward the transfer of ownership and management to a subsequent generation with favorable interest rates.[56]

A small number of more recent studies on the USA argues that listed family companies with a continuous presence of founder families achieve higher profits, if at least one member of the family remains involved in the company as CEO. However, this effect diminishes with each subsequent generation and performance of these businesses soon falls below that of companies that work exclusively with external managers.[57] What is more, family influence has no noticeable effect on market capitalization.[58] On the contrary, studies have found that the opposite is true: the financial markets tend to react negatively to an announcement that a family member will continue to exercise significant control after a generational changeover. This is a manifestation of the fact that US investors and market players consistently assume that strategic management and financial performance will deteriorate if management appointments are based on non-economic criteria such as family origin instead of skills. This is a clear sign that skepticism of family influence has become deeply embedded in the culture and mentality of the US economy.[59]

An impediment to all attempts to compare the performance of family businesses with that of non-family forms of organization is that balance sheet, revenue and earnings data on entities run as sole proprietorships or partnerships is simply not available because, at least in Germany, there were no or only partial disclosure requirements for these figures until the 21st century. Although this means that the samples on which the studies are based never meet the criterion of being fully representative, the historically very different manifestations of family businesses have to be included in the analyses. Has the family retained full ownership and all management functions? Has it continued to perform management functions as majority shareholder after a potential transformation into a corporation, or has it become a minority shareholder, exercising only a passive oversight function? Even with regard to the genesis of control structures, the problems of definition and access to statistics referred to earlier mean that studies conducted over extended periods can only produce trend descriptions.

One thing is certain: the 19th century was the century of family businesses. In both countries, almost all companies were established as family companies and managed as such for a sustained period. Early and rare exceptions in the USA are the state-owned firearms manufacturer Springfield Armory (1777) or the United States Postal Service (1792). Subsequent additions include utility companies in local authority ownership and the railway companies, which, because of their immense financing needs, were normally founded as stock corporations with large numbers of investors or, as in some German national states, were established as state-owned companies or nationalized from the 1880s onwards.

In Germany, the number of public enterprises operated by the national states was much greater. One example of a company that is still run as a state-owned enterprise is the Großherzogliche Badische Staatsbrauerei Rothaus, a brewery founded in 1771 by a Benedictine monastery and transferred to state ownership in 1806 as a result of secularization. The Königliche Hüttenwerke in Württemberg (Royal Württemberg Steelworks), which became Schwäbische Hüttenwerke (SHW) in 1921, belonged to the provostry of Ellwangen prior to 1803. From the 18th century onwards, Prussia was involved in trading, shipbuilding, mechanical engineering and banking activities under the umbrella of the Preußische Seehandlung (Prussian Maritime Enterprise). In the 19th century, the Prussian State operated state-owned mines and steelworks in regions such as Saarland and Upper Silesia.

Overall, publicly owned enterprises and corporations with a majority free float only play a limited role in both countries. A survey commissioned by the US House of Representatives of all the country's manufacturing facilities (McLane report) found in 1832 that almost all enterprises were still very small and run by families with unlimited liability.[60]

The first half of the 20th century, however, saw two major trends in the USA. First, there was a massive increase in the number of SMEs, most of which were owned and managed by families. Between 1880 and 1950, their number rose from 1.2 to 5.4 million. That was more than just a sharp increase in absolute terms; it also represented considerable relative growth in relation to the size of the population.[61] Second, a clear trend emerged in major enterprises towards the separation of ownership and control. As early as 1929, 44 percent of the 200 largest companies were run by managers, according to a contemporary study conducted by Means, and these firms accounted for 58 percent of the total capital of the companies in this sample.[62]

Table 8: Control structures in the largest US companies, 1929 and 1963 (absolute figures and percentages, excluding financial sector)

Type of control	1929 (200 companies)	1963 (200 companies)	1963 (500 companies)
Family-controlled	58.0% (116)	17.0% (34)	22.4% (112)
Manager-controlled	32.5% (65)	80.5% (161)	73.2% (366)
Special configurations*	9.5% (19)	2.5% (5)	4.4% (22)

Source: Larner, Management Control, pp. 14–17; ibid., "Ownership", pp. 781–782.

* Joint control by two or more minority shareholders or by one minority shareholder and management/unknown party.

Table 8 compares the 200 largest stock corporations outside the financial sector to determine the influence of families in 1929 and 1963 respectively, as well as the 500 largest companies for 1963. Family influence was defined relatively broadly in this context. It related to individuals, families or groups of business associates holding between 50 and 100 percent of the voting rights. Also included was the criterion of minority control, whereby these groups of shareholders, as a result of holding between 20 and 50 percent of the voting rights in 1929 and between ten and 50 percent of the voting rights in 1963, exercised significant influence over the management, for example in combination with the management positions they filled. In a small number of cases, the family retained considerable control and decision-making powers even though its interest was below this threshold. Examples for the year 1963 include IBM, in which the Watson family had a strong position, Inland Steel (block ownership), or Weyerhaeuser, a mixed group of companies that started out in the timber industry and has been family-managed since 1966, now in the fourth generation. The Federal Department Stores were an extreme borderline case. The Lazarus family, for example, held only 1.32 percent of the share capital of the department store of the same name, but the CEO, the President of the Board and five of its 19 members came from its ranks.[63] Control was also exercised through legal constructs such as pyramids, preferred shares and multiple voting rights. Companies were classified as management-controlled if their shares were held in free float and individuals, families or groups no longer held any significant influence over them.[64]

Here the figures are somewhat different from those in Means' pioneering study; but the development trend is clear: family control was on the retreat in the USA. At 58 percent, it accounted for just over half of the exclusive sample of 200 companies in 1929, but by 1963 its share had dropped to 17 percent and to 22.4 percent in the sample of 500 companies. Most of the many cases in which families controlled the company from a minority position in 1929 had, by 1963, turned into manager-controlled companies whose shares were in free float.

Table 9: Control structures in the 100 largest German stock corporations, 1934 and 1958 (in percent, excluding financial sector)

Type of control	1934	1958
Family businesses	36%	19%
Entrepreneurial	21%	25%
Manager-controlled companies	27%	45%
State-owned/publicly owned companies	16%	11%

Source: Own research on the basis of lists of companies in: Fiedler and Gospel, Top 100, pp. 7 et seq.

For Germany, the transition from the Weimar Republic to the Federal Republic also shows an increase in the number of manager-controlled companies, although the trend was less pronounced. Table 9, which is unfortunately based on a smaller sample, shows the breakdown of control structures for the 100 largest German stock corporations by number of employees for the years 1934 and 1958. The companies are broken down into three categories, primarily based on the corporate management positions held by family members. In family companies, members of the founder and owner family are found in both the management board and the supervisory board. In these companies, the family also holds more than 25 percent of the shares. Companies are classified as entrepreneurial if the family is represented on the supervisory board and holds a minority interest, and they are classified as manager-controlled if there is no recognizable family influence over the way the company is run.

Table 10: Breakdown of employees in US industry by company size, 1914–1937

Year	Companies with up to 100 employees	Companies with 101–1,000 employees	Companies with more than 1,000 employees
1914	34.9%	47.6%	17.5%
1919	29.7%	44.3%	26.0%
1923	30.0%	46.7%	23.3%
1929	30.1%	45.7%	24.2%
1933	31.3%	47.7%	20.9%
1937	26.7%	46.9%	26.4%

Source: Steindl, Small and Big Business, p. 55.

It is noticeable that the proportion of manager-controlled companies without any family influence rose from a low base of 27 percent (1934) to 45 percent (1958), but did not become nearly as dominant as in the USA, where they accounted for over 73 percent (1963). Still, even in Germany, a growing number of companies were on the cusp between family and management control. This manifested itself in the increasing relevance of the entrepreneurial category, while the presence of pure family businesses among Germany's largest companies almost halved.

The trend towards large manager-controlled corporate groups, which is more pronounced in the USA, is also reflected in the statistics of company sizes. This is because, starting in the 1920s, SMEs in the USA experienced a much-deplored loss of significance that took on crisis proportions. Although a company's structure cannot automatically be inferred from its size, SMEs were typically family businesses. As we have seen, there were still many family businesses among the major companies, but as a proportion of the total number of all industrial companies their ratio declined sharply in the middle of the 20th century. For this reason, an analysis of changes in the size distribution can provide important insights into the relative decline in the significance of family influence in the US economy.

The concentration of the US economy thus accelerated in the first half of the 20th century, with the average workforce size in US industry climbing from 207 employees in 1914 to 318 in 1937.[65] The Small War Plant Corporation, a government organization tasked with integrating SMEs into the armament program during the Second World War, complained at the end of the 1930s that the 200 largest US companies (excluding the financial sector) owned around 55 percent of the industrial sector's assets. 60 percent of all industrial capacity was attributable to only 250 industrial companies. 14 sectors were dominated by a single company, while another twelve sectors had only two prevalent companies. The First World War and the boom years to 1929 saw a huge wave of mergers, which continued during the Second World War, boosted by the policy pursued by procurement offices of giving preference to large companies.[66] 1.1 million firms, or 30 percent, of all US companies were forced to close between 1941 and 1943, while only 572,000 new companies were established during that period—an overall decline of half a million businesses. Most of the companies affected were family-managed SMEs.[67]

Table 11 demonstrates the rapid pace of concentration, especially during the Second World War. The share of industrial employees working at major companies increased from 28.4 percent in 1938 to 43.8 percent in 1943. Their share of total wages rose from 32.2 to as much as 53.1 percent. However, the table also shows that companies employing fewer than 1,000 people were by no means insignificant: though the figure reached 71.6 percent in 1938, even in 1943, these companies accounted for 49.2 percent of industrial employees. It is also easy to see that the USA's entry into the war led to a sudden shift in favor of major companies, whose share jumped from 33.1 percent in 1941 to 43.8 percent in 1943.

Table 11: Breakdown of employees and total wages in US industry by company size, 1938–1943

Year	Companies with up to 100 employees		Companies with 101–1,000 employees		Companies with more than 1,000 employees	
	Share of employees	Share of total wages	Share of employees	Share of total wages	Share of employees	Share of total wages
1938	44.7%	40.7%	26.9%	27.0%	28.4%	32.3%
1939	42.5%	38.1%	27.1%	26.2%	30.4%	35.7%
1940	41.8%	36.3%	26.6%	25.7%	31.6%	38.0%
1941	40.4%	31.3%	26.5%	25.8%	33.1%	42.9%
1942	34.5%	27.3%	26.4%	24.9%	40.1%	47.8%
1943	24.8%	32.9%	24.4%	22.1%	43.8%	53.1%

Source: *National Archives, College Park, RG 240, 570,73,28 G, Small War Plant Corp., Box 1, Office of the Chairman and General Manager, manuscript: Concentration of American Business and Finance, p. 31.*

The comparative figures on industrial employment which unfortunately only counts production sites, not companies prove that inter-war and post-war Germany did not experience the same kind of intense concentration process. It is remarkable that the number of employees working in smaller companies with up to 50 employees even increased in percentage terms, from 48.9 percent (1925) to 58.5 percent (1933), before this figure reached with 46.5 percent (1950) almost the level of 1925 again (Table 12). This is a sign that industry was more heterogeneous and fragmented into smaller operating units, and this had a positive impact on the chances of survival for family businesses. The relative share attributable to medium-sized and large companies with more than 200 employees remained—with the exception of the decrease in 1933 caused by the Great Depression—almost constant with nearly one third. The importance of truly major companies with workforce sizes in excess of 1,000 employees also remained more or less stable. This trend reflects several special factors that are ultimately traceable to (economic) policies. It is attributable first to continued support for the *Mittelstand* provided by German governments, which increased further under the Nazi regime, and second to the demerger policy applied to German cartels initiated by the Allied Occupational Forces after 1945. Overall, the German corporate landscape operated on a smaller scale and with greater stability during the entire period under review.

Table 12: Breakdown of employees in the manufacturing sector in Germany, 1922–1952 (by plant size, in percent)

Year	Plants with up to 50 employees	Plants with 51–200 employees	Plants with 200–1,000 employees	Plants with more than 1,000 employees
1925	48.9%*	19.4%	18.9%	12.8%
1933	58.5%	16.3%	16.7%	8.5%
1950	46.5%	20.4%	19.6%	13.5%

*Data from 1925.

Source: Hoffmann, Wachstum, p. 212. Without mining and saltworks. 1950: Federal Republic of Germany.

Despite the generally low levels of business concentration, the statistics concealed some dramatic changes in ownership, especially during the Nazi era. Racial discrimination and the exclusion of Jewish-German entrepreneurs from the economy of the Third Reich led to the "Aryanization" and liquidation of tens of thousands of businesses in Jewish ownership. Most of the large German (stock) corporations were "Aryanized" at a relatively early stage, starting in 1933, by forcing out Jewish management and supervisory board members and displacing Jewish shareholders. In most cases, banks and other major companies took over the property of Jewish entrepreneur families, initially supposedly on a trust basis, until it was confiscated in favor of the state and transferred to new owners in a process that began in 1938. Most smaller sole proprietorships, partnerships and family companies were forcibly liquidated or sold to non-Jewish competitors, former employees or unscrupulous profiteers. If Jewish family businesses survived at all, they were mostly taken over by non-Jewish entrepreneurs. The legal form changed only in rare circumstances to enable the acquisition to be funded by winning additional investors. The character of family-run companies was retained in most cases, despite the change of ownership.

An analysis of the private banking system gives a glimpse of the painful loss of substance suffered by the German economy as a result of the politically and ideologically motivated displacement of successful and experienced Jewish companies. Of the just over 1,000 private banks organized in the German banking association, 490 (46.4 percent) were wholly or partially in the hands of Jewish owners in 1933. Jewish companies accounted

Photo 5: The private banker Simon Alfred von Oppenheim of Cologne, his wife "Flossy" and son Friedrich Carl attend the German Derby (1929).

for 56.7 percent of the total assets of the around 1.74 billion reichsmarks attributable to sole proprietorships and partnerships in the banking sector. The five largest German private banks alone, which held total assets of more than 50 million reichsmarks each, were all owned and managed by German-Jewish banker families: Warburg, Arnhold, Hirschland, Mendelssohn and Oppenheim.[68] Between 1933 and 1938, around 80 percent of all Jewish private banks were forced into liquidation—a process that benefited their "Aryan" competitors by eliminating rivals and enabling them to acquire some of their private and industrial clients. Every fifth Jewish company—including the economically significant institutions—was "Aryanized" by way of forced acquisition. In 59 cases, the tradition-based family businesses in the banking sector were bought by individuals, and in another 32 cases they were acquired by private or major banks. The displacement of Jewish bankers went hand-in-hand with the marginalization of private banks in Germany's financial sector, and this banking segment has been unable to offset the loss of skills, know-how, contacts and business relations since 1945.[69] The banks M.M. Warburg & Co. and Sal. Oppenheim & Cie. were two of the few family-run banks to survive National Socialism. The Oppenheim family was able to transfer its business activities to a trusted partner, Robert Pferdmenges, who led the bank under his name from 1933 to 1945. Even though the family owners Waldemar and Friedrich Carl von Oppenheim were the third generation of the family to be baptized as Christians, they faced severe anti-Semitic attacks in Cologne on the basis of their Jewish heritage and were forced to withdraw from public life, barely escaping Nazi henchmen toward the end of World War II. The bank has been operating under its original name again since 1947. Its "custodian" Robert Pferdmenges held a stake in the bank until 1954, became a member of the West German Parliament for the Christian Democratic Union (CDU), and served as a key financial adviser to Konrad Adenauer, the former mayor of Cologne, who was the first chancellor of West Germany.

The situation in the two countries was completely different in 1945. The USA's continental territory was completely unaffected by military action. The Great Depression was finally overcome during the war and the ensuing widespread rise in living standards continued relatively seamlessly and at great speed in the post-war era. Having lost the war, Germany faced very different challenges. Although there was no "zero hour", there was a deep political and socio-economic rift. The country suffered considerable destruction, large territo-

Photo 6: The name of the Oppenheim banking family was erased from public view in Cologne (about 1937) as a symbolic act of anti-Semitic persecution.

rial losses and the separation of the area that went on to become East Germany, as well as the loss of assets that occurred in the process. The fundamental experience of most Germans was one of loss and uncertainty. Hardships and the will to build an existence or regain lost status became important drivers for the establishment of new family businesses. A new generation of family firms thus emerged, often from the most humble beginnings. They were joined by the businesses of refugees, who arrived in the West from Eastern and Central Germany, often bringing only their know-how, business contacts and employees. The (re)establishment of these businesses received massive support from the federal government under the burden equalization program (Lastenausgleich), and there were further schemes at the federal state level, such as the system of productive loans for refugees (Flüchtlingsproduktivkredite) in Bavaria. The combination of these factors led to a real start-up boom in West Germany after 1945.

Here are some examples: in 1947, Karl Winterhalter established a company for household goods and electric appliances in Friedrichshafen. Initially, the company manufactured household goods from war rubble. From 1959 onwards—by then based in Meckenbeuren—it emerged as the global market leader for commercial dishwasher systems for the hotel and catering industry. It changed its name to "Winterhalter Gastronom" in 1971. The company, which is managed by the founder's son and grandson, had over 1,500 employees in 2017. This is an archetypal example of a family-run hidden champion that dominates a very specific niche in the market.[70]

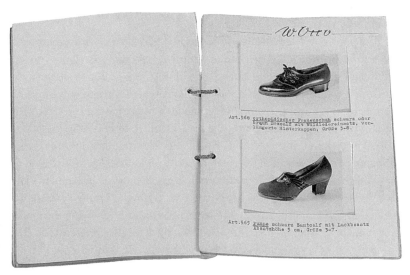

Photo 7: Small beginnings—the first "W. Otto" catalogue with hand-pasted photos (1950)

In Hamburg, the penniless refugee Werner Otto opened a shoe factory that soon went bankrupt. In 1949, there followed a mail-order company for shoes, established with seed capital of DM 6,000. Its first catalogue was issued in 1950 in a print run of 300 copies, bound by hand and with glued-in product illustrations. From these humble beginnings arose Otto-Versand, one of the world's largest mail-order groups. Today, the Otto Group is a diversified network of 123 companies in 30 countries; in 2017, it generated revenue of 12.5 billion euros and had over 50,000 employees. The company was headed by Michael Otto, the founder's son, until 2007 and owned by the family, one of the wealthiest in Germany, until 2015. After that, the majority interest in the business was transferred to a non-profit foundation controlled by the family for the purpose of preserving the cohesion of the family business.[71]

Coming from a modest middle-class background, Heinz Nixdorf, aged 26, started his own business in a cellar in the city of Essen, where he founded the one-man "Labor für Impulstechnik" in 1952. The business went on to become Nixdorf Computer AG in 1968, a family-owned stock corporation. It was one of the most important and innovative computer manufacturers in Europe, with 23,000 employees and revenue of around four billion deutschmarks (1985). However, following the founder's sudden death at the CeBIT computer trade fair in 1986, the company was thrown into an existential crisis and sold to Siemens in 1990.[72]

The poorly developed state of Bavaria benefited to a great extent from the relocation of highly specialized industries, which contributed to the industrialization of its rural areas. For example, musical instrument makers from Graslitz settled in Neustadt an der Aisch, violin and guitar makers from Schönbach in Egerland ("Sudetenland", today part of the Czech Republic) relocated to Bubenreuth, the glass industry of Haida-Steinschönau made Vohenstrauß its new home, and the jewelry manufacturers of Gabolonz moved to Kaufbeuren-Neugabolonz. A. Osmanek, Musikinstrumenten- und Saitenfabrik was a company that made musical instruments and strings. It was established in Schönbach in 1850 by a family of entrepreneurs that had employed up to 300 hand weavers and, following the mechanization of textile manufacture, had switched to a different sector. The company, which was run by the Junger family, was closed down at the beginning of the Second World War because it was "not essential to the war effort". As a result of the expulsion of Germans from their settlement areas in Czechoslovakia, Karl Junger and his son Norbert re-established the company in Bubenreuth near Erlangen. Leopold Müller, a company making pitch pipes that had also been based in Schönau and belonged to Karl Junger's father-in-law, was incorporated into the string factory. Working from Bubenreuth, Karl Junger Saitenfabrik was able to re-establish its foreign contacts from before 1939. The company expanded rapidly because, rather than produce standard models, the factory made high-quality strings according to specific customer orders. The company combined industrial and manual methods and flourished thanks to its highly specialized and highly qualified workforce. According to information provided by the company, the now renamed Pyramid Junger GmbH today ships its top-quality products to over 100 countries.[73] There are many similar examples of companies that came from rural areas and settled in similar regions of West Germany, often formed clusters, and benefited from highly qualified labor and networks from their former home and not least from targeted business development support by public authorities.

With its roots in the industrial city of Leipzig in Saxony, Karl Krause became one of the world's leading manufacturers of paper processing machines. Its third generation of owners and managers came from the Biagosch family, which left Leipzig in 1946 for the Westphalian city of Bielefeld, where from 1948 onwards the family re-established and rebuilt the company as Krause-Biagosch GmbH, a family business that went on to great success. In 1975, it was sold to another family. Jürgen Horstmann became its Managing Director and, through Krause-Biagosch, laid the foundation for the future Horstmann Group, which today has activities in the furniture and printing industries, in metal processing, bakery technology as well as IT and data processing. With locations on several continents, the company maintains a very successful position of technological innovation in the global marketplace.[74]

Table 13: Employees in the USA by company size, 1954–1987 (in percent)

Employees	1954	1963	1967	1987
1–99	51.7%	39.9%	39.9%	42.6%
100–999	9.4%	17.6%	17.5%	18.8%
over 1,000	39.0%	42.4%	42.6%	38.7%

Source: US Department of Commerce, Enterprise Statistics, year 1958. p. 32; ibid., year 1967, pp. 164–165 General Report 1958, Part 1, p. 32; US Department of Commerce, Enterprise Statistics, year 1967, Part 1, pp. 164–165; ibid., years 1987 and 1991, p. 13 in both.

While Germany saw the establishment and development of an increasing number of SMEs, the relative loss of significance of SMEs in the USA after the war continued unabated, despite the creation of a specific support organization, the Small Business Administration (SBA), in 1953. Its establishment was a response to the SME crisis, but it was unable to halt the downward trend. Revenue attributable to small businesses—defined as companies with fewer than 500 employees and revenue of up to five million dollars—as a proportion of revenue generated by all companies de-clined from 52 percent in 1958 to 29 percent in 1979.[75] At the same time, the number of SMEs increased sharply, from 1.1 million in 1958 to 2.3 million in 1975.[76] Table 13, by contrast, shows that the percentage of employees attributable to SMEs—defined here as companies with up to 999 employees—was relatively stable at just under 60 percent, slightly higher than during the war years (Table 11). That was not a sign of strength, however: given their declining share of revenue, many of the companies involved performed substantially below par.[77]

In the late 1970s and 1980s, the trend in favor of major companies was halted in the USA and SMEs regained some importance. This was mainly due to the crisis among the major conglomerates, government incentive programs and the establishment of micro-enterprises by unemployed workers. However, this resulted in a moderate rather than a dramatic trend reversal.

Table 14: Employees in the Federal Republic of Germany by plant size, 1950–1987 (in percent)

Employees	1950	1961	1970	1987
1–99	65.0%	55.7%	53.4%	57.5%
100–999	22.4%	28.4%	30.4%	29.2%
over 1,000	12.7%	15.9%	16.1%	13.2%

Source: Own calculations based on Statistisches Bundesamt (ed.), Wirtschaft und Statistik 1963, p. 540; ibid., year 1972, p. 511; ibid., year 1989, p. 703. See Berghoff, "Relikt", p. 256.

Owing to a lack of reliable data, the share of family businesses in total employment or in all companies in the Federal Republic cannot be identified for extended periods of time. Even company size categories have only been captured in long time series since 1970. Up until then, German federal statistics mostly counted plants, i.e. physical units. Companies, i.e. organizational units, were only randomly captured by the statistics. Still, the data allows at least a rough comparison with the company size statistics for the USA.

In the Federal Republic of Germany, the picture was relatively stable in the second half of the 20th century. Until 1970, the proportion of employees working in major companies increased slightly, and subsequently fell back to almost the base level of 1950. While major companies in the USA accounted for around 40 percent of all employment in most years, major companies in the Federal Republic of Germany only reached levels of between 13 and 16 percent. Although medium-sized businesses even saw a significant increase in their share of all employees in the Federal Republic of Germany, from 22.4 percent in 1950 to 29.2 percent in 1987, this happened primarily at the expense of small businesses. In many cases, smaller companies grew into the medium-size category.

Figure 4: Employee ratios of companies in the Federal Republic of Germany by business size, 1970–2012

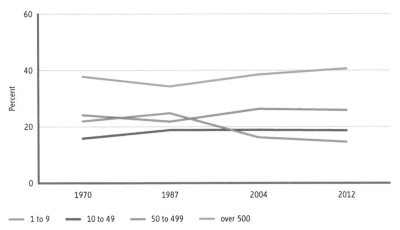

Source: Federal Statistical Office (ed.), "Unternehmen und Arbeitsstätten" Fachserie 2, Heft 11, Arbeitsstätten, Unternehmen und Beschäftigte 1987, 1970, 1961, 1950, Stuttgart 1990, p. 114; idem (ed.), Sonderauswertung des Unternehmensregisters 2004 bis 2014 im Auftrag des IfM Bonn, Wiesbaden.

At this point, it is worth noting again that the difference in company size does not equate to the difference between family and non-family companies, which is the point of interest here. However, the lack of accurate data forces us to use company size as a workaround, and the probability that a company is a family business is significantly higher for smaller companies than for major companies. To ensure that the data from both sides of the Atlantic are comparable, the 500-employee mark has been chosen as the threshold for years after 1970.[78] Companies that stayed below that benchmark are considered small or medium-sized, and most of them were family businesses. It is more difficult to justify plausibility assumptions about companies employing more than 500 employees. It is likely that some of these companies were also family-controlled and family-managed, but this link is much more tenuous because—roughly speaking—its accuracy decreases as the size of the companies increases.

The comparison of employment ratios of the different company categories does not produce exact results, but rather identifies general yet interesting trends. By reducing the threshold between large and medium-sized
to 500 employees, the statistically detectable differences diminish. SMEs
continued to carry greater weight in the Federal Republic of Germany.
On average, the share of employees attributable to major companies was
around ten percent higher in the USA than in the Federal Republic of Germany, although SMEs continued to provide the majority of jobs in both
countries.

It can therefore be considered certain that, relatively speaking, the SME
segment was and still is larger in the Federal Republic of Germany than in
the USA. This applies specifically to the category of 50 to 499 employees, i.e.
larger SMEs, which has a high incidence of hidden champions with strong
positions in the global market. Beyond that, there are convergences here as
well.

In the course of the 1970s, both countries initially recorded a relative decline in the share of employment provided by major companies. This was
caused by the interplay of several developments, which coincided in certain
phases: first, automation and the resulting use of numerical control (NC)
machines rebalanced the advantages of mass production in many sectors.
Physical labor input declined and technical set-up times were reduced, making the production of smaller batch sizes profitable. In many sectors, this
development also opened up the market to SMEs. Second, this also applies
to the pluralization of consumer wishes, which led to diversified demand.
In many consumer industries, sales were no longer generated by standardized mass products, but by more specialized goods. Here, too, niches and
opportunities arose for smaller flexible enterprises. Third, the structural crisis affecting the mining and the old iron and steel industries had a more significant impact on the major companies dominating these sectors than on
smaller businesses, which were more adept at managing the shift towards service provision than monolithic industrial companies are. The fourth point,
closely related to the third, is that the trend towards outsourcing services
and specialized production and supplier input created new opportunities for
small and medium-sized firms. Fifth, the boom in services was one of the
main reasons for the drop in capital expenditure required to establish smaller
companies. In the 1980s and 1990s, it was ultimately the spread of PCs and
the Internet that allowed start-ups to enter the market quickly. Likewise, we
will have to examine the extent to which the rise in government start-up pro-

grams, innovation incentives and the expansion of private equity facilitated the formation of new companies.

Short- and medium-term trends and countertrends overlapped at times, as indicated by the fact that major companies began to regain importance in the USA and Germany at the end of the 1980s. This trend was, however, a little steeper and started from a higher base in the USA. It also reflected the forces of the beginnings of the second wave of globalization. In its wake, massive increases in foreign direct investment (FDI) triggered a new concentration process. Between 1990 and 2007 alone, FDI outflows, i.e. the newly added controlling capital investments from domestic entities to companies abroad, increased by 13 percent per year, and the number of cross-border acquisitions and mergers rose by nine percent annually.[79] As a result of the emergence and accelerating integration of global value chains, large multinational corporations became the key players of globalization. This posed new challenges, in particular for small and medium-sized family companies, to internationalize themselves and find new sources of capital for such moves.

Figure 5: Employee ratios of US companies by business size, 1967–2012

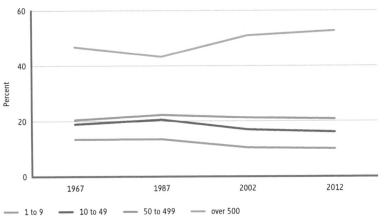

Source: U.S. Department of Commerce, Enterprise Statistics, vol. 1976, p. 164 et seq. ibid, vols. 1987 & 1991, p. 13; Company Summary: Survey of Business Owners, vol. 2002, p. 1336 et seq.; ibid, vol. 2012.

To summarize, we can say that the company sizes that are typically associated with family businesses dominated in both countries over the entire period under investigation, but shaped the national economic structures to different degrees. Without doubt, family businesses were more resilient in the Federal Republic of Germany—a phenomenon related to the consistently higher significance of the industrial sector there. Although the proportion of people employed in industry and the construction sector is on a long-term decline in both countries, it stood at 33.5 percent in Germany in 2000, while it had already dropped to 23.3 percent in the USA. In 2017, the corresponding figures were 27.3 and 18.9 percent respectively.[80] Stable productive assets in family ownership, long-term commitment to the management of companies and a high level of specialization in high-quality industrial products for which there is worldwide demand are key characteristics of the German production model, which to some extent defies deindustrialization or slows it down in some cases. The social cost of faster, unbridled structural transformation was therefore significantly higher in the USA, where entire regions ("rust belts") and population groups were virtually abandoned, and social support from the state was inadequate.

As Figures 4 and 5 demonstrate, the USA had a larger proportion of major companies, which suggests a lower proportion of family businesses, although the two countries were not all that far apart according to this admittedly imprecise criterion. In both cases, family businesses were constituent elements of the respective corporate landscapes.

The many disruptions caused by wars and political system changes in Germany's history underscored the role of family businesses as continuity-preserving entities to a greater degree than in the USA, which experienced neither an overthrow of its political system nor military rule by a foreign power. Since the Second War of Independence from 1812 to 1815, during which Washington was burnt by British troops (1814), there has to this day not been a single invasion, not even an invasion attempt, in the USA's continental territory. Family businesses play a special role in high-risk environments with unstable structures and high levels of political uncertainty.[81] Conversely, in a stable political environment they were evidently not needed to the same degree as long-term anchors of stability. Risks could—to a greater extent—be left to the mechanisms of the market. Over decades, this gave rise to the different institutional frameworks, which set the development of family businesses on different paths: market-based managerial capitalism in the USA and the economic culture of coordinated capitalism in Germany. In the following sections, we take a detailed look at these divergences and convergences in historical development.

C. Inheritance Law and the Preservation of Continuity

I.   The History of Property Rights. Differing Paths in Germany and the USA

The long-term chances of the survival of family businesses have long been affected in Germany and the US by the statutory treatment of inherited wealth. Germany has always had a "familial-social understanding of ownership", originating in Germanic law, which separated property from the individual and assigned it to the family collective. When a family member died, his or her property remained in the family. In the USA, in contrast, an "individual-meritocratic understanding of ownership" was predominant,[82] whereby inherited wealth was considered to be unearned, while assets created by the individual were held in the highest esteem. "No man should receive a dollar unless that dollar has been fairly earned", said Theodore Roosevelt in 1910, further underlining this principle.[83]

Property is a fundamental and not merely an economic principle of order. Ownership concepts shape the way a society deals with questions as to how rights to material goods should be assigned. "Property rights" within the meaning of institutional economics are therefore based on culturally more deep-rooted "property relations", that is to say, on differing forms of the perception and appropriation of property, which are used to codify legal standards. In the USA, the state enforces individually assigned titles and the proprietary regulation of as many social relationships as possible, also referred to as "propertization from above". The German legal tradition, in contrast, emphasizes the primacy of the family as an institution that is worth protecting.[84] The concept of preserving the continuity of families and the companies run by them through tax benefits and political protection is deeply rooted in Germany, but it has hardly any equivalent in the USA. Until the 1987 Supreme Court decision in Hodel versus Irving, an inheritance was not considered a natural right, unlike other forms of property. For this reason, the state was entitled to intervene without restriction in the inter-generational transfer of wealth. According to this logic, the individual possession of property that would otherwise enjoy almost total legal protection in the USA comes to an end on the death of the individual. In an explicit counterposition to the British hereditary monarchy and the dynastic accumulation of wealth, Thomas Jefferson, one of the founding fathers of the USA, reiterated his mistrust of inherited wealth and any form of long-term power exercised by the dead: "Earth belongs in usufruct to the living; the dead have neither powers nor rights over it. The portion occupied by an individual ceases to be and reverts to society."[85] As a result, the subsequent heir ties in real estate (entailed estates or fee-tail) and in other forms of wealth were abolished in one of the first laws of the new state. Land should not be removed from the market and each citizen should have equal opportunity to acquire wealth.

The circumvention of these principles by way of long-term trusts was limited by the "Rule against perpetuities" introduced in 1833 in the court case Nightingale versus Burrell. After that, the founders of a trust could only make dispositions relating to their own lifetimes or, by way of an additional limitation to a period of 21 years, dispositions that influence the wealth of heirs who had already been born at the time the trust was established. In short, trusts could only exist for a maximum of three generations or two inheritances. This rule remained in force until 2011.[86] At the same time (since 1829), the influence of the family over the trusts was weakened by the fact that the trustees were permitted to invest the moneys entrusted to them entirely at their own discretion. Even when opting for the riskiest investments, they were not bound by the instructions of the family and could rarely be prosecuted. Trusts were intended to safe keep and multiply the wealth entrusted to them during the agreed term, to the benefit of the beneficiaries; the latter received dividends, usually in order to provide for them, and also the assets themselves when the trust was terminated. In exchange, however, the families lost control over their capital assets. Trusts were therefore a mechanism for protecting family capital from wasteful consumption by the heirs, and encouraged the early separation of ownership and management that was to become so characteristic of the US economy overall.[87] A mistrust of inheritances and their negative effects, such as the increasing concentration of wealth, remained dominant in the US, and the state secured for itself theoretically unlimited access to inheritance-based transfers of wealth independent of its performance, even if it never fully utilized this scope of access prior to or even after 1916.

In Germany, in contrast, the family was considered a quasi-natural legal entity worthy of special protection. This resulted in limitations on the testamentary freedom of the testator in favor of his or her family, a privileged status of inherited wealth compared with other forms of capital gains and generally a tradition of a rather moderate taxation on inheritance. During deliberations on the first Empire-wide inheritance tax law, two principles were formulated in 1905 that continue to apply today: first of all, the principle of family ownership. Assets do not belong to individual persons but are owned by the entire family, "from which enjoyment the dying person merely steps away, without, by his death, giving something to the next of kin that they would not have possessed up to then." The following was added: "the children and the surviving spouse would have participated in the acquisition of the assets through their own work." This arrangement applied in particular to family businesses in the agricultural and commercial sectors, whose privileged status was legitimized in this way. Second, the Reichstag made a landmark structural policy decision for the benefit of the *Mittelstand*, namely that "middle segment of our society in cities and in rural areas alike" in particular were deserving of "the special attention" of the state.[88]

The Social Democratic Party (SPD) objected, saying that even large assets would also benefit from low inheritance tax. "Excessive individual wealth has accumulated to an intolerable extent from an economic point of view." The super rich apparently indulge in "excessive luxury", which presents a "social threat". Finally, the SPD drew attention to the "ever dwindling family cohesion", which takes the principle of family property ad absurdum.[89] However, these objections were played down and had no consequence, and the notion of using inheritance taxation law as an instrument of incisive socio-political reforms did not prevail.

II. The Beginnings of Modern Inheritance Law in Germany and the USA

Modern inheritance law was introduced in Germany in 1906 and in the USA in 1916. A number of strategic decisions preceded it. The Code Napoléon or Code Civil introduced after 1804 in the territories occupied by France continued to apply in many cases after the defeat of France, primarily in the areas left of the Rhine, until it was replaced in 1900 by the German Civil Code (BGB). In order to prevent the emergence of a new aristocracy, this modern Civil Code introduced the principle of the compulsory portion (of estate) based on the French model, and abolished the rule of primogeniture. The cohesive handover of lands became more difficult once all the children of a decedent had to be taken into account, as each heir could demand a portion.[90] However, the abolition of the rule of primogeniture also increased flexibility: later-born sons could now take over an agricultural or commercial business as its principal heir once it became possible to choose the most suitable successor.

This disadvantage of the principle of compulsory portion (of estate)—namely, that it could result in the fragmentation of assets and the sale of companies—was countered in the mercantile middle class by a systematic education and marriage policy based on economic considerations. Marriage between cousins was very frequent in business families in the 19th century. Furthermore, the outflow of money from compulsory portions was to be prevented: Where possible, the sons were meant to remain in the business and daughters were to marry men who would join the business or who would become strategic partners with their own businesses.[91] This ensured that in many cases the compulsory portion was not lost, but remained in the family. Inherited wealth was often tied down by way of partnership agreements, such that the community of heirs had to cooperate. It was possible to prepare the corporate constitution so as to provide for the planning of the succession process and to prevent any financing gaps that might result from payments to family members who were not joining the business.[92] Logically, then, it is likely that the provisions relating to compulsory portions pre-defined these family strategies.

Without a compulsory portion in the USA there was no such incentive, and this probably weakened the cohesiveness of families. The principle of unlimited testamentary freedom allowed not only for flexibility when choosing successors but also the complete abandonment of the business or the family—for example, by way of large philanthropic donations or bequests. This occurred very frequently, as many rich people made the principle of Andrew Carnegie, steel baron, their own: "The man who dies thus rich dies disgraced." The man who does not part with his wealth while he is alive, will die "unwept, unhonored, and unsung."[93] Wealth that has been built up by individuals must not be bequeathed, but must flow back into society in the form of charitable donations.

Photo 8: Max, Aby and Paul Warburg (M.M. Warburg & Co.) take a walk (1930). Paul Warburg married into the New York bank Kuhn, Loeb & Co. in 1895 and later was considered to be one of the primary initiators of the US central bank FED.

In Germany, the Civil Code, developed between 1874 and 1896 and introduced in 1900, provided for inheritance rules that essentially continue to apply today. During the extremely contentious debates, proposals were made to limit by state order the power of disposition of the testator beyond death or to reduce social inequality by way of sensitive inheritance taxation, but they all failed.[94] On the contrary: the limitations on testamentary freedom in place up to then were relaxed, which simplified the succession of powerful successors. In addition, the German Civil Code provided for intestate succession, which comes into play where the testator has not made a last will and testament. It regulates the size of the shares within the community of heirs by setting down the order in which relatives are entitled to benefit; that is, spouses and direct descendants of the testator starting with children, then grandchildren, then great-grandchildren etc.

Inheritance tax was introduced across the German Empire in 1906 against the backdrop of a fiscal crisis in which the Empire was faced with increasing expenditure, particularly due to building up its fleet, but was not permitted to levy direct taxes. This step had already been taken much earlier in a number of individual states: The Stamp Act (Stempelgesetz) introduced in Prussia in 1822 contained two principles that shaped the law of the German Empire: the distinction between degrees of kinship and the tax exemption of direct descendants and ancestors and of wives if they inherited together with legitimate children. Due to the exemption of most heirs and the very low taxation rates, there was virtually no redistribution effect. The idea that the nuclear family especially deserved protection was a guiding principle, and one which especially benefited family businesses.

A hereditary succession tax, which taxes the heirs, was levied both in Prussia and across the Empire. The most striking feature of this tax—and the one that distinguished it clearly from estate tax in the USA—was that it could be planned in dependency on the kinship of heirs and testators; that is to say, it offered privileged status to children and spouses.[95] The latter then became fully exempt from inheritance tax in 1906, which was one of the main reasons this tax brought in so little money. When the introduction of an estate tax was discussed in 1909, it was dropped with the argument that it would be an excessive burden on family businesses, in particular in the agricultural sector. Various initiatives aimed at increasing inheritance tax and including children and spouses also failed.[96]

In the USA, inheritances were traditionally only taxed in some federal states, at moderate rates below ten percent and without progression. In addition, this tax did not apply to children or spouses, only to collateral relatives such as brothers or cousins. At federal level, there was an inheritance taxation with a top rate of five percent on only three occasions, for a short period and during military conflicts (1797 to 1802, 1862 to 1870 and 1898 to 1902). The transition to a permanent estate tax arose, as was the case in Germany, from the increasing financial needs of the state and a contentious discussion on social inequality, because as a consequence of the "great merger movement", a very small business elite was amassing ever greater wealth. From the end of the 19th century, the criticism of the concentration of wealth by powerful "progressivism" and the Populist Party (People's Party) was as sharp as it was broad-based. In Congress in 1906, President Theodore Roosevelt called for the introduction of an inheritance tax, whose "primary objective should be to put a constantly increasing burden on the inheritance of those swollen fortunes which it is certainly of no benefit to this country to perpetuate." In the same year, in a nearly class-militant speech, he even spoke of the "malefactors of great wealth, the wealthy criminal class."[97] Initially, this was not a position able to gain majority support, but the introduction in 1909 of an excise tax on corporations and in 1913 of a permanent income tax with top rates of between one and seven percent signaled a change in sentiment.

In 1915, the concluding report of a commission on industrial relations that investigated the roots of the increasing social conflict declared that an "industrial feudalism" had emerged in the USA: entire cities and regions were apparently controlled by individual companies or families.[98] It was therefore necessary "to check the growth of an hereditary aristocracy, which is foreign to every conception of American Government …".[99] A member of the commission specifically proposed an income and estate tax which, in the upper range, would be "absolutely confiscatory", in order to prevent the creation and transfer of disproportional wealth "in the hands of any individual, group or family".[100]

III. Divergences Widen. Wartime and the Inter-War Period

In 1916, against the backdrop of these debates and of the increasing financial needs of the state, of war-related collapsing customs revenue and of the looming entry of the USA into the war (1917), a permanent federal estate tax was introduced with the Revenue Act.[101] It did not tax the acquisition of wealth by the heirs but the undivided inheritance before it was passed on. This tax was considered to be the final tax obligation of the deceased, not of one of the heirs, and was therefore referred to as an "estate tax" in contrast to the "hereditary succession tax" in Germany. All by itself, the estate tax is more significant due to the fact that deductions can be applied only once, that is, to the estate. In the case of the hereditary succession tax, each heir was entitled to deductions, and if the estate were divided across a number of heirs, there might be no tax debt at all. However, the number of heirs is irrelevant in the USA, and the higher progression levels are reached more quickly due to the assessment of the undivided estate.

The decisive difference for family businesses is that this tax does not differentiate according to the kinship of the heirs to the deceased. After a deduction of 50,000 dollars, the tax rate increased from one percent up to ten percent for assets of over five million dollars. In 1917, the top rate of tax on inheritances of more than ten million dollars rose to 22 percent and in 1924 to 40 percent.[102] Large inheritances were thus now being more heavily taxed than during wartime. There were also inheritance taxes in individual federal states, which could be credited up to 25 percent. Following heavy criticism, the top tax rate was lowered to 20 percent in 1926, and state taxes, usually around 14 percent, but at times up to 22 percent, could now be credited up to 80 percent.[103] In 1932, during the Great Depression, President Hoover raised the top rate to 45 percent, and when his successor, Franklin D. Roosevelt, introduced huge spending programs as part of the New Deal, the rate rose to 60 percent in 1934, to 70 percent in 1935 and during the war even to 77 percent. In 1934, the top income tax rate reached 63 percent.[104] This extremely severe levy by the tax authorities led to an increase in the number of trusts set up by affluent families—for example, by the Rockefellers as early as 1934.[105]

As we have already seen, trusts place the assets under the management of a trustee; the assets are tied up and the owner can no longer dispose over them. The scope for designing such a trust is enormous. The most important item was the option, available up to 1976, of lowering estate tax by skipping two generations, such that two inheritances were tax free. Instead of paying tax twice, once when the husband died and again upon the death of the wife with the subsequent transfer of the assets to a child, the estate tax was levied only once, namely on the death of the husband. The disadvantages were that the freedom of disposition over the assets was removed and that trusts could only last a maximum of three generations, that a third party, the trustee, gained influence and that the state was given supervisory rights. Nonetheless, trusts became standard instruments in the USA in the case of very large assets with the aim of reducing the tax burden and safeguarding corporate continuity—because trusts could contain clauses for the continuation of businesses. They also looked after family members who were not considered for a role in the company: that is, they kept these people, as it were, away from the company.[106]

Family foundations in Germany allow for comparable, yet also many additional benefits. As independent legal entities, they belong to themselves, so to speak. They are managed by the foundation bodies and not by external trustees, and the foundation bodies are predominantly made up of family members. German family foundations are not subject to temporal limitations. Some of the 800 family foundations in existence today, of which 100 to 150 are business family foundations, were set up 200 years ago or more. For example, the Hamburg merchant, Martin Johann Paulsen (1735–1808), stipulated in his will that all direct descendants should receive dividends from the foundation income "for all eternity",[107] and this foundation still exists today.

As is the case with American trusts, German family foundations are not subject to disclosure requirements. They can organize family businesses permanently and stably without the families losing control over the company. The transfer of all the shares in the company to the foundation provides effective protection against the fragmentation of the assets, intrusion by third parties or hostile takeovers. The will of the founder—which at times may extend far into the future—exerts great influence. In addition, such foundations may provide for family members at low rates of taxation. They also offer the advantage of enabling the outflow of liquidity to be planned. German foundation law is very flexible and allows for a high level of inheritance tax planning. In addition, up to 1974 it was possible to avoid inheritance tax permanently after the first inheritance. Business-related foundations have far greater scope in Germany than in the USA, where the separation of company and foundation is more strictly defined and offers less scope for maneuver.[108]

Apart from trusts, some of the popular options for tax avoidance in the USA were the conclusion of high-value life insurance policies, the payout for which was tax-free, or inheritance tax insurance and gifts during lifetime ("inter vivo gifts"), which were only taxed from 1924 on. The gift tax was dropped in 1926, as it was difficult to administer and easy to circumvent, but re-introduced in 1932 for situational tax reasons: the state needed money during the Great Depression and gifts were clearly being abused for the purposes of estate tax avoidance. The gift tax rate was 75 percent of the estate tax, varying between 2.25 and 57.75 percent.

Even after 1932 there was still an incentive for giving away money as opposed to bequeathing it. It was possible to divide the assets into a number of small parts and to give them to different people, for example to all one's children, instead of taxing the entire estate together. The transfer of assets either remained tax-free due to the multiple deductions now taking effect, or moved into a lower tax bracket due to being divided into a number of smaller amounts. Proposals for merging everything into one uniform transfer tax were repeatedly put on the table but were not implemented, and it was not before 1976 that the estate tax and the gift tax were harmonized.

In 1941, the top rate of estate tax for large assets from 50 million dollars upwards rose to 77 percent, a confiscatory rate that remained in place until 1976. This tax rate encouraged many family businesses to sell and switch to other asset classes. Businesses that continued to exist had a considerable level of liquidity siphoned off by the tax authorities. It is not possible to determine precisely how great this effect was or to what extent it was moderated by way of trusts and the gift tax, but the estate tax burden on family businesses is still a controversial topic. When a further increase was discussed in 1950, the Chamber of Commerce voiced sharp criticism in the House of Representatives: "The present estate and gift taxes are essentially capital levies which act as efficient brakes upon the private enterprise system." They claimed that with tax rates of up to 77 percent it was utterly impossible for family businesses to accumulate sufficient capital to set up new companies or to expand or maintain existing businesses.[109]

The consequences of the estate tax extended to the enforced liquidation or sale of family businesses in the case of inheritance or the retention of a "large readily available sum of money" in the event of inheritance which could otherwise have flowed into the company. "Such a man is often obliged to keep a large balance idle." Particularly SMEs in family ownership with a low capital cover—which was, moreover, frequently tightly bound up in machinery, real estate and inventory—were under pressure to sell in the case of inheritance. With the tax rates came an increase in the probability of a "forced sale of a family business", the "elimination of such separate business from our competitive economy" and the "growth of monopolies".[110]

One example is the sale of the Freedom Valvoline Oil Company in 1949. The two elderly majority shareholders sold up, as the descendants were not in a position to carry on the business in the event of their deaths. This news was announced to the 1,000 employees and the media accompanied by sharp criticism of the tax system and the claim that the system strengthened large businesses that were less affected by estate tax and that by contrast, family businesses "cannot be passed on to a second generation."[111]

The arguments of the Chamber of Commerce were no doubt tactically motivated and in substance somewhat exaggerated, as they did not address the possibilities for circumvention. An investigation by the Treasury in 1949/50 established that 45 percent of all inheritances over 500,000 dollars went into trusts in order to save on estate tax and to provide for family members who, due to a lack of expert knowledge, were frequently not in a position to make successful investment decisions themselves. Even if one removes those cases in which tax breaks came at the price of substantial restrictions on the power of disposition, 55 percent of all large inheritance cases remained subject to confiscatory taxes at the highest rate, which damaged large numbers of family businesses.[112]

These statistics show two things. On the one hand, a considerable number of wealthy Americans managed to avoid the grip of the state and, with the help of trusts, passed on their wealth undiminished to their descendants. The aim of the legislator to enforce the meritocratic principle across the board and to prevent a dynastic concentration of assets was repeatedly undermined. On the other hand, around the middle of the century, more than half of the larger inheritances did not appear to be using such evasive options. This probably particularly affected active, entrepreneurial families who did not want to surrender their businesses to the trusts, i.e. de facto to managers and trustees. They were faced with the choice of either paying the tax and weakening the business and their assets, or of selling part or all of the business. Overall, therefore, we see both the circumvention of estate tax and its drastic effects. Ultimately, the affected family business owners had to choose between the far-reaching preservation of their assets or the intergenerational continuity of control—and often management—of the business. As a result, American family businesses were faced with a serious problem that their German counterparts were generally spared.

With the dogma of unearned wealth established as a starting point, the discussion in the USA knew hardly any taboos. The democratic presidential candidate in 1972, George McGovern, demanded the introduction of a guaranteed minimum income for all citizens. He also wanted to introduce a progressive hereditary succession tax that would impose a 100 percent tax on inheritances over 500,000 dollars. He made himself so unpopular with this and other proposals that he failed spectacularly at the ballot box.[113]

In Germany, the state was a great deal more restrained in its grasp, especially for owners of family businesses. Here as well, the First World War and its aftermath contributed to a worsening of the burden. The bleak financial situation of the Weimar Republic forced the inclusion of children and spouses in the inheritance tax with rates of between one and 35 percent as part of the "Erzberger'sche Finanz- und Steuerreform" (finance and tax reform) of 1919. An additional estate tax was introduced too, with combined top rates of inheritance and estate taxes of 90 percent. Yet this level of taxation, extremely severe by German standards, did not last long. In 1922, the top tax rate for children was halved and spouses became completely exempt once again, though this was reversed in 1925 in the case of spouses with no children. The estate tax was dropped altogether in 1922. These measures concluded the establishment of inheritance tax in Germany and it has remained within this framework to this day, with the burden on intergenerational asset transfers lower than in the USA since that time.[114]

After the reform of 1925, the tax rate for children and spouses in childless marriages in Germany was between two and 15 percent and therefore far below the USA, where the top tax rate was 40 percent until 1926. In the most frequent cases of a marriage with children (biological or adopted) or—in the case of an early death of children—with living grandchildren, spouses were exempt from all inheritance taxes. In the USA, however, spouses—whether they had children, grandchildren or not—and children paid a maximum of 45 percent from 1932 and since the war 77 percent.[115]

The only noteworthy change introduced by the National Socialist regime was the six-fold increase in 1934 in the deduction for living descendants, which was justified as follows: "Promoting the close family unit is a demographic matter of course in a state system whose primary aim is 'people and race'."[116] The extent to which National Socialism favored individual family businesses and the frequency with which it advanced the erosion of constitutional principles was demonstrated by what was known as the Lex Krupp ("Decree of the Führer regarding the family business Fried. Krupp") of 1943, which approved an inheritance tax saving of approximately 400 million reichsmarks for the Krupp family. The prerequisite here was a change in the legal form from a stock corporation to a partnership, something that was also initiated by way of various tax incentives in over 5,000 other cases (Chapter E.III). In the case of Krupp, the tax privilege was primarily attributable to the family's personal intervention with Hitler. The text of the Führer's decree was as follows: "Fried. Krupp, as a family business, has made an outstanding and truly unique contribution to the military strength of the German people for over 132 years. It is therefore my wish that the company remain a family business." The company statutes were to be submitted to Hitler for approval. "The Reich Minister of Finance is hereby authorized to regulate the inheritance (gift) tax arising due to the death of a proprietor or the transfer of proprietorship to another proprietor within the meaning of this decree."[117] One characteristic of the dictatorship was that it replaced rule-based treatment with the purely arbitrary.

IV. Continuity and Reform after 1945

After 1945, the changes relating to inheritance law introduced by the National Socialist state were quickly eliminated. To begin with, the Allies adopted new legislation which was in line with the high tax rates in their home countries. Control Council Law no. 17 of February 1946 repealed the exemption of spouses and increased the top rate for children and spouses (tax class 1) to 60 percent with reduced deductions. Military Government Law no. 64 of June 1948, which only applied in the Western zones, lowered the rates for category 1 to a range of between four and 38 percent and exempted surviving spouses from taxation on inheritances of up to 500,000 DM, provided there was issue from the marriage. In 1951, there was a further decrease and finally in 1954 a return to the lower rates of a maximum of seven percent in tax class 1 that had applied between 1925 and 1945.[118]

As with many other things, the German system of moderate taxation was thus reinstated within a short space of time. Generally speaking, the Allies encroached deeply into the German system of production, for example, by repealing the Trade and Crafts Code (Handwerksordnung, HwO), breaking up industrial concerns and large banks and by introducing a strict ban on cartels. As with the Allied inheritance tax reforms, none of this legislation endured. In the 1950s, German perseverance proved too strong. Inheritance taxation, at times incredibly severe, was only an episode: in 1954, Germany reinstated the status of 1925, which continued to apply until the reform of 1974.

In the USA, the high tax burden under American law resulted in problems for small and medium-sized family enterprises which their German counterparts were spared. Low capital provisions regularly resulted in American family businesses not being in a position to pay their tax debt in the case of inheritance without selling considerable shares in their company or selling the company entirely or liquidating it. Not only did the high top rates of up to 77 percent introduced during the war endure until 1976, bracket creep also increased the burden in real terms, as the deductions and the threshold values remained constant for decades. The problem became particularly severe in the 1970s when inflation reached twelve to 14 percent: the top rate of ten million dollars was reached more often, which means it shrank in real terms due to bracket creep.[119]

In many cases, the high estate tax prevented inter-family succession, as the US Chamber of Commerce pointed out in 1975 during debates on tax reform.[120] As already seen, it was possible to partially circumvent the extreme burden by way of trusts, advance gifts or by concluding high-value life insurance policies. Yet such measures required good legal advisors, to which the owners of small companies in particular did not have access.

The Tax Reform Act of 1976 lowered the top rate of tax to 70 percent but increased the lowest rate from three to 18 percent. The top rate was now reached at five instead of ten million dollars, but the deduction was doubled from 60,000 to 120,000 dollars. Various loopholes such as gifts shortly before death (deathbed gifts) or skipping up to two generations by transferring assets to a grandchild, whether by way of trusts or other methods, were closed by the introduction of a generation skipping transfer tax. On the other hand, deductions increased significantly, particularly for spouses. The gift tax and the estate tax were combined to create a uniform tax: gifts during life, which were previously taxed at a lower rate, no longer brought any advantage.

A specific preferential tax treatment, the "special valuation", was introduced for the first time in 1976 for "closely held businesses", that is, small family businesses and small farms. It permitted the undervaluation of corporate assets by up to 500,000 dollars, provided a relative of the testator continued to run the company or the farm for at least ten years. There was no clear definition of what a "closely held business" is; in fact, the tax authorities had considerable discretion here and it was even possible to apply this "special valuation" to SMEs. However, as the valuation was limited to 500,000 dollars, it became less relevant as company assets increased.

One additional preferential tax treatment that was created specifically for smaller farms and SMEs was the option of deferring the payment of the estate tax under specific conditions for an extended period of time.[121] Payment could be suspended for five years and then be made subsequently over a period of up to ten years, making it possible to defer payment of the full amount until 15 years after inheritance. De facto this amounted to an opportunity in many cases of paying inheritance tax from current revenue and not from company assets. Larger family businesses did not benefit from these rules. Overall, this was a paradigm shift for the benefit of family-owned SMEs, but the tradition was retained of the high taxation of more substantial assets with a top rate of 70 percent up to 1981, thereafter 65 percent, and then between 1984 and 2001 of 55 percent.[122]

Starting in 1969, the social-liberal coalition in Germany introduced fundamental reforms, as it did in so many areas, from education to criminal law. Chancellor Willy Brandt wanted to use the restructuring of inheritance tax to redress social imbalance and relieve SMEs. Despite relatively low tax rates, family businesses increasingly reached the top rates due to their fast growth and inflation. This had a particularly negative effect, as the top rate more than doubled in 1959 to 15 percent for children and spouses. Where the inheritance was divided between a number of children, it could happen that each child had to pay 15 percent, which threatened to permanently reduce the assets of the company. The fundamental problem, evident in Germany too, was that the private wealth of the successors was often not sufficient to pay the inheritance taxes. Alternatively, it was possible to take assets out of the business or to sell all or part of the business, but this created problems with partnerships and GmbHs.[123] After all, many family businesses were undercapitalized and therefore particularly at risk. The Brandt government focused its reform policy specifically on these issues, and Brandt adopted the following guiding principles as early as 1970:

"As part of the reform of the inheritance law, an attempt to relieve small and medium-sized assets and to justifiably increase inheritance tax for large assets is being envisaged. Consideration needs to be given to preserving SMEs in the case of inheritance and avoiding liquidity problems that arise through the payment of taxes owed."[124]

Five equally potent factors were decisive in this discourse, which took place at the same time in the USA:

1. The crisis involving old industries and their large companies. 2. The perception of SMEs as special assets in economies which were threatened by stagflation and the emergence of new competitors in Asia. 3. Concerns about the increase in the concentration of economic power in the form of holding companies (trusts). 4. More attention paid to the topic of inheritance, as considerable wealth had been accumulated during the post-war years of strong growth and was now being transferred to the next generation. 5. The increased use of family foundations to avoid inheritance tax. The Federal government's goal with the reform of the inheritance tax was thus a mixture of competition policy, structural policy and social policy.

The second Tax Reform Act of 1974 increased tax rates, yet also granted generous deductions. The new top tax rate was 35 percent instead of 15 percent, but it only applied upwards of 100 million DM. Prior to that, the threshold was ten million. The deduction for children increased threefold from 30,000 to 90,000 DM, and for spouses it was now 250,000 DM, in addition to pension allowance of 250,000 DM. The principle of massive preferential tax treatment for children and spouses compared with distant relatives and non-family persons remained in place. The latter were subject to a top tax rate of 70 percent, which was just below the rate in the USA for all heirs (77 percent). From 1977 on, these rates were identical in both countries at 70 percent.

In the case of particularly large inheritances, there was certainly an increased burden in Germany: from 1976 on it resulted in a significant surge in inheritance tax revenue. The introduction at the same time of an option to defer the payment of an inheritance tax debt for up to seven years had a mitigating effect on family businesses. Even if a monthly deferred payment interest of 0.5 percent was levied, it was possible to prevent, or at least to minimize, the weakening of company assets by the forced removal of capital. The overall effect of the reform—higher tax rates, less steep progression, higher deductions, considerable preferential tax treatment for close relatives, and the introduction of deferral for up to seven years—was extremely beneficial for SMEs. In general, the reform acted as a support program for family-owned SMEs, one which was very generous compared with the reforms introduced in the USA two years later. It is interesting, however, that both countries moved in the same direction and used similar instruments.

The 1974 reform ended or complicated the tax avoidance qua family foundation that had been frequent up to then: regular inheritance tax had only been incurred when a family foundation was set up in the event of death, but not in the case of subsequent cases of inheritance. The inheritance tax now introduced was intended to prevent precisely this—namely, that the assets tied up in the foundation were entirely exempt from inheritance tax over a number of generations. It is a type of fictitious inheritance tax that feigns a transfer of assets to two children every 30 years. As a result, inheritance tax in category 1 becomes due every 30 years with two deductions being credited. However, it is possible to split the substitute inheritance tax into 30 annual amounts with interest of 5.5 percent.[125]

1974 saw the introduction of a time limitation that affected the tax appeal of the family foundation with its numerous instances of the preferential tax treatment of family businesses: if a period of more than 30 years transpired with no inheritance at all, substitute inheritance tax was owed, making a family foundation the less advantageous option, as natural living persons would not have been burdened with any form of inheritance tax during this period. Nonetheless, family foundations remain attractive: they provide long-term stability and are capable of preventing disputes over inheritance.

For example, Reinhold Würth, manufacturer of dowels and assembly technology, transferred his company to a foundation in 1987. As a result, none of the heirs can demand a payout that would remove assets from the company. The heirs only receive moderate gratuities of two to three percent of the profit, which is not a burden on the company. The foundation also provides a protective barrier against the imponderables of family life. The highest-ranking body at Würth, the foundation supervisory board, is conceived in such a way that non-family experts will hold the majority of voting rights after the death of Reinhold Würth.[126]

Figure 6: Inheritance, estate and gift tax progression in the USA and Germany after the reforms of 1976 and 1974 respectively

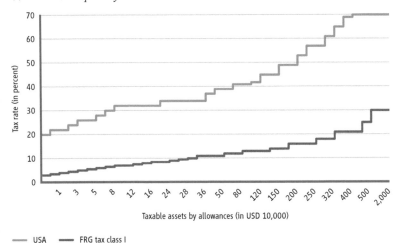

— USA   — FRG tax class I

Source: Gesetz zur Reform des Erbschaftsteuer- und Schenkungsteuerrechts vom 17.04.1974, in: Federal Law Gazette (BGBl) 42 (Z1997A), p. 940 (Section 19); Tax Reform Act of October 4, 1976; Public Law 94-455 of 94th Congress, https://babel.hathitrust.org/cgi/pt?id=uiug.30112047661969;view=1up;seq=2 (accessed: September 12, 2018). Conversions were made at the average rate of USD 1 to DM 2.5. We thank Mr Yassin Abou El Fadil for creating this graphic.

Overall, the tax burden on American family business remained considerably greater even after the reforms of the 1970s. Figure 6 compares the rates for inheritance, estate and gift tax for inheritance to children, and therefore for the standard situation of the transfer of assets, after the reforms of 1976 and 1974 respectively. Tax class 1 (children and spouses) was applied for Germany. The heirs in this case were substantially privileged compared with a similar group of people in the USA and also distant relatives and non-family heirs. At almost all levels, the tax rate in the USA was at least twice as high as in Germany and in the mid-groups three to five times as high.

V. Fiscal Policy as Structural Policy.
The Recalibration of Inheritance Taxes since 1980

In the USA, a trend towards a gradual reduction in estate tax began with the reform of 1976. Emerging neo-liberalism considered high taxes to be a barrier to growth. With that, the top rate of estate tax under President Reagan dropped in 1982 from 70 to 65 percent and in 1984 to 55 percent, but with significantly lower incremental values. From 1984 on, the top rate applied at three million dollars. At the same time the deduction increased to a still modest 325,000 dollars.[127] In 1981, the transfer of assets to spouses was generally tax-free. In 2002, the top rate dropped to 50 percent and then again in 2007 step by step to 45 percent.[128] In 2011, the rate fell to 35 percent, only to rise again to 40 percent in 2013. Despite the high level of declining top rates, from 77 percent (1942 to 1976) to 40 percent (2013 to 2017), and the long-term payment deferral option for SMEs, estate tax remains a huge barrier to the transfer in particular of large family businesses to the next generation, while spouses have been able to take over these companies without any tax burden since 1981.

With the Economic Growth and Tax Relief Reconciliation Act (EG-TRRA), in 2001 the US government under George W. Bush brought about the gradual reduction of the top rate of tax of 55 percent (2001) to 40 percent (2009). At the same time deductions of 675,000 dollars (2001) were drastically increased to 3.5 million (2009). Finally, estate tax was completely abolished in 2010. The Obama administration considered this to be an unfair privileged treatment of wealthy families. It let EGTRRA expire in 2011, and reintroduced inheritance tax with a top rate of 35 percent and of 40 percent from 2013. However, it increased the deduction to an index-linked five million dollars. By 2017, this rate was raised to 5.5 million, and eleven million dollars for married couples. The increase in the deductions by a factor of 7.4 in ten years resulted in the estate tax affecting fewer and fewer Americans and in 2013, it was levied only in the case of 0.18 percent of all deaths. Whereas in 1977, 139,115 tax returns were still submitted (7.6 percent of all deaths), by 2000 the number was only 52,000 (2.2 percent), and by 2012 this figure had dropped to 3,738 (0.15 percent).[129] After 2010, there were hardly any smaller companies or farms in the USA whose owners had to pay estate tax. In addition to the high deductions, they also benefited from the other elements of preferential tax treatment mentioned above that were introduced in 1976.[130]

The next president, Donald Trump, inaugurated in 2017, promised during his election campaign to abolish estate tax, using the misleading argument that workers, small businesses and farms were to be protected from state interference. These groups have not had to worry for a long time about reductions in their inheritances. However, it is a different matter with larger family businesses whose value is in the three-digit million range: the actual burden in this case is closer to the nominal top rate of 40 percent.

In addition, the tax burden in the federal states should not be forgotten. Up to 2000, all 50 states and the District of Columbia (D.C.) levied taxes in the event of inheritance. By 2013, only 19 states plus D.C. levied mostly estate tax but, in individual cases, inheritance tax too. In Maryland and New Jersey both taxes were levied. The top tax rate is generally 16 percent (as of 2015), with significantly lower deductions.[131] Only from 2005 was it possible to deduct these taxes from Federal Estate Taxes; prior to this, only partial deductibility was possible.[132] The lower deductions in the federal states could result in a person being liable for estate tax in his or her own state while not being subject to tax at federal level. In such cases, deductibility is worthless.

The situation in Germany was significantly more favorable due to lower tax rates, high deductions and the option of deferral. There have also been various reforms since the 1990s that resulted in additional tax breaks for family businesses. For example, an interest-free tax deferral has been granted since 1992 and in 1995 the deferral period was extended from seven to ten years.[133] In 1995, the German Federal Constitutional Court (Bundesverfassungsgericht, BVerfG) classified parts of inheritance taxation up to then as being too severe and therefore unconstitutional, which required further reforms. In its judgement, the protection of medium-sized businesses was recommended for the following revealing reason: "In addition, the legislator [...] has to take into consideration the fact that the existence of certain companies—namely from the *Mittelstand*—can be endangered as a result of an additional financial burden as may be incurred due to inheritance tax. Such businesses [...] are bound to the common good in a special way and are dedicated to acting for the common good. [...] Disposition over the business [...] is more restricted than is the case with company assets that are not tied up. The principle of equality (article 3(1) of the Basic Law, Grundgesetz) requires consideration of this reduced liquidity in the case of heirs who continue to run the company, that is, who neither sell nor give up the company but rather maintain it in its social commitment. In this case, the inheritance tax burden should be assessed such that the continuation of the business is not threatened by tax debt. This obligation [...] is independent of the proximity of the kinship of testator and heirs."[134]

Against the backdrop of the generation of post-war founders who have stepped down since the 1970s and the experience of frequently failing succession, Germany's Supreme Court elevated the intergenerational continuity of family businesses almost to the status of a national state objective. This definition allowed the conclusion of a very strong claim for protection which had—and still has—no equivalent in the USA. An inheritance tax reform followed in 1997 with retrospective effect from 1996. It introduced the following reliefs: The top rate in tax class 1 fell from the current 35 to 30 percent. Deductions were increased significantly, in the case of children more than fourfold. Provided they retained the shares in the business for at least five years, heirs of company assets received preferential tax treatment in three different ways. They were granted an additional deduction of 500,000 DM, a valuation discount of 40 percent for any assets exceeding the deduction, and, regardless of the degree of kinship, were generally placed in tax class 1.

In one stroke, the distant relatives who had been heavily burdened up to then were placed in a far better position. This reform represented a legislative reaction to the demographic trend of declining nuclear families and increasing childlessness and therefore of a reduction in the potential pool of successors. In the interest of securing succession from within the family, the conventional principle of inheritance tax law, which provided for a sharp increase in the tax burden with increasing distance between the testator and the heirs, was breached especially to encourage the transfer of family businesses. This is evidence once again of the strong political protection they enjoyed in Germany, where they are perceived to be indispensable to the economy. Fundamentally, this special ruling balanced out the unfavorable demographic trend and increased the number of potential successors within the family.

From a global perspective, Germany has taken up a unique position. According to a study from 2004, it boasted by far the lowest inheritance tax rates in a comparison of the five leading western industrial nations.[135] In 2008, additional tax breaks were adopted: while the lowest tax rates for distant relatives and other heirs increased considerably, the retention period for business heirs was extended at the same time from five to seven years together with significant or complete exemption from taxation regardless of the tax class of the business heirs. According to the standard exemption, 85 percent of the company assets were initially not taxed. At the same time, the tax liability was dropped if the businesses maintained a certain total wage bill (wages and salaries), thus rewarding the preservation of jobs. Complete tax exemption was also possible (optional relief), if 700 percent of the original wage bill was reached in total within a period of seven years. These two rules therefore provided an incentive for cost-cutting measures prior to inheritance. In addition, the deductions for children were almost doubled and the valuation discount was reduced slightly from 40 to 35 percent.[136] The result was considerable relief for heirs of business assets.

In 2014, the German Federal Constitutional Court declared the new tax breaks introduced in 1996 and 2008 to be unconstitutional "in view of the scope and the options they offered".[137] After some controversial discussions, the rules for SMEs were essentially confirmed in 2016, while at the same time being restricted or suspended in their application to larger companies. In the case of an estate worth more than 26 million euros, company heirs have to prove that the payment of inheritance tax from their private wealth would overstretch them ("exemption needs test"). Half of the latter may be used for taxation purposes. If the resulting amount is not sufficient to meet the tax debt, the excess part of the tax will be remitted. Alternatively, an heir can opt for a "dwindling valuation discount", which grants the possible discount up to a value of 26 million euros, but decreases gradually by one percent for every 750,000 euros above this threshold. There is no preferential tax treatment for an inheritance of business assets of 90 million euros and above.

Another new feature is the introduction of deduction at source, which can reduce the fiscal value of a company by up to 30 percent. The new terms for setting this have led to values that are lower than was the case to date. In contrast, the "administrative assets", that is, the non-operational assets such as financial investments, property leased to third parties, art, precious stones and, in certain circumstances, cash resources, are excluded from preferential tax treatment: they are separated from the business assets and taxed as normal. In order to prevent the exploitation of multi-layer corporate structures, a consolidated list of the assets of all companies belonging to a corporate group is now required. The option of deferral, in existence since 1977, was reduced from ten to seven years. In addition, exemption from interest was abolished and from 2016 on interest of 0.5 percent per month was introduced from the second year.[138]

This system reaffirmed the privileges of small family businesses in particular and even granted a small increase in their tax relief. Yet the situation worsened considerably for medium-sized companies if they were worth more than 26 million euros. Businesses worth 90 million euros and more were the losers in the 2016 tax reform, despite the fact that they were still in a far better position than their American counterparts.

According to a simulated tax assessment for legal status 2015 carried out by the Centre for Economic Research (ZEW) on behalf of the Foundation for Family Businesess,[139] the tax burden for children who inherited shares in large family businesses was five times greater in the USA than in Germany prior to the most recent reform. The USA is therefore in an outsider position internationally while Germany found itself in the midfield among those countries that impose an inheritance tax at all on children. Numerous European countries such as Austria, Switzerland, Sweden and Poland do not impose any such tax, while the tax rate in Italy is very low. Only Belgium and Denmark impose a considerably higher tax than Germany. Ireland and France are slightly above the level of Germany. The USA is an extreme exception, at least in relation to inheritance for the benefit of children, but in terms of inheritance for spouses with tax exemption, it is in line with a number of countries with similar rules, while Germany and above all Belgium intervene to a greater extent. However, it is the transfer to children that is decisive for intergenerational succession. If the mean value of inheritance cases for the benefit of spouses and children is taken, the burden in the USA in 2015 was still almost four times greater than in Germany. Germany was in the midfield in this ranking, while the USA and Belgium[140] showed an unusually high burden. After 2016, the gap between the two countries in terms of the inheritance by children of larger family businesses had decreased noticeably.[141]

From a long, historical perspective, the impact of path dependencies is astounding. The principles of the protection of the family in Germany and the trend of rejecting inherited wealth in favor of the high esteem afforded individual performance in the USA have characterized mindsets on inheritance tax law in both countries since the 19th century. This can be explained in Germany by way of a clear political option for the benefit of the model of intergenerational family businesses and the even more intensified support of such businesses since the 1970s. Despite the fact that the privileged status of family businesses in terms of inheritance tax was reaffirmed by the social-democratic reform chancellor, Willy Brandt, politicians of all persuasions agree that family businesses are a key component of the German economic order and that they deserve special political protection. A comparable privileged status in terms of inheritance tax exists in addition in most European countries in which similar ownership cultures also have a long-term effect.

In the USA, the insight that family businesses were worthy of protection established itself with the reform of 1976, but privileged status relating to inheritance tax was limited to smaller businesses and farms. The departure from the confiscatory top tax rates of over two thirds of the estate from the 1940s to the 1970s, deferral options over a number of years, concessions in valuation and the complete exemption of spouses marked a new direction which considerably eased the survival of family businesses in the event of inheritance. Nonetheless, the rates remained much higher than in Germany and the level of corporate tax relief continues to lag behind the arrangements applicable there. The tendency towards convergence, however, broke through in 2016, when larger family businesses in Germany lost many of their long-term tax privileges. Instead of a special protection for family businesses, the focus shifted to more competition-related preferential treatment for small businesses. The difference for SMEs is still extremely serious. In Germany since 2016, the deduction at which a 100 or 85 percent exemption from inheritance tax (maximum rate for children 30 percent) is possible is 26 million euros. After that, there are various tax benefits, but they only apply as long as the business assets do not exceed 90 million euros. In the USA in 2016 only inheritances that did not exceed 5.45 million dollars (from 2017: 5.49 million) were tax free. After that, any excess part of the assets were subject to the top tax rate of 40 percent.[142]

This may change in the future: the Trump administration is endeavoring to completely abolish estate tax. In that case, the larger American family businesses would be in a far better position for the first time compared to their German counterparts, and a long, historical divergence would be reversed. The two tax systems have converged step by step since the 1970s, yet German family entrepreneurs continue to be better placed.

D. Corporate Governance, Financing and the Development of Capital Markets

Family businesses have a special kind of corporate governance: ownership and control are only partially separated from each other, if at all. The allocation of ownership and monitoring rights depends decisively on how companies organize their financing. Exclusive recourse to internal sources of financing preserves the structure of family businesses, but these sources of self-financing—whether they are private assets or retained earnings—are usually limited. In order to ensure adequate liquidity and enable major investment spending, these companies must almost always have access to outside capital in the form of loans, tradable securities or promissory notes, or by raising equity capital on the stock exchange. Yet these options for raising funds alter the ownership and control structure of the enterprise: creditors, investors and shareholders want to safeguard their investment risks by having a voice in the operation of the company and imposing transparency and disclosure obligations. From a historical perspective, Germany and the United States developed two very different legal and institutional models for regulating these principal-agent relationships in companies. A look at the way these financial regimes arose will help explain why German and American family businesses still differ so markedly in terms of both their presence in their respective markets and the design of their corporate governance.

Over the last 150 years, extremely diverse financial systems have arisen in America and Germany. Even today, critics like to compare these two development paths as stereotypes: they stylize them as a "clash of cultures", with America's liberal market economy facing off against the more strongly coordinated principles of the social market economy (or "Rhenish capitalism").[143] The central question is: what institutional solutions did the financial systems of these two economies develop to channel investment-seeking capital towards companies and to efficiently organize the reallocation of ownership and control rights that is potentially associated with this.[144]

I.   Financial-system Duality: Market-based versus Bank-based Corporate Financing

The US economy is traditionally seen as a market-oriented system in which companies can easily access external equity and debt capital through a strong capital market. When US industry began taking off at the end of the 19th century, high standards of disclosure and investor protection were already a peculiarity of the American system, motivating private investors to invest in the capital market. As a consequence, share and bond subscriptions were more broadly dispersed ("dispersed ownership-system"), with the market assuming the dominant role as the external monitoring body of corporate governance.[145]

In German financial markets, by contrast, a more intermediary design had already begun to crystallize at the end of the 19th century. In the relationship lending system, traditional bank loans were the predominant form of corporate financing. As providers of capital, banks assumed a monitoring role within corporations or ensured the flow of information to the company owners through their close relationships as the house bank, i.e. principal bankers. Weaker investor protection and substantially smaller public capital markets thus led to greater internalization of monitoring structures and greater continuity of more concentrated ownership structures ("concentrated ownership system").[146]

Table 15: Trends in market capitalization (in percent of GDP)

	1913	1929	1938	1950	1960	1970	1980	1990	1999
Germany	44	35	18	15	35	16	9	20	67
USA	39	75	56	33	61	66	46	54	152

Source: Rajan and Zingales, "Great Reversals", p. 15.

To this day, the consequences of this institutional shift toward either a market-based or bank-oriented financial system can be demonstrated empirically at many different levels. Data on the market capitalization of stock exchanges in relation to each country's GDP provide an initial indicator: in 1913, the corresponding figures were virtually the same, but, from the 1920s onwards, the American capital market gradually moved ahead of its German counterpart. In 1980, market capitalization in the US was 46 percent, five times higher than Germany's mere nine percent. In the last two decades of the 20th century, financial and stock market values took off on both sides of the Atlantic, but the divergence in market capitalization remained striking: 152 percent in the US versus 67 percent in Germany.[147]

A further indicator is the financing preferences of companies, which have diverged for a long time. In 2012, German companies' primary source of financing was still the credit market: they met a full 60 percent of their capital requirements via external loans.[148] By contrast, US companies preferred the capital market. They generated 40 percent of their liquid funds with the placement of equity shares on the stock markets, while the issue of bonds and asset-backed securities accounted for a further 35 percent of gross domestic debt. In Germany, by comparison, listed bonds and money market instruments accounted for less than three percent in 2004, rising only moderately to 5.3 percent in 2014.[149]

A third indicator is the strong repercussions that this divergence of financial systems since the late 19th century had on the underlying types of corporate governance in each country. In the US, the fluidity of capital markets served to accelerate the spread of (stock) corporations at a very early stage. Even before 1900, 70 percent of all American companies were incorporated. That share rose to over 90 percent by 1929 and has remained at this high level ever since.[150] By comparison, just under 20 percent of German companies are incorporated even today.[151] At the same time, Germany has only half as many listed companies relative to its population as the US. According to recent studies, around 20 percent of listed companies can be classified as family businesses in the US, while the figure for Germany is around 60 percent—given that block shareholders control a significant proportion or even a majority of these companies' shares or voting rights.[152]

To analyze why different corporate governance structures in German and American family businesses have persisted throughout history, it is not enough simply to posit that market-based financing models may have promoted the separation of ownership and control rights, whereas bank-based systems helped preserve concentrated ownership structures. Rather, it is necessary to explore path dependencies in a substantially more complex framework comprising statutory regulatory regimes, institutional arrangements and culturally induced behaviors. According to recent definitions by institutional economists, corporate governance comprises a variety of mechanisms for reducing information asymmetries, transaction costs and conflicts of interest.[153] It involves classical principal-agent relationships between investors and capital seekers, between management and shareholders, and between minority and majority shareholders—as well as conflicting goals in the complex relationships between ownership, management and family.[154] From a historical perspective, it cannot be said whether the market, state legal institutions, financial intermediaries or moderating networks are the most effective way of carrying out the tasks of control and risk transformation associated with the choice of corporate financing. Instead, corporate governance systems have evolved on the basis of long-term institutional arrangements, but have often also changed rapidly in response to specific economic and, not least, political conditions. Over the following pages, we will relate these complex processes to each other in order to chart the history of the divergent presence and performance of family businesses in Germany and the United States.

II.   The Birth of Distinct Financial Systems in the 19th Century

In the late 19th century, two key factors energized the growth of the securities market in the USA. First, licensing requirements for corporations were liberalized rapidly and extensively. Under the US charter system, incorporation law was a matter for each US state and, from the 1870s onwards, competition between the federal states to attract industrial enterprises became more intense. New Jersey led the way with amendments to its company law, followed by Delaware, which dubbed itself the "New Home of the Modern Corporation"[155]. A fiscally motivated race to the bottom as regards licensing standards had begun, and the requirement whereby state governments restricted the establishment of new limited liability companies to rail- or road-building projects of public interest was abolished.[156] In addition, during the period until about 1910, the minimum rates for paid-up capital were cut to below ten percent, licensing fees were reduced and official licensing processes expedited. Nowhere else in the world at this time was incorporation such a quick and easy process. That also included the establishment of holding companies, which were allowed to acquire and hold unlimited numbers of shares in other companies.[157] Thanks to the federal structure of the US, under which a company registered in one state is allowed to do business both nationally and internationally, the strong competition between the states as regards industrialization and financing exerted an enduring pull effect for the entire process of founding and incorporating businesses. In Delaware alone, incorporation fees rose to the point where they accounted for over 30 percent of fiscal revenues.[158]

Further impetus came from the strict disclosure obligations and rules associated with investor protection that arose on US stock exchanges from the 1880s onwards. Unlike licensing requirements, disclosure obligations were not anchored in state company law: they were a purely private initiative of capital market players. Of their own accord, they agreed on business practices to ensure that detailed information could flow between investors and brokers as freely as possible. Their calls for the highest possible levels of transparency ("outsider system") were motivated much less by the allocation of operational control rights ("insider system") than by the desire to make the capital market generally more attractive for investors.[159] This focus on the rapid expansion of the securities markets during the take-off phase of US industrialization owes much to the lack of other options for satisfying the gigantic investment needs of industry. Highly fragmented and notoriously undercapitalized, the US banking sector did not have sufficient funds to finance loans to industry.[160] In order to activate the capital market as a corporate financing tool, it was thus necessary to convince as many domestic investors as possible—but especially foreign creditors—that their capital was safe in the relatively young United States by offering them securitized property rights. The geographical breadth of the country and the exceptional mobility of its population, not to mention the constant influx of immigrants, added up to substantial, country-specific risk factors, especially for foreign investors. Around 1890, some 40 percent of investors and well over 60 percent of capital came from Europe—underscoring just how international the US capital market was at an early stage.[161]

One result was a race to the top in terms of disclosure obligations as stock exchanges competed to attract investors. The New York Stock Exchange (NYSE) became the leading stock exchange in the US because of its reputation for being particularly conservative: it was the "guardian of the financial quality"[162] of the company shares that were listed on it. Modern financial reporting and international investment banking can also be traced back to the NYSE. Initially, only a handful of specialized private banks founded by immigrants—above all J.P. Morgan, Kuhn Loeb & Co, Goldman Sachs and Lehman Brothers—made use of their extraordinarily strong networks of personal contacts with European stock exchanges to act as brokers for foreign capital. They underwrote large-scale issues of securities for industrial companies, placing the vast majority with their international clients and retaining only small portions in their own portfolios. In return for their services, representatives of these banks often occupied positions on the boards of the debtor companies in order to monitor the managers and protect their investors against hidden block shareholders.[163] The original reason why they became personally involved was to strengthen investor confidence in the quality of the investment. But these practices also laid the foundations for an often close partnership between banks and industrial enterprises, one in which—as we will also show in relation to Germany—the right to monitor management was granted through personal business-partner networks. An estimate from 1912 reveals the strong influence wielded on the eve of the First World War by what was known as the "money trust": representatives of the five largest US investment banks held a total of 341 positions on the boards of 112 big businesses with total equity of 22 billion dollars.[164] At the same time, we should not overlook how strongly the combination of low licensing standards for capital raisers and high disclosure standards for investors spurred the growth of securities markets in the US. That, in turn, encouraged companies to finance themselves via the free capital market.

Photo 9: The J.P. Morgan & Co. bank at 23 Wall Street in 1910

The dynamism with which new companies were established in the US economy in the last third of the 19th century was more than astonishing. In 1872, 924 corporations started business. In 1883 alone, the figure was 3,774 and in 1910 22,122 new companies were licensed.[165] The broad dispersion of this new form of company across the US was not due solely to the establishment of large industrial enterprises requiring a lot of capital. The exceptional accessibility of the capital markets also encouraged small and medium-sized partnerships in the retail, commercial and service sectors to go public. So the percentage of corporations still in family ownership was correspondingly high. According to rough estimates for the year 1900, company directors or founding families still held the majority of the shares in 33 percent of the companies listed on the New York Stock Exchange.[166]

Nonetheless, family-based capitalism was already in decline in the US at the turn of the 20th century. Ironically, a decisive factor in weakening family businesses was the Sherman Antitrust Act of 1890, which was originally conceived to protect smaller companies against the burgeoning industrial giants. This new competition act outlawed all forms of cartel and agreements between market players. Indirectly, however, it triggered a wave of mergers, with a trend towards horizontal concentration gripping many industries. This "merger movement" peaked between 1894 and 1905, when around 3,000 companies with aggregate nominal capital of more than six billion dollars merged.[167] Many of the companies that were swallowed up were small family businesses, for whom the mergers were a highly attractive way of selling out or transforming themselves into corporations with an external capital majority. The influence of founding families was also weakened when large-scale enterprises merged with each other: for instance, US Steel came into being around 1901 through the merger of eight companies, each with strong block shareholders. But the higher capitalization of the merged company meant those shareholders lost control. The connection between ownership and management—which had still applied, if only in part—broke down altogether, giving way to a broader dispersion of equity interests. Dispersed ownership became the lasting hallmark of the market-based financial system in the United States—shifting it ever further away from Germany's system of coordinated capitalism.[168]

In stark contrast to the rigorous ban on cartels imposed by the Sherman Act, German courts had, since 1872, repeatedly affirmed their acceptability in certain circumstances. In 1888, the Higher Regional Court of Bavaria explained its rationale for restricting free enterprise: "The elevation of a branch of industry in decline by means of agreements between the members of that industry [...] is not in breach of any moral law; indeed, it is more rightly the duty of any prudent businessman. [...] The attempt to counter overproduction must thus be viewed as a battle against an economic evil [...]".[169] This opinion was confirmed and extended by the famous ruling of Germany's Imperial Court of Justice (Reichsgericht) in 1897, which enshrined not only the admissibility of cartel agreements as a means of avoiding destructive competition, but also their enforceability in court—provided such cartels did not lead to outright monopolies. Court rulings like these helped Germany become the "classic country of cartels"[170], even though such cartels often broke down and did not always produce the hoped-for recovery of ailing industries. Nevertheless, cartels and other forms of collaboration under the aegis of "cooperative capitalism" did improve both individual companies' chances of survival and long-term prospects for joint investment, research and development.

The guiding principle in Germany was fundamentally different than in the US: the persistent German legal tradition was influenced by a preference for continuity and cooperation over short-lived competition and an existential, all-against-all struggle. Whereas, in the US, companies were seen as tradable commodities that had to ensure their survival primarily in the marketplace, in Germany they were viewed also as creators of identity and meaning; as a result, the preservation of existing companies was given precedence over "ruinous" competition.[171]

This contrasted starkly with the Sherman Antitrust Act of 1890, which banned and criminalized cartels in order to protect consumers rather than producers.[172] The subsequent trend toward mergers to achieve market dominance caused many companies to forfeit their identity as family businesses. Even if the ban on cartels was far from rigorously enforced, it was the cause of a fateful path dependency that made it hard for large family businesses to preserve their autonomy in the long run.

State actors in Germany were considerably more critical of the rise of capital markets than their counterparts in America. Although calls for greater freedom to incorporate had become louder in Germany too, the governments of the individual states were initially hesitant about licensing new public limited companies. Licensing required sovereign privilege, which—as in the US—was initially granted only for capital-intensive infrastructure projects. As a result, scarcely more than 200 companies in the railway, mining and metallurgy industries were established as corporations in Prussia prior to the foundation of the German Reich in 1871.[173] As the sovereigns feared that liberalization of the stock exchanges would draw capital away from the market for public bonds and make government financing more difficult, they blocked the transition away from the mercantilist octroi model for many decades. Not until the nationwide Stock Corporation Act (Aktiengesetz) was enacted in 1870 the obligation to obtain a license from the state replaced by a normative system under commercial law.[174] This liberalizing measure triggered an incorporation boom, though one that was more subdued than in America. During the three years it lasted, 928 companies with combined nominal capital of almost 2.9 billion marks were established in Prussia alone. Across the whole German Empire, the number of company securities traded doubled. That, in turn, caused the stock markets to overheat, with speculators betting on what were often dubious stocks. The rally ended—and the bubble burst—in 1873.[175]

Subsequently, the euphoria for incorporation waned considerably: in each of the reference years 1883 and 1900, little more than 200 companies went public. What is more, the German government saw itself compelled to adopt more stringent regulation of the capital market, compensating for the loss of direct supervisory control brought about through the repeal of the licensing system. Thus indirect incorporation requirements were introduced under commercial law.

Just how strong state intervention in Germany's corporate system was can be clearly seen in four areas. First, the state established strict subscription obligations for the establishment of corporations. Germany's Stock Corporation Act of 1870 had already stipulated that ten percent of the nominal capital was to be paid up prior to incorporation and all shares in the company were to be subscribed by external investors. Experience gained in the recent crisis prompted legislators to increase the call liability to a prohibitive 25 percent (which persists to this day). What is more, company founders were also required to submit a financial prospectus, a detailed subscription plan, and proof that the majority of shareholders actually exercised their voting rights at the inaugural annual general meeting.[176] For founders, the strict deadlines and subscription obligations risked delaying the corporation's establishment and thus the financing of the investment project. They were urged to employ banks as informed intermediaries whose task was to subscribe company shares en bloc and either sell them on to their own clients or retain them in their own portfolios. The state also created special incentives for investors to acquire large blocks of shares, making it easy to defend the practice by which owners of family businesses retained majority holdings in their companies after incorporation. This was a measure that helped preserve concentrated ownership and control arrangements, as exemplified by such family-owned enterprises as Krupp, Thyssen, Wolff, Siemens and Bosch.[177]

Second, the state adopted restrictive taxation measures to limit the growth of the securities market. Following introduction of the Stamp Duty Act (Stempelsteuergesetz) of 1894 (revised in 1900), the fees payable on securities transactions tripled. This encouraged industrial enterprises to deposit shares with their house banks and to leave them there. Likewise, the banks internalized the flow of stock orders so as to avoid taxes on transfers of securities accounts and voting rights.[178] This particular legislation also strengthened the role of universal banks—which were active in both deposit and investment business—in steering and monitoring companies. At the same time, the deliberately restrictive monetary policy and low discount rates of Germany's central bank (Reichsbank) channeled corporate financing to the credit markets. For many German companies at the turn of the century, there was no rational reason to tap the free capital market in order to raise capital, as they could get loans easily via the state-orchestrated banking system.[179] The flexibility of the credit markets was a key reason for not changing a company's organizational structure, especially for family businesses constituted as partnerships.

A—very important—third factor was implementation of the two-tier management model for public limited companies, which was unique worldwide. Enacted in 1870, the two-tier system introduced a supervisory board alongside the management board, its purpose being to monitor the latter in the interests of the shareholders. Information and reporting obligations between the two bodies were designed to ensure that managers took shareholders' interests into account when making strategic business decisions. Although the reform of the Stock Corporation Act in 1884 introduced a strict separation of supervisory board and management board personnel, this governance mechanism offered majority shareholders and company founders an effective means of monitoring manager-led companies. Clearly, this German model of two separate boards meant that control rights were more strongly internalized within the organizational structure. By comparison, the unitary board system customary in America relied on the allocation of rights of disposal through the agency of the market.

These different points of focus between the two systems are just as clear in matters of investor protection. Unlike the US, disclosure regulations in Germany were governed not by capital market law, but by corporate law. Even in the General German Commercial Code (Allgemeines Deutsches Handelsgesetzbuch) of 1861, disclosure obligations were graded by type of legal entity. For over 150 years, partnerships were largely exempted from such obligations (except as regards tax accounting regulations). This aspect—which was not least one of competition strategy—slowed down the incorporation of medium-sized enterprises enormously.[180] By contrast, corporations (Aktiengesellschaften) and partnerships limited by shares (Kommanditgesellschaften auf Aktien, KGaA) had been obliged since 1884 to publish balance sheets and report profits. In addition, they were required to submit formal annual reports on their assets and "internal affairs". What stood out most in relation to corporate governance was that the annual reports did not have to be submitted to the commercial register; their sole purpose was to provide information to the supervisory board and the annual general meeting of shareholders. The limited scope of publication obligations confirms how different the German monitoring systems were from their US counterparts—and underscores the differences between the internal-stakeholder and external-shareholder models.[181]

Institutional economists trace this divergence in governance principles back to the two different legal systems. According to their theory, the Anglo-American system of common law, strongly influenced by individualism and the force of custom, gave rise to the primacy of protecting minority shareholders, which parliament and the judiciary reaffirmed on many occasions. That was a decisive prerequisite for the development of an open shareholder culture, in which ever larger swathes of the population could participate. It lent the capital market a special depth and diversity. On the other hand, investor protection remained weaker in civil-law countries, with their emphasis of subjectivism and contract law.[182] According to the theory, in an environment in which the risks posed by capital market financing were offset only in part, if at all, by rights of disclosure and protection, the players tended to reduce their uncertainty by means of socio-economic networks, including close cooperation with a house bank as well as the preservation of family-based ownership and control structures. Both generated informal trust, thus closing the governance system's normative gaps in monitoring.[183]

The low proportion of stock market listings (Figure 7) demonstrates how few German corporations opted for market-mediated control principles even at the peak of industrialization. Whereas there was a long-term increase in the overall number of public limited companies during the period of the

German Empire, companies were substantially more reluctant—especially after the legal reforms of 1884 and 1896—to finance themselves through the issue of free-float shares on the capital market.

In 1907, only one-third of public limited companies were listed on one of Germany's stock exchanges. Despite a lack of more concrete data, this trend allows us to suppose that the majority of firms were still "entrepreneurial enterprises". They steered clear of public trading of shares, preferring instead to leave the control rights with the company founders and issue shares solely to a select group of business partners and family relatives. A prime example was Siemens & Halske, where the company's articles of association of 1897 explicitly prohibited the sale of shares to outsiders. Frequently, it were only small, concentrated groups of shareholders—mostly the founders or founding families in collaboration with their universal banks—that controlled company ownership and the decision-making process.[184]

Figure 7: Listed and non-listed corporations in Germany, 1870–1914

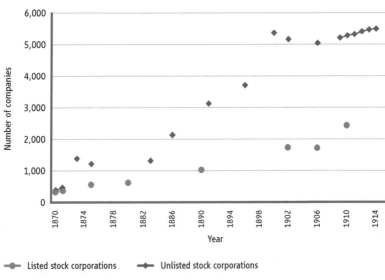

Source: Fohlin, History, p. 228.

In order to explain this phenomenon, we need to refer again to how universal banks functioned. Unlike the US banking system, where commercial and investment banking remained strictly separated, the large German banks founded after 1870 not only took deposits, but were also directly engaged in

securities and investment banking. They offered the full range of banking services, enabling them to enhance and maintain customer loyalty in the long
term. At the same time, these banks had comprehensive insights into their industrial partners' finances. If a company was at risk of overdrawing its current
account, the bank would decide whether to increase its loans to the company
or to cover part of the required financing with a bond issue. Even in the latter case, the securities were not necessarily sold to the public: in many cases,
these universal banks organized the trading of shares and bonds without recourse to the stock markets. This approach helped avoid taxes on financial
transactions, but more than that, the securities were placed with investors
among the banks' own clientele so as to ensure that the banks retained proxy
voting rights for the equity stakes deposited with them.[185] Consequently, the
banks were able to install their representatives on the supervisory boards of
industrial enterprises solely on the basis of their ability to exercise combined
proxy voting rights for their customers. Thus, even before the turn of the century, a finely meshed network of personal relationships between banks and
industry had arisen. In the interwar period of the 20th century, it was no rarity
for leading German bankers to hold 20 positions on company boards, sometimes considerably more; the delegates of the country's major banks alone
occupied more than one thousand positions on supervisory boards.[186] Entire
industries—such as iron- and steel-making and chemicals—were ultimately
steered via these interlocking networks. They promoted the creation of large-
scale enterprises and even cartels (which were by no means banned in Germany). This marked the beginning of coordinated capitalism and the birth of
the system known as "Germany Inc." ("Deutschland AG").[187]

At the same time, the interplay of universal banking, proxy voting and
interlocking directorates provided the basis for an intensive exchange of information that enabled bankers to function as intermediaries for property
and control rights. By assigning their voting rights to the financial institutions, retail investors in particular, but also large-scale investors, were ask-
ing the bankers to protect their interests "from within" the company. This
practice underscores yet again that central control functions performed by
the market in the US financial system were internalized by banks in Germany.[188] This enabled founders to preserve their influence in their companies,
provided they maintained a close and trusting relationship with their house
banks. The concentration of voting rights among a small group of players
thus served to preserve the status quo of close corporate governance system
of ownership and management.

Whereas the interdependence between banks and industry in Germany became stronger during the first third of the 20th century, the influence of investment banks in America met with growing political resistance. After the stock market panic of 1907, some federal states began passing securities laws that expanded even further the already stringent disclosure obligations for corporations. In 1912, Congress convened a special committee—the House Committee on Banking and Currency, dubbed the Pujo Committee after its chairman, Rep. Arsène Pujo—to investigate whether the "money trust" had subverted the ban on cartels enshrined in the Sherman Act. The main accusation was that the reciprocal capital and personal links between banks and big business had restricted competition to the detriment of retail investors.[189] The Clayton Antitrust Act of 1914 marked the US federal government's first attempt to regulate these banking-industry networks. By stipulating that the same person could not be a director of two or more competing companies in the same industry, the government forced bankers to relinquish at least some of their board positions. The government's initially cautious approach was coupled, however, with the open threat of placing the stock markets under rigorous state control if they were unwilling to enhance investor protection by way of self-regulation.[190]

This increased regulatory pressure was not without effect. Under the banner of "shareholder democracy", it was above all the NYSE that drew attention to the question of proportionality between property rights and voting rights. In the wake of the Pujo Committee, and even before the First World War, the American stock exchanges launched a high-profile campaign promoting the principle of "one share, one vote"—in opposition to US investment banks' patent attempts since the turn of the century to pool voting rights. Since, in purely technical terms, proxy voting rights were impossible under the US system of separate commercial and investment banks, the criticism was directed towards non-voting preference shares, "dual class stocks", "voting trusts" and "pyramid holdings", through which minority shareholders were able to secure control rights and decision-making power.[191] For the remaining family businesses in America, the discrediting of preference shares and voting trusts was a further negative development—and another step toward their increasing marginalization. They were tainted by association with the investment banks and gradually forfeited one of their key instruments for controlled market capitalization.

During the First World War, but particularly in the interwar period, the trend towards more broadly dispersed shareholdings continued in the US.

For one thing, the government levied a substantial special tax on company profits in the final phase of the war in order to prevent inflation gains and to skim off uninvested capital.[192] That made it more attractive for family-business owners to sell their company shares and diversify their assets, i.e. to exchange control rights for protection of their property.[193] For another, Liberty Bonds—which were sold via a strongly patriotic campaign and promised excellent returns—attracted a rising proportion of the United States to the stock markets. The capital market expanded after the United States entered the war, with the proportion of small investors with shares in large industrial enterprises multiplying.[194] Between 1900 and 1922, the number of shareholders in the US rose from 4.4 million to around 14 million. During the subsequent boom years until 1929, the figure reached around 20 million.[195]

But the enduring effects of these trends became apparent only in the medium term: as the number of small investors increased rapidly, a broad lobby arose in both the media and politics to push for greater investor protection. The US Congress reiterated in 1934 "[that] fair corporate suffrage is an important right that should attach to every equity security bought on a public exchange."[196] The "one share, one vote" rule was thus declared to be a fundamental democratic principle. But the regulatory authority over the assignment of voting rights was placed in formal legal terms under the business and corporate laws of individual US states and not the federal government. A very wide range of practices emerged on the state level during the entire 20th century, and "dual-class" structures were never prohibited in principle. The critical factor was that the major stock exchanges adopted the policies of the federal government. As early as the mid-1920s, the NYSE stepped up its battle against the undemocratic separation of control and property rights by refusing outright to trade securities that had no voting rights.[197] In addition to obligatory Class A shares (with simple voting rights), other types of shares that had preferred or reduced voting rights (Class B or C shares) became rarities and were accepted for trading only after being individually reviewed by the NYSE. As a result of the literal discrediting of "dual class voting rights," preference and bearer shares increasingly disappeared from the capital market along with voting trusts. According to a contemporary study published by Berle and Means, in 1930 only 21 percent of the 200 largest US companies were controlled by majority shareholders—something the authors extolled as a "remarkable diffusion of ownership".[198]

The corresponding figures for Germany, on the other hand, indicate the relative stability of family influence. In 1925, 53 percent of corporations—

or, more precisely, 842 out of a total of 1595—made use of majority voting rights to enable founders to retain control of their companies. In such cases, the owners exercised between 20 and 250 times as many voting rights as would have been the case if all the shares had been treated equally.[199] Although the period of hyperinflation in Germany provided a massive boost to the formation of corporations (due to the abundance of "cheap" money in the capital market), this did not weaken the country's preference for concentrated family ownership or its insider orientation. Very small businesses and SMEs were hardly affected by the brief outburst of incorporation: for them there were neither tax nor financial incentives for going public. In 1925, around 90 percent of all German businesses were still either sole proprietorships or partnerships.[200]

Figure 8: The wave of new corporations during the hyperinflation period: public limited companies in Germany, 1886–1943

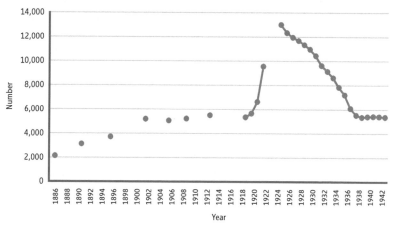

Source: Fohlin, History, p. 225; Deutsches Aktieninstitut, Factbook 2013.

By comparison, the number of public limited companies in Germany tripled between 1919 and 1923, from around 5,600 to more than 16,000. However—like the famous Stinnes Group—the majority of these were not listed, but structured either as holding or investment companies. In close cooperation with the universal banks, and on the basis of personal networks, industrial groups were established and whole industries transformed into cartels. To be sure, manager-controlled companies with dispersed ownership also experienced a boom in Germany at this time, but the underlying ownership structures remained both concentrated and largely concealed.[201] Despite growing levels of concentration—which increased in line with the rise of managerial capitalism and spawned huge corporations such as IG Farben and Vereinigte Stahlwerke—many large-scale industrial enterprises (like Siemens, Krupp, Klöckner, Wolff and Stumm) remained in the control of their founding families, in contrast to the situation in America.

In Germany, the widespread use of proxy and, especially, multiple voting rights gave family-owned corporations the scope they needed to hold their own. In contrast to the American principle of "one share, one vote", neither German stock exchanges nor legislators restricted the corporations' autonomy to assign voting rights or to reach private contractual agreements in this regard between lenders and raisers of capital. On the contrary, the German Stock Exchange Act of 1880 replaced the very specific phrase "Every share grants one vote" (from the General German Commercial Code of 1861) with the much more nebulous "Every share grants one voting right".[202] Legislators commented neither on the scope of that voting right nor on possible rules governing its assignment. This paved the way for companies to design their own personal models of insider governance in their articles of association. Especially during the hyperinflation period, the issuance of multiple voting rights became established practice. A study conducted by Germany's Imperial Bureau of Statistics (Statistisches Reichsamt) in 1925 revealed the following: of the 388 companies that made use of this tool, it was enough on average to hold just ten percent of the shares in order to control more than 40 percent of the votes.[203] In the political debate, these special rights were stylized ostensibly as a mechanism for defending German companies against takeovers by large foreign investors. They massively benefitted from the devaluation of the mark which made German corporations extremely cheap for buyers with hard currency. A reduction in the number of groups with control rights in businesses would, it was believed, preserve both economic sovereignty of German stake holders and the spirit of coordinated capitalism. But, in fact, multiple voting rights strengthened the position of the banks and, in particular, provided the owners of family businesses with a method for monitoring management.[204] They made use not only of multiple voting rights, but also of treasury shares, i.e. new share issues that were usually deposited solely with the house bank for the company's account. In addition, the example of the textile retailer C&A demonstrates that traditional, multigenerational family businesses often made use of registered shares that could not be transferred to third parties without the consent of the issuing company. This instrument was used to discipline family members with shareholdings, to limit external influence and to avoid agency conflicts.[205] "Deviations from a one-share-one-vote system, the most important of which appeared in the interwar years, greatly affected patterns of ownership and control in Germany. Because the disassociation of ownership and control allowed founders to control their firms longer than they would have otherwise, these legal changes altered the fates of families and their firms."[206]

III. Financial Systems and Corporate Governance in Times of Crisis, 1929–1945

From the late 1920s onwards, the different paths already taken by the US and German financial systems became even more accentuated. Under the influence of ingrained orientations, the economic structures and cultures in the two countries drifted further apart. The only thing the two countries had in common during this period was increasing state regulation in response to the enormous economic upheaval of the Great Depression, which bankrupted a large number of companies on both sides of the Atlantic.

In the US, the experiences of the Great Depression—which had been preceded in the roaring twenties by an almost manic stock market boom and a massive expansion in share ownership—led to highly restrictive reforms of both banking and capital market legislation. In the two-part Glass–Steagall Act of 1932 and 1933, the US government initially focused on combating the banking crisis. First, it set up the Federal Deposit Insurance Corp. (FDIC) in order to restore customer confidence in banks; second, it enforced the strict institutional separation of deposit/loan business from securities business. This considerably more stringent federal law replaced the company-law regulations of the federal states, which had been in place since the 19th century and had left banks large loopholes to circumvent this guiding principle. The initiative arose in response to the allegation that the commercial banks had used their investment-banking subsidiaries to securitize bad loans on a grand scale and sell them on to gullible small investors.[207] In order to suppress all forms of proprietary trading, the Glass–Steagall Act prohibited banks from opening branches in several US states at once and in different lines of banking business. As a result of the law, the US banking system became fragmented once again and scaled back its credit market resources, severely inhibiting the growth of bank-industry relationships. The Bank Holding Company Act of 1956 would reinforce and expand this regional and operational compartmentalization of the banking industry.[208]

However, regulators identified an even more serious problem, one that had already occupied them for several years: the lack of market transparency. Under President Franklin D. Roosevelt's far-reaching New Deal reforms, the state implemented nationwide laws to regulate financial markets, effectively replacing private self-regulation.[209] With the Securities Act (1933) and the Securities Exchange Act (1934), the US government tasked a new federal agency with overseeing stock exchange trading. The Securities and Exchange Commission (SEC) strictly enforced its "disclosure philosophy", the purpose of which was to eliminate the information deficits of (retail) investors so as to ensure that capital markets once again functioned properly.[210] Using the collapse of the nested energy, railway and real estate holding companies Samuel Insull's Midwest Holding Comp. and Van Sweringen Bros. as an example, the SEC played to the public with its renewed criticism of the hidden machinations of the industry-bank complex.[211] It insisted on exceptionally strict disclosure rules and on expanded investor protection in order to rule out any future distortions of competition to the detriment of investors. The SEC installed the world's most rigorous regime for capital market monitoring. At the same time, companies—i.e. both corporations and limited liability partnerships—were made subject to comprehensive disclosure, accounting and reporting regulations.[212] In combination with the artificial limitation of credit markets, there was hardly any incentive for US business owners not to incorporate and diversify their ownership. The fiscal policy of the New Deal also set negative signals: as of 1935, holding companies and pyramid holdings were saddled with multiple income taxes. In contrast to the intercorporate or box privilege granted in Germany, it was no longer possible to offset dividends. The reintroduction of gift tax, with prohibitive rates of up to 55 percent, made it difficult to pass on company property from one generation to the next, while income tax was also raised from a low maximum rate of 12.5–16 percent (1926) to 63 percent (1934) under the Roosevelt administration.[213] As a consequence, the proportion of first-generation and multigenerational family businesses continued to decline.

The German cooperation model—which, since the advent of the German Empire, had sought to balance the interests of owners, managers, creditors and customers by means of a finely meshed network of internal relationships—was sorely tested when the economic crisis broke out at the end of the

1920s. Several accounting scandals revealed all too clearly that the supervisory boards had not been adequately exercising their control function within the two-tier system of corporate governance. When FAVAG, one of the largest German insurers, collapsed in the summer of 1929, it came to light that the management board had for years been manipulating the accounts and speculating with shares—without the supervisory board having noticed, let alone objected, to anything. The same was true of the Nordwolle scandal almost two years later, in which the founder-manager family Lahusen deliberately concealed the company's financial difficulties with the help of its house bank. When this fact became public, it not only triggered the bankruptcy of one of the world's leading worsted spinning mills and one of Germany's five major banks (Danat-Bank), but created such upheaval that it led to a general banking crisis in July 1931 that brought about the demise of numerous industrial and banking enterprises.[214] These scandals revealed that supervisory boards had neither access to reliable information, nor the tools to sanction management, nor adequate monitoring expertise. What is more, the members of the supervisory board did not have enough time to carry out their monitoring tasks properly owing to the many positions they occupied on the boards of different companies. In some cases they were blinded by personal friendships or the prospect of compensation that was tied to the dividend, and simply allowed the managers to do as they wished.[215] Even before 1933, the German two-tier management system was considered to be faulty, and this only served to taint the reputation of public limited companies in the politically charged atmosphere of the crisis.

In direct response to the Great Depression and the banking crisis, the Brüning government issued an emergency decree in September 1931, tightening the control regulations for public limited companies.[216] A year earlier, the Ministry of Justice (Reichsjustizministerium) had published a recommendation for the revision of Germany's Stock Corporation Act. The number of supervisory board mandates that any one person could hold was capped at 20 and strict requirements were introduced regarding the self-subscription of treasury shares and the granting of loans to management board members. But the most important new provision was that company accounts were no longer to be monitored by the supervisory board alone, but also by means of a mandatory audit conducted by independent auditors. For the first time in the German corporate system, monitoring functions were externalized in order to break down the all-too-close alignment of interests within companies and neutralize it as a breeding ground for opaque nepotism.[217]

Post-1933, the National Socialist regime resumed the debate on a revision of stock corporation law and company law, giving it its own special ideological slant. The reforms introduced by the Nazis had a long-term impact in stabilizing and even expanding the significance of family businesses in the German corporate landscape. Their policy was driven by three guiding principles. First, Nazi ideology strived to strengthen the three related pillars of race, people and family ("Rasse, Volk und Familie"). Second, the regime exalted family-owned partnerships as being the ideal, "most natural" corporate form. The radical Nazi base instrumentalized the strong *Mittelstand* movement that had arisen during the Weimar Republic, painting a picture of an existential struggle between salt-of-the-earth small businesses and "anonymous" big business—often denounced simply as "Jewish"—which in their view exploited the construct of limited liability to try to shirk its personal responsibility for the success of its operations and the welfare of its employees. When the Nazis seized power, there were calls for the radical elimination of all corporations. Soon it became clear, however, that the regime would hardly be able to achieve its vision of rearmament without the help of strongly capitalized industrial groups, so the party leadership rejected all initiatives of this kind. Third, the focus shifted as a consequence to a radical reform of the organizational structure of corporations. National Socialism's corporate governance doctrine was to transpose the authoritarian leader principle (Führerprinzip) to the economy so as to close existing control loopholes and introduce clear decision-making structures. Under a series of laws passed in spring 1934 to reshape the economic landscape, a company's owner, board or managing director became the "factory leader" (Betriebsführer) and was supported and monitored by an "economic leader" (Wirtschaftsführer) of the German Labor Front (Deutsche Arbeitsfront), who represented the collective interests of the state, the shareholders and the workforce.[218] The concept of individual leadership enhanced the status of the business owner and favored owner-based corporate structures.

In the following years, these ideas were entrenched via massive changes in stock corporation and company law. The Law Governing the Transformation of Companies (handelsrechtliches Umwandlungsgesetz) of July 1934 promised corporations and private limited companies (GmbHs) discounts on their sales, trade and corporation taxes if they reversed their incorporation and became partnerships. Although transformations of this kind had been possible prior to the new law, they were expensive and time-consuming, as they required the existing company to be first liquidated and then re-established. This step now became superfluous, thus also reducing the consequent tax burden.

From December 1934 onwards, the Act Governing the Profit Distribution of Corporations (Anleihestockgesetz) significantly reduced the volatility of Germany's capital markets by capping the amount that could be paid out in dividends to between six and eight percent. Companies that exceeded this threshold were forced to transfer their undistributed profits to Deutsche Golddiskontbank, a (semi-)public financial institution. In order to circumvent this, companies began retaining a large portion of their profits as hidden reserves. The goal of the regime was to make the subscription of company shares unattractive for private investors, thus freeing up capital market funds to finance the state's rearmament plans.[219]

Finally, in 1937 a new Stock Corporation Act raised the barriers for establishing and operating public limited companies. The new law made disclosure obligations for corporations and private limited companies substantially more stringent and raised the minimum amount of paid-up capital for corporations from 50,000 to 500,000 reichsmarks. The regime now took direct action to suppress public limited companies, forcing those with less than 100,000 reichsmarks in capital to transform themselves into general partnerships or private limited companies within three years. The Nazis continued to accept public limited companies only in the arms-related sectors of large-scale industry—and only on condition that the personal decision-making competencies of "factory leaders" were strengthened and the rights of the supervisory board and shareholders curtailed. A further component in the Nazis' package of measures was the formal ban on multiple voting rights under the Stock Corporation Act of 1937—but with generous exemptions for family businesses. By way of compensation, public limited companies were even allowed for the first time to issue up to 50 percent of their shares as non-voting preference shares, which promised higher dividends to shareholders who refrained from exerting any influence on the company's management.[220] Both of these measures strengthened the position of blockholders and existing shareholders, as companies could now be endowed with capital without altering their underlying control structures. It is telling that the new laws were drafted together with commercial lawyers, ministerial officials and leading representatives of German industry, such as Carl Friedrich von Siemens, Willy Tischbein (Continental), Hermann Schmitz (IG Farben) and Wilhelm Kißkalt (Munich Re). It was these "factory leaders" of private industry, strengthened in their claim to leadership, who were able to preserve and even expand their entrepreneurial autonomy in the reform process despite many ideologically motivated directives from the Nazis. Even large family businesses tended to benefit from this strengthening of hierarchical control structures and succeeded in consolidating their positions. As a result, the core of Germany's insider-oriented corporate governance model remained intact even during the National Socialist era and, at some levels, was even considerably enhanced.

Partnerships extended their dominant positions, profiting from the suppression of corporations. As already shown in Figure 8, the number of German public limited companies almost halved between 1931 and 1939, falling from about 10,500 to just over 5,500. Private limited companies, too, which the Nazis likewise combated because of their limited liability, decreased in number from 55,000 (1934) to 25,625 (1938). In view of this massive intervention—and the politically induced corporate transformations, especially of commercial and industrial SMEs—one might argue that manager capitalism in Germany had been transported back to a state similar to that before the First World War. As a result of the state-controlled arms and war economy up to 1945, the free capital market almost dried up completely, while loan financing for industry boomed through the covert creation of money and the central bank's indirect discounting of bills of exchange on a massive scale.[221] Where corporations remained in place (as was the case with universal banks and large-scale industry), the close personal links between companies were hardly reduced at all, despite—or even because of—state interference. Instead, they continued to exist within the established collegial system of two-tier management.

IV. The Era of Reconstruction. Corporate Financing on Established Paths, 1945–1980

After the Second World War, continuity as regards corporate structures, company law and the design of the financial system was surprisingly pronounced in West Germany. It is remarkable, for instance, that the number of public limited companies continued to decline despite the incipient economic boom—from around 5,000 in 1943 to just under 2,600 in 1957, before ultimately falling to an all-time low of just over 2,000 in 1983. At the same time, the ratio of listed corporations declined as well, ostensibly underscoring the irrelevance of this form of company, which had been on the decline for many decades. But on closer analysis, we can discern big differences in this trend in terms of company size. In 1957, 87 of the largest German companies were corporations, while a further nine took the form of private limited companies.[222] Thus, the continuity of the period after 1945 was that of the strong separation between incorporated large-scale enterprises and partnership-based SMEs.

Figure 9: German public limited companies and partnerships limited by shares, 1960–2012

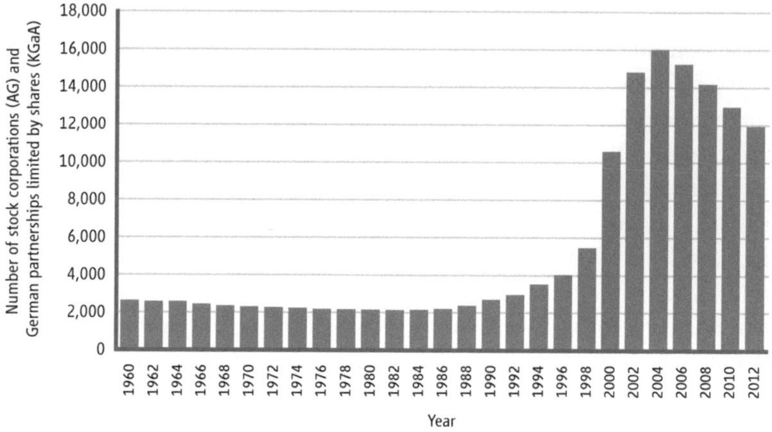

Source: Deutsches Aktieninstitut, Factbook 2013.

West German policy continued to support this trend, albeit not for ideological motives. For instance, the Transformation Acts (Umwandlungsgesetze) of 1956 and 1969 not only perpetuated the regulations introduced in 1934, but made it easier for public limited companies to re-establish themselves as general partnerships or private limited companies. The laborious civil-law process that individual shareholders had been compelled to pursue in order to obtain compensation for the loss of their shares was also simplified. The (re)transfer of ownership was streamlined to suit the needs of the new company owners, and was made simpler and clearer in cases where virtually all of the original company's capital was transferred.[223]

The state also retained patriarchal control with incorporations: after 1945, a national commission comprising representatives of the central bank (Bundesbank) and of the ministries of finance and economic affairs continued to determine whether a company could list on the stock exchange. This commission took a very restrictive approach, especially in the early postwar years. Instead of serving the needs of corporate financing, the capital market was primarily expected to provide capacity for the bonds and covered bonds that, given the immense war damage, were needed to finance urgent infrastructure measures (housing and roads).[224] The "leader principle" was not officially abolished until the minor reform of the Stock Corporation Act in 1965. At the same time, the law stipulated that, by ministerial decree, multiple voting rights could again be used for the personal assignment of control rights. In this way, German stock corporation law once more distanced itself from the "one share, one vote" principle applicable in the US and made it easier for blockholders to exert influence.[225]

Figure 10: Share ownership in West Germany, 1960–1992 (in percent)

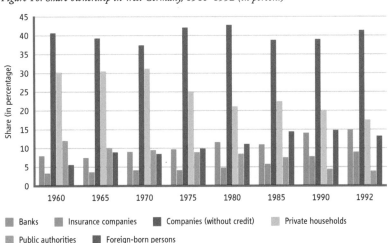

Source: Fohlin, History, p. 233; Deutsches Aktieninstitut, Factbook 1996, Table 0-81; Deutsche Bundesbank, Geld- und Bankwesen, 1976, p. 300 et seq.

Until well beyond the end of the 1980s, two metrics indicate the persistently high levels of family influence on German companies: the high number of partnerships and the concentrated ownership structures of corporations. Figure 10 shows the increasing retreat of private households from the stock market. Whereas small investors still subscribed around 30 percent of traded shares in 1960, by 1992 that figure had fallen to 17.6 percent. Even in 2000, only ten percent of German households invested in the stock market, whereas 25 percent of American households invested their savings in shares.[226]

This figure alone underscores the narrower dispersion of commercial property ownership in Germany. Instead of small investors, it was commercial and industrial business and, increasingly, banks and insurance companies that together held the majority of company shares: well over 50 percent in 1960 and even more than 65 percent in 1992. In the second half of the 20th century, the German capital market served largely to intensify the cross-holdings within "Germany Inc.".

Table 16: Ownership structure of the 100 largest German companies by revenue, 1988–1998 (in percent)

Companies	1988	1990	1992	1994	1996	1998
Majority owner (>50%)	54	54	51	53	52	57
Other top-100 company	1	2	0	0	1	0
Foreign investors	16	17	16	18	14	17
State	13	8	11	13	13	13
Individual investor, families, foundations	21	23	19	17	19	18
Other	3	4	5	5	5	9
No majority owner (<50%)	46	46	49	47	48	43
Over 50% free float	28	30	29	29	27	22
No stake over 5%	18	16	20	18	21	21

Source: Fohlin, "History", p. 243.

Underlying this process, at the level of individual companies, the concentration of control and ownership continued to grow. Table 16, which casts light on the ownership structures of the 100 largest German companies, clearly demonstrates that less than one third of these companies had a free-float majority in 1988. By contrast, more than half of all corporations were dominated by individual majority owners. In 20 percent of companies, the founders, their families or family foundations held the majority of shares. In individual cases, they had almost complete control over their companies, holding up to 80 percent of the shares. At a further 18 companies, several owners, again usually the original founder or founding family, held significant stakes of over five percent of the total capital, enabling them to monitor the company's management.[227]

Even though institutional investors—in the shape of banks and industrial enterprises—were on the rise, families remained one of the most important shareholder groups. As was the case with Bosch, Krupp, BMW or VW, they exerted tremendous influence on management from their supervisory board positions. It is hardly surprising, then, that in 1990 17 of the 21 largest private fortunes were attributable to the ownership of companies founded by the family in question.[228] For a long period of time, the German corporate governance system evidently offered majority shareholders a consistently positive environment. As a result, they saw hardly any need to diversify their assets or to turn their backs on the companies founded by their own families.

This argument can also be applied to financing strategies. If we view market capitalization in relation to the volume of loans raised by the private sector (non-financial companies only) (Figure 11), we can see that, until the end of the 1980s, the credit markets were the primary source of liquidity in Germany.

Figure 11: International financing structures: stock market capitalization in relation to volume of bank loans, 1960–2010 (private sector)

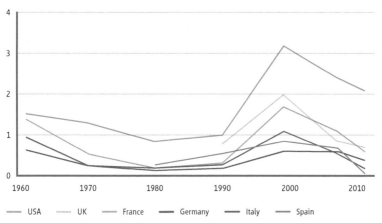

Source: https://www.true-sale-international.de/abs-im-ueberblick/abs-und-mittelstand (accessed: November 15, 2018).

Compared with the market-oriented Anglo-American financial system, but also with the other leading industrial nations of Europe, German companies accessed external equity capital much less often. This was particularly so during the economic downturns of the 1970s, where both companies and private investors tended to steer clear of the stock markets due to the high risks involved. As a result, the German capital market was underdeveloped. In 1980, the total value of shares in listed companies in Germany amounted to only nine percent of GDP. If we leave aside the National Socialist period, that represented a new all-time low; by contrast, the market capitalization of US companies was 56 percent of GDP as of the same date.[229]

Even though there are no historically long statistical series available on family businesses, we can still point to a relevant interrelation in this context: compared with America, the extremely strong presence of family businesses in Germany ensured that their skepticism towards market-based forms of financing slowed the development of German capital markets. Even at the end of the 1980s, family businesses were still virtually unaware of the capital market as a potential form of financing. This was due, on the one hand, to the structural dominance of bank loans in the intermediary-oriented German finance system and, on the other, to very tangible peculiarities of the financing behavior of family businesses established as either corporations or partnerships. The capital structure theory of finance alone cannot explain the preference for financing solutions that are so far removed from the market. It assumes that the overwhelming majority of profitable companies will make use of debt capital given the potential tax deductions. What is more, there is an almost asymmetrical burden on dividends and interest payments, profits and losses.[230]

In practice, however, the motives of family businesses are significantly more complex, and their actions are not based—at least not primarily—on tax considerations. In the classical three-circle model comprising company, family and shareholders, decision-makers were faced with a much broader set of strategic, but also emotional, goals when procuring liquidity.[231] The persistent dominance of the credit market for the financing of German companies leads us to the conclusion that it was precisely the large number of family-owned SMEs that preferred to take on external debt because it posed the least danger to their established governance structures. This practice of risk minimization comprised two aspects. First, one related to competitive strategy, namely to avoid reporting and disclosure obligations where possible. Second, one focusing on control considerations, namely to avert potential agency conflicts posed by preserving a largely homogeneous and stable ownership and monitoring structure. In this context, the emotional bond between the founding family and the company—a multigenerational project—had a reinforcing effect on this behavior.[232]

Figure 12: Pecking order: factors influencing financing decisions

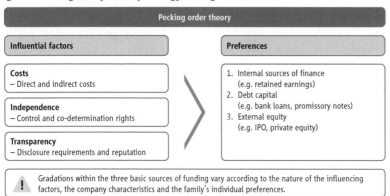

Source: Stiftung Familienunternehmen, Kapitalmarktfähigkeit, p. 41.

This weighing up of financial and institutional-economic cost considerations gave rise to a clear pecking order as regards the financing preferences of German family businesses (Figure 12). This model presupposes that family businesses will finance themselves through retained profits for as long as their success enables them to do so. If we ignore the stagflation crisis of the early 1970s, the underlying conditions for such an approach were quite favorable throughout the postwar period, with its long phases of high growth that enabled companies to accumulate wealth. For example, between the reference years 1963 and 1979 alone, own funds accounted for around 90 percent of gross capital expenditure by non-financial companies in Germany.[233] If taking on debt was unavoidable, then family businesses preferred to borrow external capital in the form of bank loans. "Relationship lending" from a company's house bank offered a well-balanced option for corporate financing, as only the lender had a say in matters and needed to be provided with information. This personal contact with the bank's representatives, who in the case of corporations might also be supervisory board members of the client, enabled owners to preserve the trust-based internal control of their companies.[234] By contrast, the raising of external equity capital was considered to be by far the least attractive option because it posed the strongest threat to preserving the status quo as regards control structures and the owners' ability to pass on the business to the next generation without interference. In this way, risk aversion, an orientation towards the long term, and the desire for independence created specific financing patterns among German family businesses.

Admittedly, this model reflects only trends in the complex reality of financing. In fact, the use of particular financial instruments differed in each individual case and was dependent on the particular motives of the families, on situational requirements and, last but not least, on characteristics such as the age and size of the company and the industry in which it operated. Diverse studies conducted from the mid-1980s onwards revealed that both German and American family businesses displayed a considerably more conservative approach to debt than manager-led corporations with a large free float.[235] The finding that the level of debt depended on profitability and correlated positively with a company's size is not so surprising. But the relatively new research into family businesses uncovered something quite startling, namely that the older the firm, the greater the recourse to internal sources of financing.[236] This was evidently how family businesses stabilized themselves structurally after a highly critical establishment phase. At the same time, however, the older they became, the more family businesses appeared to gravitate towards the pecking-order model. Thus, the longer the bond between the founder family and the business, the stronger the desire to preserve control rights.

If we combine this observation with data on the incorporation process, a serious difference becomes apparent, one that allows profound insights into the divergent financing cultures in Germany and America. As we have seen, initial public offerings (IPOs) played only a minor role as a financing option in postwar Germany: until 1983, there were only three to four a year. What is notable, however, is that these few companies were on average 53 years old when they went public. By contrast, companies in the US and UK went public, on average, just ten years after their establishment.[237] Whereas even founders sought to access the capital market quickly in the Anglo-American sphere, German companies that went public were already in their second or third generation of family ownership or, more to the point, in majority ownership far removed from the market. The penetration of the economic and financial system with this traditional "idiosyncratic financial logic",[238] i.e. a concentrated connection between ownership and control rights in the hands of just a few players, was thus much more pronounced.

V. New Paths? Financial Systems in the Era of Globalization, 1980–2012

Not until the 1980s and 1990s did this clear structure of bank-based corporate financing begin to falter in Germany. A shift from loan- to securities-based financing began to emerge—mostly of a cautious kind, but at times dynamic (Table 17).

Table 17: Financing structures of the private enterprise sector, 1970–2008 (in percent of total financing)

Year	1970	1980	1990	2000	2008
USA					
Equities	55	49	39	63	52
Credit	15	13	18	10	9
Bonds	14	17	18	14	20
Other (bills of exchange, provisions)	16	21	25	13	19
Germany					
Equities	27	20	31	49	41
Credit	47	52	42	37	37
Bonds	3	2	2	1	4
Other (bills of exchange, provisions)	23	26	25	13	18

Source: Bundeszentrale für politische Bildung (ed.), Finanzierungsstruktur G-7-Staaten, http:// www.bpb.de/nachschlagen/zahlen-und-fakten/globalisierung/52587/finanzierungsstruktur-g-7 (accessed: November 15, 2018).

At first glance, a certain convergence is apparent if we look at the trends in financing types between the two countries since 1970. In America, equity financing initially declined in significance into the 1970s and 1980s, while the proportion of debt financing (via loans and bonds) rose slightly. This trend had reversed markedly, however, by the turn of the century. What is notable about Germany is that market-placed bonds were of only marginal importance throughout this entire period. Another obvious feature is that external equity capital jumped from 20 percent in 1980 to 49 percent in 2000. Despite the financial crisis, it was still at 41 percent in 2008, showing that German companies used it much more intensively as a source of liquidity than ever before. At the same time, the significance of bank loans initially declined, but then stabilized at 37 percent, a high level compared with the US.

These new trends had diverse causes. In general terms, there has been a trend towards more international financial markets since the 1990s, in tandem with the globalization of production and trade flows. America was the first country that dared to allow cross-border capital flows in the early 1970s. The UK and Japan soon followed suit, with the main European economies doing the same with a delay of about ten years.[239] It is interesting to note how quickly the trend in dismantling trade barriers increased openness to foreign investors and stimulated direct investment. The "cross-border transfer of capital and control"[240] rose in volume by an annual average of 13 percent from 1990 to 2000 alone. In 1990, it amounted to 0.2 billion dollars; ten years later it had risen to 1.4 billion dollars (FDI outflow only). Simultaneously, the absolute number and value of full acquisitions, i.e. international mergers, rose enormously.[241]

Many German companies, too, were swept along by this trend—one that politicians came to view ever more critically. In 2005, SPD party chairman Franz Müntefering used his now famous "locusts" metaphor to warn against the growing power of private equity funds and hedge funds, which were buying companies with expectations of short-term gains. His criticism was triggered by the takeover of Siemens Nixdorf Informationssysteme by Goldman Sachs and Kolberg Kravis Roberts & Co., a US investment firm. The new investors quickly took the computer and ATM manufacturer, which had been family-owned until 1990, public. They made millions through the IPO, only to systematically hollow out the already crisis-ridden company in order to skim off profits.[242] In the face of the capitalization of German stock markets driven by a new group of local and foreign investors, the traditional system of corporate governance—ring-fenced and bank-based—seemed to be breaking down.

From our vantage point today, however, the polemics of the turn of the millennium, which gave vent to growing unease about "American" shareholder value, look more like a battle against spirits that had been deliberately invoked a good 20 years earlier. A critical examination of the financial situation of German companies after the crises of the 1970s provided the trigger for opening up German capital markets in the 1980s. There was broad concern among politicians and economists that German companies had too little equity capital. Indeed, with an average equity ratio (ratio of equity to total assets) of 18.7 percent in 1981, German firms lagged behind their competitors from abroad, which had equity ratios of over 50 percent.[243]

This "equity gap", as it was termed, was blamed on the house-bank system, which offered too little flexibility. According to the critics, the banks had failed to adequately alleviate the financial bottlenecks that many companies—in particular SMEs—had experienced during the crisis years. Given the rapidly rising number of insolvencies, which jumped from just over 2,000 in 1970 to almost 13,500 in 1985, it seemed an economic necessity to facilitate German companies' access to the capital market.[244]

In the following 20 years, successive German governments enacted new laws, amendments and reforms at exceptionally short intervals, all of which were designed to achieve three goals: to expand securities trading, to improve investor protection, and to raise control and accounting standards to international levels.[245] A start was made in 1987 with a reform of stock market law, which lowered the entry barriers for companies wanting to list on an official stock exchange.[246] There followed four Financial Market Promotion Acts (Finanzmarktförderungsgesetze) between 1990 and 2002, which were flanked by further new regulations under stock-market, stock-corporation and company law. Fiscal changes included the abolition of stock exchange turnover tax in 1991 and bill stamp duty a year later. The Tax Relief Act (Steuererleichterungsgesetz) did away with capital gains tax in 2000 and, in 2002, profits from the sale of equity investments became tax exempt. As a consequence, the cross-shareholdings that were characteristic of "Germany Inc." were gradually dissolved. Banks and financial investors now showed greater willingness to trade their equity investments more quickly in the marketplace, which had a negative impact on the stability of ownership, especially at family-controlled corporations.[247]

As of 1995, state regulation of securities trading increased in order to enhance investor confidence in Germany as an international financial center. A decisive signal was the German government's establishment in 1995 of a dedicated supervisory body for securities trading, which was renamed the Federal Financial Supervisory Authority (Bundesanstalt für Finanzdienstleistungsaufsicht, BaFin) in 2002 and also given oversight of the banking and insurance industries. Under the aegis of this new authority, a clear trend emerged towards combining German capital-market and company law. Strict reporting and disclosure requirements were introduced, expanding investors' insights into the ownership and control structures of companies. As early as 1995, for instance, shareholders were obliged to report their ownership interests and voting rights to both the supervisory authority and the listed company in question as soon as they exceeded certain thresholds. This was designed to enhance information flows regarding ownership structures both within and outside companies, so as to prevent abuse, opportunism and hostile takeovers. Shortly afterwards, insider trading was banned and issuers of financial instruments were obliged to make ad hoc disclosures. We could list many more control measures that were taken to create a transparent market, but probably none had such an existential effect on family-owned corporations as the abolition of multiple voting rights. The Control and Transparency in Business Act (Gesetz zur Kontrolle und Transparenz im Unternehmensbereich) of 5 March 1998 banned any further issues of shares of this type and stipulated that multiple voting rights already extant were to be eliminated within five years. This put paid to one of the key mechanisms used by families to retain control of their companies. Just how strong economic policy makers intended this break with German corporate ownership to be is underscored by the fact that multiple voting rights were not only largely abolished, but were explicitly ostracized as a barrier to market transparency in the first German Corporate Governance Code (Deutscher Corporate Governance Kodex), which is legally underpinned by the Stock Corporation Act—a clear indicator of how the "one share, one vote" paradigm had gained ground in Germany.[248]

Only in rare, justified cases were companies permitted to retain their voting-right status quo. Against this backdrop, many companies sought refuge in complex structures built around foundations in order to preserve family influence. According to the Intes Family Business Academy, by 2010, 40 of the 100 largest family businesses had transferred their assets to non-profit foundations, business owner foundations or, in particular, private equity foundations (Beteiligungsträgerstiftungen), which could also function as umbrella companies for the family holdings.[249] Successful family foundations include Bertelsmann, Hertie, Heraeus or Haniel, while shareholder or private equity foundations include Schickedanz Holding, Diehl-Stiftung & Co. and Würth-Familienstiftungen. Since the reform of foundation law in 2002, corporate foundations have become a viable alternative for many family-owned SMEs too.[250]

The reforms made it easier for foundations to be granted non-profit status, exempting them from inheritance, gift and all income taxes.[251] Unlike the US, where the criteria have been relatively restrictive since the Tax Reform Act of 1969, German foundation law is extremely liberal. Non-profit family foundations not only prevent the disintegration of family wealth when families break up or fail to produce successors, they also secure family influence in their companies. A prime example of this is Bertelsmann AG, which may be majority-owned by the Bertelsmann Foundation, but is still significantly controlled by the Bertelsmann family.[252] A corporate structure of this type would be illegal in the US, where the prime objective of the Tax Reform Act was to stop abusive tax planning and conflicts of interest of persons associated with both the company and the foundation.[253]

Just as the promotion of capital markets in America since the late 1920s led to massive state intervention in order to regulate the market and improve investor protection, the more stringent regulations introduced since the 1990s in Germany widened the range of financing instruments available to companies there. In the debate surrounding the "equity gap", the main complaint of German business owners was that many family-controlled SMEs did not have adequate channels for accessing the capital market. It was viewed as a structural problem of the bank-based financial system that house and issuing banks had for a long time shown little interest in organizing IPOs for such small enterprises. The low profiles of the companies in question were deemed an obstacle to attracting sufficient external capital.[254]

From the late 1990s onwards, novel access channels to the capital market were opened up for SMEs. Though greeted with much optimism, they were fraught with difficulties—as time would show. In March 1997, Frankfurt-based Deutsche Börse AG, which runs the Frankfurt Stock Exchange, set up a new segment: Neuer Markt (NEMAX 50) was devoted entirely to the issue of innovative shares in "new economy" enterprises. In April 1999, the SMAX (Small Cap Exchange) segment was established for second-line stocks from the Official Market and Regulated Market, followed two months later by the SDAX, a new index for 50 lower-value small caps. But the NEMAX 50 and SMAX enjoyed only fleeting success. The NEMAX 50 got off to a very positive start, buoyed by the general stock market euphoria generated by the IPO of Deutsche Telekom. The latter was advertised as a "stock for the people", attracting thousands of small-scale retail investors to the capital market. Between 1996 and 2000 alone, the number of shareholders in Germany almost doubled, from 3.7 million to 6.2 million. This growth was driven mainly by 276 new issues of start-ups and small, future-oriented tech companies.[255]

The NEMAX 50 boom was initially fueled by considerable underpricing effects, but in the medium term the segment was dragged down by the bursting of the dot-com bubble in spring 2000. News reports of insider trading, false ad hoc disclosures and fraudulent accounting at some of the companies listed on the index led to a huge loss of trust and, ultimately, to the closure of the segment, followed soon afterward by the demise of the SMAX as well.[256]

Table 18: Balance sheet structure of German companies, 1997–2012 (in percent)

Year	1997	2000	2003	2006	2009	2012
Large-scale enterprises (revenues > €50 million)						
Tangible assets	47.1	42.0	37.9	36.6	35.9	35.3
Receivables	52.9	58.0	62.1	63.4	64.1	64.4
Total assets	**100.0**	**100.0**	**100.0**	**100.0**	**100.0**	**100.0**
Equity capital	25.7	26.0	28.0	28.1	28.3	29.8
Borrowed funds	74.3	74.0	72.0	71.9	71.7	70.2
Total liabilities	**100.0**	**100.0**	**100.0**	**100.0**	**100.0**	**100.0**
SMEs (revenues < €50 million)						
Tangible assets	59.3	57.8	57.4	54.9	56.6	56.7
Receivables	40.7	42.2	42.6	45.1	43.4	48.3
Total assets	**100.0**	**100.0**	**100.0**	**100.0**	**100.0**	**100.0**
Equity capital	7.3	10.6	14.1	17.7	20.8	24.0
Borrowed funds	92.7	89.4	85.9	82.3	79.2	76.0
Total liabilities	**100.0**	**100.0**	**100.0**	**100.0**	**100.0**	**100.0**

Source: Bendel et al, "Entwicklung Unternehmensfinanzierung", p. 41.

Ultimately, only the SDAX survived as a special segment for SMEs. It took further government requirements regarding investor protection and disclosure obligations to get the stock markets back on a sound footing after the crisis. In 2007, Deutsche Börse carried out a reorganization that resulted in the current segments of the Prime Standard (DAX, MDAX, TecDAX and SDAX) and General Standard (SMEs of the Regulated Market), each with graded rules as regards transparency. Only after many detours, then, was it possible to answer the question of how innovative SMEs and family businesses should gain access to the public capital markets. The stock market crash, and then the financial crisis of 2007/08, had a lasting impact on family businesses' view of control and risk when it came to their actually taking advantage of these new access channels.

As the rough comparison of balance-sheet structures in Table 18 shows, the opening up of capital markets did achieve the intended goal of strengthening equity bases, especially those of SMEs. Between 1997 and 2012, the average equity ratio grew from 7.3 to 24 percent. At the same time, levels of external debt fell.

Still, as regards company financing structures, it is worth noting that higher levels of equity, in turn, led to a comeback for traditional bank loans after the stock-market and financial crises. The higher equity ratios of many small companies improved their creditworthiness, thus reducing the default risk for banks extending credit or placing bonds in the market. What is more, the higher return on equity demanded by investors meant that borrowing gained in significance again. The leverage effect helped raise profitability, provided the interest rate remained below the total return on investment—as has been the case in the low-interest-rate period since the banking crisis of 2007. For majority-owned family businesses, this meant that, once they had closed the equity gap, they found it much easier again to utilize intermediary types of financing. As a result, the classical concentrated corporate governance structures of the German model have stabilized again in recent years.[257]

We can confirm this statement by taking a look at the significance of family businesses in the group of public limited companies listed in the CDAX. Between 1995 and 2006, a general decrease in ownership concentration in these companies was observable,[258] with the proportion of voting rights controlled by the respective largest shareholder falling from 55.1 to 40.4 percent. The same was true for the measurable voting rights of the three largest shareholders, which declined from 66.4 to 52.1 percent. In parallel, the proportion of companies with a broad free float increased by twelve percentage points to 44 percent. If we order the companies not by ownership criteria alone, but by the characteristic control and management functions of family businesses, it becomes apparent that, despite the many IPOs since the end of the 20th century, the significance of family-based companies has risen. If the criteria taken are exercise of at least 25 percent of the voting rights and one identifiable representative of the family on a company board, the proportion of family businesses increased from 28 percent in 1995 to 55 percent in 2000, stabilizing at around 48 percent after that (Figure 13).

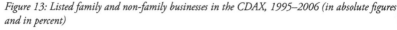

Figure 13: Listed family and non-family businesses in the CDAX, 1995–2006 (in absolute figures and in percent)

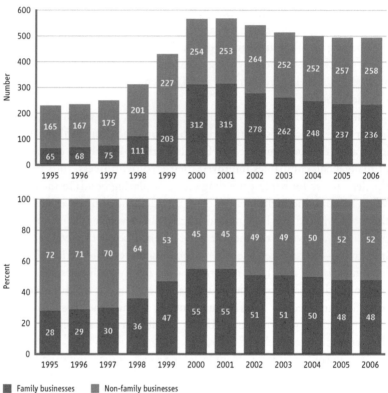

Family businesses   Non-family businesses

Source: Ampenberger, Unternehmenspolitik, p. 237.

Evidently, the founder families succeeded in retaining their influence in their companies even after an IPO. In Germany, the average founder-family-owned stake was 38 percent, putting those families among the most important shareholder groups of listed corporations. In America, around the same time, founder families held an average of only 18 percent of their companies' equity. Further, in the S&P index, which is comparable with Germany's CDAX, not even one-third of the companies were "family-influenced"—even when we apply the most liberal possible definition, namely control of five percent of the voting rights.[259]

That the two corporate governance models continue to differ so markedly is surprising, especially when we consider that the convergence processes that arose in the 1990s did not consist solely in Germany adapting its standards to match America's. In institutional terms, the US financial system also underwent decisive changes that, in certain points at least, indicate a departure from traditional principles. Starting in the late 1980s, the Federal Reserve under its new chairman Alan Greenspan began softening the strict separation between different types of banks. Commercial banks, which the Glass–Steagall Act had banned from investment banking for more than 60 years, were again allowed to transact this sort of business. In fact, American banks were already drifting towards the practices of universal banks before President Bill Clinton officially rescinded the separation in the Gramm–Leach–Bliley Act of 1999. Whereas the commercial banks began getting involved in international equity business, many investment banks withdrew from their positions of control in US big business and began transacting a large number of investment and private equity deals for their own account.[260] Critics saw this trend as a key reason for the distortions in the banking and capital market that ultimately led to the collapse of Lehman Bros. in 2008, triggering the global financial crisis. Since then, there has been a lively debate in America about reinstating the Glass–Steagall Act. The Obama administration took the first steps in this direction with its reform of Wall Street. Investment banks were made subject to stricter regulation and their fundamental weaknesses eliminated by refinancing through the Federal Reserve. But the policy of the Trump administration now points in the opposite direction.

A second aspect of convergence has emerged since the 1980s with the easing of the strict "one share, one vote" principle with respect to voting rights. In 1984, the NYSE set up a "Subcommittee on Shareholder Participation and Qualitative Listing Standards", a panel with the task of renegotiating the eligibility of preference shares and voting trusts.[261] The debate was triggered largely by major US media companies such as the Washington Post, News Corporation or Rupert Murdoch's 21st Century Fox. They argued that a concentration of voting rights through the issuance of non-voting dual class shares was necessary to protect the journalistic integrity of their work despite the dispersed holdings of their shares. This line of argument was drawn from past debates: In the United States—much like in Germany—special treatment of the media and the transport industry had been discussed for decades under the heading of general social interest. Against the backdrop of the strongly growing wave of mergers and acquisitions since the 1980s that would radically reshape national and international business landscapes, the debates being waged on the assignment of company control rights became a matter of principle. In a test case in 1984, General Motors and major family-owned companies such as Ford and Mars joined media companies in calling for governance rules to be liberalized.[262] A wider range of share classes was said to help fend off hostile takeovers, establish control over self-acquired subsidiaries and cement the relationship between companies and their founders. As early as 1988, the US Securities and Exchange Commission also adopted a position in which the control interests of entrepreneurs were weighed in a new way against the interests of short-term investors. Working closely with the NYSE, the SEC revised Rule 19c-4 of the Securities Exchange Act of 1934. The new regulations permitted the issue of shares with no or reduced voting rights that could be alphabetically classified as A, B or C shares with disparate voting rights.[263] At the same time, it specified that no existing shareholder rights could be diminished as part of the issue of dual class shares. Furthermore, Paragraph 19c-4 expressly stated that disparate shareholder structures should be used during mergers and acquisitions if they served a "bona fide business purpose." This vague language created broad interpretive leeway when evaluating issuance requests.[264] Ultimately, though, the SEC could issue only recommendations; the final regulatory authority remained in the hands of the states. Nonetheless, Rule 19c-4 served as a guide for stock exchange practices in subsequent years. Particularly since the beginning of the new millennium, the number of companies with a dual class voting structure has risen strongly in the United States. In 2012, about ten percent of companies listed on the S&P 1500 indexes used this instrument—among them the Ford Motor Company, a family business, which had been granted an exemption from the NYSE in 1956 and secured the family's influence by issuing Class B shares with multiple voting rights. Between 2006 and 2010, Ford restructured its ownership and control rights once again as part of a capital increase. Today, members of the family hold less than two percent of the company's share capital, but control 40 percent of its voting rights.[265]

Another very noticeable trend especially in recent years among the visionary founders of new high-tech and social-media companies is the use of dual class structures to prevent their long-term strategy decisions from being subjected to pressure by the interests of short-term investors. Mark Zuckerberg is probably the most prominent representative of this trend. Zuckerberg and some of the others who helped him launch Facebook hold special Class B shares that have ten votes each, a feature that solidifies their control of the company.[266] It remains to be seen whether this trend will ultimately have any impact on succession at family businesses. And it is not without a certain irony: As shares with multiple voting rights emerged in the United States at the end of the 20th century, they were being abolished in Germany in 1998 by the Control and Transparency in Business Act (Gesetz zur Kontrolle und Transparenz im Unternehmensbereich, or KonTraG) for the purpose of introducing the firmly established US principle of "one share, one vote" into German capital market law.

A third developmental direction emerged in the regulatory areas of accounting transparency and disclosure. In response to the Enron and Worldcom scandals, the US administration passed the Sarbanes–Oxley Act in 2002, the first federal law to directly intervene in the corporate governance of US companies. These advances towards a patriarchal form of state supervision not only restricted the individual states' sovereignty in company-law matters, but essentially swept aside the previous practice of self-regulation through the market. The new regulations mainly concerned accounting requirements for public limited companies. Since 1930, various private accounting bodies of the auditors' associations had been working on defining Generally Accepted Accounting Principles for the United States (US GAAP). In 1973, in an effort to strengthen investor protection, the SEC ultimately recognized the recommendations of the Financial Accounting Standard Boards (FASB) as standards for the entire US economy. The voluntary commitment to observe the basic "true and fair view"-principles of the FASB entailed considerable disclosure obligations. However, gaps in monitoring appeared in the market-based system of private control by rating agencies, auditors and bank analysts. With the Sarbanes–Oxley Act, US regulators put an end to the method of internal self-control practiced by auditors and companies. In order to restore investor confidence in markets after the dot-com crash, private auditors were prohibited from providing companies with both accounting and consulting services simultaneously. The peer-review principle of auditing financial accounts was to give way to external monitoring. Companies were obliged to put in place a cost-intensive internal control system for accounting and to have their financial statements evaluated by an independent regulatory authority, the Public Company Accounting Oversight Board. At the same time, reporting and disclosure obligations were once more considerably expanded and standardized under federal law. Harsh sanctions, including removal from the market and even long prison sentences, were introduced for breaches of accounting regulations.[267]

The effect of these measures is still the subject of debate. While the strict regime of disclosure and auditing undoubtedly enhances investor protection and market transparency, the practice of constant control puts ever greater pressure on managers and owner families not to put their financial leeway, or even their companies' existence, at risk with a negative analyst's report. In this respect, market-based control—for all its efficiency—encourages decision-makers to maximize profits in the short term. This sort of connection is likely to discourage German family businesses from accessing the capital market and changing their legal form. Nevertheless, as financial markets, value chains and corporate structures become more globalized, there is a clear trend towards internationalizing disclosure and accounting practices. Against this backdrop, German lawmakers found themselves compelled to tighten accounting regulations around the middle of the first decade of the 21st century. The Accounting Law Reform Act (BilReg, 2005), the Accounting Control Act (BilKoG, 2005) and the Accounting Law Modernization Act (BilMoG, 2009) all introduced decisive reforms, e.g. of the legal norms for accounting and the companies' record keeping. The goal was to make annual financial statements more informative and align them as far as possible with the International Financial Reporting Standards (IFRS). As the new legislation also anchored these stricter disclosure obligations in the German Commercial Code, family businesses, more than ever before, face a serious question when choosing their financing models, i.e. to what extent they can meet demands for greater disclosure without forfeiting their freedom of control and decision-making.[268]

The problem of greater pressure for disclosure is not one confined to large family-controlled enterprises seeking external funding, it is a fundamental problem that increasingly impacts the conventional loan financing of many small and medium-sized family businesses that are partnerships or private limited companies. In this case, it is the much more stringent equity requirements introduced by Basel II and Basel III in the wake of the financial crisis of 2007 that have led to more restrictive practices in the granting of loans. Companies are increasingly faced with the choice between accepting higher risk premiums and taking out loans at significantly more expensive terms, or proving their creditworthiness by agreeing to disclose inside information about their business operations and possibly even submitting to external auditing of their management and control systems. At present, it is not at all clear to what extent these stricter obligations to provide evidence to banks and capital markets will cause family businesses to reorient themselves as regards their financing strategies.[269]

From the historical perspective, then, we can conclude that the US and German financial systems have been converging over the last 30 years or so, but that this process has by no means eliminated the differences between the two that have existed for decades. The typical institutional characteristics of the corporate governance systems on both sides of the Atlantic are still clearly visible. This is true not only of the differences as regards the dispersed versus concentrated ownership and control structures of companies, but their preferences for capital-market versus credit-market financing as well as a marked divergence in the presence of family-based companies. The different types of capitalism practiced in Germany and America that persist to the present day can be traced back through history along well-worn paths of legal regulation, regulatory governance and, last but not least, cultural practices of corporate organization.

E. Family Businesses and Economic Policy

There may be no direct equivalents in English for the two terms "Gewerbe-förderung" (trade and business promotion) and "Mittelstandspolitik" (small and medium-sized enterprise policy), but they have nonetheless had signal character for economic policy in Germany. These two things have never referred explicitly to family businesses, but they hold out the promise of particular public-sector support for these businesses.

I. The Long-standing Tradition of Trade and Business Promotion in Germany

Trade and business promotion includes a broad spectrum of structural policy and regulatory instruments, which serve as direct and indirect aids to ensure the establishment, survival and ongoing development of companies. The 19th century saw the evolution of country-specific institutional structures, which laid the foundation for the corporatist economic regulation model in Germany and the more market-based one in the USA that characterizes corporate landscapes to this day. The various German states were heavily involved in trade and business promotion at an early stage: the mercantilist traditions of the pre-modern era made these territories compete against each other in order to attract trades and other businesses to their regions and secure the resulting tax and concession revenues. Furthermore, the catastrophic experience of Prussia's defeat by Napoleon (1806), which resulted in losses of territory and onerous tribute payments, caused the collective feeling of economic backwardness to spread. Given the lack of raw materials and colonies, investments in the educational system advanced to become an important means of offsetting these disadvantages and accelerating the process of catching up with Great Britain. Public educational institutions for trade and industry therefore played an early and important role in trade and business promotion. As early as the 1820s and 1830s, many technical colleges were established to train engineers. Twenty vocational schools with a total of 1,000 students were in operation by 1835 in Prussia alone. The best graduates each year were awarded government scholarships to attend the Commercial Institute in Berlin, which opened in 1821 and was known from 1879 onwards as the Technical University. The Polytechnical School in Karlsruhe similarly took on the character of a technical university in the 1830s. The German states thus met the growing demands of the business community for structured, technically and practically relevant training of professionals. What is more, as vocational schools and universities spread relatively widely throughout Germany, they became real hotbeds of innovation and entrepreneurial spirit, producing countless family business owners like machinery manufacturers August Borsig and Carl Hoppe.[270]

State and local authorities also started publicly advocating the organization of trade fairs and industrial exhibitions to ease the sharing of knowledge about modern industrial manufacturing methods. The states awarded travel grants to entrepreneurs who wanted to study the latest machines made in progressive Great Britain or Belgium, or showcase their products abroad. The public authorities often acted in close coordination with new, regional trade associations, which simultaneously functioned as lobbies and information networks for the business community. Promotional tools included support for the launch of technical journals and information services, for the establishment of sample stocks and industrial museums featuring machines and products. Competitions and innovation contests served as motivational aids for potential start-ups. Even more important was tangible assistance for founding businesses and other capital support, export subsidies and loans that, as public money, frequently made up for the lack of private investment resources. Forward-looking trade and business promoters like Peter Christian Beuth in Prussia, Ferdinand von Steinbeis in Württemberg and Albert Christian Weinling in Saxony launched smart programs that created and boosted private companies with the help of state aid. These endeavors were not state capitalism. Instead, the aim was to help businesses to help themselves through seed capital, information and the communication of technical knowledge. Prussia and Württemberg thus purchased machinery from abroad and made it available to potential start-up entrepreneurs and interested manufacturers free of charge, on condition that trade secrecy was set aside and other local businesspeople were also permitted to inspect the plant and equipment—i.e. spread this state-of-the-art technology rapidly.[271]

There were no parallels in the USA to this broadly based policy of promotion. In the 19th century the structures of US statehood were still rudimentary—both in the federal states and in the emerging and still discordant central government in Washington, D.C. State intervention was often met with rejection, as it seemed unnecessary or detrimental to the free development of the market in this resource-rich, fast-growing country. Technical education remained dependent on private initiatives alone. Precisely this conspicuous deficit in the technical college landscape led in 1862 to the Morrill Land-Grant Acts: Washington donated 120 square kilometers of land to each federal state, which was to finance the establishment of institutes of higher education from the proceeds of the sale of that land. Colleges were subsequently established in many places and they later evolved into universities. One of them, modelled on technical universities in Europe, was the Massachusetts Institute of Technology (MIT), yet it endured chronic financial hardship until 1914. During the course of the 20th century these predominantly privately financed top US universities became the world's leading research and educational institutions, producing large numbers of innovative entrepreneurs—and leaving their German role models well behind.

In contrast to the USA, the promotional programs provided by German states included direct financial assistance for business and its institutions at an early stage. Often it was established public-sector commercial and trade organizations that grew into this role. In Prussia, for instance, the state-owned "Maritime Commerce Company" (Seehandlungsgesellschaft), which was set up in the 18th century, turned into a kind of development bank that pursued an active industrial policy from the 1820s onwards. In Brunswick-Lüneburg, Baden, Silesia and many other German states, it was initially state-owned banks and semi-public regional banks and banking associations that made important financial contributions to the development of industry; in particular, they ensured the necessary expansion of the transportation and traffic infrastructure. Private banks slowly began to take on this role in the middle of the century,[272] but government funding continued to flow freely. In 1866 the state parliament of Saxony approved the princely sum of 1.5 million talers to make advance payments to manufacturers and merchants. While low bureaucratic hurdles and liberal licensing requirements were intended to encourage the establishment of industries in US states, the German states opted for tangible material incentives—always coupled with the mercantilist idea that the public authorities should retain control over economic development.

In Germany it was immensely helpful to the SME business sector and therefore to family businesses in particular that they were able to rely on an expanding network of savings and cooperative banks, where loans were provided in the context of close personal bank-client relationships. A distinction needs to be made between two segments—the mainly municipal savings banks, of which there were about 2,500 around the year 1900, and the institutions initially referred to as credit cooperatives or disbursement societies and later named cooperative banks. The latter provided the SME business sector with reliable, local support, initially financing craft and trade enterprises. But as steady partners, they grew alongside their customers as smaller businesses were transformed into major industrial conglomerates. The private commercial banks that evolved in parallel also became a significant presence in the region. Towards the end of the century, the major banks took over numerous smaller financial institutions and branches of regional banks. They were then represented throughout Germany by branches, which eased personal contact between family business owners and their house banks—a system still in use up to the present day. In contrast, American savings banks and commercial banks were unstable and fragmented. They had virtually no regional branches and were not permitted, usually because of their articles of incorporation, to transact industrial financing business: the risk was believed to be too high. Furthermore, they were almost always short-lived and at risk of going bankrupt. The major US investment banks dealt mainly with major corporate clients, such as heavy industry and the railway companies. Relationships between banks and companies were significantly more distant and anonymous, which in structural terms meant fewer incentives to retain traditional family business structures.

The chambers of industry and commerce, the constitutions of which made them statutory institutions, represented another important component in Germany's institutional set-up. Compulsory membership in these chambers, which was legally endorsed in 1870, meant that they included almost all tradespeople. Through these chambers, entrepreneurs gained institutionalized access to official channels and politicians, which ensured that their interests and concerns were heard. The chambers were the business community's regional lobbying and advisory bodies as well as functioning as lower-ranking government administration departments, establishing very efficient flows of information in both directions and laying an essential institutional foundation for German-style cooperative capitalism. The Association of German Commerce (Deutscher Handelstag, DHT), a national umbrella organization of chambers with a central office in Berlin, was set up in 1861. In 1918 it was renamed the Association of German Industry and Commerce (Deutscher Industrie- und Handelstag, DIHT).[273] Freely organized industry associations and business and trade associations likewise formed the second pillar of the business lobbying infrastructure in Germany from the mid-19th century onwards. The business networks that were created—for instance, within the Berlin mercantile community or in the mining associations of the Ruhr region—eased informal cooperation outside of the corporate acquisition and market competition circles, thus indirectly safeguarding the independence and longevity of family-based corporate structures.[274]

In contrast, chambers of commerce in the United States never achieved a similar degree of commercial importance. They were only amalgamated to form a national organization in 1912 on the initiative of President Taft, who wanted one key partner in the business community and a counterbalance to the increasingly powerful labor movement. The American Chamber of Commerce was created as an amalgamation of local chambers and regional associations in which membership was voluntary. These associations were comparatively weak and fragmented and did not act on behalf of the government. Although they also provided important coordination and information services, they lagged well behind the thoroughly organized German chambers and associations in terms of institutional effectiveness. As a result, they did not become established economic policy pressure groups able to effectively channel and champion the interests of their business constituencies vis-à-vis public institutions. Even the degree of self-organization and therefore the formation of informal networks was considerably less developed in the United States. In this constellation, it was easier for the market paradigm to prevail over the relics of pre-modern economic organization.

II. *Mittelstand* Policy. A Legacy of the 19th Century

The German term *Mittelstand* (small and medium-sized enterprises) is still in common currency in Germany. It embraces the concept of laws and norms of a static social order, and is rooted in the system of values of a feudally structured society in which each class has a firmly allocated place that may not be challenged. In an economic context, the term *Mittelstand* is very blurred: In 1901 the legal advisor to the Breslau Chamber of Commerce, Georg Gothein, remarked tartly: "If you can't define it, you refer to it as *Mittelstand*."[275] Thus the term incorporates a broad spectrum of the commercially and agriculturally self-employed, ranging from farmers to shop owners and craftsmen. During the 19th century,[276] the call for an active government *Mittelstandspolitik* or SME policy meant the term became a major political rallying cry.[277] *Mittelstand* policy was a conservative reflex to the challenges of the modern era, a response to industrialization, which energized the process of social change and generated massive economic upheavals. The argument was that the *Mittelstand* had to serve as a guarantor of stability at the heart of society. As a "healthy core sandwiched between rich and poor", it was entitled to receive particular protection from the state according to small business owners and conservative circles.[278]

SME policy seemed to be a panacea for safeguarding the monarchy and with it the status quo of the existing social order. It was intended to act as a bulwark against social democracy, against unbridled competition and against the threat posed by anonymous capital, often decried as "Jewish". As with trade and business promotion, a whole arsenal of direct and indirect support instruments hid behind the term "*Mittelstand* policy", including competition and regulatory matters as well as socio-political aspects. The initiatives had three broad objectives: ensuring the continued existence of SME structures, offsetting the disadvantages faced by SMEs in competition with their major industrial rivals and ensuring a sustainable pool of businesses through succession and new foundings.

In practice, this SME policy turned out to be a pendulum that oscillated between preservation and measures for modernization. One example was the structuring of the Trade, Commerce and Industry Regulation Act (Gewerbeordnung), in which not all the far-reaching demands of small and medium-sized enterprises for protection were implemented, but many concessions were made, even on fundamental regulatory issues. Thus the 1897 Skilled Crafts and Trades Act (Handwerksgesetz) restricted key aspects of the principle of freedom of trade that had prevailed since 1869 and established long-term path dependencies. Following traditional German guild ideals, master craftsmen were now able to set up craft guilds (Innungen) with compulsory membership, if the majority of self-employed craftsmen in a particular district agreed. Restrictive admittance of new master craftsmen gave them the means of self-regulating their market position and the intensity of regional competitive pressure. Citing the conservation argument, extensive use was made of these means of undermining market mechanisms.

The Empire boosted the self-governing ambitions of small and medium-sized enterprises. Chambers of Crafts and Trades were established as self-governing public bodies, which required all craftsmen in a particular district to join them and pay membership dues. Like the CICs they were self-governing institutions, lobbying organizations and liaisons with the government apparatus all at the same time. The principle of compulsory membership and their merger in 1900 into the Association of German Chambers of Skilled Crafts and Trades (Deutscher Handwerks- und Gewerbekammertag) put craft trades in a strong position,[279] and even resulted in 1905 in the tendering system in Prussia being changed to awarding public contracts preferably to local master craftsman businesses.[280] In 1908 the influence of skilled crafts and trades was manifested by the introduction throughout the Empire of the "partial certificate of professional competence" (kleiner Befähigungs-nachweis), which continued to tie training accreditation firmly to the master craftsman's certificate.[281] This too was primarily a building block in the process of (self-)regulating market access, which had wide-ranging education and industry policy implications, because this approach enabled practically relevant vocational training with professional instruction to be systematized and applied to the industrial apprentice system. In 1912 the legislature even classified businesses employing several hundred people under certain circumstances as "large-scale skilled crafts and trades" and in the 1920s made huge efforts to incorporate what was often unregulated industrial training into the traditional structures of the skilled craft apprentice system. Ultimately, these provisions laid the foundations for sustainably high training standards in Germany. Given that around 2.5 million skilled craftsmen were working in industry and the service sector in 1926/27 alone, and that 19th century industrial factory schools adopted the master craftsman training model, these protective measures had an impact far beyond the SME sector.[282]

In the USA, the handicraft sector and the vocational training remained unregulated to a large extent, i.e. subject to market mechanisms. That ensured more competition and higher fluctuation, but also resulted in unclear, often relatively low standards of qualification. Short periods of on-the-job training for workers were the norm. In contrast to organized professional training, this practice generated fewer trade-off effects for the establishment of independent small businesses, and encouraged a process of concentration of big businesses instead of continuous renewal in the *Mittelstand*.

There were also ambitions in Germany to prevent predatory market competition in the commercial sector. From 1899 onwards various German states imposed special taxes on department stores and cooperative societies to protect the retail trade. Even vending machines at railway stations and some elements of street vending were regarded as a threat to stationary retail and were strongly regulated or even prohibited. In 1911 the Hessian government summarized the rationale behind these measures[283] as follows: It is "in the state's interest to ensure the existence of as many small and medium-sized enterprises as possible."[284] However, the real economic ramifications of these protective measures remained modest: Many small tradesmen continued to suffer hardship and became industrial workers. Public procurement offices regularly circumvented the tendering rules. And the importance of department stores and consumer cooperatives continued to increase. Some retail businesses thrived along with them, but others found themselves trapped in a precarious existence or even had to close.[285]

The imponderables of the flourishing industrial market economy could not be remedied through SME policy. That became very clear during the First World War, when rationalization efforts of the armaments production led to a preference for major industrial businesses in terms of resource rationing and the awarding of contracts. Material supply bottlenecks, the massive growth of large corporations and the consequences of postwar inflation all fueled the concerns of independent SMEs, which constantly saw their existence under threat during the eventful years of the first German democracy—the Weimar Republic. Following its establishment in 1918/19, the republic even explicitly made the promotion of small and medium-sized enterprises a national objective: Article 164 of the Weimar Constitution stated: "Independent small and medium-sized enterprises operating in agriculture, industry and commerce are to be supported in legislation and administration terms and protected against overburdening and absorption."[286] The recently established Reich Ministry of Economic Affairs underlined its regulatory ambitions by initially establishing a special *Mittelstand* department in 1921, which was institutionally upgraded in 1925 by the appointment of a Reich Commissioner for Skilled Crafts/Trades and Small Businesses (Reichskommissar für das Handwerk und Kleingewerbe). This prioritization was motivated by the idea that the reorganization of economic, political and social interaction could not happen if small and medium-sized enterprises, as the core of the German economy, were permanently weakened.

Governments in the Weimar Republic interpreted their constitutional mandate to the effect that they had to accommodate the social-protectionist interests of small and medium-sized enterprises and, at the same time, reform the system of occupational rules in the spirit of the "social economy" (Gemeinwirtschaft) ideal. However, the attempt to balance the interests of powerful trade unions, chambers of commerce and associations of skilled craftsmen, small business and large industry, and migrate them all into a state-facilitated restructuring of the economy, failed miserably. Neither the modernization of the vocational training system nor the envisaged reform of the crafts and commerce statutes (Handwerks- und Gewerbeordnung) succeeded. Towards the end of the Weimar Republic, the state saw itself caught up between increasingly radicalized self-serving interests. On the basis of their rights to be protected, the SME organizations demanded increasingly more extensive measures and wanted to upgrade their trade associations to regional cartel-type occupational groups that dictated terms and conditions, delivery and pricing. Since the beginning of the 1920s, they had expected the government to deliver sweeping competition policy intervention, the suspension of the minimum price principle for public tenders to the benefit of skilled crafts and trades, the elimination of competition from department stores, itinerant traders and consumer cooperative societies, and strict controls on the power of the conglomerates and industrial cartels. Although Weimar Republic governments were very SME-friendly and at least willing to contemplate partial intervention in the competition, they could not fulfill these exaggerated demands. Even direct subsidies of SMEs, provided by a special government loan program worth 34 million RM set up in the summer of 1925, were barely able to pacify the powerful *Mittelstand* lobby.[287]

Yet the proponents of the *Mittelstand* did achieve an important taxation policy success. As far as family businesses were concerned, there were plans in Prussia prior to 1914 to put the limited liability company (GmbH), the typical legal form of a family-owned incorporated enterprise, on an equal footing with the joint stock company (AG). This would have led to a twofold tax burden, because profits would have been applied both at corporate and at owner level, ensuring a significant increase in income tax. In 1905 the "Centrale für GmbH" organization was set up by the legal advisor of the Cologne Chamber of Commerce to lobby against these proposals, and it temporarily succeeded in preventing this double taxation burden. Although GmbH companies became liable for tax in the future, the tax liability apportioned to their partners was offset against their personal tax burdens, putting them in a considerably more privileged position than the joint stock companies. This preferential treatment, which could be justified in structural policy but not in terms of tax systems, was maintained beyond the change in the political system until 1920.

Germany found itself in a severe financial crisis after 1918. The Erzberger tax reforms in 1919/20 were a reaction to that crisis: they harmonized what had previously been a very fragmented system of taxation law. In addition to establishing the Reich Ministry of Finance, the reform also created an extensive network of around 1000 regional tax offices. At the same time, taxes were increased sharply. As part of these reforms, income tax revenue was passed to the Reich. A separate corporation tax for legal entities was introduced for the first time in 1920, initially with a tax rate of ten percent. The law exposed the partners of a GmbH to a twofold tax burden, but on the initiative of the "Centrale" in turn, it created a reduced rate of tax for proprietors with lower incomes, i.e. bestowed a privilege on the owners of smaller family businesses, which were deemed particularly worthy of protection. This benchmark was upheld in the 1925 amendment to the corporation tax law. From that date up until 1935, limited liability companies were liable for a standard corporation tax rate of 20 percent, while smaller businesses, irrespective of legal form, were only liable for the much lower rate of ten percent (progressive scale up to 20 percent). Here the legislature again opted de facto to give smaller family businesses preferential treatment.

Double taxation also became a reality in the USA, with a progressive scale of corporate tax from eleven to 14 percent from 1936 onwards, though this was still lower than Germany's 20 percent. However, a direct comparison is not possible owing to the option of significantly higher write-downs in Germany—a diverse range of small concessions that benefited SMEs without giving them massively preferential treatment. Most striking are the differences in lobbying: a key hallmark of "cooperative capitalism" in Germany was the ability of companies to organize themselves in influential associations that entered into dialogue with the state and were able to force compromises. Nevertheless, SME owners feared losing their livelihoods, given the general crisis in the economy of the Weimar Republic and the sense of a particularly severe threat. Sociologist Geiger spoke of a "panic within the *Mittelstand*".[288]

III. National Socialism, the New Deal and the Wartime Economy

The situation deteriorated seriously from 1929 onwards as a result of the convulsions caused by the global economic crisis, and any loyalty that the *Mittelstand* had retained with regard to the Weimar Republic was quickly abandoned. The Nazi Party (NSDAP) was quick to exploit these dashed hopes. It was easy to build bridges between the Weimar Republic's *Mittelstand* activists and Nazi ideologues within the framework of a shared trade mentality, an anti-big-business approach, a strong preference for state control, and the call for a new national social(ist) romanticism. From the end of 1932 onwards, the "National Socialist Militant League for the *Mittelstand*" (Nationalsozialistischer Kampfbund für den gewerblichen Mittelstand) aggressively championed a crackdown on consumer cooperatives and department stores.

Promoting the German *Mittelstand* therefore became a core theme of the Nazi Party's political manifesto. Coupled with the ideological exaltation of family, kin and race, this generated a basically positive attitude towards family businesses. Because they epitomized individual responsibility, personal "leadership" and financial solidity, they were regarded as the better alternative to anonymous public limited companies, which had been discredited from 1929 onwards as a result of spectacular bankruptcies and management failures. At the party's rank-and-file level, radical "Kampfbund" officials were increasingly vocal in their demands for department stores, consumer cooperatives and anonymous corporations to be pushed out of the economy. Their approach was driven by an aggressive anti-Semitism that ultimately found an outlet in the frenzied boycotts of Jewish businesses in March 1933. Once National Socialism was established, however, its leadership rejected increasingly vocal ambitions to abolish public limited companies, because it required big business to help it fulfill its military build-up plans.[289] The left wing of the Nazi Party, which had been influential before the party came to power, was led by Gregor Strasser, who preached the model of a corporate-state socialist economic system based on SME structures. However, he was unable to gain support for his ambitions.

The Nazi regime retained the basic private-enterprise constitution and relied on an equally pragmatic as well as symbolic political system of economic incentives, commercial law reforms and (party-) state controls to get companies to commit to its objectives. The ideal was still the small to medium-sized owner-managed family business. Distinguishing features of this approach included the symbolic promotion of company directors to the rank of "factory leader" ("Betriebsführer") with the aim of ideologizing hierarchical leadership structures (familiar from the patriarchalism of early family businesses) and applying them to the entire economy. At the same time, the laws governing the corporative (ständische) reorganization of the economy, which were passed in 1934, ensured that conflicts between employees and employers were disavowed by using the smoke-screen propaganda terms "Gefolgschaft" ("followers") and "Betriebsgemeinschaft" ("factory community"), but at the same time enabled company directors to be monitored more closely by what were called "Treuhänder der Arbeit" ("trustees of labor"). The compulsory incorporation of all skilled craft, commercial and industrial businesses into supervisory sector and professional groups (Wirtschafts- und Fachgruppen) as well as regional guilds and chambers reinforced the self-administrating bodies of the economy, provided them with the opportunity to develop cartel-like structures, but at the same time made them submit to state control and the primacy of rearmament.

This fact alone demonstrates that economic policy in Nazi Germany was characterized by numerous contradictions and conflicting objectives. It was characterized primarily by a relatively unprincipled pragmatism aimed at serving Nazi Germany's military build-up, where the situational prerogative often swamped or even contradicted or frustrated ideological, regulatory objectives. This applied in particular to corporate law priorities. Indeed, both public limited companies and GmbHs were forced to convert to partnerships through massive fiscal incentives, as illustrated in Chapter D. However, intervention in company statutes always focused on the goal of maximum efficiency in the provision of armaments. Although the number of public limited and limited liability companies was reduced,[290] they were retained as an effective form of large-scale industrial organization, especially in sensitive manufacturing segments. There was no comprehensive forced conversion of joint-stock companies.[291] As we have seen, public limited companies were given a more restrictive legal form, but limited liability companies, which were also criticized as being "anonymous", were not. Initial ideas for creating a dedicated, uniform type of enterprise for family businesses that was intended to supersede the GmbH never left the drawing board. For family business owners, this meant they were able to defend and enhance their status quo. They continued to have the option of operating under the legal form of a GmbH in order to derive benefit from the advantages of this specific mixed form—the lack of disclosure obligations, a low level of authorized capital and the safeguarding of family business succession.

Initiatives by the Nazi regime to benefit skilled craftsmen and small businesses likewise turned out to offer both advantages and disadvantages. A long-held wish of the skilled craft sector was fulfilled in 1935 with the introduction of the "major certificate of professional competence" (großer Befähigungsnachweis), which made the master craftsman's certificate a prerequisite for the independent management of a skilled craft business. However extensive demands from *Mittelstand* circles were disregarded. Despite an establishment and expansion ban, department stores and mail order businesses were not abolished in order to boost family-owned retail outlet businesses, even if many consumer cooperatives were closed down on account of their close relationships with the labor movement. As early as 1933, a fixed discount rate of three percent was set and extras were prohibited in order to create a level playing field for small and large commercial enterprises. Nevertheless, skilled craft businesses were required to adopt rational, always verifiable operations management methods as a result of the introduction of accounting obligations in 1937, and were thus exposed to an increased tax liability.[292] Tax policy initiatives by family businesses, which demanded the simplification of tax law and the abolition of double taxation through corporation and income tax, proved futile. On the contrary, the state increasingly asserted its authority and tax-levying powers here too.

Although Walther Funk, Hitler's economic advisor and future Reich Economics Minister, announced very vocally in 1929 that corporation tax for family businesses would be reduced,[293] the exact opposite occurred after 1933. Given the "Third Reich's" massive financial requirements for its military build-up, taxation of corporations increased, with tax rates rising in 1936 from 20 to 25 percent and in 1937 to 30 percent. From 1938 onwards, an element of progression was built into the tax system that depended on the level of profits made, analogous to the approach taken in the USA two years previously. As tax audits tended to become more rigorous, the tax on profits in excess of 100,000 RM increased to 35 percent, then in 1939 to 40 percent, in 1941 to 45 percent and finally in 1942 to 50 percent. Despite the sliding scale, and given the universally increasing tax burden, this cannot be regarded as effective preferential treatment of the German *Mittelstand*.[294]

In the USA the New Deal and military build-up caused corporation tax to increase from 13.8 (1932) to 40 percent (1942). To spare smaller companies, a progressive system with a considerable spread was introduced in

1936. The New Deal included a momentous reform of taxation policy, which weakened some family businesses considerably. President Roosevelt wanted to combat trusts and the families behind them.[295] His solution, which took effect with the 1935 Tax Reform, was to eliminate the tax appeal of pyramid structures that families used to control several interconnected companies: after 1935, "intercorporate dividends" were subject to double taxation. Corporation tax regimes in most other countries did not include double taxation. For example, in Germany from 1916 onwards (apart from an interruption between 1923 and 1925), parent companies were able to offset profits generated by companies in which they held stakes of 20 percent or more against their own tax liability. In 1923 this provision was also extended to local business tax.[296] This kept groups of companies from bearing an additional burden compared with stand-alone companies, but it also made it easier for individual families to control interconnected companies. Yet while the Nazi regime did not challenge a provision that benefited family holding companies, the US government started to break the dominance of families over multiple interconnected companies. As we have seen, the Nazi regime did not generally favor holding company and group structures; instead, it provided massive tax incentives for converting from joint-stock companies to partnerships. This intercompany (box) privilege lasted until 1977. It meant that for example a parent company could receive dividends from an affiliate company whose shares it owns without attracting additional corporate taxes. The minimum requirements for this rule were even reduced. After 1977 this privilege was replaced by a system in which double taxation was avoided through a tax imputation procedure, the half-income method from 2001 onwards and the partial-income method from 2009 onwards. In effect intercorporate dividends were tax-free or were only moderately taxed, which favored pyramid structures used by family firms to retain control of their commercial property.

Attempts by the Nazis to safeguard family businesses against liens or pledges, as in the agricultural sector, were abandoned. The Academy for German Law (Akademie für deutsches Recht), which was established in 1933, seriously discussed the creation of "hereditary business estates" ("Erbhöfe"). Analogous to the "Reich Hereditary Farm Law" ("Reichserbhofgesetz") that applied in the agricultural industry, these "estates" were intended to prevent legacies from being weakened through hereditary estate fragmentation and from being burdened by new debt in the form of mortgages or bonds. In return, heavily indebted businesses would be allowed to benefit from an exemption from judicial enforcement—a provision that emphasized the sustainability of small and medium-sized enterprises, but would have hampered the modernization investments necessary to ensure their renewal. Ultimately an end was put to these deliberations by the argument that such long-term ties are not expedient in the business world, because, in contrast to agriculture, they are subject to faster transformation processes and premature determination of a successor contradicts the principle of merit-based selection.[297]

The Nazi regime in particular destroyed the basic principles of the rule of law and governed in a blatantly despotic manner under the guise of the normative state. Discrimination against and the expulsion of Jewish entrepreneurs destroyed one of the pillars of the German business middle class. The overwhelming majority of Jewish firms were driven into liquidation, which caused thousands of family businesses to disappear. Private-sector self-administration organizations and state and party authorities were actively involved in deciding whether a Jewish business should be closed down or should continue operating under "Aryan" ownership. This was an effective method of getting rid of unwelcome competition using the spurious argument of the "overcrowding" of industries and economic regions, and many non-Jewish family business owners benefited indirectly from this elimination of Jewish businesses.

The emerging "Aryanization market" also provided unscrupulous profiteers with the opportunity to acquire parts of Jewish companies at well below their true value for the purposes of expanding their own businesses or going into business on their own. Prominent "Aryanization cases" such as Joel/Neckermann or Felina/Greiling are representative of the hundreds of corporate takeovers in the German *Mittelstand*.[298]

However, the opportunities that arms and "Aryanization" transactions provided contrasted with the Nazi state's massive steering of the market, which narrowed the freedom of action of family businesses. The Nazi regime started to favor major industrial enterprises even before the war broke out in order to ensure that the manufacture of armaments was as productive as possible. Companies that were willing to pursue the regime's economic objectives and to fit in, ideologically speaking, did good business. On the other hand, the regime's arbitrary measures also included the enforced closure of non-strategic businesses and forced conversions to armaments production. Overall, National Socialism exploited and burdened the economy. Smaller businesses, especially those of little military relevance, were severely disadvantaged. This was clearly evident in the allocation of raw materials and manpower for production and of foreign currencies for export business. During the war, "combing-out campaigns" ensured withdrawals of staff—all the way to enforced closures.

Photo 10: Plant roll-call at FAG Kugelfischer in Schweinfurt (1939, photo from the plant magazine "Unser Werk und Wir")

The example of Württemberg manufacturer Fritz Kiehn, who had demonstrated massive personal and financial commitment to the Nazi Party's cause since 1930, shows how much entrepreneurs of the *Mittelstand* who believed the Nazi Party's promises could be disappointed. Kiehn's efforts to fundamentally extend his business clout via the Party failed miserably. He attempted to acquire the majority shareholding in Magirus AG with the aid of political protection and to convert it to a family business in the legal form of a general commercial partnership (OHG). However, during the takeover battle he faced competition from major companies like Deutsche Bank, Daimler Benz and Klöckner, and Magirus was ultimately purchased in 1936 by the Klöckner Group. Although Kiehn made a substantial speculative profit on shares acquired early on in the takeover process, he was put under political pressure and forced to donate most of the profit to the Nazi Party and to the SS in particular. He was able to compensate somewhat through "Aryanization transactions"—such as brutally forcing the owners of the SME Papierwarenfabrik Fleischer to sell at well below true value.[299] However, on the whole not even an "old campaigner of the NSDAP" ("alter Kämpfer") such as Kiehn with excellent connections to party leadership was able to join the ranks of the business elite and to expand his company substantially. His strategy did not pay off and the social advancement he dreamed of never happened. Despite all the SME rhetoric spouted by the Nazis, the hopes of family business owners were often cruelly dashed. For instance, they remained under-represented in the steering committees of the Nazi economy: in 1941 only five of 17 members of the Reich Association Industry (Reichsgruppe Industrie) advisory board were family business owners, and they all came from larger family businesses, including three joint-stock companies.[300] In contrast, there were plenty of family business owners in the occupational groups (Reichsgruppen or Fachgruppen) of the commercial and banking sector who had a significant influence on the "Aryanization" and restructuring of the entire sector.[301]

Despite a wide range of symbolic concessions, the pragmatism that characterized the dirigistic wartime economy of Nazi Germany impeded a genuine strengthening of small and medium-sized commercial enterprises. In fact, Nazi economic policy initially focused on combating unemployment, then on a military build-up with the assistance of big business and on eliminating so-called "enemies of the people", whose number included numerous Jewish family business owners. The regime's SME protectionist "mission statement" was an ideologically unifying thread, but it did not deliver any tangible regulatory reforms. Small and medium-sized enterprises were to some extent courted by the Nazis, but also hemmed in and repeatedly abandoned once the regime realized that its goals would be more easily achieved with the help of big business. This gave rise to a parallelogram of forces in which some SMEs benefited, depending on their industry, location and ownership arrangements, while just as many lost out.

IV. From Highly Regarded Small Business Ideology to Unpopular Small Business Administration

For a long time in the USA, there were no protective mechanisms for smaller family businesses at all. In the 19th century, a belief in the self-regulating capability of the markets and fragile administrative structures of the young state prevented the development of distinctive business promotion programs and social-protectionist strategies. Nevertheless, a kind of small business ideology had existed since the inception of the USA.[302] Thomas Jefferson believed that only a distribution of property that was as broad as possible would guarantee the survival of democracy, and that an excessive concentration in the hands of just a few would inevitably lead to tyranny. The topos of the USA as a "nation of shopkeepers" endures to this day, and it was joined by the cult of the self-made man, the belief that anyone could achieve affluence through his or her own efforts. This mentality explains the high regard for the *Mittelstand* and individual entrepreneurship as well as the absence of state support for these businesses, but it began to change in the late 19th century as emerging major corporations were coming under increasing criticism. "Progressivism" saw a cardinal problem in the increasing concentration of economic power, which had to be stopped politically. Trusts began to seem like dark forces that were using their financial muscle to take over the state and undermine democracy through lobbying and by bribing members of Congress. The big industrial cartels appeared to block the path of millions of Americans to entrepreneurship as family business owners, and shackle them under the yoke of proletarian dependence. So it was SME owners above all who spoke out in favor of the Sherman Act (1890). However, the prohibition of cartels (Chapter D) achieved exactly the opposite, providing de facto incentives for creating increasingly larger corporations.

As in Germany, the spread of large retail chains symbolized the threat to small and medium-sized shopkeepers. In the 1920s and 1930s, they made huge inroads into rural areas and became all-too-powerful competitors to local retailers. In 1936, a first protective law benefiting independent store businesses—the discount restrictions in the Robinson–Patman Act—was enacted as part of the New Deal in the USA, practically at the same time as half-hearted attempts were being made by the Nazis to protect shop owners against major companies. Another (and, as in Germany, largely unsuccessful) attempt to offset their competitive disadvantages was the Miller–Tydings Act of 1937, which permitted resale price maintenance and thus granted an exception to the Sherman Antitrust Act in order to prevent smaller companies from being severely crippled in price wars. This was a reaction to the situation in which "mom-and-pop stores" had been forced to stand by helplessly since the 1920s as major retail chains undercut them on price. Special taxes were even imposed on retail chains in some US states. These measures were preceded by debates that resembled those in Germany: Progressivists and populists argued that small, family-run stores were the backbone of the US economy and that they had to be protected against unfair competition, which would ignite a ruinous process of pushing them out of the market.

Senator Tydings, one of the initiators of the 1937 price-setting law, also regarded small and medium-sized enterprises as indispensable socio-cultural institutions within US society. In his view, they represented local ties and interpersonal solidarity, were a manifestation of rural living environments and sound, trust-based business practices. Therefore they constituted the opposite of unscrupulous big business. Tydings argued that "the independent producer and the independent distributor [...] is an American institution. They are just as much a part of the life of every community as its church or schoolhouse. They know when there is sickness in the neighborhood [...] They are local business with a heart, [...] I see this great humane and worthy institution, this bulwark of democratic Government—the small independent businessman."[303]

Resale price maintenance had been widespread practice in Germany since the 19th century, and was legalized by the Emergency Monopoly Decree (Kartellnotverordnung) of 1930 despite the disadvantages it brought for consumers. By contrast, the prohibition on price maintenance in the USA was not changed until 1937 as part of the New Deal, as noted above. This comparison again shows that this SME need for protection in Germany had previously been tolerated and legally acknowledged. Resale price maintenance was not completely abandoned until 1974 in Germany and 1976 in the USA.[304] Besides disadvantaging consumers, it was not able to guarantee effective protection for independent retail businesses and their numbers declined dramatically in the postwar period. Producers, however, were frequently unable to enforce their pricing specifications.

The New Deal marked the temporary rejection of an almost unbounded belief in the superiority of a laissez-faire approach and an orientation towards state interventionism, which had previously been unheard of in the USA. When the time came to combat the economic crisis in both countries, the economic policies adopted seemed at times to be related, even if the relationship was a distant one.[305] In both countries, major corporations became the bogeymen. President Roosevelt blamed them for the global economic crisis and the rise of fascism in Europe and regarded them as a danger to democracy in the USA. That is why he wanted to promote and assist family businesses. The battle against monopolies and a relaxation of the antitrust law did in fact benefit small and medium-sized enterprises, which considered themselves threatened in the 1930s by the parallel betterment of trade unions, the introduction of various welfare benefits and tax increases. Given the persistence of the Great Depression, which would not be overcome until after the Second World War had broken out, SMEs were provided with targeted assistance for the first time. The Reconstruction Finance Corporation (RFC), which was set up in 1932 by President Hoover and substantially expanded by Roosevelt, was intended to compensate for the weaknesses of the banking sector. However, it was a controversial institution that channeled tax revenues into recapitalizing beleaguered companies and into promoting investment on a grand scale. This concept was so alien to many critics that they referred to it as "socialism" or "bolshevism".[306] The money flowed mainly to banks, insurers and railway companies, as well as to large family-run corporations such as Kaiser, and to SMEs, which also benefited from various job-creation schemes.

The National Recovery Administration (NRA) created in 1933 introduced centrally planned economic and corporatist elements to the American economy. The aim was to prevent cut-throat competition by having companies, unions and the state reach agreements on prices and "fair practices". Such practices included minimum wages; a ban on child labor, a step that was taken very late in comparison with Germany; and a limit on work hours. Cartels were permitted. Hugh S. Stephenson, the director of the NRA, viewed his organization as an alternative to the "murderous doctrine of savage and wolfish competition and rugged individualism."

In under two years, the NRA produced approximately 3,000 regulations that filled more than 10,000 pages, and exercised strong control over the economic system in the United States. The conditions under which millions of people worked were regulated. Membership in the NRA was voluntary, but companies were subjected to intense pressure to join it. Those who did join were permitted to display a blue eagle, the symbol of the NRA, on their packaging and store windows, whereas those who did not join faced disadvantages that extended all the way to boycotts. In general, the NRA favored large listed companies over smaller family businesses. As a result, the former were able to expand their monopolistic positions and cope better with the avalanche of red tape issued by the agency. In 1935, the US Supreme Court unanimously declared the NRA law unconstitutional and the agency was forced to close. But some of the laws that had emerged from it, particularly those favoring unions and workers, remained in force.[307]

Photo 11: The emblem of the National Recovery Administration (1933–35), which companies could display in order to prove that they fulfilled their patriotic duties

As a rule, lobbying on behalf of smaller companies remained weak, because the many older associations or indeed those now emerging were fragmented along regional, industry or political orientation lines and most were very small. Given their diversity, they were barely able to agree on guidelines for common lobbying policies. A contemporary observer called them "the most confused group"[308] in American politics, and one study of a political scientist even issued the verdict: "There is no small business interest."[309] 390 legislative proposals to support smaller businesses were submitted to Congress between 1933 and 1942, of which only 24 were adopted.[310]

Thus, it took until the autumn of 1940 to establish a dedicated point of contact for SMEs, the so called Senate's Special Committee to Study and Survey Problems of Small Business Enterprises—a step that was less the result of lobbying by the affected entrepreneurs than for tactical armaments-related reasons. The Committee was therefore initially disbanded in 1949 and revived in 1950 under a new name, today the Committee on Small Business and Entrepreneurship. Family business owners thus had a point of direct contact on Capitol Hill to which they could address their concerns, for instance through consultations, and through which they could float legislative proposals. For some time, however, this committee played only a minor role in Washington's political environment: its committee initiatives only increased sharply in the 1970s, and not until 1975 was it was upgraded to a "permanent standing committee".[311]

Four days after Germany declared war on the USA, on December 15, 1941, the Committee opened four days of hearings involving representatives of smaller companies. In November 1941, Democratic Senator O'Mahoney warned in a radio broadcast, very much to Jefferson's way of thinking: "If we let little business go down in a total effort to defend democracy, we shall let the very foundation of democracy perish."[312] The issue here was how the SME sector, which accounted for around half of the US economy, could be integrated into the wartime economy. One could say that only under the pressure of war did Washington start to take an interest in the problems of smaller family businesses, because it reckoned that the war could not be won without them. At any rate, the minutes of these hearings totaled 1,045 pages.[313] The list of complaints was long, ranging from inadequate supply of raw materials to insufficient consideration for arms contracts, which—as seen in Chapter B—significantly increased the level of concentration in the US economy. It appeared as if the war effort would result in a cartel involving a small handful of major corporations and in SMEs perishing in vast numbers. Furthermore, there were complaints about inadequate access to capital and information, the withdrawal of manpower and bureaucracy at government procurement agencies that small businesses were not really equipped to cope with.

In order to remedy these shortcomings, Congress established the Smaller War Plants Corporation (SWPC) in February 1942, which provided loans to help smaller industrial companies convert to arms manufacturing. In order to integrate them into the wartime economy, major contracts were split into small segments and passed on to SMEs, financial assistance was provided, contacts with procurement agencies made easier and technical advisers were made available.[314] There were exemptions from cartel prohibition laws for production pools involving several smaller companies. Only industrial businesses were provided with assistance. How large they were allowed to be was initially disputed: the Senate Banking and Currency Committee attempted to define the term "small business", "but could not do so".[315] After much debate, the upper limit was set at 500 employees.

The establishment of the SWPC represents a US economic policy milestone, because there was for the first time a central government agency that dealt with the concerns and interests of smaller companies. However, its raison d'être was disputed right from the start. Entrepreneurs, journalists and politicians of a free market persuasion, mostly Republicans, regarded the SWPC as a symbol of anti-market dirigisme. Its funding and human resources were inadequate, loan application processing took too long and there was plenty of rivalry with affiliated government agencies. The Head of the SWPC was replaced at the beginning of 1943 less than a year after the corporation's establishment. President Roosevelt then appointed a "big businessman", Robert Wood Johnson II, chairman of family business Johnson & Johnson, which was established in 1886. Johnson expanded the SWPC substantially, set up 14 regional boards and added 400 additional hires. By May 1943, the SWPC employed 1,100 people. But in September 1943, Johnson stepped down, as he was no longer able to identify with the direction in which the institution was heading. As an entrepreneur, he fundamentally disliked the bureaucratic way of working in particular. In his opinion companies didn't need the SWPC, because they would have made a good job of integrating into the wartime economy on their own—and indeed, most SMEs flourished. Johnson concluded from this that there was no reason for state intervention on behalf of SMEs and that one could have faith in the market. And he was not the only person with this attitude, which is firmly rooted in the American way of business thinking.[316]

Photo 12: Maury Maverick, a staunch New Dealer and the chairman of the Smaller War Plants Corporation

Johnson's successor, Maury Maverick, was a Democratic congressman, an "ardent New Dealer" who thought along completely different lines. He did his utmost to enable the SWPC to continue as a permanent institution once the war was over. However, there was considerable political opposition to his plans, and his attempt to mobilize companies to back this undertaking failed. Less than 100 family business owners attended the meetings that were organized for this purpose. Business was booming, many SMEs were highly optimistic and they no longer wanted the swollen bureaucracy of the war years, trusting that market mechanisms were enough in peacetime. President Truman therefore decided in December 1945 to close the SWPC down in January 1946. Its loan scheme was transferred to the Reconstruction Finance Corporation (RFC). When in turn the much criticized, scandal-ridden RFC was liquidated in 1953, its responsibilities were transferred to the newly created Small Business Administration (SBA). This agency was established under pressure exerted by the Senate Small Business Committee and due to the dramatic decline in the importance of SMEs after 1945. The equally politically contentious SBA, which was regarded with skepticism even by SMEs, had initially received a 3-year mandate, but was given permanent status in 1958 following a 2-year extension.[317]

The SBA provided loans and guarantees, brokered public contracts and advised SMEs. Initially these programs were pretty modest in terms of volume and their impact tended to be limited: in its first year the SBA only provided loans worth 35 million dollars. The first Director of the SBA explained that his authority had to work "with and not against the spirit of self-reliance".[318] In 1954, few businesspeople were aware of the SBA and what its function was, and the ongoing problem of defining what "small" meant was still not conclusively solved. In practice the SBA applied the threshold of 1,000 employees to industrial companies, while the Pentagon insisted on the old threshold of 500 for military contracts.

A considerably greater impact than the modest activities of the SBA was achieved by the 1944 Serviceman's Readjustment Act, which in common parlance was called the "G.I. Bill" and was intended to reintegrate and reward soldiers returning home. Not only were millions enabled to obtain a university education and build houses, which they would have otherwise not been able to afford; around one million veterans also set up their own businesses with the assistance of this law.[319] The bulk of these were small businesses. The opportunity to obtain low-interest loans to set up businesses and buy homes was widely advertised.

Photo 13: Advertising low-interest loans for former soldiers (about 1941–1945)

Promoting SMEs to a greater degree was also regarded as unthinkable immediately after the war because major corporations enjoyed a kind of "hero status" during this period. On the business front they had, it seemed, won the war all on their own. 76 percent of all Americans interviewed in a 1950 survey stated that they viewed major corporations in a positive light. The "antitrust agenda" had faded into the background. Only eight percent of those interviewed were able to define the term "monopoly". University graduates thronged to join the "corporate giants", avoiding the risks of starting up their own businesses. A survey of graduates in 1949 came to the straightforward conclusion: "no longer is small business the promised land"; major corporations were now the predominant model. Social scientists argued that the SME's time had passed. David Lilienthal, who had once declared the family business to be a superior model, bade farewell to his "old dream: the independent man in his own [...] business. [...] There is a new dream: a world of great machines", which are controlled by corporations and would promote "human freedom and individualism".[320] Technocratic feasibility fantasies and the adulation of size as a badge of success went hand in hand with a belief in the superior capabilities of managers. It was a philosophy that predominated well into the late 1970s to an extent that went way beyond similar perceptions in the Federal Republic of Germany.

Many family business owners were staunch proponents of the "laissez-faire" doctrine and didn't believe that Washington bureaucrats could help them. A fear of "big government" continued to be strong. But the cultural influence of standing on one's own feet proved to be a long-term impediment to the creation of strong pressure groups. Even in the 1970s interviews with SME owners highlighted their "overriding sense of self-sufficient individualism".[321] There were even several SME associations that expressed their opposition to direct assistance in their favor, because, as the National Federation of Independent Businesses, for example, argued in 1950, this involved "socialism and communism"[322]. Also, some associations were founded that pretended to speak on behalf of SMEs which in fact were covertly financed by major corporations. Their objectives were to thwart the rekindling of the old issue of the anti-concentration of economic power, and to prevent government structural policies that benefited SMEs.[323]

The political track record of the postwar years was negative for SMEs. Despite receiving moderate support from the SBA, they declined in importance. The share of "small businesses"—defined as companies with fewer than 500 employees and a turnover of up to five million dollars—as a proportion of the overall sales volume of the US economy declined from 52 to 29 percent between 1958 and 1979.[324] In other words, concentration made rapid progress. In 1962 political scientist John H. Bunzel noted "that small business is not looking particularly healthy." It is "weak, though not abysmally so" and will therefore not disappear either.[325] Senator Sparkman was somewhat more florid when speaking about SMEs: "during the so-called fabulous fifties, the bright sun of business prosperity has been for them behind a dark cloud."[326] Despite that, there were also plenty of profitable SMEs and their total number increased. Even so, the major corporations grew considerably faster by comparison.

The debate about the future of the SBA started around 1955. The National Association of Manufacturers (an industrial umbrella organization), the US Chamber of Commerce and the American Bankers Association all argued in favor of closing the SBA—a circumstance that would have been absolutely unimaginable in Germany. Ultimately, though, the agency was granted another two years and a substantial increase in its still meagre financial resources, and in 1957 it received permanent authority status and an indefinite mandate, although many politicians and businesspeople as well as affiliated ministries had spoken out against such a move. What was key was the backing given to the SBA by President Eisenhower, who wanted to raise his profile as an ally of SMEs.[327]

The SBA survived, but remained a weak institution that was also misused for the purposes of political patronage and regularly criticized for its inefficiency. Its level of human and financial resources improved but remained inadequate. Between 1954 and 1960 the SBA granted loans worth 1.05 billion dollars, and between 1954 and 1965 its headcount increased from 545 to nearly 4,000.[328] The SBA enhanced its standing, because on the one hand it deliberately opted to use crisis rhetoric and was keen to exaggerate the problems faced by SMEs in order to exploit sympathy "for the small guy". Nevertheless, it did not manage to pursue an all-encompassing promotional policy: its assistance programs only reached a fraction of all US SMEs, and nationwide there were fewer than 100 advisers available to provide "management assistance". In the 1960s and 1970s the default rate on SBA loans increased from 25 to 40 percent, because as the loan scheme was expanded, credit checks were often not performed to the due degree of diligence.[329] In 1971 an investigation by the Government Accountability Office ("Comptroller General") for Congress revealed a range of "serious problems". Various SMEs withdrew from the SBA programs, complaining about "an excessive amount of red tape" and "regulations which are cumbersome or too strict."[330] Criticism of the SBA never ceased.

V.   *Mittelstand* Policy and the German Economic Miracle

In West Germany on the other hand there was no need to fight battles in order to gain acceptance of government assistance for SMEs. There was no equivalent of the SBA, because *Mittelstand* policy was, as in the Weimar Republic, firmly on the agenda of the Ministry for Economic Affairs, and was handled by Department II from 1956 onwards. There were also special Ministry project groups and a Bundestag committee for specific *Mittelstand* issues. However, demands for a dedicated SME ministry were rejected. From 1963 to 1966 the Ministry for Economic Affairs was headed by no less a figure than the CDU's leading SME politician, Kurt Schmücker, himself a family business owner. This high regard for the *Mittelstand* was also manifested in the establishment of the "Institut für Mittelstandsforschung" (IfM) in Bonn, which was founded in 1957 at the instigation of the federal government, in particular its Minister of Economic Affairs, Ludwig Erhard, and by the State of North Rhine-Westphalia. Its mandate was to provide politicians with facts to enable the latter to give SMEs targeted assistance.

In East Germany (the German Democratic Republic or GDR), wholesale condemnation of major corporations as "Nazi criminals" meant that many SMEs were not initially nationalized and most remained in family ownership until 1972, provided the owners had not fled or been deemed to be Nazi activists or war criminals. However, they were subjected to multiple forms of discrimination, such as higher taxation and planned-economy paternalism. Skilled craft businesses were compelled to join production cooperatives. But the regime of East Germany's Socialist Unity Party of Germany (SED) basically accepted private-sector small and medium-sized enterprises, initially out of necessity, and followed the tradition of regarding them as an alternative model to big business. In other words, the GDR was at least willing to tolerate SME businesses as part of its socialist planned economy. Furthermore, it was obvious that the GDR would have had far more serious economic problems if it had chosen to insist on socialist structures in the *Mittelstand*. In contrast to all the other socialist economies in the Eastern Bloc, private-sector SMEs remained a part of the economic system in the GDR—a peculiarity that underlines how firmly entrenched SMEs are in Germany.

Differences in SME policy on either side of the Atlantic can also be attributed to differing wartime experiences. The North American continent was spared the devastation of the war; indeed, it helped overcome the impact of the Great Depression in the USA with a highly dynamic rate of growth that continued after 1945. In contrast, Germany had hit rock bottom. Given the war of aggression it had unleashed and the apocalyptic crimes against humanity it had committed, Germany was morally discredited, occupied by the Allies and had lost its national sovereignty. Promoting the *Mittelstand* sector, which was vocal in putting its interests on the political agenda, was a vital and undisputed aspect of reconstruction. The barriers to entering the skilled craft and commercial sectors remained in place or, as in the former American zone, where general principles of free enterprise had temporarily applied, were reintroduced. The lobbying efforts of powerful skilled craft and retail trade pressure groups were very successful: In 1953 the master craftsman's certificate was made obligatory for managing a skilled craft business throughout West Germany.[331] In this regard the Bundestag committee responsible noted that the Skilled Crafts Code (Handwerksordnung) can "only be shaped according to German ... needs" and not based on "Allied or even American perceptions."[332] The Skilled Crafts Code was an endorsement not only of the principle of occupational protectionism but also of the dual education system. This ensured that the skilled labor force was highly qualified. The result was, in essence, the rebuilding of one cornerstone of German cooperative capitalism.

An active *Mittelstand* policy was quickly adopted and pursued, although the promotion of small and medium-sized enterprises was not included in the constitution, as it was during the Weimar Republic. However, the fact that SMEs required additional financial assistance to offset disadvantages and thus ensure a more level playing field when competing against larger companies has basically been undisputed since 1949.[333] These disadvantages, so it was argued, resulted from banks being cautious about lending money to SMEs, which was attributed to poorer availability of information relating to their financial strengths and the dependence of these businesses on their owners.

Where the interests of big industry collided with those of the *Mittelstand*, the latter always drew the short straw. In 1952 the Investment Aid Act (Investitionshilfegesetz) enacted a forced loan to be provided by the entire West German economy to support the mines and steelworks of the Ruhr-region—in essence, a redistribution from SMEs to big industry. It resulted in an unsuccessful appeal by 256 mostly medium-sized businesses in the Federal Constitutional Court. Even so, the loan came with increased depreciation options, which lessened the burden. On the other hand, the expansion of primary industry, which was afflicted by capacity bottlenecks, was also in the *Mittelstand's* interests.[334]

Business start-up programs had a long history at the level of the individual German states. What was new was that the federal government itself put major programs in place to ensure the sustainable regeneration of sole proprietorships and small family businesses. The most well-known of these was the ERP Special Fund that was established as part of the Marshall Plan (officially known as the European Recovery Program). Marshall Plan aid from the USA helped plug the habitual dollar gap, providing German companies with financial assistance in this key currency that enabled them to purchase urgently needed raw materials abroad. Yet importers did not get this dollar aid for free; they had to pay domestic-currency amounts into counterpart funds, resulting in the creation of the federal government's ERP Special Fund, which it used to finance start-ups, investments and exports via the state-owned development bank Kreditanstalt für Wiederaufbau (KfW), which was established in 1948. In 1950 the Fund was worth 1.6 billion dollars.

The Marshall Plan came to an end in 1953, and that year the London Debt Agreement stipulated that the Federal Republic only had to repay just under a third of the three billion dollars it had received. This figure was paid out of the federal budget, so that the ERP Special Fund did not decrease. Instead, it grew until 2005 through capital repayments of previous loans and interest to twelve billion euros and was transformed into a revolving fund for long-term, low-interest investment loans. To this day, its purpose is to finance the funding priorities of Federal German economic policy. In the past these priorities included infrastructure expansion, development aid, environmental protection as well as *Mittelstand* promotion and assistance. While the focus in the early 1950s was still on funding infrastructure and primary industries, priority was given after 1955 to promoting small and medium-sized enterprises primarily in economically underdeveloped regions such as the borderland between the two German states.

A portion of the roughly twelve million refugees benefited particularly from the ERP business start-up programs, the development loans of the Equalization of Burdens Act (Lastenausgleichsgesetz) and federal state aid. 36 percent of these refugees had had their own businesses in 1939, while only 7.7 percent were self-employed in 1950. "There was plenty of unexploited self-employment potential here."[335] Refugees therefore availed themselves of KfW business start-up assistance on a large scale. It is one of history's ironies that a massively effective funding instrument of this kind was financed, at least initially, mainly by the USA, which itself kept assistance to American small and medium-sized commercial enterprises on the back burner. Only when it came to reintegrating war veterans back into civilian life did the G.I. Bill breach this tradition, funding business start-ups on a huge scale.

Photo 14: Advertising for the Marshall Plan. In this poster a small family receives large deliveries of supplies from the United States.

Given sustained rapid growth, assistance activities in both countries tended to be cut back in the 1960s. In contrast to the Federal Republic, US economic policies, which relied primarily on market self-regulation, treated American SMEs as poor relations. Although the increasing concentration in the economy was viewed critically, American belief in the superiority of manager-run major corporations and conglomerates was still widespread. SMEs were frequently regarded as relics of earlier times with a low ability to innovate. The American Chamber of Commerce was vocal in its attempts to dispel these preconceptions.[336] At a congressional hearing, it accused the politicians in Washington of being responsible for the "decline of this nation's most productive element" and thus for a renewed increase in concentration. "Unfortunately, these vital segments have been neglected [...] and it is time that Congress considered updating many of the laws, rules and regulations, which at times so harshly affect that segment today."[337] Complaints like these were not heard with the same degree of stridency in Bonn.

Associations representing American SMEs remained fragmented and lacked political influence. In Germany there were likewise no influential associations specifically representing SMEs or family businesses either. As in the USA, this can be attributed to the diversity of family businesses, but it also owes much to the relatively firm entrenchment of SME policy in the German government apparatus, which made political mobilization especially for SMEs unnecessary. The Arbeitsgemeinschaft Selbständiger Unternehmer (ASU) was founded in 1949 and was renamed Die Familienunternehmer – ASU in 2007. The Bundesverband Junger Unternehmer (BJU), known today as Die Jungen Unternehmer, was established in 1950 as a young entrepreneurs' organization and was followed in 1954 by the Vereinigung von Unternehmerinnen, now known as the Verband deutscher Unternehmerinnen (Association of German Women Entrepreneurs). In each case, these were not powerful lobbying organizations that might have exercised major influence on the national political stage. Instead, these associations primarily had an internal impact, creating networks, advancing training opportunities and working on image promotion on behalf of their members.

Indicative of the major political importance of family businesses in the Federal Republic of Germany is their very visible presence in the country's industrial umbrella organization, the Bundesverband der Deutschen Industrie e. V. (BDI), established in 1949 and 1950. This association is very highly organized. It was established and headed for 22 years by family business owner Fritz Berg, the proprietor of an ironmongery plant established in 1853/85 and based in Altena (Westphalia). Berg was a member of an informal circle of businessmen that met regularly with leading politicians in the German government. The Frankfurter Rundschau newspaper even described him as the "Federal Chancellor's most listened-to economic adviser."[338] In 1953, Berg, along with Robert Pferdmenges, initiated an informal "Adenauer kitchen cabinet". This group gave the entrepreneur Berg and the banker Pferdmenges the opportunity to discuss and influence decisions on central

Photo 15: Konrad Adenauer and Fritz Berg, family business owner, president of the BDI and member of Adenauer's influential "kitchen cabinet"

questions related to West Germany's economic system.[339] Berg played a key role in shaping the West German economic system. The fact that the 1957 Act against Restraints of Competition (Kartellgesetz) contained so many exemption clauses that de facto undermined the ban on cartels can largely be attributed to his commitment. The law therefore fell well short of the English-speaking Allies' expectations and of the practices of the early years of the Federal Republic.

Table 19: BDI presidents classified according to business background

Period in office	Family businesses	Public limited companies with wide share ownership, cooperatives
1949–1971	Fritz Berg (Wilhelm Berg GmbH)	
1972–1976		Hans-Günther Sohl (August-Thyssen-Hütte AG*)
1977		Hanns Martin Schleyer (Daimler Benz AG)
1978	Nikolaus Fasolt (Wessel Werke)	
1978–1984	Rolf Rodenstock (Optische Werke G. Rodenstock)	
1985–1986	Hans Joachim Langmann (E. Merck OHG)	
1987–1990	Tyll Necker (Hoka GmbH)	
1991–1992	Heinrich Weiss (SMS Schloemann-Siemag AG)	
1992–1994	Tyll Necker (Hoka GmbH)	
1995–2000		Hans-Olaf Henkel (IBM)
2000–2004	Michael Rogowski (Voith GmbH & Co. KGaA)	
2005–2008	Jürgen R. Thumann (Heitkamp & Thumann KG)	
2009–2012		Hans Peter Keitel (Hochtief AG)
2012–2016	Ulrich Grillo (Grillo-Werke AG)	
Since 2016		Dieter Kempf (Datev)

* family business until 1968

Source: BDI, "The BDI and its Presidents, 1949–2016", https://bdi.eu/der-bdi/historie/#/artikel/ news/der-bdi-und-seine-praesidenten-1949–2016/ (accessed: May 1, 2018).

Berg also regarded himself as a representative of heavy industry, which initially dominated the BDI. By making campaign donations, preferably to the CDU/CSU and the FDP, the BDI asserted its influence over the selection of candidates for elections. Berg's power was sometimes very substantial, but also had clear limitations, and he frequently clashed with Minister of Economic Affairs Ludwig Erhard. When the deutschmark was revalued for the first time in 1961 against the wishes of the BDI and despite Berg's personal intervention with Adenauer, Berg was so indignant that he temporarily suspended the 100,000 DM monthly payment to the CDU.[340]

Even after he stepped down, the BDI continued to be headed mainly by family business owners, who mostly came from smaller major companies rather than SMEs. This focus distinguished it from its Weimar Republic predecessor, the Reichsverband der Deutschen Industrie, which was dominated completely by industrial magnates.

It would certainly be a misrepresentation to claim that the amazingly large number of BDI Presidents from family businesses implies a specific BDI focus to the benefit of these companies. But conversely it is evident that family businesses definitely played an important role within the BDI, and were able to use it to have their concerns put on the political agenda. That was manifested, for example, in the debate about the reform of inheritance tax. The presence of family business owners at this exalted level also explains why specific associations for SMEs did not play an important role.

VI. *Mittelstand* Policy as a Reaction to Crises in Germany and the USA since 1970

In both Germany and the USA, SME policy significantly increased in importance during the crisis decade of the 1970s. The oil-price crises symbolized the gradual end of the postwar boom. In the light of structural transformation in industry, the rise of new competitors in Asia, soaring bankruptcies and the return of mass unemployment, a new employment policy approach caught on. It sought to replace those jobs that were being lost in traditional sectors of big industry by means of a "company size-focused structural policy".[341] People had high hopes of SMEs, which pledged a return to full employment, and in West Germany the number of *Mittelstand* policy initiatives increased dramatically in the 1970s. Traditional social protectionism finally faded into the background to make way for a structural and employment policy mindset. A very diverse array of funding and assistance instruments was employed at federal government level and increasingly at state government level. It ranged from business start-up and innovation funding, loans, subsidies and guarantees, increases in cartel-formation leeway through to the financing of consultancy services.

The first milestones were put in place in 1970 in the form of the action program for enhancing the performance of SME enterprises and the ERP investment program.[342] They enabled banks and equity investment companies to obtain inexpensive refinancing if they provided loans to SMEs. These interest-rate subsidies lowered their capital costs. The 1973 antitrust law amendment also added a specifically SME policy component to West Germany's already very weak antitrust law: by allowing "*Mittelstand* cartels", it provided small and medium-sized enterprises with additional opportunities to join forces for the purposes of improving performance and increasing competitiveness.[343] Since 1979 the equity capital assistance program (Eigenkapitalhilfeprogramm) has been providing SMEs with government loans that partly had the character of debt capital and partly that of liable equity capital. These loans were marked by subordination of government claims, interest-free and grace periods, and interest rates well below market levels.[344] The institutions that implemented this company size-focused structural policy in practice were the existing development banks: KfW and Deutsche Ausgleichsbank (Lastenausgleichsbank up until 1952). The programs were funded by the ERP Special Fund, the Equalization of Burdens Fund and through financial resources provided by the development banks.

In 1972 the federal government unveiled the main features of its assistance agenda in an "SME Guide" (Mittelstandsfibel). The rhetoric of social protectionism was gone. Instead, the guide espoused structural, competition and modernization policy arguments as well as the argument of offsetting disadvantages. The introduction said: "Markets are being interlinked across national borders and continents. The old is being dismantled. Structures are changing. Large businesses are often better able to keep up with this pace. It is often tougher for small and medium-sized business owners." What matters here is "helping people to help themselves. [...] Government assistance never rewards a lack of proactivity, but only supports active entrepreneurs."[345] Funding for the purposes of "enhancing SME performance" and "occupational training and education" featured alongside financing assistance. In both cases the focus was on advice, advanced training and joint research.

Table 20 provides a breakdown of loans from 1969 to 1971 that had terms of up to 20 years and initially granted grace periods lasting several years. The direct financial assistance provided amounted to a considerable 1.3 billion DM, which, as a result of substantial coupling effects, ultimately generated investment totaling around 4.9 billion DM.

Table 20: ERP loans to the Mittelstand, 1969–1971 (in DM million)

Program	Quantity of ERP loans	Total of ERP loans	Investment triggered by them
Regional aid (incl. inner-German border region assistance)	7,839	809.5	2,920.9
Business start-ups by young entrepreneurs (aged 21–42)	5,115	157.1	479.2
Setting up businesses in new residential areas	2,006	151.0	833.7
Introduction of EDP/IT	782	54.2	152.5
Self-employment for refugees and war-affected persons	1,842	122.9	382.4
Miscellaneous	182	43.0	147.4
Total	**17,769**	**1,337.7**	**4,916.1**

Source: *Bundesministerium für Wirtschaft und Finanzen, Mittelstandsfibel, p. 23.*

Table 21 reflects the long-term performance of the ERP program. Its total volume grew by a factor of 15 between 1965 and 1995, while the proportion of funding provided for SMEs rose from 30.9 to 66.7 percent, which in absolute figures corresponds to an increase by a factor of 33. The upheaval of the late 1970s is manifested clearly once again. SME funding volumes increased almost fivefold between 1975 and 1985 and, as a proportion of the total ERP, these funds rose from 18.8 to 61.5 percent. The next major expansion after German reunification had the aim of facilitating business start-ups in the former East Germany. In 1990, 43.8 percent of total SME assistance was channeled into the new federal states. In 1995 the record total of 5.7 billion euros was distributed. This was followed by a significant reduction, although it was considerably overstated in the table as a result of a change in data collection methods. The KfW's priorities were now environmental protection and the housing industry, and in these segments SMEs received additional funding.

Table 21: ERP Special Fund assistance to SMEs, 1965–2010 (in € million)

Year	Total ERP resources	SME assistance	SME assistance as a percentage
1965	556.8	171.8	30.9%
1971	1,035.4	184.1	17.8%
1975	1,295.1	242.9	18.8%
1980	1,559.4	867.7	55.6%
1985	1,888.2	1,161.1	61.5%
1990	5,492.8	2,940.4	53.5%
1995	8,540.6	5,695.8	66.7%
2000	n.a.	1,787.4	n.a.
2004	n.a.	2,004.1	n.a.
2010	n.a.	1,457.0	n.a.

Sources: Bundesministerium für Wirtschaft (BMWi), ERP-Hilfe zur Wirtschaftsförderung 1965, pp. 23 and 34–37; idem, ERP Programm, vol. 1972, p. 7, vol. 1976, pp. 12–13, vol. 1980, pp. 12–13, vol. 1985/86, pp. 14–15, vol. 1992, pp. 12–15, vol. 1994/95, pp. 13–14; KfW Group, Annual Report, vol. 2001, p. 42, vol. 2005, p. 53 and vol. 2010, p. 45.

27,531 loans totaling 2.3 billion DM or 1.1 billion euros were provided to SMEs from the ERP Special Fund in 1985. In the same year, the cumulative total of sureties, guarantees and other warranties issued by the federal government amounted to 228.7 billion DM alone. The amount of financial assistance provided has risen remarkably since the 1970s. The federal government's subsidy reports provide a record of subsidies paid to SMEs and independent professions, and between 1975 and 1985 these increased from 253 million to 1.3 billion DM. Expenditure on SME policy measures therefore increased a staggering 46.9 percent on average per annum.[346]

In 1975 the federal government passed a *Mittelstand* assistance law modelled on the laws applicable in various federal states. It incorporated improvements to capital provision and training and codified preferential treatment for small and medium-sized enterprises in the awarding of public contracts. Overall, the result was a very confusing array of assistance programs. There were 180 types of assistance in the business start-up programs alone that could be combined with other programs at both federal and state level. State and federal assistance as well as EU aid, which was increasingly available from 1990 onwards, were not coordinated or synchronized. According to one analysis, government subsidies were only provided in less than ten percent of business start-up cases, so that the impact on business start-ups was modest despite rapidly increasing subsidies.

Table 22: Mittelstand assistance provided by the Federal Ministry for Economic Affairs, 1975–1990 (in DM million)

Year	Assistance for Mittelstand	Asset assistance programs	Regional assistance	Total
1975	140	114	349	603
1980	588	362	422	1,372
1985	728	230	364	1,322
1990	456	375	528	1,359

Source: De, Bestimmungsgründe, pp. 50–56.

Table 22 illustrates just the assistance provided from the budget of the Ministry for Economic Affairs. Added to that are activities by other ministries, e.g. the Federal Ministry for Research and Technology (BMFT) in particular, as well as separate budgets provided by the KfW and Deutsche Ausgleichsbank. Table 23 collates the SME-related funding volumes provided by these institutions.[347]

One can clearly see that between 1975 and 1980 there was a sharp increase in federal government expenditure on *Mittelstand* assistance. Expenditure by the Ministry for Economic Affairs alone rose by a factor of 3.6. After moderate decreases in the 1980s, there was another spike in the 1990s, which can only be partially attributed to assistance for SMEs in the new federal states of the former GDR. Overall, federal government expenditure on small and medium-sized enterprises rose faster than the entire federal budget.

Furthermore, the assistance provided by the federal states, which also increased but overall fell well short of what the federal government provided, needs to be taken into account too. One method that was frequently used

Table 23: Mittelstand-relevant federal government assistance, 1975–2010 (in € million)

Year	BMWi	KfW	Deutsche Ausgleichsbank	BMFT
1975	89.4	99.1	4.3	n.a.
1980	322.2	107.4	15.6	n.a.
1985	390.8	141.4	28.0	368.6
1990	260.1	325.8	117.8	116.1
1994	1,247.1	450.9	191.2	292.9
1995		450.8	169.3	
2000		746.7	226.4	
2005		1,423.4	–*	
2010		1,680.9	–	

* Ausgleichsbank was incorporated into KfW in 2003.

Source: De, Bestimmungsgründe, p. 65. In line with calculation details in: ibid., p. 64–65. Augmented by: KfW Group, Annual Reports 1998–2010; idem., Annual Report 1995; Deutsche Ausgleichsbank (DtA), Annual Reports 1995–2000.

in the federal states was the establishment of specialized promotional organizations. Lower Saxony, for example, set up a limited liability company to that effect in 1967, with 52.5 percent of its shares held by the state government and 23.75 percent each by the state bank (Landesbank) and the savings banks. This structure again demonstrates the importance of house banks as points of contact for financing. From a government standpoint, their involvement, which was also provided for in a wide range of federal government and KfW programs, helped prevent or substantially reduce any friction—and therefore lost opportunities—between the parties involved. A trust-based relationship existed between companies and their house bank. Furthermore, the banks—usually savings or cooperative banks—had in-depth knowledge about their corporate clients. For small and medium-sized enterprises, they were the first port of call for raising government funding. As a rule, the funding institutions did not enter into a direct contractual relationship with companies but only with their relationship banks. This method, which is still used, is called an "onward-channeling transaction" (Durchleitungsgeschäft). It proved successful because these established local relationships exploited the knowledge that house banks had about their borrowers and thus limited any misallocation of capital. A similarly stable structure never existed in the USA due to the fragmentation and weakness of the regional banking sector. Complaints about bureaucracy and inefficiency, which resulted from direct contact between companies and government promotion and funding agencies, never ceased.

Cooperative capitalism had a comparatively effective structure for providing assistance to small and medium-sized enterprises, but that is not to say that things were generally tougher for people setting up businesses in the USA. Indeed, they benefited from the fact that the private venture capital/private equity sector was far more developed in their country than it was in Germany or Europe in general. One could argue that government assistance programs in the early years of the Federal Republic made up for unavailable private sources of funding, which produced much greater yields in the USA.

The first equity investment companies existed in the USA as early as 1946, while in Germany they did not appear on the scene until 1975. The venture capital sector in both countries underwent rapid expansion in the 1980s, when it began to play an important role in Germany as well. Starting from a very low base, it grew even faster than in the USA, where it still plays a far greater role. In 1999 venture capital was—in relation to the national product in each case—more than four times as great in the USA than in Germany.[348]

Starting in Baden-Württemberg, assistance was also provided in several German states to maintain the continuity of family businesses. As a reaction to the growing problem in the 1990s of finding corporate successors, programs that paved the way for and mentored the succession process were put in place. Financial resources corresponding to those for business start-ups were made available if companies changed hands. In 2005 Baden-Württemberg provided subsidized loans worth 495 million euros, divided among 3,300 business start-up and succession cases, for these two purposes alone. Just under one third of these funds went to people and entities taking over companies. This financial assistance was augmented by numerous other offers. The spectrum ranged from advice and training to the involvement of succession mediators. In addition public guarantees and the acquisition of dormant and explicit shareholdings by the state's own development bank (L-Bank) were facilitated.[349]

An SME policy renaissance also occurred in the USA during the final quarter of the 20th century, though with a certain time lag. The background to this was the fact that the US Fortune 500 companies had shed around five million jobs between 1970 and 1984, and the USA was in deep crisis. SMEs were now regarded as beacons of hope, which, as in Germany, were believed to be capable of overcoming unemployment and recession. Scientists proclaimed the "end of mass production" and elevated the "flexible specialization" of SMEs to the new growth paradigm.[350] Major corporations, which very recently had been much admired, were suddenly regarded as dinosaurs whose lack of adaptability had condemned them to extinction. In 1984 Business Week wrote: "Small is Beautiful Now in Manufacturing."[351] SMEs were regarded as creative and flexible. The 1980s saw the launch of two magazines aimed specifically at people starting their own businesses—"Inc." and "Venture". Together, they quickly reached a circulation of one million copies.[352] Professorial chairs of "entrepreneurship" were set up at business schools and universities, and scientists increasingly turned their attention to SMEs and family businesses.

Although distrust of state intervention in the markets remained high, there was a quantum leap in funding policy terms. In 1978 the policy of supporting SMEs to help them win public contracts, which had been pursued since the 1930s, was stepped up by enabling government departments to exclude major corporations from certain tenders by means of "set-asides". The objective of awarding SMEs 20 percent of the volume of all state contracts was defined in 1988, and increased in 1994 to 23 percent.

Five percent are reserved for companies owned by women. There are other quotas in place for veterans, minorities and disadvantaged regions. In 2015 the actual quota for all SMEs was 25.8 percent, which equated to a contract volume of 90.7 billion dollars.[353]

As early as the 1970s the annual volume of loan guarantees provided by the SBA increased from 450 million to 3.6 billion dollars.[354] In 1982 the Small Business Innovation Development Act created the Small Business Innovation Research (SBIR) Program.[355] It staged contests that rewarded SMEs for successfully developing and commercializing innovations, and familiarized other government agencies with these innovations. Since then several government departments have been obliged to spend a portion of their budgets on assisting SMEs with research.

Since the Small Business Investment Act of 1958 there has been a department within the SBA that has acted as a "venture capitalist". It created the Small Business Investment Company (SBIC) program, which took stakes in SMEs via funds and provided them with assistance in the form of low-interest, long-term loans as well as tax breaks. Between 1958 and 2015 there were 2,100 such funds. They received 72 billion dollars worth of assistance and financed 166,000 investments.[356] 1964 saw the launch of the Equal Opportunity Loans Program (EOL), which was specifically aimed at poor people who wanted to set up their own businesses. In 1971/72 a "minority business enterprises" fund was also set up. As President Nixon's "executive order" stated, it was aimed at "negroes, Puerto Ricans, Spanish-speaking Americans, American Indians, Eskimos, and Aleut people."[357] Asians and veterans were also added later as target groups. The absolute numbers may be impressive: between 1958 and 2014 more than 118,000 SMEs received a total of 73.3 billion dollars worth of loans and equity.[358] However, given the size of the USA, it is obvious that only a small fraction of all SMEs actually received such assistance.

In 1975 the Government Accountability Office (GAO) put its massive criticism of the SBA in writing. The GAO alleged that there were no clear criteria for the granting of the SBA's loans, which were often arbitrarily approved, and that there were many instances of loan misallocation, which was rendered evident by a very high default rate.[359] These negatives contrasted with a series of spectacular success stories. Thus, for example, family business owner Frederick Smith received funds from the SBIC program after he established a small courier service called Federal Express in 1973, which advanced to become a global logistics corporation named FedEx (since 1994). In 2018 Smith was still CEO, but he only held a minority interest in FedEx's share capital, almost all of which was widely dispersed or in the hands of large investment companies. Once again we encounter the pattern so typical of the USA, in which fast-growing start-ups often do not even survive the change from the first to the second generation as family businesses.

With help from an SBIC and various private equity firms, Thomas Stemberg established the discount office supplies retailer Staples in 1985, which in 2014 generated sales of 22.5 billion dollars in more than 2,000 superstores with some 90,000 employees. Staples went public just four years after it was established. Stemberg stepped down as CEO in 2005, and in 2017 Staples disappeared from the stock exchange list when it was acquired by a private investment company. Other success stories where SCBI assistance helped transform small family businesses into major corporations involved Amgen, Compaq, Apple, Whole Foods, Intel and Sun Microsystems. To this day, these companies make absolutely no mention in their PR material of the fact that they received state aid; they only refer to private equity investors. Although they accepted government funds, they were apparently ashamed of having done so.

Despite these thoroughly positive examples, however, an investigation into business start-up assistance in the USA came to the conclusion several years ago that the majority of SBIC funding and assistance projects ultimately failed. This was attributed to the fact that good, viable companies meet their financial needs sufficiently in the capital markets, and that SBIC funds, in turn, were frequently channeled to less promising companies. Furthermore, the incompetence of the SBA administrators was constantly criticized. Only 197 of the 782 SBICs set up between 1976 and 1997 were still actively involved in the market around the year 2000.[360] The SBICs therefore delivered mixed results, with the most vocal criticism coming from the Republicans.

Many politicians and entrepreneurs regarded (and regard) the SBA as a foreign object in the free market economy. In 1996 the Republican-controlled House of Representatives attempted unsuccessfully to close the SBA down. The Bush administration also made repeated attempts, but they failed each time in Congress. Painful budget cuts made the SBA's work more difficult before the Obama administration upgraded it. President Trump has made very disparaging statements about the SBA, but has not (yet) abolished it. In contrast, assisting and promoting SMEs has in principle never been a controversial issue in Germany. German companies have also been able to access EC and EU (from 1992 onwards) SME programs. These achieved a notable dimension with the first action program for SMEs in 1986, and 250 million DM in subsidies were made available between 1990 and 1993. A Europe-wide network of advisory centers was set up, of which 27 were located in Germany. In 1990 a dedicated Directorate General for the *Mittelstand* was set up, followed in 1993 by a second action program and in the 2000s by a considerable increase in funding volumes.[361]

However, heroic inventor-entrepreneurs continued to dominate the self-image of the US economy. Silicon Valley as a new SME-supported growth model matched this ideal perfectly. The incredible rise of the San Francisco Bay region to become the world's most important IT and high-tech industry location was—at least superficially—not initiated by economic policy. But although the Valley has been celebrated as an example of free enterprise, it did benefit substantially from taxpayers' money, especially during its infancy. In the 1960s the Pentagon's willingness "to pay almost any price for compact [...] electronics for its missile programs stimulated the infant semiconductor industry. This early and cost-insensitive purchasing helped companies pioneering the technology to move down the learning curve."³⁶² Silicon Valley was not just the work of innovative developers from whose garages many SMEs and even major corporations like Apple or Hewlett Packard (HP) emerged, but also the result of subsidies provided by the US Department of Defense and the NASA space agency.

To this day, such hidden subsidies represent a special kind of business promotion in a country that otherwise pays homage to free enterprise. That applies in particular to the dual-use applications of aviation and space travel, satellite and telecommunications technology as well as to medicine and nanotechnology. The EU regards this as massively unfair competition: indeed, in 2010 the USA's military-related research expenditure exceeded that of all EU member states put together by a factor of 6.4.³⁶³

Photo 16: From a garage company to a tech giant—the rented garage of company founders William Hewlett and David Packard, now with a different coat of paint (2002)

The dominant pattern of a rapid transformation from family business to corporation with widely dispersed share ownership can also be observed in Silicon Valley. Almost all the successful corporate projects relinquished their family business status as early as the first generation. In 1939 Stanford graduates William R. Hewlett and David Packard started up their electronics business HP in a garage. In 1947 a corporation emerged from this partnership. The company grew as a result of winning movie industry contracts, and from the 1950s onwards primarily as a provider of electronic measuring instruments and pulse generators for the US defense and space industries, later supplying computers and then printers. HP went public in 1957 and was traded on the NYSE from 1961 onwards. Initially Hewlett and Packard each held around 30 percent of the company's shares, which however transitioned to scattered ownership in the 1960s. Packard in particular was politically very influential and served as deputy defense minister under Nixon from 1969 to 1971. His appointment was regarded as scandalous and as evidence of the power of the military-industrial complex. He returned to the company in 1972 and was Chairman of the Board until 1993. At Amazon the transition from family business to corporation with scattered share ownership was completed even faster. In 1994 Jeff Bezos used money from his family to set up the online bookstore Amazon in a garage and floated the company as early as 1996. By 2018 nearly 78 percent of the shares were in scattered ownership.

Outside of Silicon Valley, too (as in Germany), there has been a wide range of local, regional and state initiatives since the 1970s. These included technology transfer programs to help SMEs collaborate with universities; very successful examples include the Research Triangle in North Carolina, where a science park was set up back in the 1950s jointly with regional universities like Duke and Chapel Hill. It was then massively expanded and attracted technology start-ups. In 2002 a comparative study came to the conclusion that funding and assistance policy in the USA had focused on "knowledge-based production", while Germany concentrated even more on subsidizing the preservation of existing companies.[364]

Germany also lagged behind as far as protection against bureaucratic intervention was concerned. The US federal government's 1980 Regulatory Flexibility Act exempted SMEs from a wide range of regulations that burden major corporations. The 2012 Jumpstart Our Business Startups (JOBS) Act provided SMEs with generous exemptions from the strict accounting regulations contained in the 2002 Sarbanes–Oxley Act and from SEC guidelines. Companies generating gross sales of less than one billion dollars were now classed as emerging growth companies. On admittance to the stock exchange they were exempted for five years from certain disclosure obligations. Start-ups that wanted to raise up to 50 million dollars worth of capital were even exempted from all disclosure obligations.

In Germany there were no similar initiatives to assist start-ups by cutting back on formal regulations. On the contrary, the German Industrial Relations Act (Betriebsverfassungsgesetz) of 1988 stipulated that companies with more than 100 employees had to set up an economic committee (Wirtschafts-

Table 24: SME funding and assistance provided by federal agencies of the USA, 1955–2015 (in USD billion)

Year	SBIC payments	SBIR/STTR* payments	SBA** loan guarantees
1955	–	–	–
1960	–	–	–
1965	–	–	0.4
1970	0.2	–	–
1975	0.1	–	–
1980	0.3	0.05 (1983)	3.4
1985	0.5	0.2	2.8
1990	0.6	0.5	3.6
1995	1.2	1.0	8.3
2000	5.5	1.2	10.1 (1999)
2005	2.8 (2004)	2.0	20.3
2010	1.2	2.5	22.4
2015	2.5	9.3 (2014)	33.3

* Small Business Innovation Research Program (SBIR) or rather Small Business Innovation Research (STTR) since 1982.
** Guaranteed Loans, SBA Program 7 (a) and 504.

Sources: SBA, Annual Report 1965, p. 11, vol. 1970, pp. 6 and 24, vol. 1976, p. 4, vol. 1980, pp. 24 and 31, vol. 1985, p. 18, vol. 1990, p. 18; SBA, State of Small Business, vol. 1996, pp. 279 and 303, vol. 1999–2000, pp. 22–23 and 130, vol. 2001, p. 49; vol. 2005, p. 39, vol. 2004, p. 34, vol. 2010, pp. 50–51 and 95; SBA, Agency Financial Report, vol. 2009, p. 8, vol. 2010, p. 7, vol. 2017, p. 13.

ausschuss) as well as a works council. Companies employing five people or more are required to set up a works council.[365] The regulatory jungle in Germany, ranging from occupational health and safety to protection against dismissal, from approval timescales to commercial inspectorates, is a great deal denser and is therefore a particular hindrance to start-up businesses. The SBA also provides business start-up funding and assistance as part of efforts to combat poverty, in order to relieve pressure on the social welfare systems. This approach was embraced much later in Germany, namely in 2003 as part of the Hartz II reforms.[366] Conditions for start-ups and recently established

SMEs are much better in the USA, which explains the higher rate of start-up activity.

This SME policy awakening in the USA was also reflected in funding volumes disbursed by the various SBA programs. Starting from a very low base, the 1980s saw substantial increases that were continued in the 1990s and rose again massively in the 2000s. While in 1990 volumes for both funding lines— the SBIC (established in 1958) and the SBIR (established in 1982)—were still less than one billion dollars, much higher volumes were achieved in the 1990s and 2000s. Even then, however, government seed funding remained modest compared with privately raised funds: in 2000 the venture capital market alone provided 105 billion dollars of new funding for the entire economy.

Overall, SME funding and assistance policy has tended toward broad coverage and convergence in both countries since the 1980s, although it still plays a bigger role in Germany. A good example of this is export promotion, which reinforced tendencies that already existed: a focus of corporations on the global market in geographically smaller Germany and a concentration on the huge domestic market in the vast USA. According to a study by the Department of Commerce on export promotion, the USA ranked last or next to last, depending on the indicator used, in a 1987 league table that also included Canada and six European industrialized countries. Measured by the export promotion expenditure as a proportion of total central government outlays, Germany spent more than twice as much on export promotion than the USA.[367]

In the USA export promotion is handled by the Export-Import Bank of the United States (Ex-Im Bank), which was established in 1934 as part of the New Deal and operated from 1945 onwards as an independent government agency. It was extremely controversial and was the source of many scandals, for instance when companies that were about to go bankrupt were given loans or when there were suspicions of politically motivated favors. Ex-Im Bank's closure was prevented just in time in 2015 and its existence was secured until 2019, but it remains to be seen whether it survives the current Trump era. President Trump has repeatedly made extremely negative statements about the bank, and other Republicans have described the bank as the "epicenter of crony capitalism" and, given its preferential treatment of a few major corporations, as the "Bank of Boeing".[368] A second export promotion pillar is the Overseas Private Investment Corporation (OPIC), established in 1971 as a government authority that helps companies to reduce their political risks through government liability commitments. It has been financially independent since 1984, has repaid all the taxpayers' money it received and has transferred huge surpluses to the Department of the Treasury in the past few years; thus, the OPIC does not come in for very much criticism. However, in 2018 its abolition was likewise seriously discussed, as it was accused of "crony capitalism".[369]

In Germany export promotion is handled using a generally acknowledged mechanism that is a textbook example of cooperative capitalism. In 1927 the Reich concluded a contract with private-sector Hermes-Kreditversicherungsbank AG. The state absorbed the risks of bad debt, while Hermes handled processing and issued insurance policies to exporters. The system was reintroduced in 1949 and massively expanded in the 1950s. Since then, Hermes, known as Euler Hermes since 2002, and Deutsche Treuhand-Vereinigung, renamed PricewaterhouseCoopers AG WPG in 2005, have reduced the risks of financial distress for German companies as a result of nonpayment by foreign business partners. In 2014 up to 165 billion euros were provided for export credit guarantee purposes, of which 24.8 billion euros was accounted for by contracts primarily in emerging markets, equating to 2.2 percent of total German exports. The program has not operated at a loss since 2006 and by 2014 it had generated a profit of 3.9 billion euros for the German government.[370] Hedging of financial risks was paralleled by a global network of very active Chambers of Foreign Trade (2018: represented in more than 80 countries), the Germany Trade & Invest network (2018: 50 locations) and the Federal Ministry for Economic Affairs' SME market development program, launched in 2012. Export promotion was important particularly for the many hidden champions, because these generally small to medium-sized family businesses served global markets, and the federal government not only made market entry easier by providing loans, credit protection and organizational assistance, but also reduced risks to current operations through default guarantees. This highly developed system of export promotion is a key component in the remarkable global market success enjoyed by small and medium-sized German family businesses.

In summary one can state that in Germany the government intervened in the economy earlier and to a considerably greater degree and focused particularly on SMEs. Even though the USA caught up, initiatives were often half-hearted and controversial, while in Germany they were mainstays of cooperative capitalism. Many programs such as export promotion or ERP loans have proved successful over many decades, so that there is no debate about their raison d'être.

The starting point for programs in both countries was the recognition that in many respects SMEs suffered from disadvantages, in particular as far as access to the capital market was concerned. However, the economic impact of these assistance programs is unclear: they were always accompanied by deadweight effects and bureaucratic inefficiency as well as misallocation of resources. The bankruptcy rates for business start-ups are high in both countries. SME promotion was often primarily used by politicians as a means of raising their profiles, and was characterized to some extent by non-systematic, non-transparent approaches. The sheer number of programs and players alone makes it utterly impossible to assess the efficiency of SME promotion.

Even so, the focus of each set of economic policies did not cause the differences between the corporate landscapes in both countries; rather, it amplified existing divergences. It was above all the differences in business culture that were reflected in business regulation and promotion policies. The USA tended to make things easier for start-ups rather than protecting existing companies. In Germany the opposite tended to be the case.

In the USA SMEs often complained about being politically disadvantaged. However, they achieved key successes particularly as far as anti-cartel and fair trade policies were concerned. They attracted attention in Washington on specific issues through lobbying by industry associations and by pooling political donations. And federal authorities had targets that required them to award a quarter of their contracts to SMEs. Such massive intervention in market activities to the benefit of SMEs does not occur in Germany. Nonetheless, the rhetorical esteem in which SMEs have been held in the USA since the 1930s and 1950s was not commensurate with the financial support that they received, although the latter has been increasing very substantially since the 1980s.

VII. Political Power Open to Owners of Large Family Businesses

In contrast, owners of larger family businesses had considerably more influence in specific cases—not as representatives of the family business sector, but as advocates of particular interests. They used their foundations to engage in agenda-setting and supported projects that appeared to them to be useful or worthwhile. For instance, funding for universities served in both countries as a method of enhancing the skills base of potential employees. Direct or indirect election campaign donations enabled financial resources to be transformed into political influence. In both countries, family business owners with the necessary funds regularly participated in the political process. Given that money plays a much larger role in US politics—the 2016 election campaign devoured some 6.5 billion dollars and election campaign costs are not reimbursed out of taxpayers' money, as in Germany—wealth of any kind secures disproportionately large opportunities to wield influence. Thus, compared with the USA, the nexus between money and political power tends to be moderate in Germany. In the context of cooperative capitalism, lobbying was usually conducted in Germany at the collective level of industry associations as well as by means of individual donations and contacts or through the exercise of public office, though on a much smaller scale than in the USA.

In the USA, lateral entry to higher positions within the apparatus of state was and is open to family business owners, who often seized these opportunities after retiring from their business careers. Examples of this include Bechtel National Inc., a construction group established in 1898, which is now in the fifth generation of family ownership. As one of the world's largest construction groups handling mega-projects such as airports, motorways or nuclear power plants, close relationships with public-sector clients were always very important. A corporate history of Bechtel is rightly called "Friends in High Places", because business involving such gigantic projects required political connections. During the Reagan presidency, the relationship between Bechtel and the government was characterized by outright revolving door practices. The company's legal advisor, Caspar Weinberger, became US Secretary of Defense, while the president of the Bechtel Group, George Shultz, was appointed US Secretary of State. Conversely, executives from the government-owned Export-Import Bank who had also supported Bechtel and its clients were appointed to lucrative positions within the group.[371] In Germany such career paths were practically unheard of due to the relatively watertight separation of the higher echelons of the civil service and the political classes. The list of US family business owners who were appointed to ambassadorships—in Germany a domain reserved for experienced professional diplomats—is long.

A particularly striking example of a politically influential, extremely wealthy family business owner is Henry Kaiser. His various companies benefited from major government contracts during the New Deal era (dams and roads) and during the Second World War (warships). Kaiser's close personal relationship with President Roosevelt turned out to be beneficial and lucrative as far as these exorbitantly priced government contracts were concerned. Government purchase commitments and price guarantees as well as cheap loans enabled Kaiser's companies to make no-risk profits, sometimes without having to invest any appreciable capital resources. After the Republicans assumed the reins of government in 1946, Kaiser, who had very recently been regarded as an acclaimed defense contractor and candidate for the Vice Presidency, had to face accusations of wartime profiteering before a congressional committee. Nonetheless he managed to benefit from public programs again.[372]

There are also specific examples in Germany of politically influential, extremely wealthy family business owners. Friedrich Flick (1883–1972) forged a heavy industry empire during the Weimar Republic years. In 1932 he managed to sell the mining company Gelsenkirchener Bergwerks AG to the Reich at a triply inflated price. Shortly beforehand, he had made large payments (450,000 marks) to members of the Cabinet to help their candidate—Hindenburg—in the presidential election campaign. The sale of the mining company restored Flick to financial health, but triggered a scandal.

From 1933 onwards Flick channeled his donations to the Nazi Party and joined "Heinrich Himmler's circle of friends" ("Freundeskreis Heinrich Himmler"), which provided business owners with access to the new political elite in return for donations. His good contacts with the Party enabled Flick to benefit to a much greater degree than many of his competitors from the expropriation of Jewish assets, the armaments boom and the use of forced labor. After 1945 Flick was sentenced to a lengthy prison term, but was freed after serving just five years. The bulk of the Flick Group's industrial assets were returned to the Group in 1952 and until 1985 it was Germany's largest group of companies in family ownership. Flick rose to become Germany's wealthiest man during the "Economic Miracle" years. Close political links remained one of the trademarks of the Flick story. In 1981 the Group was granted a tax break worth just under one billion DM by the Federal Ministry for Economic Affairs. Word subsequently got out that Flick had bribed politicians of all parties represented in the German Parliament, the Bundestag. The "Flick Affair" ended with prosecutions for bribery and corruption as well as tax evasion, which resulted in both FDP Economic Ministers, Hans Friderichs and Otto Graf Lambsdorff, being fined and the CEO of Flick KG, Eberhard von Brauchitsch, being given a suspended two-year prison sentence.

The frequently emphasized transatlantic differences are also clear in any comparison of these two government contractors: Kaiser was very open-

minded about the capital markets and at opportune moments did not hesi-
tate to float parts of his empire on the stock market and content himself with
owning around a third of the shares. In the interest of rapid growth, he allowed business associates and partner businesses to invest in his companies
and accept 50:50 arrangements. Although he placed leadership of the Group
in the hands of his son and the family initially still remained majority owners, the link between the family and the Group dissolved during the postwar years.

Flick, on the other hand, attempted to keep his companies entirely in
family ownership. In contrast to Kaiser, he did not involve external capital
and ensured in all his companies that the family retained its controlling interest. He also disinherited one son (Otto-Ernst) and weakened the position
of his other son (Friedrich Karl) by instructing in his will that an external
manager (Eberhard von Brauchitsch) be brought in to help run the business. This family strategy did considerable damage to the company, and in
1985/86 the Group was sold to the Deutsche Bank after an unsuccessful in-
terlude by the second generation. The era of this particular family business
ended when the transition to the second generation failed because of inheritance disputes and succession problems. In Kaiser's case, on the other hand,
the family or rather the family foundation retained a stake in the group of
companies for a long period, although it soon found itself in a minority
shareholder position.[373]

Kaiser, Bechtel and Flick represent extreme examples, but they demonstrate that wealth can be transformed into political influence in both countries. This was and is an easier and more direct process in the USA, because
the political system is geared, among other things, to the private funding of
election campaigns and these are a great deal longer and more expensive than
in Germany. However, although this fact explains spectacular individual cases, it does not account for the different make-ups of the US and German corporate landscapes and their diverging political preferences. While politicians
in Germany viewed it as a key mission to promote family businesses and
SMEs in particular much earlier, in the USA it took until the Second World
War and the crises of the 1970s before equally sizeable assistance programs
were put in place and—as in many other areas—before a process of convergence between both countries began. Irrespective of that, there were cases
in both countries of politically influential family business owners, although
given the election system in the USA, Americans were on average better able
to make their wealth count.

F. Path Dependencies.
Historical Genesis and Critical
Junctures over the "longue durée"

Historical circumstances worked in favor of family businesses in both countries, but they were more numerous and exerted a greater influence in Germany.

I. Family Businesses in the Traditional World of Europe— the Case of Germany

1. The Long History of Family Businesses

The existence of older, successful family businesses, especially mercantile companies and banks, but also manufacturing enterprises such as breweries, textile houses and manufactories, had an enduring influence on the German corporate landscape. One need only think of large family firms such as Fugger, Welser, Hochstetter and the like. The family business had been firmly established in Germany since the Middle Ages and it continued to serve as a model. Looking back on the genesis of his company, Werner von Siemens wrote: "From my young days it has always been my ambition to build an enterprise of world standing in the style of the Fuggers, which would give not only me but my successors power and authority in the world."[374]

The tradition of craft guilds, with the respective trades vigorously defending their monopoly positions, also exercised a decisive influence. Craft businesses were, as a rule, passed on within families rather than being bought or sold; even widows could run the business in order to bridge gaps in the line of inheritance. If there was no male heir, the principal method of passing on ownership was to bring in an outsider to marry the widow or a daughter of a deceased master craftsman. The longevity of these businesses was due to the protection they enjoyed from competition and the collectively enforced high standards of training and quality. Despite the increasing competition from non-guild businesses, especially in rural areas, and the introduction of free enterprise—in Prussia by the Stein-Hardenberg reforms of 1810 and in the North German Confederation (Norddeutscher Bund) by the 1869 industrial code—many elements of the old craft business structures continued until well into the 20th century thanks to the compulsory membership of master craftsman in chambers of crafts.[375]

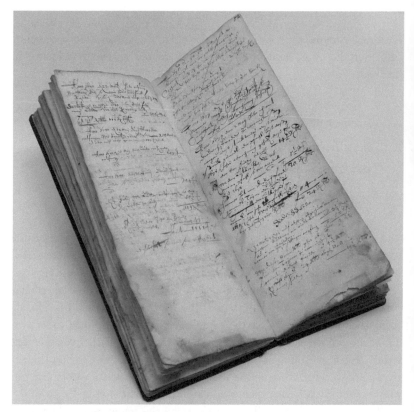

Photo 17: Account book of the Harkort merchant company (about 1705)

Agriculture was also typically organized in the form of family enterprises, with regional laws of succession broadly divided into two camps. In areas in southern Germany where the partible inheritance system (Realteilung) predominated, farms were divided up between all the heirs, which led to the fragmentation of farmland and the rise of secondary occupations in agriculture. Primogeniture, by contrast, usually favored the eldest son, or occasionally also the youngest son (ultimogeniture), so that a farm was kept intact over multiple generations. And the primogeniture form of inheritance seems to have provided the basic model for non-agrarian enterprises too.

2.   The Model of the Aristocracy

The dynastic principle was fundamental to the aristocracy. The autonomy and continuity of the family collective were paramount and any divergent individual preferences had to be subordinated. The interests of the individual, and especially later-born siblings, were expected to give way to the overall interests of the dynasty. "The needs of the family [...] greatly transcended those of the individual."[376] This principle was most significantly expressed in relation to property, where the legal institution of fideicommissum, or entailment, under ancient Roman Law was often applied. It limited testamentary freedom and was designed to preserve the wealth and social status of an aristocratic family over generations. A testamentary disposition usually created special family assets that were both indivisible and could not be used as security for loans. As a rule, these assets were inherited by the first-born son, with all other heirs being provided for through civil service posts or strategic marriages. This legal construct was binding on all subsequent generations. It protected and immobilized the assets; the successor inherited only the right of usufruct within defined limits. He was not allowed to sell the estate or encumber it with debt, nor could he bequeath it to whomever he pleased, as the family as a whole retained ultimate ownership (Obereigentum) and the original dispositions had to be followed. In other words, the successor was merely the custodian of the collective family wealth. Such entailed estates not only protected landholdings and manor houses, but also the aristocracy's many other undertakings, from mines to breweries, mills and ironworks.[377] According to the legal scholar Carl Friedrich von Gerber, this form of inheritance (Fideikommiss) created "the foundations for a family history" and "sociality" between the generations.[378] The second half of the 19th century saw a considerable increase in the number of such estates in tail male. Exactly 143 years after entails were abolished in the United States, the Weimar Constitution of 1919 specified the dissolution of entailed estates, but they continued into the 1930s, and even until 1945 in many cases.

Although they represented essentially a much criticized privilege of the aristocracy, the model of "Fideikommiss" also had a wider impact. Bourgeois families began to follow suit and entail their own family estates. Johann Caspar Harkort II, owner of a hammer works and farm near Hagen, did so as far back as 1732. His descendants, and especially Friedrich Harkort (1793–1870), were to play a key role in the industrialization of the Ruhr region in the 19th century. To emphasize the principle of primogeniture, the family's first-born sons were always named Johann Caspar and, like aristocrats and monarchs, were referred to using Roman numerals. Not until the generation after Johann Caspar IV (1753–1818), the father of Friedrich Harkort, was this custom discontinued.[379]

Photo 18: Advertising for the Faber-Castell company (1921)

In the interests of preserving their wealth, family businesses also modelled themselves on the aristocracy by laying down certain rules of succession or articles that established foundations or registered pre-emptive rights that were enduringly binding on their descendants. Along with cultivating family origin myths, preoccupations with investigating genealogy, designing family crests and drawing up family trees also all led in the same direction. The family was perceived as a collective that conferred continuity to which short-term interests had to be subordinated.

Even though engagement in industrial firms was considered as not befitting the status of the nobility, a minority of German aristocrats did become involved in business activities that extended beyond agriculture. Particularly in sectors that had direct links to land ownership (mines and brickworks) or forestry and agricultural (wood processing, mills, breweries, sugar and potato factories), they founded companies and owned or operated them, in some cases for generations.[380] In addition, some middle-class entrepreneurs were elevated to the ranks of the nobility, which represented the highest level of social recognition and was a very desirable goal for most entrepreneurs in the 19th century.

Photo 19: Count Anton-Wolfgang von Faber-Castell (1941–2016) in front of the family castle

In 1758, the carpenter Kaspar Faber settled in Stein near Nuremberg and in 1761, he began to produce lead pencils. His great-grandson Lothar turned the company into an industrial operation. From his takeover to the time of his death in 1896, the workforce grew from a staff of 20 to about 1,500 people. He sold his pencils as brand-name products, acquired the sole rights to a graphite mine in Russia and entered the international market. He was considered to be one of the most important and richest entrepreneurs in Bavaria—and was ennobled as a baron in 1881.[381] His only son, Wilhelm, died at an early age in 1896, leaving the family without a male heir, and the company then passed to Lothar Faber's widow, Baroness Ottilie von Faber. Their granddaughter, also named Ottilie, initially took over as proprietor of the family entail, but inherited the company in 1903 after the death of her grandmother. She married Count Alexander zu Castell-Rüdenhausen, who joined the company's management two years later and changed his name to Faber-Castell, which became the company's new name in 1928.

As early as 1843–46, Lothar had a castle built in the neo-Renaissance style. This was followed from 1903–06 by the construction of the "Neue Schloss" (New Castle), whose facade included neo-Roman elements and was linked to the old castle by a tower. This building, which went by the nickname "pencil castle," was frequently used to reinforce the company's image and to underscore its solidity and long history.

The company was led by direct descendants of the family for many years. Count Anton-Wolfgang von Faber-Castell managed the company in the 8th generation for nearly 40 years. He died in 2016, and in 2017 for the first time, an executive was appointed CEO who was not a member of the family, but Countess Mary von Faber-Castell continues to represent the family on the Board of Management and plays an active role in the company's leadership. Members of the 9th generation are already working in the company or are preparing externally for future managerial roles.[382]

3.   The Supreme Importance of the Family

While classical economics, prominent in the Anglo-American world, had elevated individualism to its pre-eminent status and defined the individual as the ruthless maximizer of individual profit, in Germany this was considered undesirable—and prompted counter-models that focused on the collective good and the "community" (Gemeinschaft).[383] If the rampant individualism of classical economics appeared to threaten the moral foundations of society, the family was seen as the nucleus of society and a guarantor of its future survival. Most influentially, the German idealist philosopher Georg Wilhelm Friedrich Hegel considered the family collective to be a better alternative to the unchecked possessive individualism of "the mere individual".

"It is not only property which a family possesses; as a universal and enduring person, the family requires permanent and secure possessions, i.e. it requires wealth. The arbitrariness of a mere individual's particular needs is one aspect of property in the abstract, but along with the selfishness of desire, it is transformed here into something moral, into care and gain for a common interest. As its head, the husband must represent the family as a legal personality in relation to others. Furthermore, he is responsible for [...] controlling and administering the family's wealth. This is the common property of all family members, none of whom has property of their own, but each has a right in the common property."[384]

Hegel thus posits the principle of familial continuity, which the father as custodian of the family's wealth is responsible for safeguarding. Accordingly, as with the entailment of Fideikommiss, individual family members have no right to this wealth. In this philosophical tradition, the family is a separate and most precious legal personality that merits the special protection of the state.[385] This idealistic position became highly influential among legal scholars and had significant consequences for inheritance law, which used statutory shares in Germany to severely constrain testamentary freedom in favor of the family.[386]

4. Ties to Place and Homeland

Although the population was by no means static and Germany had experienced some major migratory flows, in the 19th century there were many families who had lived in one place or one region for centuries. A similar degree of allegiance to place was impossible in the United States: the country's development was driven by mass immigration and a steady stream of large-scale internal migratory flows—generally from east to west. Until the frontier finally ceased to exist in 1890, the US had been expanding its territory, constantly offering recent arrivals new opportunities in areas that were being settled for the first time. Cheap or free land acted as a powerful magnet to settlers. In Germany, by contrast, there was far less mobility and small-scale structures predominated. Forces here tended more toward continuity, which also led to the perpetuation of family businesses and their strong ties to a particular place.

5.   Distrust of Entrepreneurs

In Germany, companies were initially regarded with a great deal of skepticism in the 19th century. They therefore possessed very little social prestige, and the entrepreneur was not idolized as in the US, but rather greatly distrusted. Entrepreneurs in the 19th century were viewed extremely critically in leading social circles—the aristocracy and the civil service—but also by those who believed they were likely to be the losers of this development: craftsmen and farmers. After all, entrepreneurs disrupted the traditional order of things. Similarly antagonistic attitudes were not found in the US. There, expansion into new territories that had no established structures meant there was no breeding ground for resistance born of the desire to protect vested rights. After all, there was enough space for everyone.

In Germany, the distrust of market forces led to various constraints on freedom of trade (Gewerbefreiheit), which became even more restrictive again following the failed revolution of 1848. Relics and remnants of the old class system were everywhere. Some businesses required a state license before they could commence operating. Until 1870, individual licenses were required to found stock corporations. After that date, incorporation law was more liberal, but rigorous scrutiny was still required, especially as the "crash of 1873" (Gründerkrise), during which many financially unstable companies collapsed, durably reinforced the skepticism with which entrepreneurship was regarded. In particular the educated middle classes in Germany looked down on business people with disdain and contempt, and the aristocracy simply considered work in industry as beneath their social rank. Consequently, aristocrats and academics stayed well away from commerce and kept their sons from taking up careers in the "lower realms" of business, where they might become "tradesmen" or "money men", or "soulless materialists" lacking cultural ambitions.[387]

These attitudes held sway for a long time, but were not strong enough to hinder industrialization, and began to weaken naturally after the 19th century came to an end. However, the entrepreneurial bourgeois family often formed a protective enclave as far as societal prejudices were concerned, as evidenced by socially endogenous marriage practices. Preferred marriages were those arranged between entrepreneurial families that had complementary business interests. Men often married their cousins in order to prevent the fragmentation of the family's wealth and the associated business complications. It would appear that the greater external pressure on German family entrepreneurs led to stronger cohesion.

II. Family Businesses in the "New World" of the United States

The United States was and remains a country of family capitalism, but in comparison with Germany, it was less deeply culturally ingrained or established for the long term. Instead, it was shaped by the exceptionally strong founding culture of the first generation and a generally transient structure. There were seven reasons for this:

1. The Anti-aristocratic Founding Credo of the United States

The new state deliberately did not create any aristocracy. In addition, in 1776 the Bill for Abolition of Entails drawn up by Thomas Jefferson specifically abolished entailed estates created during the colonial period. His reasoning is telling, and instituted a tradition:

"The transmission of this property from generation to generation, in the same name, raised up a distinct set of families, who, being privileged by law in the perpetuation of their wealth, were thus formed into a Patrician order, distinguished by the splendor and luxury of their establishments. [...] To annul this privilege, and instead of an aristocracy of wealth, of more harm and danger, than benefit, to society, to make an opening for the aristocracy of virtue and talent, which nature has wisely provided for the direction of the interests of society, and scattered with equal hand through all its conditions, was deemed essential to a well-ordered republic. [...] a repeal of the law [...] would authorize the present holder to divide the property among his children equally, ... and would place them, by natural generation, on the level of their fellow citizens."[388]

The US was to be a meritocracy, structured by the capacity of individuals who had a right to equal opportunities. Inherited property or class privileges, by contrast, were disapproved of. Instead, there prevailed the already highly regarded British utilitarian principle that the dead should not exercise power over the living. Jefferson was in favor of an "aristocracy of virtue and talent", based on the individual, not on dynastic family groupings. Another factor that counted against entails was that they prevented the use of land as security for loans, which would be a serious, potentially growth-restricting disadvantage in the emerging credit economy. The development of a real estate market that was as free as possible enjoyed a higher priority.

The fact that these ideas were not fully realized and that rich family dynasties nevertheless arose does not contradict the cultural force exerted by the ideas of the founding fathers. As instruments to protect dynastic wealth, many family trusts and foundations were established in the 19th century, but they did not have the same effect as entails: they did not remove land from the market, since it could still be freely sold by the trustees.[389] The key point was that there was no aristocracy, and social status based on birth and inherited privileges was considered deeply un-American.[390]

2.   The Cult of the Self-made Man

US society tended to idolize the upwardly mobile and look down on inherited wealth. Since the 1860s, the writer Horatio Alger had celebrated the American dream in over 130 dime novels, most of which became bestsellers. Poor, hard-working, honest youths succeeded in rising above their humble origins by performing acts of bravery that attracted the attention of wealthy benefactors. Nothing seemed to fascinate American society more than a rags-to-riches story. However, the previously mentioned maxim of Carnegie, that the man who dies rich dies disgraced, still applied: the wealth that an individual had accumulated should not be passed on to heirs, but should flow back into society through charitable giving. This cultural tradition continues to this day, as demonstrated by the Bill & Melinda Gates Foundation or the Chan Zuckerberg Initiative for example. The United States is a country of philanthropy. For enterprises, however, this usually results in a substantial outflow of resources, a diminution of the inheritable estate, or even the disengagement of the family—in other words, it tends to weaken family businesses.

Despite the Horatio Alger myth, in the 19th century many entrepreneurs were sons of entrepreneurs, and wealthy dynasties sprang up that preserved and increased their wealth over several generations.[391] However, the proportion of upwardly mobile individuals seems to have been much greater than in Germany.[392] This may be due to the openness of the country as a land of immigrants and the lack of any mechanisms and traditions that would constrain mobility. For instance, there were no guilds and no chambers of crafts that encouraged people to remain in their traditional roles, and the model of the aristocracy that was so important in Germany was entirely absent.

With the wealth of resources and the openness the country afforded, it appeared that social advancement was possible for everyone. An elevated status could be acquired within one generation much more easily than in Europe, thus intergenerational strategies played a much less significant role and, as already indicated, inherited wealth had more negative connotations. While in Europe the position of an individual in the order of succession was key to whether he could be an independent farmer or craftsman, this social constraint did not apply in the US, as there were usually many other options available for securing a livelihood.[393]

3. The Wealth of Opportunities and Openness to the New

Since emigration was inherently highly risky, on the whole immigrants tended to be more willing to take risks than those who stayed behind. Living in the United States required people to come to terms continually with what was new. Immigrants frequently moved around and changed occupation as the expanding nation steadily provided more new land and created new opportunities. In fact, internal migration and changing occupations became a mass phenomenon. Social advancement seemed possible for many, and did indeed become reality for a sizeable minority. There was less old wealth and fewer people who insisted on preserving the status quo and blocking change. All this created an unprecedented dynamism and a readiness to embrace the unknown. A willingness to pursue new ventures rather than rest on one's laurels became the predominant trait of many Americans. Heritage and preserving continuity were less important than in the more strongly socially stratified Germany.[394]

4. Economic Independence and Business Acumen

Economic independence and business acumen rank among the core fundamental values of the United States—a fact that foreign visitors and immigrants often noticed. In 1835 Alexis de Tocqueville, who travelled across the US on behalf of the French government from 1831 to 1832, wrote in an exceptionally perceptive analysis that society in the New World was characterized by a love of freedom, individualism and the pursuit of prosperity. "It is strange to see with what feverish ardor the Americans pursue their own welfare."[395] He attributed this to the lack of an aristocracy and of a serious unequal distribution of land as in Europe, which was true at least during the early years of the US when the culture was becoming established. In today's terms, we would speak of greater social mobility and a society less concerned with ossified status boundaries. "Almost all the tastes and habits that the equality of condition produces naturally lead men to commercial and industrial occupations." He was fascinated in particular by the legion of small businesses run by families. "But what most astonishes me in the United States is not so much the marvelous grandeur of some undertakings as the innumerable multitude of small ones."[396]

Two years later a German immigrant wrote that Americans had a more entrepreneurial mindset than any other people. "Business is the very soul of an American, he pursues it … as a fountain of all human felicity." Immigrants had to adapt to this obsession with business and should not hanker after the "sociable idleness of Europe".[397]

5. The Size of the United States and the Mobility of Citizens

As the British historian Mary Rose has demonstrated with reference to the cotton industry, the size of the country and the great geographical mobility of the American population considerably weakened the cohesion of families and the ties that bound their businesses to particular locations. In her study of British and American family businesses, she was able to show a clear difference between the two countries. In the US, people operated within a more fluid and dispersed environment and frequently made use of networks across families.[398] The barriers to entry were lower, as there were very few formal obstacles; indeed firms enjoyed freedom of trade everywhere. The pace at which businesses were founded and moved was further accelerated by the large numbers of immigrants streaming into the country who had no geographical ties.[399] As a result, the dynastic motives that were deeply rooted in Europe were less pronounced. In a study of the American values system, Thomas Cochran states: "High mobility, both geographic and social, also weakened family ties; men expected to leave home early, and in many cases the farm of their early childhood memories was soon sold. The same was true of family business firms. Few sons felt the obligation, common in continental Europe, to perpetuate the farm or firm as a family enterprise. Money, or 'economic rationality' rather than land and family ties, was the common measuring rod of the society. New opportunities drew away the ablest young men, and partnerships continually changed."[400] Persistently high internal migration weakened the sense of family and the authority of parents. "Such home relations probably tended to enhance individual initiative."[401]

6.   The Dynamism of Immigrant Entrepreneurs and the Strength of their Networks

Along with family relationships, ethnic networks among migrants created further trust-based mutual support structures. In many cases they complemented those of the family, but they also often served as substitutes, for example if most family members had remained in Europe or were living in other parts of the US. Immigrant entrepreneurs thus gained a measure of stability, especially in the first generation when they were in the process of establishing their businesses. Living in Little Italy or Polish Hill, in the French Quarter or Swede Hollow, in Over-the-Rhine or Kleindeutschland gave these entrepreneurs access to a non-family resource that resulted in a lessening of the economic importance of the family in the long term. The ethnic foundations of trust led to the establishment of many partnerships between immigrants from the same country of origin who were not related to each other. This route offered an alternative that in the long run, that is to say after ethnic enclaves weakened and disintegrated in second and subsequent generations at the latest, was to strengthen individualism. Many partnerships between co-ethnics were also dissolved after a short time, with the partners continuing either alone or together with another compatriot. Partnerships were also formed with members of one's own family, but this was by no means the only option.

7.   Autonomy and Property as Core Values of US Society

The concept of the economically autonomous settler family figured prominently in the beliefs and traditions of the United States. The homestead or family farm was specifically supported by US land sales policy from the Land Ordinance of 1785 through to the Homestead Act of 1862. Jefferson prevailed over his rival Alexander Hamilton, who favored a land sales policy that was designed to generate as much income as possible for the state and encourage immigrants to move to towns and take up the trades practiced there. Jefferson, by contrast, thought that a large number of independent farmer families would create the foundations for the future social order. Land was therefore to be parceled in such a way that it could be managed by one family in each case, who would then be able to ensure their subsistence on their own property. Jefferson considered the relatively equal distribution of land to be the prerequisite for a republican community. As a political project, this attempt at social engineering did not in fact succeed, as land speculation resulted in the creation of large landholdings. Nevertheless, there were also many small family farms, even if the families were often not the initial purchasers and had to take on large amounts of debt. They soon cast off the narrow corset of the subsistence economy and went on to supply local and distant markets. The logic of the monetary economy, the practice of borrowing and the calculation of profits swiftly spread even to the furthest reaches of the country.[402]

Of foremost importance was the availability of large areas of land, the mostly free market in land, the existence of a capitalist agricultural system, and the emergence of small-scale agrarian structures. From 1787 onwards, yeoman farmers were able to acquire property without restriction. These farmers were not burdened with compulsory levies as was the case in many parts of Germany, where they were accustomed to many restrictions and taxes as well as to very small areas of land. The result in the USA was market-driven entrepreneurial farmers who were not tied to the land, i.e. if necessary, they could and did sell their farms and move on elsewhere. Sons also often left to set up their own farms.

These factors resulted in very powerful path dependencies and are a good example of the "longue durée" of historical constellations which still—even in entirely different circumstances—influence behavioral dispositions to the present day. As an interim conclusion, it can be said that the conditions for family businesses were favorable but different in both countries. The great emphasis on individualism in the United States tended to work against long-term intergenerational strategies, whereas a pronounced family orientation made the multigenerational family business the model in Germany. The next chapter examines the consequences of the path dependencies outlined here on the various types of business and family cultures on both sides of the Atlantic.

G. Cultural Identities. National Trends in Family Business Cultures

When the US retail giant Wal-Mart ventured into the German market at the end of the 1990s, the management echelons of this family business from Arkansas were confident of success. With a strategy mix comprising stringent cost and logistics management, a rigorous focus on customer service and a "personnel policy that emphasized loyalty and a strong identification with the company"[403], they believed they had a tried and tested formula that would enable them to swiftly conquer this new market. The "Wal-Mart way", however, failed spectacularly in Germany. In 2006, barely eight years later, the company was forced to pull out, selling all its stores to the Metro Group.

The reasons were manifold. Wal-Mart had not studied the particular features of the German retail market in sufficient detail beforehand. Having to compete with the discounters in the ALDI or Schwarz groups, both likewise family businesses, would inevitably make it very difficult for the US company to succeed. Wal-Mart never achieved strong enough sales revenues and the bargaining power to push through higher margins with wholesalers and brand-name manufacturers. But it was not merely its market strategy that was at fault, its entire corporate philosophy was poorly adapted to the conditions in Germany. With missionary zeal, Wal-Mart had set out to establish service standards in German supermarkets on a par with those that US shoppers were accustomed to. This meant, among other things, obligatory "greeters" at the store entrance, a free bagging service and the "ten-foot rule", which encouraged employees to speak to customers unsolicited while they were walking round the store. However, practices like these, which aimed at boosting Wal-Mart's image as a service-focused retailer, were more likely to disconcert than please German shoppers, who had their own shopping habits.[404]

Similar difficulties arose with respect to labor relations. Through shared symbolic practices, the management sought to implement an American model of corporate culture in its German stores, a model that centered on the idea of the "Wal-Mart family" developed by the company's charismatic founder Sam Walton in the 1960s.[405] In ritual-like morning assemblies, which began with everyone joining in the company chant, employees were expected to celebrate being part of the corporate family and declare their willingness to always give their best, work hard and be friendly to customers. To strengthen team spirit and symbolize flat hierarchies, sales staff were referred to as associates. The participative elements of the corporate philosophy were accompanied by a strict code of conduct, however. The company prescribed in detail how employees were to dress, spend their break time and communicate with each other. Even in their private lives, they were expected to identify wholly with the values of the company, or rather those of the religious family that owned it. Compulsory celebrations and communal leisure activities were intended to ensure that employees' personal family lives blended as closely as possible with the company community. These practices, which Germans found rather strange, even went as far as imposing moralizing rules such as a ban on flirting at the workplace and an open request to employees to report co-workers who broke the rules. The company also circumvented consultation with works councils which are prescribed by the German Works Constitution Act. It was implacably anti-union, and saw any form of workers organizing to represent their interests as a breach of trust. As a result, Wal-Mart had to deal with numerous labor courts and high staff turnover rates. From the point of view of employees, the "Americanized" corporate culture lacked authenticity; it did not live up to its own expectations of what an employer should be. Instead of giving work meaning, Wal-Mart's values and standards remained alien.[406] So in the end, it was the differences in attitude and cultural disparities that hampered Wal-Mart's entry into the German market. As an article in German weekly newspaper Die Zeit commented in 2006, the retailer had failed because it had sought "to integrate its employees fully in its own corporate culture rather than agreeing on working conditions rationally in consultation with the social partners as is otherwise customary in Germany".[407]

The example of Wal-Mart demonstrates two things: first, operating in foreign markets forces multinational companies to face the difficult challenges of intercultural management. Choosing a market strategy and shaping relationships with internal and external stakeholders requires sensitive adaptation to the institutional environment, cultural traditions and different attitudes that are specific to the country in question. Clearly, then, companies are more than merely organizations that optimize economic value-creation processes. They are also—and perhaps above all—sociocultural constructs whose functioning depends on the social relationships of their members, their emotional cohesion and their motivation to cooperate.[408] Without the integrative power of a shared corporate culture, enterprises are at risk of fragmentation.

Second, the case demonstrates that family-based corporate cultures in the US and Germany have clearly developed along different historical pathways and within different structures. For instance, in family businesses it is often the case that the guiding principles of the social system of "family" are carried across to the economic system of "company". However, the assumption of universality and the expressive over-emphasis of the family concept that characterized Wal-Mart's business philosophy was perceived as "typically American" as there were no equivalents among companies within the German cultural framework, nor were there enough points where they coincided to enable any positive effects to emerge.

Against this backdrop, tracing the divergent paths in the social formation of family businesses requires examining both the commonalities and the differences between their national identities and mindsets. To what extent have cultural predispositions led to different forms of family influence on corporate culture? How did the different economic, political and social environments of their countries of origin affect the company's social constitution? At what points did they intersect? Compared with the United States, the strong presence of multigenerational family businesses that continues to this day in Germany alone suggests that the family aspect is more deeply rooted and more widely accepted as a means of shaping management, labor relations and personnel policy. Based on this, our working hypothesis is that the cultural form of the family business was particularly compatible with the coordinated capitalism found in Germany. In the American type of liberal market economy, this cultural form apparently gradually diminished in importance, fragmented, and underwent a transformation, although it did not disappear altogether. This is true of the British model too.

The task of describing these development pathways presents numerous challenges. There is no *one single* family business culture, but rather a considerable variety.[409] National models of corporate culture are also not homogeneous. Likewise, there is no one "German" or one "American" corporate culture that can be compared universally and independently of sectoral, cluster or regional contexts.[410] In her studies, Mary Rose has convincingly argued that a national comparison must take account of the different degrees of influence of political and societal context factors, but need not pay too much heed to the contrast between the corporate cultures in the individual sectors and local regions where they were frequently blended and blurred.[411] And the USA is still home to successful family businesses such as Mars Inc., National Cash Register or Cargill Inc., whose business philosophies (unlike Wal-Mart) are closely related to those of German family enterprises. Methodologically, therefore, we will proceed by combining an examination of several relevant case studies with a systematic chronological analysis of key historical trends. To begin with, we will investigate the historical roots of the fundamental principles that have shaped corporate culture since the era of family capitalism in the 19th and early 20th centuries. We will then go on to follow the transformation processes of family-based corporate cultures in the course of the modern age up through the present day. We will trace characteristic trends in the socioeconomic and cultural histories of the two countries in order to identify the factors that, to a greater or lesser extent, drive continuity and change.

I.   Paternalism: Forms and Functions of the Archetype of Corporate Culture

Herbert Matis defines corporate culture as the "totality of common values and standards plus shared modes of thinking [...] that influence the decisions, actions and activities of the members of the organization".[412] Metaphorically speaking, corporate culture is the spirit and style of the company. It is based on shared influences and preferences for how things should be done and how they should be. The constitution of the company, which is based on formal and informal codes of conduct, assumes an important steering function for managing operations and for integrative and motivational tasks with respect to labor relations.[413] The essential purpose of corporate culture is to create a sense of "belonging to a community" that reins in individual opportunism and enables people to work together to achieve a specific purpose. For family businesses, these bonding aspects are closely interwoven on all three systemic levels of family, ownership and management. The set of shared values is first a central means of engendering a sense of purpose and cohesion within the entrepreneurial family. The family cultural identity is the glue that continually legitimizes the multigenerational project and sustains the willingness of the company's owners to preserve the family line of succession. Second, it underpins the decision-making hierarchies and structures within the company and provides models for corporate governance. Third, it influences the relationships between family and employees, and as a cultural social constitution ideally also engenders motivation, loyalty and emotional attachment. For the comparative historical analysis, all three levels of family, governance and work culture[414] in companies will be examined.

When companies were becoming established at the threshold to the modern industrial era as a form of collective entity for doing business, the family played a central role as the organizational model for a company. Against the backdrop of companies operating in an economically low-trust environment in which neither the market nor the state provided sufficient assurance for the enforcement of contracts, early governance models were based on the established social system of the bourgeois family. One of the common historical factors is that in both Germany and the United States, the majority of firms adopted a paternalistic corporate culture during their founding and establishment phases. This type of culture is characterized by the interplay of elements of autocracy, guardianship and welfare. Paternalism carried, so to speak, the governing and responsibility model of relationships from the domestic social group across to the factory floor. It was based on the pre-industrial ideal of the paterfamilias, which crystallized into a "master of the house" attitude and elevated the entrepreneur to the head of the "works family".[415]

Women as entrepreneurs were an exception during the 19th century. The companies they started were generally small and focused on the production of household goods or toys. At the turn of the century, Margarete Steiff, the daughter of a lower middle-class master builder from the south-western town of Giengen, succeeded in creating a global toy brand. Disabled since her youth, Steiff was a creative tailor who used highly inventive niche and advertising strategies to sell toys. During the developmental phase of her company, she established a management style characterized by discipline and a duty of care for her primarily female workforce. With similarly innovative product ideas, Käthe Kruse and Melitta Benz became highly successful entrepreneurs—and yet, typically for the times, they handed the reins of their companies to men in successor generations.[416] A focus on the guiding principles of the middle-class family played a major role here as well. Women were supposed to be in charge of the domestic sphere.

Photo 20: A view of the Krupp monument against the backdrop of the Krupp plant in Essen (1928)

This analogy with familial roles was deeply rooted in the socialization patterns of everyone concerned and was familiar to every employee from the lowliest worker through to the most senior manager. Family culture helped shape the forms of management and labor relations. From this the paternalistic corporate culture derived collective purpose, trust and control. For instance, in a speech to his employees in 1872, Alfred Krupp asserted "I will be and remain master in my house, as on my property".[417] Gustav Selve, the owner of one of the largest German metalware factories Basse & Selve (Altena), placed his credo "Loyalty begets loyalty" in big letters above the entrance to his office where all his employees could clearly see it.[418] At the height of family capitalism, four elements characterized paternalistic labor relations and a patriarchal business style:

First, an autocratic leadership style. Following the seniority principle, all decision-making powers led upwards through the hierarchy to the company manager.[419] Economically, this form of organization was legitimized by ownership, management and responsibility all resting in the hands of the company's owners. Culturally, this organizational philosophy coincided with the customary role models of an emerging middle class that had internalized the authoritarian and work ethic of Protestantism.[420] The link between a patriarchal style of management and social paternalism was the original and most lasting characteristic of family-based corporate cultures.

There are many descriptions of autocratic leaders on both sides of the Atlantic, from the industrial revolution well into the 20th century. For instance, John Henry Patterson (1844–1922) was notorious for his authoritarian style. The founder of the National Cash Register factory (NCR), which is now considered the oldest IT company and which was owned and managed by four generations of his family right up until 1986, did not tolerate any dissent and was quick to fire workers or managers who did not follow instructions.[421] This behavior was similar to that of many German factory founders such as Alfred Krupp, Friedrich Karl Henkel and Robert Bosch.[422] They shared the then commonly held belief that paternalistic leadership was the best way of maintaining order in the growing industrial conglomerates. However, this leadership style was by no means solely confined to firms that—as was later to emerge—remained in family control for a long time. It could also be found among the managers of large stock corporations. Walther Rathenau, son of AEG's founder as well as a director and member of the supervisory board for many subsidiaries of the electrical company, considered paternalistic autocratic leadership to be the best form of management as it "does not jeopardize business, ensures control, holds workers in check, and gives prosperous citizens their due".[423] A specifically German variety of this self-image was to differentiate the patriarchal hierarchy along the same lines as ranks in the civil service or the military. For example, at the family businesses of Krupp, Freudenberg and Siemens, salaried employees entrusted with managerial and administrative tasks were referred to as officials ("Beamter" or "Privatbeamter") until well into the 20th century, and were usually guaranteed regular promotions and a job for life. Company owners provided safe salaries and welfare services and expected loyalty from their employees in return.[424] Such hierarchical structures that imitated government ranks were unknown in the United States.[425] Here the social order was already giving rise to cultural differences that were to diverge even further over the course of the modern era.

Second, this form of sociopaternalistic welfare provision formed a key element of the corporate culture. In 19th century middle-class circles, providing for the moral and social well-being of employees, their upbringing and education was considered to be one of the principal duties of the paternal factory owner.[426] However, welfare was always a means of instilling discipline as well. It was to be used to counter fluctuations in the workforce, opportunistic slowdowns in production or—in the worst case—trade union "machinations". At the same time, it served to provide motivational and loyalty incentives, which saved on management, control and implementation costs.[427] Family entrepreneurs admittedly never had a monopoly over incorporated companies with respect to corporate social policy. Nonetheless, as they were strengthened by a values-based family logic, their commitment was more idealistic and the emotional ties went deeper. However, it is not easy to draw a clear line here in relation to the legal and country-specific organizational forms of companies. Detailed studies on the genesis of corporate social policy show that even the "family businesses developing into entrepreneurial enterprises with strong management [...] usually preserved their patriarchal-authoritarian style of social commitment into the 20th century".[428]
In the United States, autocratic NCR founder Patterson was one of the pioneers of occupational health and welfare institutions. In 1890 he built the first "daylight factories" with ceiling-high windows and ventilation systems for his plants. A health fanatic himself, he devoted a large part of his fortune to creating better working conditions for his workforce. At the same time he began to build parks and theatres for the education and recreation of NCR employees and their families.[429] By the end of the 19th century, an extensive catalogue of corporate social policy measures had evolved from the early family entrepreneurial cultures on both sides of the Atlantic. The spectrum ranged from more equitable arrangements for weekly payment of wages instead of monthly, to company sickness, pension and disability insurance schemes, improvements to occupational safety, right through to com-

pany housing estates.[430] Given the largely precarious nature of work and life for workers at the time, these measures sprung both from economically rational reasons and a sense of social responsibility. On the one hand the morality of bourgeois family culture required companies to improve the daily working conditions of their workforce, while on the other hand they also sought to increase productivity and ensure the loyalty of employees despite (or indeed because of) the increasing institutionalization of union representation. The master-of-the-house viewpoint led to the widespread conviction in both German and American companies that for reasons of self-interest, company owners must retain the welfare-providing role for themselves.[431] They saw state intervention and the "machinations" of trade unions as unwarranted interference. One example is the Weinheim leather tannery owner Hermann Ernst Freudenberg, who in 1905 reacted with great incomprehension to the agitation of unions in his company, and consequently started a voluntary supplementary welfare fund to strengthen the paternalistic relationship structures in the company.[432] Like the family business Selve in Germany or shortly thereafter Mars Inc. in the United States, Freudenberg also introduced a "long-service bonus" (Dienstprämie) that provided employees with extra pension and bonus payments depending on how many years they had been with the company in order to "bind them for the future".[433] Family continuity in company management was thus to be reflected in the continuity of the corporate family.[434]

Photo 21: Production room with machinery of the National Cash Register Co. in Dayton, Ohio (1904)

Family culture furthermore meant that patriarchs expressly favored the employment of their factory workers' children in the company as well. Along with individual aptitude, a factor considered in job interviews was the ideal of a community of values, the integrative power of which could be cultivated across generations. "Hire for aptitude and attitude [and] keeping the large band happy"[435]—these principles were formulated as far back as 1880 by the family that owned Cargill-MacMillan. This US agricultural and pharmaceutical concern is currently in the hands of the fifth generation of the family and counts as one of the heavyweights in the sector.

Clearly, then, the elements that shaped labor relations—paternal authority and group welfare—led to a focus on the needs of the family's own business world. This also included segregating the intimate inner family sphere and with it that of the family business. This desire for privacy was considered morally justified as it enabled company management to focus entirely on its business and social responsibilities. Private, personal matters were to be subordinated to the interests of the collective.[436] The desire for anonymity was also reinforced by a reluctance to comply with disclosure obligations and an interest in protecting company secrets—a concern that was vital not only during the early years of the modern industrial era. The glue binding this special form of business undertaking was a strongly emotional replication of the ties that existed as integrative mechanisms both at the heart of business families and in the extended context of the workforce family.[437]

Third, the co-evolution of family and company was thus based on a wide range of symbolic instruments that used emotionality to create a sense of community within the inner family collective of the owners and within the extended "works family". The hidden matrix of corporate culture was formed by "group-bound values and norms, mindsets and attitudes that first arose from the interaction of people with the internal and external corporate world, second influenced the perceptions and actions of the workforce, third existed in symbolic form, and fourth were handed down as company traditions".[438]

A typical characteristic of family cultures is that they feature strong historical references to the founding phase of the company's history. In existing family businesses these are references to traditions, the legacy of the generations, and the entrenched canon of values that lend this form of organization legitimacy and stability. Even in long since manager-led stock corporations of a certain age with a family-ownership background, traces of the family are often still to be found in the company's DNA. Regardless of national contexts or their current legal form, historicity is thus the factor that reveals common roots in the social model of the family.

One characteristic of the human resource strategies of family businesses was and is that they are underpinned by non-material practices that lend them meaning. Centre stage is usually reserved for the firm's founder, whose entrepreneurial and moral example sets the tone for enduringly influential values. These traditional historical role models serve as a point of orientation and motivation for the continuance of the company project and are directed both at the family heirs and at the company community as a whole. Family businesses often have written guidelines or rule booklets as objectified artefacts of a corporate philosophy that has evolved over time. An example from NCR illustrates the close ties between economic and social strategic norms: in this case a booklet was produced on the basis of a handwritten sketch by founder John Patterson. This included instructions for the company's management along with moral rules of behavior for family members and empowerments for staff. Known internally as "the Bible", these guidelines—with few amendments—were handed out to every employee until the 1980s.[439] Mars Inc.'s five principles of management, originally formulated by the first heir Forrest Mars in the 1940s, are distributed in the firm's worldwide subsidiaries in the form of posters or brochures.[440]

By means of such objects the company itself went on to develop its own timeless, larger-than-life personality. It would appear that the few big US corporations still remaining in family hands, such as Walmart, Mars, NCR or Cargill, currently publicize such family history artefacts much more widely and utilize them to promote their image more extensively than is the case in Germany. This phenomenon can hypothetically be explained by the fact that family businesses in the US are subject to much greater pressure to justify their existence in an environment dominated by manager-led firms, which leads them to emphasize their traditional business philosophy. Whitney MacMillan, heir to the Cargill concern, still argued in 1996: "Cargill is proud of its privacy. Its managers contrast the alleged short-termism of America's public companies with the attention their firm pays to job security for its workers."[441] [...] "Deep know-how, institutional memory, leadership continuity, and personal networks are built through long-term employment and by promoting from within. Most corporations lay off people during bad years, destroying social capital. At Cargill, we held on to our employees and concentrated on growing out of our problems."[442] He went on to argue that with its strict family-oriented values, Cargill felt more like a Japanese or German company in a foreign and family-hostile environment.[443]

As more recent studies on German family businesses have shown, the sense of family is often reproduced here in more intimate and informal objects. In her research, Christina Lubinski mentions the role of family graves and the ubiquitous rows of ancestor portraits in the meeting rooms of German family firms.[444] Family trophies and family trees, and in some cases also historic production pieces, artistic posters or jewelry, were often ceremoniously passed on to the next generation at family gatherings so that subsequent generations would carry the legacy forward.[445]

Buildings also serve as places of remembrance. Often they are modest homes where founding families lived before their social advancement, and that now serve as museums or destinations for "pilgrimages" where later generations and employees can experience the heritage of the family. Examples include the "ancestral homes" of the Krupp family in Essen and the Siemens family in Goslar. Similar treatment awaits a company's first business sites, as the example of Walmart shows (Photo 1). Early machinery or products are also venerated as a type of icon. The goal is always to lend a tangible quality to a company's history, to bring it to life and to make it palpable.

Photo 22: Mausoleum of the founder of Mars, Franklin Clarence Mars, and his son Forrest Edward Mars in Minneapolis

The mausoleum, whose roots can be traced to ancient models, is an immense grave that combines the elements of a building and a monument. Mausoleums were originally used for monarchs and other persons of high rank and were intended as reminders of their importance, fulfilling the functions of commemorating and representing the dead and issuing an appeal to posterity. Family mausoleums underscore the unity of a family by providing all its members with a final shared resting place. For these very reasons, many family businesses have elaborate mausoleums to highlight the binding nature of the family tradition.

Rituals, traditions and storytelling also played a very important role as they intensified the family bond over generations. According to company legend, John Henry Patterson demanded that his sons and senior managers assemble every morning for exercises before work, and go for rides on company-owned horses. He saw himself as a "pioneer and conqueror", which is why, like Napoleon, he always rode white horses. In this case the canon of values of the company owner was almost religious in nature.[446] To this day, work meetings are held in private informal settings, and communal sport and health programs for the workforce are part and parcel of NCR's corporate culture. As relics of the past, in practice such attitudes continue to be reproduced and employed every day to preserve the family and work culture.

Among the most common narratives are observations on the personal leadership style of the founders, their industriousness and innovativeness, thriftiness and morality. In both Germany and the United States, descriptions of entrepreneurial family cultures contain virtually identical references to 19th century Protestant middle-class ideals.[447] Irrespective of whether they represent the historical truth or not, what is important is the message they subtly use to appeal to subsequent generations to stand on the shoulders of their forefathers, not only in relation to their business dealings, but also in matters of morality and ethics too. Often a romanticized founder myth and the repeated telling of such stories at family and company celebrations were, and remain, a central element that emotionally underpins the values attached to company ownership.[448] The narratives reproduced the sense of family and assigned individuals the roles traditionally ascribed to them.

The above-mentioned characteristics of family-based corporate cultures can be neatly encompassed by the concept of socioemotional wealth[449] which has become established in the field of business and sociological research into family firms. Added to what we have deduced of its historical genesis, it is evident that the family has influenced business philosophies as follows:

Photo 23: Goblet of the Stollwercks as a symbol of the family and business tradition

First, the identification of the family with the business arises from the need to maximize autonomous control over its wealth and preserve this autonomy in future too. Second, there is a collective group interest in maintaining the longevity of the multigenerational project. An intimate knowledge of the history of the business, free access to information about all company operations, along with personal ties to all objects (factories, original site, products) and subjects (family members, senior managers, workforce) are psychological mechanisms that can generate feelings of affiliation across several generations. Third, the historicity of the object, that is to say the duration of the connection between family, ownership and business, becomes a decisive factor. The longer the family or an individual owner feels associated with the company, the stronger the sense of psychological ownership.[450] Fourth, and closely related to this, the shared business project appears to be socially more valuable when not only past owners, but also the present and future owners develop the feeling that, through work and private sacrifice, they have invested a part of themselves in the company. From a historical-theoretical perspective, the experiences of the founders and predecessors feed into the expectations that future generations will continue the business. Put simply, the step into the future is relatively strongly rooted in the history of the company and the family. In contrast to young manager-led firms, strategic economic decisions are taken on the basis of a broader set of basic principles, rules and world views which have expanded over time. These may represent a burden, but are also an important resource. Fifth and fundamentally however, the symbolic storytelling culture and a living familial memory constitute key hinge points at which the family spirit can develop an awareness of the need to preserve, reproduce and perpetuate traditional family, governance and work cultures.

Photo 24: Workforce photograph at the Robert Mühle company in Glashütte, Saxony (around 1900)

As demonstrated, paternalism forms the original link, deeply ingrained in everyday 19th century bourgeois culture, between the social systems of the family and of the business. The traditional paternal role model predicated the desire for sole decision-making sovereignty, legitimized an autocratic leadership style and tied it to responsibility for the welfare of the extended company family. On both sides of the Atlantic, these family cultures served to compensate for serious legal and structural deficits in the organization of markets. As a consequence, a family orientation was the only plausible way of solving early management problems, handling labor relations, acquiring capital and recruiting successors.[451]

The close relationship between bosses and "their people" was a core element of paternalism. In photo 24, the sons of company founder Robert Mühle can be recognized by the suits they are wearing. Approaching the boss was not a great hurdle. His door might have been always open to his "people". The boss and his employees knew one another well, both at work and privately. The Mühle family, for instance, had lived in the region for centuries. The business they founded in 1869 initially built measuring instruments for watchmakers in Glashütte. With the emergence of automobiles in the 20th century, it specialized in speedometers and rev counters. Even though the company was expropriated twice by East German communists, the 5th generation of the family is still active in the industry, producing wristwatches and nautical instruments.[452]

It comes as no surprise that during industrialization, that is to say when patriarchal corporate cultures were being established, there were more similarities than differences between Germany and the United States. It was only after this period that clear divergences began to emerge and country-specific characteristics became more obvious. The US and Germany experienced political upheavals to very differing degrees. The economic institutions and market systems followed different development paths, and the liberalization and pluralization processes of modern consumer societies took place at different speeds. At the same time, ideas about the family and the paradigms that shaped social and labor relations changed too. Against this backdrop, the corporate culture of family businesses also underwent complex transformation processes and proved to be capable of dynamic change to a greater or lesser degree. In the following section we will determine why and to what extent the marginalization of family businesses in the United States led to the disintegration of family-based corporate culture there, while in Germany family business philosophies proved to be much more resilient to the changes around them.

II. Footholds and Transformation Processes of Family Business Cultures in the 20th Century

Patterns of behavior and the way businesses are organized are pre-formed by institutional and cultural frameworks, which in turn are the result of historical influences. As Colli and Rose put it in a nutshell: "… these influences, by affecting the expectations and attitudes of businessmen, themselves mold the culture of individual firms leading to significant international variations in business behavior. In many ways it is a truism that business organization is the product of economic and social conditions. It means that although the structure of a country's enterprise is partly shaped by the extent and constraints of both product and factor markets, the legal framework, governments, value systems, and attitudes are also critical determinants of business forms and strategies. [...] The institutional environment represents the backdrop against which business behavior must be viewed [...]."[453]

Given that business and family cultures evolve depending on the macrostructures around them, in the course of the "varieties of capitalism" debate, authors from various disciplines have attempted to describe the specific national forms in which company and business cultures developed. Highly influential, although undoubtedly very sketchy, is the model of Alfred D. Chandler, the doyen of comparative business history. He described the transition to "managerial capitalism" as the ideal institutional solution which entrepreneurs in the United States were the first to embrace in response to the challenges of running complex large companies. He contended that the family business was replaced by market-driven financing models and outside managers who would supposedly manage companies more professionally and more effectively.[454] His core thesis is that familial emotionality and informality, as well as the limits to the financial and human resources of individual families once an enterprise had reached a certain size, fundamentally impeded rational management based on professionalism and productivity. He maintained that the need to preserve the close psychological ties between ownership and control, that is to say the need to constantly align the often irrational logic of the family system with the rational requirements of the business system, created unnecessary costs in comparison with the market-based regulation of principle-agent relationships. As recently as 2010, a group of international industrial sociologists offered an opinion on familial governance models: "Joint family and firm optimization, however, may result in substantial costs. The potential inconsistency of family norms with business rationale may lead to epic and emotional rivalries. Families tend to favor equality among members, while productive organizations base rewards on productivity. Hiring based on blood and not on merit considerations hinders efficiency. Needless to say, firing and comforting one's child may be difficult. Furthermore, some of the attractive features of family firms require undisputed family control. As a result, family firms may also be at a disadvantage when financing large projects or at hiring talented employees."[455]

According to Chandler writing in the early 1980s, in Germany companies had only partially distanced themselves from pre-modern forms of family-based business management. As a result, they had embraced modernization only half-heartedly. Thus, the business landscape developed into a hybrid mix. Traditional corporate cultures of "personal capitalism" remained, while cartels, close bank-industry relationships and political networks led to a corporate capitalism in which not only financing models, but also above all work, personal and managerial relationships continued to be shaped in part outside the market.

Focusing more closely on the grey areas of such rigidly typologizing models of capitalism, since the 1990s a whole series of industrial sociologists have examined how the corporate cultures of family businesses have changed over the years against the backdrop of such trends. Common to all is that they assume a differentiation and partial blending of traditional and modern types of culture. Dyer's model appears helpful; this expands the original "paternalistic culture" to include three manifestations, supported by American case studies such as Cargill, Levi Strauss or Teflon. With the "laissez-faire culture", the family continues to see its role as laying down guidelines, but allows executive managers and employees wide-ranging autonomy to pursue the economic and social objectives of the company. He uses the term "participative culture" to describe (more rarely encountered) egalitarian company cultures in which traditional top-down hierarchies are replaced entirely by group and team-based decision-making processes. The family retains ownership, but pulls back to the integrative function of instilling a sense of community. He assigns to the category of "professional culture" family businesses where the owners have hired outside managers to run the company and where family relationships are replaced across the whole field of corporate governance by individualized models of creativity, innovativeness and performance.[456]

Dyer analyzed the development of the corporate cultures of over one hundred US family businesses at the end of the 1980s with reference to these categories. Of interest is his finding that approximately 80 percent of the firms in his sample that had been founded since 1900 continued to adopt a paternalistic company culture during the early years of their existence. Although his sample also included many firms established in the period after 1945, only around ten percent of these displayed a laissez-faire or participative culture during their establishment phase.[457] Only a single company started out with a professional corporate culture from the outset, with the owning family immediately stepping into the background. This confirms that paternalism in the United States continued to be present as the basic form of start-ups well into the last decades of the 20th century.[458]

Two observations of Dyer are insightful for the purposes of identifying the reasons for the divergent developments in Germany and the US. First, in young companies, strong ties are created between the founding family and the business. Second, a decisive factor determining whether patterns of behavior and resources are carried over from the social system of the family to the business organization is whether this connection is maintained beyond the lifetime of the founder and across generational changeovers. There are clear differences between US and German firms in relation to persistence. For instance, in the US three-quarters of all companies studied by Dyer switched to a professional culture and threw off their personal familial roots almost entirely within two subsequent generations.[459]

As shown in Chapter B, at around only twenty percent, the proportion of German family businesses that switched to professional, manager-led control was substantially lower. Thus the founders of start-ups in the US created their companies more often with no intention of establishing multigenerational family businesses, but as short or medium-term investment projects that were to be sold on as soon as possible whenever the market was favorable. This trend emerged significantly earlier in the US in the 1920s, and only increasingly began trickling across to Europe since the 1990s. During the second globalization phase and under the impact of tertiarization and digitalization, these non-simultaneous historical trends were followed by an increasing convergence of founders' mindsets. For the traditional type of family business aimed at multigenerational continuity, this transformation became a problem. The appeal of founding a business, earning a quick fortune, and then moving on creates competition for potential managers and successors. After all, an organically growing company might be seen as less attractive than a glamorous start-up.

Where family businesses underwent the transition to a professional corporate culture, the family culture lost its significance as an agent for giving purpose to the collective and coordinating its economic activity. In particular, its internal impact on management principles, personnel and labor relations lessened. Where still present, from the middle of the 20th century family culture had increasingly begun to assume a more passive role in many US firms and was used primarily for externally directed marketing and image-enhancing purposes.[460] By contrast, in the majority of German companies the family culture became established as an enduringly active steering mechanism even up to the threshold of the post-modern era—by which time this was the case in only a minority of US companies.

The attempt to compare national patterns of development of corporate cultures and examine divergences and convergences must be seen from a historical perspective. In particular, the embedding of company models in their respective political, social and cultural environments resulted in very different historical dynamics. Three factors were essential for the differing degrees of importance attached to family-based corporate cultures in the two countries in the 20th century: first the duration and depth of historical embedding and the degree of cultural acceptance of the family business model, and second its situative adaptability or resilience to economic and societal change. A further consideration is the specific impact of national models for organizing business enterprises. Here the study adapts the concept of institutional isomorphism as found in modern organizational research,[461] which states that, on closer examination, companies tend to imitate organizational forms that are seen as having fitted very well in the past with the institutional frameworks of the respective legal, economic and social systems. This mimetic pull effect may provide a plausible explanation as to how and why family businesses tended to be sidelined in the prevailing system of managerial capitalism in the US, whereas they flourished more widely in Germany.

1.   Family Collective versus Individualism. The Historical Foundations of the Entrepreneurial Family Spirit

The first point of differentiation is the impact of enduring traditions that facilitated the perpetuation of family businesses in Germany. The ties between family and company were more deep-rooted here. Family-based structures already present in pre-modern craft, industry and mercantile organizations were carried across to industrial and service companies in the modern era. One example is the guild system: the centuries-old practice of passing on craft trades by sons taking over as master craftsmen on the death of their fathers strengthened the acceptance of family-based forms of business and led to a deep-seated preference for the intergenerational transmission of wealth, knowledge and skills.[462] This traditional guild system of training gradually evolved into organized industrial apprenticeships. The patronage relationships between apprentices and masters persisted and laid the foundations for the paternalistic form of labor relations to be found everywhere from small businesses to the emerging large industrial enterprises.[463] At the same time, the traditional European concept of a household, which was understood not solely as a biological but also as a socioeconomic collective, strengthened the notion of a "works family" based on authority and responsibility for the welfare of workers.

There were no such deep cultural precursors to family entrepreneurship in the United States. There were also no models of aristocratic or feudal economies where at least the rules of succession and the symbols and customs used to perpetuate family ties could rub off on the mercantile middle classes.[464] Society in the US was much more strongly focused on individualistic role models. Becoming an entrepreneurial pioneer garnered greater respect than taking over a father's farm or factory. The ideal of personal advancement through hard work acted to hinder or lessen interest in multigenerational business projects—a sociocultural pathway also manifest in the much more open trial-and-error mentality of American start-up projects.[465] Likewise, business failures and opportunities to rapidly switch careers in the US fitted much more naturally with an entrepreneurial biography, as cultural historian Scott Sandage so pertinently pointed out a few years ago.[466]

Even when business projects resulted in bankruptcy, those involved were not stigmatized. This economic culture of "failure and forgiveness"[467] found expression in the unique insolvency law of the United States. As forerunner legislation in individual federal states had already done since the middle of the 19th century, the first federal bankruptcy law of 1898 specified that the foremost objective was to restructure the company, not determine guilt or legally wind up the remaining assets for the benefit of creditors. In contrast to all European countries, a highly debtor-friendly approach to handling failure evolved in the US. In France, Germany and Great Britain there were strict legal sanctions if company managers did not promptly report insolvency. In the event of bankruptcy, trustees were appointed and companies were taken under the strict supervision of the courts. In the case of negligence or omission, salaried managers could also be held fully liable for any financial losses to creditors. This was traditionally not the case in the United States. Bankrupts were not to be pushed into admitting insolvency by the threat of severe punishments, but rather were to be encouraged by lenient liability provisions and allowed a great deal of latitude to actively manage the crisis or pursue a fresh start. With the Chandler Act of 1938 and the Bankruptcy Code of

1978, US legislators created the famous "Chapter 11" bankruptcy procedure which offered company heads the opportunity to remain at the helm while they reorganized the company and restructured the debt themselves.[468] The most important argument in favor of the US system is that it enables entrepreneurs to make a fresh start and encourages a greater willingness to take risks.[469] Thus the possibility of failure was neither socially, politically or legally proscribed, but was seen as the natural consequence of market exigencies.

In Germany, on the other hand, for many years breaks or gaps in an entrepreneurial biography were socially sanctioned as failures, as they resulted in almost the complete loss of one's professional and social reputation.[470] The "second chance", which in America was extended to everyone who strove for success and showed a willingness to work hard and take on personal risk, was rarely granted in Germany.[471]

In view of this significantly higher risk, there were far fewer incentives for heirs to family businesses to stray off the familial beaten track. Innovation and creativity tended to be harnessed within the company for expansion into new business areas or optimization of processes or organizational aspects, rather than considered an individual opportunity to break out. Then, too, in the event of failure, insolvency law could result equally for both incorporated and unincorporated firms in severe personal consequences, state intervention and a strict creditor-oriented repayment of debt. In Germany, the imperial bankruptcy code (Reichskonkursordnung) of 1877 continued to apply unchanged for over 120 years until 1999. A company head who demonstrably acted improperly faced not only criminal prosecution but also civil proceedings that could result in his or her personal liability for a period of 30 years. Even those who had incorporated their own start-ups were only partially better off, because if they were convicted in insolvency proceedings they would face the prospect of a de facto exclusion from employment for up to five years[472]—likewise a poor incentive for the more risky path of striking out on one's own. It is only since the new millennium that the legal systems have converged in this area by attempting to create a new balance between the interests of debtors and creditors.[473]

Private insolvency of the type relevant to small businesses—that is, a way of freeing oneself of debt that offers the possibility of a fresh start—has only been available in Germany for about twenty years, whereas it has been an option in the United States since the early 19th century and was standardized across all states by the 1898 Bankruptcy Act.[474] There is hardly any other country in the developed world that has such a high a number of insolvencies as the United States.[475] Over 200,000 cases a year were recorded as early as the end of the 1960s. Between 1945 and 1970 the debt-income ratio, that is to say the level of personal debt as a percentage of income, saw a massive increase from 14 percent to over 50 percent.[476] In American society, debt-freeing private insolvencies became increasingly routine, and are currently used by over a million people in some years. In Germany they were not possible at all prior to 2000. Although the figures are rising, they are still relatively rare compared with the US, and bankruptcy remains tainted with the stigma of enduring personal failure. The story the figures (Table 25) tell is clear. In the United States the number of people affected by private insolvencies is far higher than in Germany, both in terms of absolute figures and as a percentage of the population. Here, too, a certain convergence trend is once more evident, while clear divergences remain.

Table 25: Private insolvencies in the US and Germany, 1990–2015 (absolute and percentage of population)

Year	US absolute	FRG absolute	US as percentage of population	FRG as percentage of population
1990	718,107	0	0.3%	–
1995	874,642	0	0.3%	–
2000	1,217,972	14,024	0.4%	0.02%
2005	2,039,214	99,711	0.7%	0.1%
2010	1,536,799	139,110	0.5%	0.2%
2015	819,760	107,919	0.3%	0.1%

Source: American Bankruptcy Institute, Annual Business; Statistisches Bundesamt, Insolvency Statistics.

It can clearly be seen here that differences in mentality and business cultures influenced the behavior of family entrepreneurs. The same was also true of societal trends. For instance, there were often significant differences in relation to the institutions underpinning the stability of family businesses. Family businesses experienced existential problems not only as a result of succession crises, but also due to internal family conflicts, especially divorces, which often go hand in hand with legal disputes and the fragmentation of wealth. It is difficult for fractured and disintegrating families to keep a business intact in the long term. Although no statistics can be recorded for internal family constellations, well-documented divorce frequency figures can serve as an indicator of the average durability of families in the two countries.

Figure 14 shows that for a long time divorce rates were much higher in the US than in Germany. The division of family assets that often accompanies divorce can weaken a family business, and in extreme cases can result in it being carved up, sold or even liquidated.[477]

Less stable families have less stable companies. Despite the sharp decline in divorces since 1980, the US had one of the highest divorce rates in the Western world at the end of the 20th century. The decrease in divorces was presumably due to people choosing to marry later, the general acceptance of cohabitation without marriage, and the increasing number of singles. In Germany, the number of divorces, which started from a lower base, continued to rise, narrowing the previously clear gap between it and the US. Since the late 1990s, as with so many other areas examined in this study, a significant convergence trend is evident.

Figure 14: Divorce rates in the US and the German Empire/Federal Republic of Germany, 1870–2014 (per 1,000 residents)

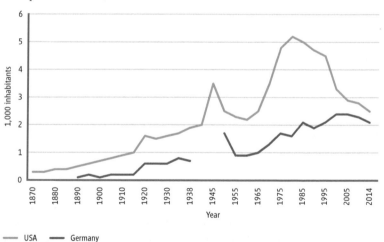

The figures from 1950-1985 include only the former West Germany.

Sources: Statistisches Bundesamt (ed.), Ehescheidungen im Zeitverlauf, https://www.destatis.de/DE/ZahlenFakten/ GesellschaftStaat/Bevoelkerung/Ehescheidungen/; Besser, Christoph, Grunddaten der Bevölkerungsstatistik Deutschlands von 1871 bis 1939, https://histat.gesis.org/histat/table/details/98A1BFDCBF8E69DAC7F4CFC5EBED536F; US Census Bureau, Population Estimates, http://www.census.gov/popest/estimates.html (accessed: November 20, 2018); 144 Years of Marriage and Divorce in the United States, in: Washington Post, June 23, 2015.

It remains the case, however, that marriages were clearly less stable in the US than in Germany over a long period of time, thus it is reasonable to assume that the chances of a multigenerational family business surviving in the US were therefore significantly worse.

2.   Emancipation versus Continuity. The Dynamics of Social
      Liberalization and their Impact on Family and Work Cultures

The second and less historically distant cause of transatlantic divergences is the different times at which social liberalization trends emerged in the course of the 20th century. The liberal and individualistic values that are now considered typical of Western societies became established in the US several decades ahead of Germany. This can be inferred from the earlier establishment and general acceptance of a democratic system of government, and also from the fact that the US had already taken the leap forward to a modern mass consumer society in the 1920s. Following the enormous economic growth in the "roaring twenties", American citizens witnessed a very rapid transformation of their everyday worlds. Different lifestyles proliferated based on increasingly complex consumer desires. With the economic and social rise of a broadly-based middle class, the rigid differences in status evident at first glance that were associated with traditional class-bound societies tended to fall away. Class barriers now appeared to be surmountable with the aid of ostentative consumption and freely available credit. The relative importance of leisure and consumption over work greatly increased. Life goals such as self-fulfillment, recognition and participation became more important.[478]

This shift in values was reflected in changed social relationships within companies. Both in theory and in practice, by the end of the 1940s at the latest, novel industrial sociological human relations concepts had become common which set out to improve working conditions, particularly those influenced by Ford-style mass production methods in the United States, and involve employees more closely in decision-making processes.[479] These views infiltrated companies from society in the form of young, well-educated employees who increasingly rejected rigid hierarchies, calling instead for greater team orientation and a stronger voice in management. Specifically with respect to US family businesses, Dyer argues that traditional paternalistic corporate cultures increasingly found themselves on the defensive in this regard. As a result, numerous companies disassociated themselves from their traditional models entirely, or enlarged or adjusted their family cultures to en-compass participative business philosophies.[480]

Photo 25: The allure of the new consumer society—a Dupont employee demonstrates the abilities of plastic in 1949.

One example of such a hybrid corporate culture was the Mars Corporation. Forrest Mars, the son of the founder, continued the authoritarian leadership principles of his father, but at the end of the 1950s he also established flat hierarchies at the employee level alongside strong feedback and job enrichment mechanisms.[481] Since then the company has not differentiated between administrative and production employees in pay and social insurance matters. The way his own office was furnished mirrored exactly that of the newly introduced open-plan offices in which ordinary staff and managers now sat together. The message was that neither the boss nor the managers were to be granted material privileges. This model was celebrated by the business press in the 1960s as "cozy and paternalistic corporate culture".[482] At least as a phenotype, parallels can be seen here to many modern start-ups in the technology and service sectors which, like Mark Zuckerberg at Facebook, effectively re-enact this style of leadership for the wider public.

Yet this early and enduring social liberalization did not just affect labor relations and company social constitutions, it also made it more difficult to retain ownership and control functions within the inner circles of business-owning families. In the US, the traditional models of the family eroded much earlier than in Germany, which gave greater impetus to the emancipation endeavors of potential successors. The breakout forces exerted by the consumer and multi-option society made it much more difficult and costly for US family businesses to maintain the emotional ties between family and company. There was a rising tendency of successors to take capital out of the company in order to pursue their own life projects within and outside business—especially as the financial markets lured heirs, and even founders, with the prospect of making high financial gains on selling, and the booming stock market offered lucrative alternatives for financing the business.

German companies were faced with similar challenges. However, these transformation processes took place around three decades later when, from the late 1960s onwards, German postwar society started down the road to mass consumerism and—as Jürgen Habermas put it—its social and political "fundamental liberalization"[483]. During the years of the "economic miracle", the traditional models of family-based corporate cultures had initially become re-established. The historically discontemporaneous nature of the transformation processes in the social environment was a key factor in making family business cultures more lasting and consequently more resilient to external drivers of change.

3.   The Phenomenon of the Second Founding. The Restoration
     of Family Business Cultures in Postwar Germany

A third and closely related differentiating aspect is that the family culture in
Germany experienced a cultural and economic renaissance during the National-Socialist era, but especially also in the immediate postwar period. Cohesion was greatly strengthened in and around business-owing families when
the country was faced with the challenges of dealing with the massive political, social and economic upheavals of the demise of the Nazi dictatorship.

In contrast to the United States, where the connections between family,
work and company were tending to become weaker, the collective experiences of war and shortages, insecurity and austerity resulted in a strengthening of the social-conservative model of the family across the German society
as a whole.[484] In order to survive and shoulder the work of rebuilding the
country, the daily lives of workers, salaried employees and entrepreneurial
families were all oriented toward the family as a safe space and community
of economic solidarity. Strengthening the ideal of the family reflected the
desire for bonds of commitment and closeness, and this was carried across
from the social sphere to the business world. As a result, family businesses
became anchors of stability that stood for continuity and dependability in
uncertain times.

The upheavals had strengthened the identification of the owner families
with their businesses, and lent greater weight to the importance of protecting and preserving their inheritance, leading to a stabilization of the family
concept as a model for managing a company. The fear of losing the hard-
won gains of previous generations provided a strong motivation to get family firms up and running again. Against this backdrop, an emotional renewal
of a sense of duty among family members to carry on the multigenerational
project became evident. This applied in particular to cases where companies
had been lost as a result of flight and expropriation in the former territories
of eastern and central Germany and their owners had started afresh in West
Germany. Such families had been forced to leave all their non-monetary assets, machinery and property behind, but they had the know-how, customer
contacts and above all the unbending drive to continue the family business
tradition. This model enjoyed a wide appeal, so much so that former workers
literally moved with the company to start afresh at a new location. Ten thousand of these "refugee companies" injected a significant amount of growth
into the West German economy after 1945. A prime example of this is Otto-

bock, the current world-market leader in orthopedic technology. When the family lost all its private wealth in Königsee (Thuringia) following expropriation in 1948, its members fled to Duderstadt in Lower Saxony and began again from scratch. Product knowledge and ties to employees and customers were their most important capital for this fresh start.

It is a singular aspect of German family business history that reconstruction by the owners following the Second World War represented a kind of second founding, literally for refugee companies, and symbolically and psychologically for existing West German companies. The political and economic crises in the first half of the 20th century led to a revitalization of family business cultures, focused as they were primarily on security and stability. Examples are Werner Bahlsen, Hans Riegel jun. or Reinhold Würth, who were all the second or third generation to manage their companies in the 1950s. These entrepreneurs of the "economic miracle" years saw it as their life's work to lead the family firms out of the turmoil of war into a successful future. In doing so, they developed an intensive personal identification with their work analogous to the processes that had engendered a spirit of purpose for the founder generation. One manifestation of this was also the fact that family entrepreneurs who had taken over around the middle of the 20th century usually held on to the reins for a very long time and kept their companies as independent as possible.[485]

The fates of many family businesses in East Germany were also quite remarkable in this context.[486] Until 1972, around 11,000 private companies employing over 50,000 people existed in the German Democratic Republic under the constant threat of nationalization by the socialist government. The families that owned them carried out vital reconstruction work during the postwar years, usually making rare high-quality and niche products. In total they accounted for an impressive 15 percent of the GDR's industrial production before they were suddenly nationalized after Honecker came to power in 1971. Despite this massive political intervention, many family entrepreneurs tried not to lose the connection to and control of their companies, for example Pommer Spezialbetonbau (Leipzig), Julius Blüthner Pianofortefabrik (Leipzig), Robert Mühle (Glashütte) or Auhagen Modellbahnzubehör GmbH (Marienberg). The former owners lost their property rights but stayed on as employees, and in some cases even remained in charge as works managers. The particular circumstances of the immediate postwar years and the renewed threat to the companies under socialism strengthened family cohesion and motivated even the children to continue to identify with "their" company. Following the collapse of the GDR, family ownership of the afore-mentioned companies was restored, and they exist to this day, now under the management of the fourth or fifth generation. This phenomenon perfectly illustrates how resilient the family connection proved to be in the face of the most serious political turbulence, and how these upheavals in German history also led to the strengthening of family entrepreneurship.[487] It is an irony of history that the massive attacks on private ownership ultimately contributed to its invigoration.

In the United States, due to the political continuity and the absence of wars conducted on the American continent, there were no such "unintended consequences". There, with a largely stable political and economic backdrop, the market-based governance models of managerial capitalism continued their victory march, while in Germany family business cultures witnessed a revival.

Analogously to the way in which the German economy had harnessed the family social system to compensate for the structural deficits of the market in the 19th century, during the political and economic crises of the 20th century it fell back on the formative power of traditional leadership models. Seen from a macroperspective, therefore, in the German economy the principles of family-based management underwent a second anchoring phase during the postwar era which the US did not experience in this form.

Family businesses also benefited from the fact that Germany's strongly family-based society initially still supported the acceptance of patriarchal corporate cultures. During the economic boom of the 1950s and 1960s very few in the successor generation of owner families sought to emancipate themselves from the family and its business. The recollection of shared values strengthened the integrative power of entrepreneurial families. If reconstruction required the help of the next generation, then its members subordinated themselves to the higher goals of the collective, even if this meant giving up their own career plans.[488] As Mark Spoerer notes in the case of C&A for example, entrepreneurial families intensified their use of symbols and customs in the 1950s in order to revitalize family principles and their strongly conservative-religious orientation against a backdrop of insecurity caused by societal collapse.[489] The Braun family in Melsungen started to pass on shareholdings to the next generation when they were still young children so they would develop a sense of custodianship for the family legacy.[490] In only a few companies, such as Bosch for example, did succession issues lead to complex internecine power struggles.[491] Generally speaking, the patterns of hierarchical seniority-based management were fortified and accompanied by a great willingness on the part of the extended owner families to patiently leave their capital tied up in the company to aid reconstruction. The marked statistical decline in incorporations in the two decades following the Second World War (Chapter D) underlines the revival of family influence in the German economy.

Nevertheless, there were not merely emotional, but also solid rational economic reasons for a reconnection of families with entrepreneurial activities. Under the drive for deconcentration during the period of allied occupation, many large family-owned enterprises were faced with the prospect of being broken up. Keeping companies in the hands of families, even converting them back into unincorporated firms as in the case of Krupp for example, was one feasible way of avoiding demergers in accordance with US anti-cartel laws.[492] In the postwar era, emphasizing the highly personal style of management characteristic of family businesses was also an important way to gain the trust of potential business partners through informal networks and private contacts. In view of the ongoing liability and legal uncertainties, as well as a largely stagnant capital market, the personal reputation of the family entrepreneur offered dependability. In particular, often longstanding contacts with the firm's local bank could be reactivated in order to obtain loans to repair factories and resume production. Analogous to the cooperative economic model that had emerged in Germany during the interwar years, family firms proved to be business undertakings that were very compatible with the economic, political and social conditions prevalent during reconstruction.[493]

With regard to labor relations, too, lines of economic and cultural development that originated in the German Empire and the Weimar Republic continued. Starting from the paternalistic ideal of the works family, particularly in the *Mittelstand*, the corporatist notion of the works community had become established. It was founded on the idea that labor relations in a company should not be conducted solely on the basis of market mechanisms and formal contracts, but should also be built on "cooperation based on mutual respect and recognition"[494] between employers and employees. The *Mittelstand*—and with it specifically the organizational form of family business—appeared to be the ideal nucleus for anchoring cooperative interest groups moderated by industrial associations, trade unions and the state.[495] The concept of the social partnership (Sozialpartnerschaft), which was warped during the National-Socialist era under the banner of a factory community ("Betriebsgemeinschaft") into an ideological industrial relations straitjacket, was revived again after 1945. The image of the works family was again linked to the paternalistic-authoritarian roots of an entrepreneurial self-concept based on values of welfare and loyalty. As companies were now widely perceived as communities of destiny and solidarity for the shared new beginning, the emotional ties between the entrepreneur and the workforce intensified. The family orientation of society, the idea of social partnership (Sozialpartnerschaft), and also the mindset of obedience and camaraderie cultivated during the period of dictatorship and war, made the patriarchal corporate culture in postwar Germany into a highly socially compatible and plausible form of management. In complete contrast to the United States, the governance models based specifically on the social system of the family acquired a new legitimacy, proving to be a very good fit for the conditions prevalent in the immediate postwar decades.

From the point of view of the individualistic US, this must have seemed very anachronistic indeed. In 1951 a young American PhD student by the name of David Landes, who went on to become one of the most prominent American economic historians, described the distinct difference between American and European corporate cultures with respectful astonishment. In his travel report, he highlighted the strong influence of the traditional family business on the central European model of capitalism. The family business seemed to him to be "solid as a rock" in an uncertain, turbulent world. Landes stressed the characteristic positive labor relations and personal style of management. These qualities ensured that the US orientation he was familiar with—namely, hard, rational market mechanisms—was tempered by the soft factors of reputation and a willingness to cooperate. "Run like a household"[496], family businesses here were focused on maximum independence. They were therefore relatively risk-averse and less driven by growth and profit. At the same time, Landes highlighted particular features of the production system: it was characterized by a greater production depth and quality-oriented specialization analogous to the European tradition of craftsmen and skilled workers. As he summarized his observations, "the ideal of quality is almost a fetish"[497]. He believed this was one of the key reasons why the market was not so fiercely competitive. In Germany the focus was not so much on mass production and cut-throat price competition, but first and foremost on differentiation and innovative products, product segmentation and high-quality manufacturing.[498]

4. Quantity or Quality? How Divergent Production Systems Shaped Corporate Culture

This observation reveals a fourth influencing factor: historic links can be traced between the divergent forms of production systems and the national characteristics of corporate governance models. The starting point for this is the simple observation that the size of the domestic market was significantly different in the US and Germany. Unlike many American companies that concentrated on serving the large domestic market until the end of the 20th century, German companies went down the export route very early on. As a consequence, they focused on high-value products and specialized technical investment goods.

This is exemplified by the strong representation of technical industries such as engineering, chemical equipment and machine tools, electrotechnology, or metal and materials processing in the SME segment. It has meanwhile been established that these industries still feature the highest density of family businesses in Germany today.[499] By contrast, the services sector dominates in the United States. 71 percent of family businesses are involved in consumer products and retail, while 15 percent are active in media and entertainment, and eleven percent operate in the real estate, hospitality and construction sector.[500]

The focus on quality enabled German export-oriented family businesses to be flexible and highly specialized, sometimes carving out technological niches for themselves. While mega-corporations rose up in the US, where the focus was—not uncoincidentally—on mass production along the lines of Fordism developed during the 1920s, the business landscape in Germany tended to be dominated by smaller entities and specialization strategies.

The focus on quality correlates with a certain tradition of corporate social relations. The training and qualifications of skilled workers and their long-term loyalty to the company was accorded much more importance in Germany than in the United States. Here, too, the enduring allegiance to a particular location can be attributed to efforts to secure the company's own pool of qualified know-how and resources built up through in-house training. In this context, the ideal of high-quality production logically resulted in many small and medium-sized German companies developing a keener sensibility for employer/employee relations and the integrative power of paternalistic family cultures.

By way of example, the 1914 travel impressions of the family entrepreneur Hermann Ernst Freudenberg express a German counterview of the inner workings of the growing American mega-corporations. On visiting the Ford plants in Dearborn, Freudenberg commented with a great deal of skepticism and moral incomprehension: "The whole organization is both amazing and unique, and the worker is degraded absolutely to a machine. In return he receives at least five dollars a day, and if he cannot keep up with the work, a bell is rung. Despite the generous wages, the people do not seem uplifted or happy [...]. This is going too far, a man is not a machine [...], his personality suffers, and all the more so as the factory does not concern itself with his private life."[501]

Fordism, and with it the purely structural rational factory models rigorously driven by keeping down costs and optimizing output, did not become widespread in Germany until well after the Second World War, but once it did become established it was with a corporatist paternalistic slant.[502] Typical of this combination of modernizing and traditional elements among models of company management is the example of the family entrepreneur Hans Bahlsen, a trained engineer from Hanover. In the 1950s, he wrote many internal documents on labor relations that included modern human relations concepts he had picked up from a management course at Harvard Business School in 1954. According to Bahlsen, it was important to create a positive environment at work by including workers more, encouraging their creativity, and allowing them greater latitude. However, his work also reproduced the ideals of the works community (Werksgemeinschaft) and showed the deep-seated attachment of the German company to traditional family role models. According to Bahlsen, workers should "feel like followers who have a bond with and are responsible to their benevolent company leader ['Betriebsführer']".[503] This once more demonstrates that the 1950s and 1960s in Germany can be understood as a reconstruction phase for family-oriented models during which traditional governance practices took deeper root.

At the same time, the focus on quality also influenced succession practices in family businesses. According to figures produced by the Deutsches Industrieinstitut in 1956, around three-quarters of all chief executives and managing partners of German companies had obtained their qualifications through the traditional route of vocational in-house training. In family businesses in particular, one model was dominant: the designated successors received technical or business training in the family firm or in a company operating in the same sector to which the family had close business or frequently even friendship ties. Following their journeyman years, the young entrepreneurs returned to the family firm to take up their first management roles.[504] The emphasis on the practical side of successors' education reflected the traditional ideals of the family-based apprentice/master training and an obligation to serve the business needs of the family's company. In the early years of the Federal Republic, a small minority of future company heads additionally enjoyed an academic education, predominantly (over 40 percent) resulting in science-based or engineering degrees.[505]

In the United States, by contrast, the academicization and professionalization of the managerial profession had commenced at a much earlier date. As far back as the beginning of the 20th century, colleges and universities, such as Harvard Business School for example, had offered business administration courses specifically designed to offer qualifications for future company leaders. Even the economic and legal university degrees established during the interwar years became a common stepping stone in the career of top managers, thus helping to create a larger pool of individually trained entrepreneurial talent and underpinning the manager cult in the United States. The result was a labor market for company executives that utilized mechanisms for selection and competition rather than family ties.

This, too, illustrates the divergent pathways in the development of the business cultures. In the US, the recruitment of successors on the basis of ancestry and family membership was increasingly perceived as posing a risk to the company's success. It was thought that the suitability of leaders should be tested by the market and demonstrated by external qualifications, with greater weight being attached to administrative rather than technical ones. In Germany on the other hand, practical vocational training remained the rule, and this prolonged the pattern of recruiting from within the family. Kinship ties and informal networks were still primarily used to acquire knowledge resources for the business.[506]

5.   The "1968" of Paternalism. Transformation of Familial Governance
      and Social Constitutions

It was not until the end of the 1960s that these attitudes began to be questioned in Germany. In a widely read study entitled "Der deutsche Unternehmer. Autorität und Organisation", the Münster-based economic sociologist Heinz Hartmann painted a gloomy picture of the future of German entrepreneurship. He criticized the patriarchal authoritarian concepts that had become established both among German SMEs and large industrial enterprises. He accused the generation of "economic miracle entrepreneurs" of hanging on to the reins for too long. Their tenure had been marked by too great an emphasis on security, lack of strategic innovativeness and rigid organizational hierarchies.[507] Following on from the criticism of established management structures, during the 1970s a broader and much more public debate emerged about the technological backwardness that threatened to overtake German *Mittelstand* in comparison with capital-rich US industrial concerns.[508] When in 1975 the Kiel-based economics professor Herbert Giersch presented the caricature of a company owner who had generated high profits during the postwar decades but had not reinvested them, choosing instead to lay them aside as security in order to preserve independence and unfettered decision-making control, he was implicitly attacking German family entrepreneurs.[509]

Even if his provocative thesis was too blatant a generalization, contemporary analyses clearly showed that the environment for family-based entrepreneurial cultures had also begun to change in Germany. The bankruptcy of Herstatt Bank and car manufacturer Borgward, the demise of the Neckermann and Stollwerck companies, and even the Volkswagen crisis, showed that monolithic governance structures inherently carried a high risk of internal rigidity. A documentary series that ran in *manager magazin* from 1971 demonstrated how much the model—praised for providing stability until just a few years prior to that time—had come under fire. It identified authoritarian organizational structures as the primary reason for mismanagement at over sixty family and stock corporations. The accusation was that individual (and often deficient) strategic decisions taken by the "old guard" had undermined the flow of information, the creativity and the synergies of team-based working. As a result, talented managers and up-and-coming entrepreneurs had become increasingly distanced from such traditional business cultures and—as happened at Neckermann, Stollwerck or VW at the end of the 1960s—turned their backs on the company.[510] Such studies indicate that in Germany now too, organizational hierarchies centered on individual people appeared to be becoming increasingly discredited and less accepted than functional company models.

One profound historical explanation of this phenomenon is offered by Christian Kleinschmidt's observation that in parallel with the arrival of pluralistic mass consumer societies, the experiential worlds of German entrepreneurs underwent a radical change as a result of "the managers' 1968".[511] The now strong admiration for American human relations concepts led to the old models of personnel management being questioned by a self-confident young generation of managers and employees. And as the economic reconstruction process came to an end, the prolonged acceptance of paternalistic organizational principles also waned. New challenges emerged, not solely but especially for family businesses that had been built on the broad foundations of traditional company cultures. Potential areas of conflict also arose as societal liberalization processes began to gain traction in companies too.

When comparing German and American corporate cultures during the last third of the 20th century, the central point remains that the trends were marked by new convergences, but lasting divergences also remained. The cultural identities of family businesses remained bound to their national pathways. Although a certain amount of blending took place as a result of transnational transfer and transformation processes, ultimately the oft-debated "Americanization" of German governance and social constitutions did not materialize.[512] The family influence in German companies proved to be more deeply ingrained and more resilient to the temptations of market-oriented organizational models.

If we first examine the internal cohesion of entrepreneurial families, it can be seen that since the 1960s German companies experienced an erosion of traditional family models such as their US counterparts had done several decades earlier. This gave rise to two issues: first the society-wide trend towards individualization made it more difficult to tie successors down to serving the needs of the company. Second, if they did decide to stay in the family firm, the young successor generation also made a determined push for faster participation at the managerial level. Strong resistance to seniority and authority principles began to emerge within the family. Decision-making at the shareholder level became more complicated. Whereas in the past the proposals of the paterfamilias had unanimously been passed on the nod at gatherings of co-owning family members, there were now often heated discussions or even showdown votes.

In response to this dynamic of disintegration, German and American family businesses now invested a lot of effort in harnessing symbolic rituals to strengthen the emotional ties of the family members. When looking back on the 1980s, Pamela Mars-Wright, the current owner of the Mars Corporation, commented that her company had once been at risk of losing its family foundations. Ever wider gulfs had formed within the family and in its relationships with employees. She maintained that, as a means of saving the traditional company so to speak, she had reminded everyone of the Five Principles that her father had formulated in the 1960s. According to her, when it seemed that the company was about to fall apart, it was evident "that we weren't living the Five Principles. We weren't the company we thought. We weren't the company we thought our Associates thought we were. So, there were these five words [Quality, Responsibility, Mutuality, Efficiency and Freedom] up on a wall. Everybody could repeat them. Anybody can repeat five words. It's not that complicated, but we weren't living them. So we decided to go back to the Five Principles and to really focus on them."[513] To renew the emotional bonds between the family and the company, all 13 heirs agreed to sign a booklet setting out the shared principles to be followed by all employees.[514]

The family business of Bagel offers a similar example from the German context. Its chief executive Peter Bagel used the occasion of the company's 175th anniversary in 1976 to make an emotional speech in which he told the still very young next-generation family members personal stories from the firm's history that illustrated the close ties between the company and the family that were indissoluble for him. He aimed to reactivate the familial memory in order to induct the children into the role of custodians of the family's values and traditions. To embody this idea, he presented each child with a jewelry case that symbolized their responsibility for preserving the family business in its original form.[515]

The Hengstenberg vinegar and pickles factory based in Esslingen is a very typical family business in many respects. It was founded in 1876 with Hengstenberg's wife's dowry as seed capital and the family crest as its trademark. In 1970, in the wake of the social and political change at the time, it became clear that the hitherto paternalistic corporate culture was under threat. In an interview with a journalist in 1972, as a sort of legacy for his family and workforce, the founder's grandson Richard Hengstenberg outlined the things that had become established practices and needed to be preserved.

What was important to him was that the Hengstenbergs were "an ancient Westphalian family" whose history could be documented all the way back to the 14th century. "Firmness and steadfastness [...] have been handed down to the present day [...]. Tradition—that means sticking to tried and trusted business principles." These included an autocratic leadership style and staying focused on high-quality sauerkraut, red cabbage, vinegar and gherkins made with ingredients from the region. Some of Hengstenberg's farmers had been supplying the company for several generations. At the time it was being debated, Richard Hengstenberg categorically rejected the abolition of retail price maintenance, which would have removed the protection from aggressive price competition that Hengstenberg as a supplier of brand-name products enjoyed. He likewise rejected worker co-determination, which would lead to "control by incompetents", calling it a "potent trend of the times" that threatened the success of the Federal Republic. To him, family entrepreneurship was a buttress that stood for enduring solidity. "What we have accomplished should not be here today and gone tomorrow. It should be something that lasts, something that grows and survives over time. [...] The best foundation for this is the family. [...] The care for one's offspring inherent in human nature [...] motivates people to work to achieve something lasting from the outset. And at the same time, the hope that one's descendants will continue the work that has been started and carry it through to the end gives a purpose that goes far beyond today and today's profit. Neither a feeling of futility nor the desire to play Vabanque may be indulged." Identification with a centuries-old dynasty and a sense of duty to past and future generations offered a stable sociocultural reference framework. However, people now had to be explicitly reminded of this. For Hengstenberg, selling shares was out of the question: "the family duty in all its aspects" obliged him to turn down offers from all over the world to purchase the company or acquire shares in it. "As long as there are sons [...], who would dare, unless forced to, to break the chain in which the individual is but one link? And so it will continue through the generations."[516]

In the 1970s, many may have found this protest about the dangerous "trend of the times" old-fashioned and somewhat pathetic. However, what is fascinating and telling as regards the cultural appeal of family entrepreneurship in Germany is that his descendants have embraced Richard Hengstenberg's legacy in many respects. The company is still 100 percent family-owned and in 2018 employed around 500 workers in Germany. As representatives of the fifth generation, the cousins Steffen and Philipp Hengstenberg sit on the board of directors chaired by Albrecht Hengstenberg (fourth generation). In this triumvirate, Philipp is also responsible for procurement and production. The family thus not only exercises its rights of control, it is also constantly involved in the management of the company, albeit with the assistance of non-family managers since the 1990s. The company's website proudly presents farmers from the region who have supplied Hengstenberg with high-quality ingredients for many decades. At the same time, this serves to highlight the strength of its own history. In 2016 the company moved its headquarters back to its original location, in part to symbolically underline its deep-rooted traditions.[517]

These examples can admittedly only show a small selection of the many approaches family entrepreneurs adopt to this day to revive the value attached to family ownership. Collectively, however, they illustrate that consecutive succession and recruiting the company head from within the family were by no means to be taken for granted, but required active legitimation. This applies to both countries, albeit earlier in the United States and later in Germany.

One point specific to Germany, however, is that while internal family succession remained the norm since the 1970s, much more robust structural and organizational preparations were made before passing on the business assets. It is notable that the generational transition following the "second founders" was frequently characterized by a cohabitative interregnum phase during which the representatives of the old and the new generations were actively involved in running the company. This model, also referred to as "dual generation leadership", proved to be a hybrid of traditional patriarchal company management and cooperative team structures. The objective was to avert leadership crises at an early juncture. A wide range of examples such as Grundig, Bagel, Rodenstock, Lambertz, Benteler and Diehl show[518] that since the 1960s, new forms of leadership bodies have been formed in which both incumbents and successors work together. Whether in the form of expanded executive management, an advisory council, managing board or supervisory board, the general partners worked together with family partners designated as successors, and often also with outside executive directors as well. By virtue of the established seniority principle, the senior partner continued to play a dominant role in decision processes within the new leadership structures, while the successors tended to remain passive. Nevertheless, the inclusion of successors in the leadership echelons also represented an important token of family integration and offered them the opportunity to grow into their future roles. As a consequence, dynastic, hierarchical and also co-educative integrative functions overlapped in these handover practices that enabled ownership and management to remain in the hands of the family.[519]

The intensive efforts of German family businesses since the 1970s to maintain the link between ownership and control could only be explained with reference to the historical context. Here the integrative forces of psychological ownership grew all the stronger, the longer the family's values, views and symbols had formed the basis of its corporate culture. This applies both to the rules for corporate succession and to the willingness of family partners and family shareholders to continue patiently leaving their capital to work in the collective family project and not withdraw it for reasons of personal preferences.

Nevertheless, the integrative forces of entrepreneurial families were in danger of weakening, not least because, under the influence of the societal pull to individualization, individual members were freeing themselves from the family collective and thus threatening the continuity of the multigenerational business. Organizational challenges additionally arose from the exponential growth of family dynasties themselves. Family businesses that had mastered the transition into the third or even further generations had to cope with an ever growing number of people with a say in how the business was run. In the case of American agricultural concern Cargill, in 1950 it was owned by a group of twelve people; by 1970 this had reached 30, and by the end of the century over 70.[520] In the case of companies such as C&A, Haniel or Miele that had been founded prior to 1900, the family base dissipated into multiple, often heterogeneous family branches that were very difficult to keep track of. The familial right to equal treatment for all children ran counter to the entrepreneurial logic of concentration and the optimum structuring of control and ownership relationships. In such circumstances, dynamic adaptation of organizational models was necessary to preserve the identity of families, avoid conflicts, and ensure the selection of suitable directors. Managing family complexity necessitates the creation of family committees to serve as interfaces between the family and the company. Such advisory boards, foundations or special administrative institutions may be encountered early on in the history of German family businesses, at Haniel or Krupp for example.[521]

Here we can mention only a select few of the many manifestations of such entities. What is striking, however, is that from the 1960s onwards it is possible to recognize a trend for codifying in writing what had previously been only informal codes of conduct for large families, that is, creating family or company constitutions as legally binding organizational principles. Take for example the moral and religious views of the German-Dutch Brenninkmeijer family, which founded the retail chain C&A. The family code evolved over the years into what became known as the "Unitas rules" when codified in the 1960s. They set out governance principles that ranged from the amount of capital shareholders were obliged to leave tied up in the company, to inheritance and successor rules, all the way down to instructions for managing employees.[522] The overarching objective was to harmonize the interests of the family and the company, while at the same time reinvigorating the collective spirit of purpose. Regular meetings of the internationally widespread family branches were intended to aid communication and the symbolic renewal of the familial memory. To the present day, the Brenninkmeijer family has been vigorous in its efforts to actively counteract the threat of disintegration. The most recent example is its 2010 initiative to create a haven for family interaction in Mettingen, the small town in North Rhine-Westphalia where C&A started, complete with an archive and museum to house objects representing the family's shared values and history.[523] Over many years, such measures have helped preserve the ties between the many branches of the family.

Rumors circulating since the spring of 2018 that some parts of the family are in favor of selling off the company to the Chinese, however, cast doubt on whether these integration efforts will continue to be successful in future.[524]

While Chandler rather one-sidedly interpreted the increasing complexity of management tasks as an economically rational impetus for restructuring ownership and control structures, the expanding family collective also generated pressure to dynamically contain the family business culture on a structural level and find a new legitimacy for it on an emotional level, without—as Chandler implied—necessarily giving up family control.

As the Mars example shows, initiatives designed to maintain the family's influence can also be found in American family firms. Nonetheless, the breakout forces exerted by the social and economic environment had a much greater and more dominant impact on families in the United States. At the latest since the 1950s, the powerful forces of institutional isomorphism began to emerge in the US. Here the entrepreneurial landscape offered a different solution for dealing with the problems of family and company complexity as state and legal regulations determined the organizational environment of companies. Since the Second World War, anti-cartel, inheritance and taxation legislation, along with the infrastructure of the financial system and the outsider control system, had ensured that market mechanisms and formal regulation took priority over informality and familiarity. However, a normative pressure to conform also arose from the idealized model of the manager and from a desire to emulate the business success of expanding US megacorporations. Many US family businesses now followed suit and opted for a growth strategy likewise based on mass production, diversification and international expansion. The trend toward the horizontal and vertical integration of value chains, not least by means of direct investment in Germany and Europe, resulted in the replacement of functional, owner-financed organizational models. Even companies such as Ford or Otis that for many years had articulated a strong founder myth were now floated on the stock exchange. In the United States the old models of dynastic leadership were replaced early on. During the transition into multinational industrial conglomerates, the question of how the equality expectations of the family could be aligned with the company's interests was often answered by family members withdrawing from active management, bringing in professional managers and looking to external equity providers and the stock exchange to finance any necessary expansion.

From a rational economic point of view, this must be seen as a perfectly reasonable option for obtaining greater flexibility. On the other hand, it also gave the family partners greater freedom: they were able to pursue risk diversification strategies with their private capital, investing in potentially more profitable businesses and avoiding being dependent on a single asset. If expanding family firms required further injections of capital in order to grow, the individual owners were then also faced with the fundamental question: were they still willing to bear the automatically greater liability risk of financing expansion from cash flow, private means or bank loans? Entrepreneurs in the US increasingly decided in favor of an investment strategy focused on their own individual interests, outside the collective holdings of the family business.[525]

In many sectors, medium-sized family businesses in Germany experienced similar economic pressures to change, but not until much later. The excellent export opportunities and the booming sales markets of the economic miracle years had long guaranteed stable company growth. When looking around at their competitors within the same industries and sectors, they continued to see other highly profitable family firms. The mimetic dynamics thus tended to favor sticking with the status quo rather than changing or exiting. It was not until the "long 1970s" that companies began to experience crises again. Structural change in industry, automation, new consumer expectations and turf wars with foreign, usually Japanese, competitors now all combined to present complex challenges. In Germany, too, these changes in the business climate prompted many to critically question existing organizational forms. However, this happened at a time when family culture was still present in the collective memory as a stabilizing force for crisis management.

This emphasis on preservation was to have a lasting influence at all levels of management and labor relations of family business in Germany until well into the last third of the 20th century—as can be seen in prominent large family enterprises such as Bertelsmann, Schaeffler or Messer. At the end of the 1960s and beginning of the 1970s, they all opened up to alternative management-led organizational concepts in which family control and the companies' independence were ensured by means of complex holding structures and foundations. This was possible owing to the particular provisions of German foundation law that, in addition to family foundations, permitted a particular legal form of foundation-controlled companies (stiftungsverbundene Unternehmen) in which family shares could be pooled. This simplified the succession issue and enabled a family to continue actively controlling the company. Moreover, for a long time multiple and preferential voting rights allowed under German Stock Corporation Law protected family and institutional block ownership.[526] Even if the family's own financial strength was no longer sufficient to furnish the company with urgently needed investment and expansion capital and external equity providers increasingly became involved, these constructs minimized the worrying risk of losing control of the company. For instance, in 1977 the early preparations for a generational transition in the Bertelsmann corporation were expressly designed to prevent the withdrawal of the family from the strategic side of day-to-day business. Still immersed in the debate about whether to float on the stock market, which had flared up again at the end of the millennium, the family around the patriarch Reinhard Mohn rejected the idea of allowing external investors to have voting rights and a say in the running of the company. It was argued that such a step would not only jeopardize the independence of the company, it would also destroy the stable corporate culture that had so far steered it safely through many crises.[527] The family even accepted the need for the company to borrow heavily in order to buy back externalized investor shares following the collapse of the "new economy" so that it could regain full control.[528] To generalize, during crises German firms did not run to the capital markets, but rather chose to tentatively explore new financing models while falling back on proven familial governance models.

This reflex had also been evident in labor relations and the social constitutions of family businesses since the 1970s. Irrespective of sector-specific developments, general structural changes in the labor market made it increasingly difficult to maintain personal ties in human resource management. Occupational profiles changed in line with increasing specialization and differentiation in production, microelectronic automation and rationalization. Highly qualified technicians and skilled workers replaced workers accustomed to the employer-as-caretaker model. The societal ideal of staying at one company for one's entire working life, from training right through to retirement, was destabilized owing to lay-offs following crises and structural redundancies designed to shed less skilled jobs. This led to great insecurity among the workforce and an upsurge in labor disputes. Although mitigated by business associations and trade unions in Germany's corporatist model, the erosion of the works family narrative proved unstoppable.

At the same time, the new pluralistic mass consumer society lessened companies' influence on the everyday lives of employees. Based on the companies Bagel and Rodenstock, Christina Lubinski's studies provide notable insights into how society's reorientation toward individualized lifestyles weakened the cohesion between owner families and workforce. Company celebrations and shared leisure activities with colleagues after work became less popular, and consequently important informal elements of the communal relationships within companies were lost. In people's everyday working lives, the shift in social values towards post-materialistic self-fulfillment goals resulted in the diminishing importance of the traditional conservative virtues of discipline, obedience and allegiance to the company.[529] Instead, greater emphasis was placed on motivating a workforce that increasingly did not perform physical but rather mentally demanding work through a leadership style oriented to participation and individual advancement.[530] German family businesses now also found themselves having to justify their internal leadership culture in order to meet the new expectations of the workforce. Albeit at a later juncture in comparison with many US firms, Germany also witnessed a dismantling of hierarchies as well as family businesses adopting participative corporate cultures. The appointment of non-family managers was often the first step in this process. If at all, the process of relinquishing ownership—and consequently control rights—usually did not take place until much later.

It would nevertheless be erroneous to interpret these convergence trends as a fundamental weakening of German family cultures during the orientation crises of the 1970s. The fact that the public has perceived German family businesses as "safe havens" or as countermodels to the American-style of impersonal, purely market-driven risk capitalism has benefited them to this day. Owing to their strong allegiance to a particular locality and more cautious approach to expansion, family businesses remained attractive employers because they tended to avoid radical rationalization, sudden relocations of production, or outsourcing strategies. The familial long-term stability and quality cultures stood for a stronger rules-based orientation and ritualization of labor relations. Such socioindustrial inertia tendencies bore an inherent risk of organizational rigidity. At the same time, however, they represented stabilizing elements for firms' social constitutions, which proved to be highly beneficial during phases of transformation. Their established image and the good training and professional development opportunities for employees were valuable assets for recruiting and retaining the skilled workforce required.

To date there is a lack of conclusive empirical studies that have compared country-specific aspects and analyzed how national corporate and family cultures influenced each other. Only the research conducted by the Dutch organizational anthropologist Geert Hofstede provides, in the form of a snapshot from the 1980s, initial findings on how companies were influenced by their cultural environments.[531] On the basis of employee surveys at various IBM sites, Hofstede defined four cultural dimensions for scoring the behavior preferences of industrial actors. The "power distance" (Machtdistanz) dimension rated how important employees found equal participation in decision-making processes. He showed that authoritarian approaches and a hierarchical unequal distribution of power were now rarely to be found in either the United States or Germany. Even in Germany, the liberal-democratic values of participation and cooperation had ousted the old patriarchal autocratic modes of thinking. The dimension of "performance ideals" (Leistungsideale) indicated that the business worlds of the two countries were both characterized by marked competitive and assertive traits.

While the two corporate cultures showed evidence of convergence in these first two points, there were lasting differences in the other dimensions of "individualism" and "uncertainty avoidance" (Unsicherheitsvermeidung). In the United States, managers and workers rated the importance of group decisions and collective consensus-building much lower. An individualistic mindset was seen as an important driver for leveraging the creativity and innovation potential of the individual for the company. In Germany on the other hand, a sense of community was more strongly internalized, which can also be interpreted as an emphasis on the guiding principles of conformity, compliance and security. Later studies on divergences between national and corporate cultures confirm that German companies tended to attach greater weight to experiential knowledge when developing plans and forecasts for estimating future market risks. The "emotional-psychological need for a structured environment"[532] resulted in traditional norms of behavior and a collective cautiousness becoming firmly established.[533]

If one transposes this rather general finding to the role of the family business, ultimately the persistence of the latter in Germany appears to be due to a characteristic national business culture. The way family businesses were structured in Germany had proved to be compatible with the stability and security expectations of society. In this reading, until the 1990s risk aversion phenomena or the patient capital (geduldiges Kapital) at the corporate level found their societal equivalent in a much higher savings rate than in the US. Then, too, especially the older generations in Germany have a far greater tendency to "keep together" the money they have earned in order to pass it on to help their offspring get a better start in life. This also indicates that there were and still are tangible cultural differences between the two societies. The greater disinclination to leave something to one's heirs in the US is also reflected in the widespread uptake of reverse mortgages, which enable one to sell one's real estate while retaining the right to live there for life, in return for a monthly payment or an additional pension. On death, it either becomes the property of the bank or the heirs pay off the loan. While this model enables the older generation to enjoy a higher standard of living, it does so at the expense of the heirs ("spend before you end"), and is thus unpopular in Germany, where the first providers did not appear on the market until 2007/08.[534] In 2007 there were a mere 200 contracts in Germany, whereas in the same year there were 879,708 in the US, the world's biggest market for these products. Reverse mortgages have been offered in the US since 1960, and have even been backed by government guarantees since 1989. The UK represents the biggest European market and the second largest in the world. The varieties of capitalism are relatively clearly mirrored by the extent to which the intergenerational transfer of wealth is seen to be desirable.[535] These general differences in mindset also influenced the succession practices of family businesses.

The less pronounced individualism and the clear preference for group-based internal and external cohesion in coordinated capitalism made it easier to sustain the paradigm of the family as a leadership and organizational model for companies. On the flip side, the far more widely accepted model in the US of spending the fruits of one's labor on personal hedonism resulted in a certain disregard for the beneficial aspects of the intergenerational transfer of corporate wealth for society as a whole. Against this backdrop, the strongly individualistic nature of American society appears to make it much more difficult to persuade company founders and their potential heirs and successors to support a multigenerational project.

In the light of the massive political and economic upheavals Germany experienced in the 20th century, it was the security aspect in particular that appeared to become deeply ingrained in the sociocultural DNA of the corporate landscape. Initially marked by the period of postwar shortages, since the 1970s the increased awareness of the social and economic risks of the modern post-industrial era ensured that family businesses were again perceived, at least in part, as anchors of stability. As sociologist Ulrich Beck incisively noted, societal leisure and consumption trends blended with the contours of a "risk society" (Risikogesellschaft) that was highly sensitive to the potential for new conflicts in the distribution of work, property and knowledge. Family businesses had to adapt to both trends by changing their internal and external structures.

The picture as a whole is completed by the concept of corporate culture as a dynamic and highly heterogeneous construct. If we look at the micro-level in companies themselves, the differences between the company cultures of long established family businesses such as Mars and Bahlsen, Cargill or C&A are minimal. The families developed similar patterns of identity and the same mechanisms for preserving family ties. However, there are distinct differences in the pace and intensity of the forces that externally impacted family businesses during the period examined. For instance, we tend to find fundamental divergences between social and business cultures at the macro-level. Here the historical overview highlights stark contrasts between developments in the respective countries: while political stability, generally higher economic output, and the early emergence of a multi-option society resulted in a tendency for family business cultures to become destabilized in the United States, in Germany the huge upheavals in the first half of the 20th century and the lag in the development of the affluent consumer society repeatedly (re)stabilized family firm identities. As a consequence, the structural divergences can ultimately only be understood with reference to the distinctive history of these experiences and mindsets in the two countries. Nonetheless, the durability of family businesses appears to be gradually waning even in Germany. In the wake of the dynamic globalization process and the hyper-individualization of society, new convergence trends appear to have emerged over recent decades. Although they have always been present to a certain extent, the problems of succession are now more frequent in Germany too. This indicates a weakening of the bond and the sense of purpose that family businesses instill within the family collective. This is illustrated, for example, by the conflicts at Bertelsmann and in the latest splits in the Becker brewery dynasty in Cologne, the venerable biscuit-maker Bahlsen or the Oetinger publishing group. In the meantime, research institutes predict that between 2018 and 2022 only about half of family businesses will find a successor from within the family. In around 20 percent of cases, an internal handover to employees may be possible. However, approximately every third medium-sized family firm is openly considering selling the business to an outsider due to the breakout forces acting on the family, a growing shortage of successors in the pipeline, and the high capital requirements of international competition and digitalization.[536] Far-reaching changes in the social and business environment are once more confronting corporate family cultures with adaptation challenges.

H. Conclusion. Two Development Paths

Family businesses were and are constitutive elements of the economic systems of Germany and the United States. It is not difficult to identify commonalities in their historical development and current manifestations. One central feature is their multigenerational nature: family businesses succeed in preserving an entrepreneurial family spirit and ensuring continuity of ownership, management and control over long periods of time. For instance, Antonius Cramer founded the Warsteiner Brewery in the Westphalian town of Warstein in 1753. The company is now managed by the ninth generation of the family—Catharina Cramer. In 1829 David G. Jüngling opened the Eagle Brewery in Pottsville, Pennsylvania, which has been operating under the name of D.G. Yuengling & Son ever since 1873. Today, fifth generation owner Richard (Dick) Yuengling runs the business, and all four of his daughters work in the company, two in management, paving the way for the sixth generation of leadership in this wholly family-owned enterprise.

Beyond the giant multinational beer conglomerates, these two companies are among the most important supraregional breweries in their countries. They are both 100 percent family owned and, according to the families, will stay that way for a long time to come. Both have deep roots in the small towns where they have been based for over 250 (Warsteiner) and 180 (Yuengling) years, during which time they have steadfastly cultivated strong patriarchal corporate cultures. Their advertising emphatically highlights their traditional heritage and the personal involvement of the family, which stand as a mark of quality and solidity. For the first time in Warsteiner's history, a woman has taken over the helm, and this will soon be happening at Yuengling too. Yuengling's four basic rules could likewise serve as maxims for Warsteiner and many other long-established family businesses: "1. Stay small. 2. Don't go public. 3. Avoid big cities. 4. Keep it in the family."[537]

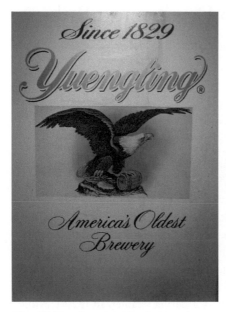
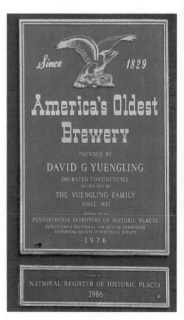

Photo 26: Yuengling advertising that touts the company's position as the oldest brewery in the United States

Photo 27: Plaque recognizing the Yuengling brewing company as a historic place that has been continuously operated by the family

One marked difference is in their attitudes to employee representation. The works council has played a constructive role at Warsteiner for many decades—in 2017 the company was even awarded a "workplace democracy" prize[538] by the German Trade Union Confederation (Deutscher Gewerkschaftsbund, DGB). Yuengling, by contrast, banned trade unions altogether from his company in 2006. As a result, various labor organizations called for a boycott which is still in force today.[539] While Warsteiner plays by the rule of cooperative capitalism, Yuengling still operates very much in the tradition of entrepreneurial individualism. For such individualists, the right of non-organized labor to work, which is upheld in many US states, is seen as a fundamental right and is cited when defending the company against the "nannying" interference of external organizations in its internal affairs. Yuengling's triumphal self-presentation as a billionaire said to be worth 1.9 billion dollars, and ranked 361st on the Forbes 400 list of richest Americans in 2016, stands in contrast to German entrepreneurs' greater discretion about their fortunes: the Cramer family, whose assets are estimated to amount to between 500 and 600 million euros, is much more reticent when it comes to its wealth.

And while Yuengling's long and unbroken family tradition is treated as an almost curious exception in the US media, the continuity of the Warsteiner family over nine generations—also a rarity—attracts much less attention in Germany. Here, people are used to long-lived family businesses and do not see them as anything out of the ordinary. Media reports about these companies tend to be more matter-of-fact, even while acknowledging their achievements. These two examples reflect the key findings of this study.

Germany has a higher number of owner-led family businesses, and these are considerably older on average than their US counterparts. The United States, meanwhile, has long produced significantly more start-ups, and those that survive have generally been floated quickly on the capital market. The result is that the original owners lose control over the business—i.e., from that point on, ownership and management are separated, particularly in the case of larger companies.

These differences—representing trends to which there are some notable exceptions—are attributable to a complex set of historical circumstances. In general, however, the institutional and cultural framework in Germany has supported multigenerational family businesses, while the US environment has favored the dynamism of young companies.

The study illustrates these differences, beginning with inheritance law. While German legislators have traditionally protected the collective interests of families and thus also of their businesses, the legal frame of reference in the United States has always been the individual, who ultimately has to prevail on his or her own behalf. This led to the significantly higher taxation of inherited wealth in the US which, at its peak between 1941 and 1976, reached confiscatory proportions—a maximum rate of 77 percent—for the families concerned. What flowed into state coffers as "unearned wealth" or into philanthropic ventures in the US, remained in Germany for the most part in the hands of entrepreneurial families, whose unbroken ties to their companies were seen as highly beneficial. In the United States, the dynastic approach to preserving assets was deeply frowned upon by the founding consensus of the country itself, which, as a former British colony, defined itself by its anti-aristocratic values. This attitude encouraged the children of entrepreneurial families to build their own fortunes through their individual achievements and to start their own businesses. Though families were still able to circumvent tax law and the anti-dynastic culture to pass on wealth, for example using trusts, this had a high price: control of the company usually passed to the trustees. Even from the 1940s to the 1970s, inheritance tax thus made up only a small share of total tax revenue in the US. At the same time, the tax system could considerably weaken family businesses, in some cases even forcing their sale. It was only towards the end of the 20th century that this policy came to an end; the tax burden was substantially reduced and there was a degree of convergence between the American and German inheritance tax systems where family businesses were concerned.

Early on, the far greater size and efficiency of the US capital market encouraged family businesses to turn into listed stock corporations with free-floating shares—a trend that was particularly apparent among large companies beginning in the late 19th century. This contrasted sharply with the German system of bank-based financing, which enabled long-term relationships between family businesses and their house banks, creating conservative corporate structures. While relatively strong investor protection became established in the US and facilitated anonymous financing in the capital market, in Germany the focus was on internal control and the continuity of concentrated ownership structures. This was further encouraged by the acceptance of cartels in Germany, followed as of 1957 by relatively lenient rules prohibiting cartels, rules with many exceptions. By contrast, in the US the Sherman Antitrust Act of 1890 placed a strict ban on cartels, which often encouraged concentration through mergers instead, bringing family control to an end.

It was only with the "second globalization" from the 1980s onwards that these national differences in the institutional frameworks of corporate finance and corporate governance began to soften. In Germany, the capital market began to gain ground against bank loan financing. A pivotal moment for family businesses that are stock corporations (such as those registered as an Aktiengesellschaft or AG) was the abolition of multiple voting rights. In complete contrast to their American counterparts, German families had long been able to use such rights to secure control over their businesses even when they no longer owned the majority of shares—a legal arrangement that had immensely strengthened the position of family businesses in Germany over many decades. From the 1990s, new rules on transparency and disclosure led to a convergence in the two countries' financial systems. In practice, however, there are still many differences in the way German and American companies do business.

Politically, the German state soon saw a role for itself in ensuring the fortunes of the country's industry, and especially the *Mittelstand*, a trend that reflected Germany's economic model of cooperative capitalism. In the liberal market economy of the US, meanwhile, faith in market self-regulation remained strong. German family businesses could rely on the local savings and cooperative banks, which—unlike the more volatile US savings banks—were sound partners that were strengthened in part by the support of local government and solidarity organizations. Germany also created a broad-based system of technical education from as early as the 19th century, and restrictive rules governing entry to manual trades secured high standards in training for these trades over the long run. It is a historical irony that this backward-looking approach produced progressive outcomes and laid the foundations for a culture of productivity and quality. In both countries, however, measures aimed at pure social protectionism proved to be a dead-end. Another pillar of the German institutional landscape were the associations that represented almost all the trades. The rules on how to do business in Germany were traditionally negotiated between the government, businesses and unions rather than following pure market principles. Strong personal networks and influential lobbies such as business associations and unions created the foundations for both formal and informal coordination and also helped medium-sized family businesses to assert their interests. Though present in the US, such collective institutions never achieved comparable importance there.

National Socialism did not systematically improve the position of family businesses despite its propagandistic promises. Instead, its intrusions into the economic fabric caused many stock corporations to (re)convert into partnerships. The resulting decline in the number of joint stock corporations continued long into the post-war period and was only reversed in the 1990s, when various liberalization measures simplified admission to the stock market. The destructive character of National Socialism was particularly evident in its obliteration of the significant segment of family businesses in Jewish hands. The owners were deported and murdered and the businesses "Aryanized". Germany's total military defeat meant that the business landscape suffered physically as well, with many cities reduced to rubble. It is testimony to the resilience of family businesses that they not only survived the political upheavals, but that large cohorts of companies were (re)established in the wake of 1945 and 1990.

Although the United States saw itself as a "nation of shopkeepers", the state long refrained from market intervention to help small businesses: the large influx of immigrants in the 19th century, many of whom became entrepreneurs, seemed to render systematic support for new businesses unnecessary. The disproportionately large number of self-employed people among immigrants remains a trend to this day, even if immigration policy has been more restrictive since the 1920s. Yet this never-ending supply of potential entrepreneurs brought instability as well as dynamism. Competition was often ruinous and many entrepreneurs failed, but there was no shortage of new founders or second and third attempts—and thus little need for the government to provide incentives. This experience led to a long-lasting political reluctance to intervene in the market on behalf of small and medium-sized businesses.

It would take the impact of the Great Depression of 1929, the growing concentration of big business, and the process of rearmament during the Second World War to change this. At that point, institutions were created for the first time specifically to protect and promote SMEs, although they remained rather weak for many years. A major turning point was the creation in 1953 of the Small Business Administration, which was made permanent a few years later and served as an institutional framework that created support programs enabling small and medium-sized enterprises to grow relatively quickly in the 1970s and 80s. However, aid measures for SMEs were long a source of political controversy, especially among family business owners themselves, who viewed state intervention of any kind as alien to the US system. In West Germany, by contrast, SME policy was an integral part of cooperative capitalism and had a firm place in the economics ministry, and state funding for SMEs was never seriously questioned. After 1945, it was, ironically, an instrument created with US aid as part of the Marshall Plan—the Special Fund of the European Recovery Programme (ERP)—which proved to be an effective lever to rebuild the economy and especially to support SMEs. Administered by the "Reconstruction Credit Institute" (Kreditanstalt für Wiederaufbau, KfW), the Special Fund was not wound up once the reconstruction effort had been completed, but enlarged and turned into a permanent fixture of economic policy in the Federal Republic.

In the crisis-ridden 1970s, support provided to SMEs in Germany rocketed as part of the government's employment and structural policies: the crisis affecting large companies in traditional industries and the enormous increase in insolvencies among SMEs led to widespread fears of permanent damage to the corporate landscape. This trend soon emerged in the US, too, resulting in a convergence in the two countries' policies towards SMEs from the 1980s onwards—though the US put a clear emphasis on supporting start-ups, while Germany focused on the conservation of existing businesses and succession issues. And in the strategically important area of export promotion, the German government's efforts went far beyond what was acceptable to politicians in Washington.

In Germany, the state was thus involved earlier and more intensively in supporting the economy, and gave particular attention to SMEs as central to the country's economic model. However, this finding should not be interpreted as a criticism of the United States. Rather, German policy was, in many respects, a reaction to an underdeveloped capital market. In other words, the "deficits" of American SME policy were more than offset by the considerably more developed private venture capital sector. Even so, the two countries had different ways of generating growth. In Germany, the incentive lay in the continuation of existing businesses, thus the government provided active support to help companies flexibly adapt to new markets. In the US, the focus was instead on market-based creative renewal, in which the old was superseded by the new. Accordingly, the number of new businesses remained extremely high well into the early 21st century. As a share of the total population, the United States produced more than twice as many company founders as Germany over the period studied.[540] Successful businesses remained in family hands for a significantly shorter period of time than in Germany, as the capital market was highly receptive and many founders did not share the aspiration of German business owners to manage their businesses for generations.

Political turbulence, which was rife in 20th century Germany, led to widespread insecurity, and in such times of crisis family cohesion was seen as an anchor in the storm—a belief that also extended to family businesses with their promise of safety and continuity. The great age of German family business began in the years after 1945, as old companies pulled closer together and numerous new ones were founded. Among large businesses, too, maintaining or reinstating family control was a survival strategy to help undermine the deconcentration measures planned by the Allies. In the US, by contrast, the two World Wars were periods of relative order and continuity, and did not provide any additional impetus to family businesses: there was simply no need for them to provide a stabilizing role like the one they performed in Germany. We must agree with Harold James when he says: "Family capitalism has been particularly important in countries and societies with profound shocks and discontinuities."[541] In simple terms: an unstable environment led to the stabilization of the family business model in Germany. In the United States, meanwhile, the greater stability of the system as a whole tended to undermine the presence of family businesses.

Yet the national differences in corporate landscapes have more than just socioeconomic causes; they have cultural and historical roots that date back centuries. In Germany, feudalism left a long legacy: the dynastic principle of the nobility had a lasting formative power. The tradition of craftsmen organized in guilds was engrained in the fabric of the German economic system. This distanced the trades from market forces and competition, but also brought high standards of training. Some German family businesses had roots reaching far back into the early modern period (about 1500 to 1800), and were regarded by many families as an ideal organizational model. Continuity conferred dignity and prestige, and families strove for the recognition and fulfillment it provided. While these ideas were by no means alien to established families in the United States, they were less important than individual achievement. The continuous flow of immigrants meant the arrival of new families whose old-world histories meant little in their new homeland: they had no other choice but to look forward. Thus the US has always been a meritocracy that prizes the individual: it is the self-made man, not the guardian of tradition, who garners the most respect. This is no wonder in a society whose fundamental experience was one of virtually unlimited land and resources. In this context, the idea that any hard-working man could go from dishwasher to millionaire—whatever country or family he came from—became a popular narrative. New companies embodied a sense of promise, fueling the business acumen that foreign observers soon came to see as a very American trait. Germany's relative compactness, its lack of land and natural resources, and its widespread skepticism towards entrepreneurs meant that people looked to a much greater degree to the solidarity of the family and the safety of home regions and tradition.

Corporate cultures in family businesses on both sides of the Atlantic held many similarities. Companies were often paternalistic and maintained their own traditions and rituals. However, this model began to erode relatively early in the US: the future seemed to belong to companies owned and managed by professionals and controlled by the capital market. In the 20th century, a belief in the family business as a multi-generational project seemed to lose credibility even with the owners themselves. In Germany, on the other hand, the ties between families and their companies remained closer. This was a function of the strong individualism and greater social mobility in the US, but also the lesser importance that American business owners generally attached to long-term thinking or the desire to leave something behind for their children. There were always opportunities to pursue a new project of one's own, and that had higher value than the preservation of an existing business. US insolvency law, which favored borrowers over creditors, reinforced this attitude. In contrast to Germany, failures were not a cause of social ostracism, but a sign of self-initiative—and often a starting point for the next project. Legally and culturally, there was greater focus on opportunities than risks. In Germany, owners found it much more difficult to step away from a flourishing family business into a completely new project.

The social and economic context played a prominent role here: with their enormous domestic market, US businesses could count on Fordistic mass production. In Germany, meanwhile, where the local market was smaller, companies soon began to concentrate on the export of high-quality, complex products, making continuity a highly effective strategy, particularly in businesses built on highly qualified skilled labor and specialist knowledge developed over many decades. Hierarchical structures modelled on government were replicated in many companies and had a stabilizing effect, and the state assisted companies with social programs and diverse aid, especially for small and medium-sized businesses. This cooperative capitalism, which allowed a major role in corporate life for the government and other external actors, especially the unions, facilitated the creation of stable, enduring structures. In the US, the free-market principle prevailed. "Money talks," and its voice was all the louder and more ruthless given the absence of the sort of external stabilizers created in Germany. This allowed a more vibrant process of "creative destruction" and meant that state support for SMEs arrived late in the day and was relatively restrained.

The United States experienced a fundamental social liberalization and the emergence of mass consumerism earlier than Germany, opening up opportunities beyond the workplace and traditional family roles: leisure, hedonism and self-fulfillment became more important in people's lives. Investing capital and time in the family business was no longer a matter of course. Selling shares was simple and attractive, and there was no shortage of appealing lifestyles away from the traditional world of work. These trends were further reinforced by the mythology of the professional manager. Free from family ties, he could supposedly dedicate himself with great competence and rationality to improving economic efficiency. In other words, the model of the multi-generational family business now found itself culturally on the defensive much sooner than it did in Germany.

It was not until the 1960s that the process of fundamental liberalization began here as well, leading to the erosion of traditional family models, and the problem of succession did not become a major issue until the 1980s. Succession within the inner family circle was always the primary objective, even if professional managers increasingly took over the running of family businesses or they were sold off. Such cases, which again demonstrate a degree of convergence between the two countries, were regarded in Germany as "failed succession"—a marked contrast to the more relaxed view in the US, which regarded these as normal developments.

Overall, this comparative look at the history of family businesses in Germany and the United States provides many new insights. The study shows the expected contrasts, but also reveals many parallels and related developments. It is clear that the model of the family business is more than just a special form of corporate culture: the difference in the prevalence of family businesses today is the manifestation of complex historical differences in the development of economic structures and cultures on either side of the Atlantic. The ties between families and businesses are embedded in, and contingent on, long-term social currents, political path dependencies and notions of how the economy should be organized. Multi-generational family businesses have a historical and a contemporary dimension. The legacy of the predecessors, especially the founders, commits the current generation to the company. At the same time, each member of the family needs to live up to the current demands of the company. This points to the principle of achievement, which must always be fulfilled, regardless of tradition.

The idea of the family business was born in the pre-modern age to counter the institutional deficits of the market, cushion the risks inherent in economic activity and direct family resources into economic life. From the 19th century onwards, America's individualistic ideals and belief in the self-regulating forces of the market led more and more businesses to leave the family safety net behind. In Germany, by contrast, family ties were more deeply engrained in the social structure, and instilled themselves into the guiding principles of a coordinated, informally managed model of capitalism. Sharp divergences thus emerged in the institutional set-ups of the two economies, with greater or lesser consideration given to the interests of family businesses as a result. Only from the 1970s and the second phase of globalization do we find increasing convergence of the two countries' legal and financial systems. However, large cultural differences remain. These still have an enduring practical impact on decisions about corporate succession, financing and strategy. The history of family businesses is thus not only reflected in the traditions of individual companies, but is a useful lens through which to examine the present day. Closely intertwined with the wider institutional context, this history continues to shape businesses in Germany and the United States in various ways today. Exploring these historical connections helps us gain a closer sense of where we are and to objectively consider future options for the development of family businesses. In the process, it becomes clear that all economic models have their strengths and weaknesses and that there is no ideal path. This, too, is one of the lessons of history.

Endnotes

1   See Family Firm Institute, Global Data Points, https://archive.org/details/perma_cc_CF89-K2JB (accessed: December 13, 2018).

2   Morck and Steier, "Global History", p. 8.

3   See La Porta, De Silanes and Shleifer, "Corporate Ownership"; Morck and Yeung, "Family Control"; see also the more balanced appraisal in James, "Family Values"; Colli, *History*; Berghoff, *Familienunternehmen*.

4   See Whittington and Mayer, *European Corporation*, pp. 99–110 and 120; Bell, *End*, p. 41.

5   See Stiftung Familienunternehmen, *Bedeutung*, p. 10.

6   In a survey of the entire segment of medium-sized companies in Germany, ZEW in Mannheim even quotes shares of 65 percent (family-controlled) and 60 percent (owner-managed), but offers no comparative figures for other countries. See Stiftung Familienunternehmen, *Bedeutung*, p. 17.

7   This survey also reveals that family businesses in which the CEO is chosen chiefly on the basis of primogeniture—i.e. that the eldest child almost automatically takes over the family business—generally perform worse than when other criteria are used to select a CEO.

8   http://beta.fortune.com/fortune500/ (accessed: July 20, 2016).

9   http://top500.welt.de/list/2014/U/?i=10&p=1 (accessed: July 20, 2016).

10   See Global Family Business Index (as of May 2015), http://familybusinessindex.com/ (accessed: July 20, 2018). The revenue and size data relate to the period 2013–2015.

11   See ibid. The St. Gallen definition is: "We define a family business as follows. For a privately held firm, a firm is classified as a family firm in case a family controls more than 50% of the voting rights. For a publicly listed firm, a firm is classified as a family firm in case the family holds at least 32% of the voting rights."

12   See Simon, "Speerspitze", pp. 875 et seq.; idem, *Gewinner*.

13   Hermann Simon speaks of a share of 90 percent. See Simon, "Faszination", p. 146.

14   Second edition: Simon, *Hidden Champions*.

15   Venohr, Fear and Witt, "Best of German Mittelstand", p. 6.

16   See Hannah, "From Family Firm", p. 121.

17 See Klein, *Familienunternehmen*, pp. 106–112.
18 See Berghoff, "Varieties of Financialization".
19 See Roberge et al, "Lengthening", p. 2. See Venohr, Fear and Witt, "Best of German Mittelstand", p. 15.
20 Own evaluations on the basis of the Global Family Business Index (see Note 10). Comparative international studies also highlight the particularly long life span of German family businesses: See Fernández Moya, Fernández Pérez and Lubinski, "Test of Time", p. 233.
21 See Ward, *Keeping*, pp. 2 and 268.
22 See Stamm and Lubinski, "Crossroads", pp. 120–121.
23 Of the 4,400 companies surveyed, 408 provided data. See Lamsfuß and Wallau, *Größten Familienunternehmen*, pp. 11–12.
24 See Klein, *Familienunternehmen*, p. 35.
25 See ibid, pp. 42–43 and 111.
26 Quoted from https://en.wifu.de/en/research/definition-of-family-business/9187-2/ (accessed: September 21, 2018).
27 See Shanker and Astrachan, "Myths and Realities", p. 108.
28 Ibid, pp. 109 and 113.
29 See Klein, "Family Businesses", p. 158.
30 Ibid.
31 Ibid.
32 See Stiftung Familienunternehmen, *Bedeutung*, p. 52. The top 500 group comprises 587 companies.
33 Quoted in "500 Jahre Unternehmensgeschichte. The Coatinc Company", p. 20 [our translation].
34 See *Handelsblatt*, August 7, 2007; *Der Treasurer. Nachrichten für die Finanzabteilung*, August 21, 2015; https://www.prym-group.com/index.html (accessed: October 14, 2018); example in Plate et al, *Familienunternehmen*, pp. 475 et seq.
35 The authors wish to thank the Foundation for Family Businesses for providing information on the oldest German family businesses.
36 See N.N., Familie; Plate et al, *Familienunternehmen*, pp. 63–71; generally also: Köhler, "Wirtschaftsbürger", pp. 116–143.
37 See presentation of Berenberg Bank's areas of business at https://www.berenberg.de/en/berenberg/ (accessed: August 20, 2018).
38 See Scranton, "Build a Firm".
39 Griffen and Griffen, "Family", p. 335.
40 Landes, "French Business", demonstrates this using French family businesses as examples. Similar treatment in Sawyer, "Entrepreneur".
41 Griffen and Griffen, "Family", p. 328.
42 See ibid., pp. 333–334.
43 Both quotations from: Griffen and Griffen, "Family", pp. 325 and 337.
44 Bell, *End*, p. 41.

45 See Fairlie and Robb, "Families".
46 See Berghoff, "Immigrant Entrepreneurship", and the literature referred to there.
47 See Scranton, *Novelty*, pp. 241–259 and 319–327; Carnevali, "Social Capital", p. 911.
48 See Scranton, *Novelty*, pp. 323–327.
49 Carnevali, "Social Capital", p. 925. See Scranton, *Novelty*, pp. 319–327.
50 See Winkler, "Protest", p. 780.
51 See Will, *Selbstverwaltung*, pp. 577 et seq.
52 See, among others, Richter, "Friendly Co-operation".
53 See Berghoff, Köhler and Wixforth, "Navigation", pp. 448 et seq.
54 Weber, "Werttreiber", p. 158 [our translation].
55 This paragraph is largely based on Weber, "Werttreiber".
56 See Ehrhardt, Nowak and Weber, "Running in the Family".
57 See Amit and Villalonga, "Performance", p. 174, and table 9.1, p. 159.
58 See Anderson and Reeb, "Founding-Family Ownership", p. 1303.
59 See Ehrhardt, Nowak and Weber, "Running in the Family", p. 7.
60 See McLane, *Documents*.
61 See Soltow, "Origins", p. 6.
62 See Means, "Separation", pp. 94–100.
63 See Larner, *Management Control*, p. 19.
64 See ibid., pp. 9–17.
65 See Steindl, *Small and Big Business*, p. 50.
66 See National Archives, College Park, RG 240, 570,73,28 G, Small War Plant Corp., Box 1, Office of the Chairman and General Manager, manuscript: Concentration of American Business and Finance, pp. 31 and 17–18.
67 See Hagley Library, collection 1a11 NAM, Series 16, Box 221, Financing Small Business, in Commercial and Financial Chronicle, November 14, 1946.
68 See Köhler, *"Arisierung"*, p. 92.
69 See ibid., p. 542–543.
70 See https://www.winterhalter.com/de-de/unternehmen (accessed: November 12, 2018).
71 See https://www.ottogroup.com/en/die-otto-group/daten-fakten/Historie.php (accessed: September 21, 2018).
72 See Berg, *Nixdorf.*
73 See http://pyramid-saiten.de/de/about/firmenhistorie.php (accessed: December 12, 2018).
74 See Müller, "Familien- zu Parteibetrieben", p. 182; http://www.horstmann-group.de/gruppe/ (accessed: December 12, 2018).
75 See Blackford, "Small Business", pp. 5–6.
76 Figures based on information from the Internal Revenue Service (IRS), in Hagley Library, collection 1960, American Chamber of Commerce, Box 84, Background Information on Anti-Business Day.

77 See Bunzel, *Small Businessman*, p. 59.
78 Unlike the German figures, US statistics use 500 employees as the upper threshold, with the result that the threshold of 1,000 employees used in Figures 13 and 14 can no longer be applied.
79 See WTO data in: Koch, *Globalisierung*, p. 28.
80 The World Bank, Data Bank, World Development Indicators, http://databank.worldbank.org/data/reports.aspx?source=2&series=SL.IND.EMPL.ZS&country=USA,DEU (accessed: December 15, 2018).
81 James, "Family Values", pp. 75 and 79.
82 Wischermann, "Erbschaftsteuer", p. 174; Beckert, *Vermögen*, p. 20; Miller and McNamee, "Inheritance", p. 1 [our translation].
83 In contrast, wealth earned by a person himself was worthy of protection and legitimate, "if it is honorably obtained and well used", quoted from Theodore Roosevelt, New Nationalism Speech, August 31, 1910, http://teachingamericanhistory.org/library/document/new-nationalism-speech/ (accessed: December 12, 2018).
84 Siegrist, "Propertisierung", p. 17 [our translation]. Fernández Moya, Fernández Pérez and Lubinski, "Test of Time", p. 252.
85 Quoted from: Chester, "Inheritance", p. 24. See Johnson and Britton Eller, "Taxation".
86 However, from 1979 it was weakened in some Federal states and repealed almost everywhere after 2000. See Hall and Marcus, "Why Should Men", p. 150.
87 See ibid.
88 All quotes in this paragraph: Verhandlungen des Deutschen Reichstages, 11. Legislaturperiode, II. Session, 1. Abschnitt 1905/06, 5. Anlageband, Aktenstück 360, Bericht der VI. Kommission über die Besteuerung der Erbschaften, pp. 3973–3974 [our translations].
89 Ibid. [our translation].
90 See Dorn, "Erbrecht".
91 For example, the Haniel family managed this very impressively. See James, *Familienunternehmen*, pp. 81–127.
92 See Zeumer, "Nachfolgefinanzierung", p. 206
93 Carnegie, "Wealth", p. 664.
94 See Dinkel, "Erben", p. 89.
95 See Beckert, *Vermögen*, pp. 247–248.
96 See ibid., p. 264.
97 Quoted from Johnson and Britton Eller, "Federal Taxation", pp. 71–72.
98 Manly, "Report", p. 113.
99 Ibid., p. 32.
100 Garretson, "Statement", p. 295. The main report took the same direction. See Manly, "Report", p. 32.
101 See Johnson and Britton Eller, "Federal Taxation", pp. 71–79.

102 See Beckert, *Vermögen*, pp. 214–219; Jacobson, "Estate Tax", p. 122.

103 See National Archives, College Park, RG 56, 450 62 34 1, Records relating to the Excess Profit tax and Estate and Gift tax, 1942–1961, Estate and Gift Tax Program 1949–1950, Note of February 28, 1949. The top rate of income tax was 77% in 1918 and dropped to 25% by 1925.

104 The deductions for spouses were 60,000 dollars and, since 1948, 120,000 dollars.

105 See Marcus and Dobkin Hall, *Lives in Trust*, p. 280; Beckert, *Vermögen*, pp. 222–227.

106 See National Archives, College Park, RG 56, 450 62 34 1, Records relating to the Excess Profit tax and Estate and Gift tax, 1942–1961, Estate and Gift Tax Program 1949–1950, Note of February 28, 1949; Marcus, "Law"; Jacobson et al., "Estate Tax", p. 122 [our translation].

107 *Die Welt*, November 27, 2009, https://www.welt.de/welt_print/vermischtes/article5342902/Verschwiegene-Gesellschaften.html (accessed: December 12, 2018) [our translation].

108 See Fleschutz, *Stiftung*, pp. 70–76.

109 Hagley Library, Collection 1960, American Chamber of Commerce, Publications Box 84, The Administration Tax Proposals. Testimony of Chamber Representatives before the House Committee on Ways and Means, February 28, 1950, 6, p. 13.

110 Ibid., pp. 13–14.

111 Quoted from ibid., p. 14.

112 See ibid., p. 5.

113 See Beckert, *Vermögen*, p. 231.

114 See ibid., pp. 275 and 228; Schardt and Weiler, *Erbschaftsbesteuerung*, p. 16.

115 Apart from that, in 1922 the gift tax was incorporated into the inheritance tax and placed on a level with it.

116 Quoted from ibid., p. 53 [our translation].

117 Reichsgesetzblatt 1943, I, p. 655. Bertha Krupp became the sole proprietor and transferred all her shares to her son, Alfried. See also James, *Krupp*, p. 214 [our translation].

118 See Frank, *Erbschaftsteuer*, pp. 49–52.

119 See Jacobson et al., "Estate Tax", p. 122.

120 See contribution Walker Winter, House of Representatives 94th Congress, Second Session, Public Hearings and Panel Discussions before the Committee on Ways and Means on the General Subject of Federal Estate and Gift Taxes, March 15–23, 1976, p. 660.

121 See Abou El Fadil, *Erbschaftsteuergesetzgebung*, p. 71. In this case, at least 65% of the overall estate to be taxed had to comprise company assets.

122 See Beckert, *Vermögen*, pp. 237–238.

123 Pieper, "Dauerbrenner", p. 42.

124 Willy Brandt, Grundsätze einer Strukturpolitik für kleine und mittlere Unternehmen, Drucksache des Bundestages 06/1666 of December 29, 1970, p. 12 [our translation].

125 See Bianchini-Hartmann and Richter, "Besteuerung".

126 See *FAZ*, December 17, 2003.

127 See Jacobson et al., "Estate Tax", p. 122.

128 See ibid.

129 See US Congress, Joint Committee on Taxation, History, Present Law, And Analysis Of The Federal Wealth Transfer Tax System, Report for the Public Hearing, March 18, 2015, JCX-52–14, in particular p. 25, https://www.jct.gov/publications. html?func=startdown&id=4744 (accessed: December 12, 2018).

130 See Center on Budget and Policy Priorities, Ten Facts You Should Know About the Federal Estate Tax, May 5, 2017, https://www.cbpp.org/research/federal-tax/ten-facts-you-should-know-about-the-federal-estate-tax (accessed: December 12, 2018).

131 See https://taxfoundation.org/does-your-state-have-estate-or-inheritance-tax (accessed: December 13, 2018).

132 See http://www.taxpolicycenter.org/briefing-book/how-do-state-estate-and-inheritances-taxes-work (accessed: December 13, 2018).

133 See Seer, "Betriebsvermögen", p. 215.

134 BVerfG-Beschluss of June 22, 1995 (2 BvR 552/91), BStBl. 1995 II, p. 671 [our translation].

135 See Ehrhardt, Nowak and Weber, "Running in the Family", p. 3. and also Appendix I.

136 See Pieper, "Dauerbrenner", p. 42.

137 BVerfG-Urteil of December 17, 2014, 1, BvL 21/12, Rn. (1–7) [our translation].

138 See the Stiftung Familienunternehmen, *Erbschaft- und Schenkungsteuerrecht* (2016), for a very detailed presentation of this complicated matter.

139 See Stiftung Familienunternehmen, *Country Index* (2016), pp. 139–161.

140 In Belgium, a significantly reduced inheritance tax rate of three percent is now levied which applies to all family businesses regardless of their size. See Stiftung Familienunternehmen, *Country Index* (2019), pp. 14–16.

141 See also Stiftung Familienunternehmen, *Country Index* (2017), pp. 24 and 28.

142 In Germany, if the value of the estate exceeds the tax exemption limit of 26 million euros, the entire company assets are subject to tax.

143 See, among others, Hall and Soskice, *Varieties of Capitalism*; Abelshauser, *Kulturkampf* [our translation].

144 See Klein, *Familienunternehmen*, p. 78.

145 See La Porta et al, "Law and Finance", pp. 1113–1155; Coffee, "Rise", pp. 18 et seq.

146 Ibid.; Ampenberger, *Unternehmenspolitik*, pp. 80 et seq.

147 See Coffee, "Rise", pp. 18 and 20.

148 See Gischer et al, *Geld*, p. 30.

149 See Hennerkes, *Familie*, p. 368 et seq.; Bendel et al, "Entwicklung Unternehmensfinanzierung", p. 43.

150 See Soltow, "Origins", p. 32; Blackford, *Rise*, p. 81.

151 Data on Germany from: https://de.statista.com/statistik/daten/studie/237346/umfrage/unternehmen-in-deutschland-nach-rechtsform-und-anzahl-der-beschaeftigten/ (accessed: November 12, 2017).

152 See La Porta, López de Silanes and Shleifer, "Corporate Ownership", p. 508; Ampenberger, *Unternehmenspolitik*, pp. 2 and 5.

153 See Schmidt, "Corporate Governance", p. 388.

154 For the three-circle model of family businesses see, among others, Lubinski, *Familienunternehmen*, p. 15; Wimmer et al, *Familienunternehmen*, pp. 6 et seq. and 96 et seq.

155 See also with reference to the present day: www.delawareinc.com (accessed: December 15, 2018).

156 Lamoreaux, "Partnerships", p. 66.

157 See Friedman, *Law*, p. 50.

158 The same was true of the institutional infrastructure. The Delaware Court of Chancery was established in 1899. It is still the best-known, and certainly the most liberal, court in the United States in matters of corporate law. See Friedman, *Law*, p. 51.

159 Kirchbach, *Publizitätspflichten*, pp. 2–4; Ampenberger, *Unternehmenspolitik*, p. 79 [our translation].

160 See Fohlin, "History", pp. 26 et seq.

161 See Coffee, "Rise", p. 8.

162 Hawkins, "Development", pp. 166–167.

163 See Dunlavy and Welskopp, "Myths", pp. 42–43; Chernow, *House of Morgan*, pp. 31–32. According to Coffee's calculations, an investment bank on the board of a company adds around 30 percent to its market capitalisation (Coffee, "Rise", p. 29).

164 See Geisst, *Geschichte*, p. 153.

165 See Passow, *Aktiengesellschaft*, pp. 18–19; Heberton Evans, *Business Incorporations*, pp. 99–113, 120–126 and 134–144. A more recent data compilation can be found in: Dunlavy and Welskopp, "Myths", pp. 52–53.

166 See Hannah, "Divorce", p. 428.

167 See Blackford, *Rise*, p. 85 and Hannah, "Mergers", p. 306.

168 See O'Brian, "Factory Size"; Bell, *End*, pp. 42–43.

169 Quoted from Richter, *Wirkungsgeschichte*, p. 65. [our translation] For the development of case law see ibid., pp. 61–77.

170 Böhm, "Reichsgericht", p. 212 [our translation].

171 See Albert, *Kapitalismus*, pp. 103–127 [our translation]; Hau, "Traditions", pp. 44 and 48–49.

172 See Spindler, *Recht*, pp. 224–256.

173 See Guinnane, "Ownership", p. 702.
174 See Fohlin, "History", pp. 259 et seq.; also Gehlen, "Aktienrecht", p. 167.
175 See, among others, Gömmel, "Entstehung", pp. 153–55 and 160.
176 See Spindler, *Recht*, pp. 56 et seq.; Dunlavy and Welskopp, "Myths", p. 53.
177 See Fohlin, "History", pp. 227 and 259.
178 See ibid., p. 259.
179 See Coffee, "Rise", p. 55.
180 See Pellens and Fülbier, "Anforderungen", pp. 437 et seq.
181 See Klein, *Familienunternehmen*, p. 79.
182 See Coffee, "Rise", p. 24.
183 See Ehrhardt, Nowak and Weber, "Running in the Family", p. 5.
184 As confirmed by Fohlin, "History", p. 228.
185 See Ziegler, "Modell", p. 284.
186 Ibid., p. 285; Wixforth and Ziegler, "Bankenmacht"; Fohlin, "Rise", pp. 307–333. For a detailed analysis see also Fohlin, *Finance Capitalism*.
187 See Reckendrees, "Wurzeln", pp. 57–84.
188 See Fohlin, "History", p. 259.
189 See Schader, *Steuerungsfähigkeit*, p. 183.
190 Ibid.; Geisst, *Geschichte*, pp. 165–166f; Fohlin, *Finance Capitalism*, p. 29.
191 See Means, "Separation", pp. 76–78.
192 See, among others, Stamm, *Bundesfinanzen*, p. 123.
193 See Becht and DeLong, "Block Holding", p. 641.
194 Between 1900 and 1928 alone, the number of shareholders of the 31 largest industrial companies increased fivefold, from about 227,000 to 1.4 million. See Becht and DeLong, "Block Holding", p. 641; Means, "Diffusion", pp. 563–65.
195 See O'Sullivan, *Contest*, p. 76 and Rutterford and Sotiropoulos, "Rise", pp. 485–535.
196 Securities Exchange Act of 1934, Section 14 (a), quoted in: Bainbridge, *Corporate Governance*, p. 35.
197 See Coffee, "Rise", p. 37.
198 See Berle and Means, *Modern Corporation*, p. 109.
199 See Fohlin, "History", p. 262.
200 Data from Gömmel, "Entstehung", pp. 152 et seq.
201 For the persistence of network-based, often family, influence see Ziegler, "Kontinuität", pp. 46 and 52.
202 Dunlavy and Welskopp, "Myths", p. 56 [our translations].
203 See Pross, *Manager*, pp. 84–85.
204 See Fohlin, "History", p. 254.
205 See Spoerer, *C&A*, p. 58.
206 See Fohlin, "History", pp. 261–262.
207 See same author, "Investment", p. 29.
208 See Schmidt, "Corporate Governance", p. 7.

209 In this context, there were also attempts to abolish the charter system of the federal states, but both Theodore Roosevelt and William Taft were unable to enact a Federal Incorporation Law. Friedman, *Law*, p. 50.

210 Kirchbach, *Publizitätspflichten*, pp. 2–4.

211 See McDonald, *Insull*; Becht and DeLong, "Block Holding", pp. 642 et seq; Means, "Separation", pp. 75 et seq.

212 See Kirchbach, *Publizitätspflichten*, p. 4.

213 See Marcus and Dobkin Hall, *Lives in Trust*, p. 280; Beckert, *Vermögen*, pp. 222 et seq.

214 See Gall et al, *Deutsche Bank*, pp. 294 et seq.

215 For more details, see Bähr, "Corporate Governance", p. 64f; Fiedler, "Netzwerke", pp. 93 et seq.

216 See "Notverordnung des Reichspräsidenten über Aktienrecht, Bankenaufsicht und über eine Steueramnesie" of September 19, 1931, in RGBl (Imperial Law Gazette) I, 1931, pp. 493 et seq.

217 See Habersack, "Abschlussprüfer", p. 695.

218 For information on these laws, see, among others, Bähr, "Corporate Governance", p. 67.

219 See Tooze, *Ökonomie*, pp. 137–138.

220 See Hein, *Rezeption*, p. 188, for a general treatment of the Stock Corporation Act of 1937, and also pp. 169 et seq.

221 For an overview, see Buchheim and Scherner, "Role"; Spoerer, *Scheingewinn*.

222 Data from Deutsches Aktieninstitut, Factbook 2013, Table 01–1a and 01–08.

223 See Löffelholz, *Repetitorium*, p. 600.

224 See Fohlin, "History", pp.231 et seq.

225 For more details, see Fey, *Unternehmenskontrolle*, pp. 43–44; Wittgens, *Spruchverfahrensgesetz*, p 8.

226 See Fohlin, "History", p. 232.

227 Ibid. p. 235.

228 See Joly, *Großunternehmer*, p. 21.

229 See Coffee, "Rise", p. 18.

230 See Stiftung Familienunternehmen, *Bedeutung*, p. 39.

231 See Tagiuri and Davis, "Attributes"; Gersick, *Generation*; Moores, "Paradigms"; Wimmer, *Familienunternehmen*.

232 For more detail, see Wimmer and Groth, *Erfolgsmuster*.

233 See Mahr and Eisen, *Volkswirtschaftslehre*, p. 79; Beier, *Zeitraumanalyse*, p. 166.

234 See Berthold, *Familienunternehmen*, p. 80.

235 See Myers and Majluf, "Corporate Financing", pp. 187–221; Barton and Matthews, "Small Firm", pp. 1–7; for an overview, see also Koropp, *Financial Behavior*, pp. 17–18.

236 See *Koropp, Financial Behavior*, p. 18.

237 See Frantzke, Grohs and Laux, *Initial Public Offerings*, pp. 1 and 5.

238 See Koropp, *Financial Behavior*, p. 18. What is more, prior to their incorporation the majority of family businesses had placed only minority shares on the stock exchange, which led to price discounts on issue, ultimately resulting in poor share performance.
239 See Coffee, "Rise", p. 22.
240 See Jones, *Globalization*, p. 144 [our translation].
241 See, among others, Koch, *Globalisierung*, p. 28; Coffee, "Rise", p. 20.
242 See article "Münteferings Heuschrecken-Liste", *Der Spiegel*, April 29, 2005.
243 See Luttermann, *Unternehmen*, p. 12.
244 See Köhler, "Havarie", p. 260; Burghof and Hunger, "Access", p. 2.
245 For a general overview, see Berghoff, "1990er Jahre".
246 See Burghof and Hunger, "Access", p. 3.
247 See Ampenberger, *Unternehmenspolitik*, pp. 90–91.
248 Ibid, pp. 92 and 95.
249 See Leendertse, Julia "Stiftungen boomen wie nie zuvor", *Die Zeit*, January 20, 2010.
250 See also Bundesverband Deutscher Stiftungen, *Zahlen*, pp. 16–17; Schneider, *Unternehmensstiftungen*, p. 307.
251 See Schielke, "Vertrauen", p. 96.
252 See Berghoff, "Blending Personal."
253 See Fleschutz, *Stiftung*, pp. 72–74.
254 See Berthold, *Familienunternehmen*, p. 83.
255 See Burghof and Hunger, "Access", p. 13.
256 For further details, ibid., pp. 18 et seq.
257 See Bendel, Demary and Voigtländer, "Entwicklung", p. 41.
258 See Klein, *Familienunternehmen*, p. 234.
259 See Anderson and Reeb, "Founding-Family Ownership", p. 1302.
260 See Fohlin, "Investment", p. 32.
261 See Katz, "Securities Exchange Act of 1934", pp. 3–4; Bainright, "Short Life", p. 577.
262 See Bainright, "Short Life", p. 565.
263 It should be noted that the assignment of voting rights follows no clear pattern. Depending on the company and the share prospectus, Class A, B or C shares can be associated with different rights.
264 See Bainright, "Short Life", p. 583.
265 See Zellweger, *Managing the Family Business*, pp. 135–136.
266 See Commander, Using Different Classes.
267 See Burmistrova, *Corporate Governance*, p. 3; Moritz and Gesse, *Auswirkung*; Frugier, *Einrichtung*, pp. 2 et seq.
268 See Schmidt, "Corporate Governance", p. 3.
269 See also Berthold, *Familienunternehmen*, p. 86; Stiftung Familienunternehmen, *Kapitalmarktfähigkeit*, p. 47.
270 See Wernicke, *Kapitalismus*, p. 366; including Lundgreen, *Techniker*, pp. 7–132.

271 See Boelcke, *Glück*, pp. 74–87; Lundgreen, *Techniker*, pp. 133–217; Wernicke, *Kapitalismus*, pp. 357–377.

272 See Ziegler, "Zeitalter", pp. 253–254.

273 See Ullmann, *Interessenverbände*, pp. 2–3.

274 See Biggeleben, *Bollwerk*, pp. 31 et seq.

275 Gothein, *Mittelstand*, p. 7 [our translation].

276 Blackbourn, "Mittelstandspolitik", p. 116.

277 For history of the term, see Conze, "Mittelstand".

278 Blackbourn, "Mittelstandspolitik", p. 115.

279 See Berghoff, Köhler and Wixforth, "Navigation", p. 447.

280 See Wernicke, *Kapitalismus*, p. 352.

281 See Lenger, *Sozialgeschichte*, pp. 154–159.

282 See Grunberg, *Mobilization* (1941), p. 329.

283 A detailed overview is provided by Wernicke, *Kapitalismus*, pp. 151–392.

284 Quote as per Blackbourn, "Mittelstandspolitik", p. 117. See ibid., pp. 114–17 [our translation].

285 See Spiekermann, *Basis*.

286 Huber, *Verfassungsdokumente* (Vol. 4), p. 176 [our translation].

287 See Aufmkolk, *Mittelstandspolitik*, pp. 84–85; Berghoff, Köhler and Wixforth, "Navigation", p. 482.

288 See Geiger, "Panik".

289 Cf. Bähr, "Corporate Governance", p. 66.

290 The number of public limited companies declined during the 1931–1939 period from 10,437 to 5,535. The number of limited liability companies declined between 1934 and 1938 from 55,000 to 25,625, just to avoid the obligation to make public disclosures. See Bähr, "Corporate Governance", p. 78.

291 But tax authorities were definitely able to enforce conversions.

292 See Winkler, "Stand".

293 See Funk, *Befreiung*, pp. 19–20.

294 The provision that stated that replacement purchases could be written off entirely with immediate effect from 1933 onwards only brought partial relief. This also applied to non-durable assets from 1934 onwards. See Schröder, *Steuerlastgestaltung*, p. 88.

295 See Morck, "Double Taxation".

296 See Spindler, *Recht*, pp. 15–16.

297 See Lange, *Erwerb*, pp. 294–295.

298 See Köhler, *"Arisierung"*; Kreutzmüller, *Ausverkauf*; Bajohr, *Arisierung in Hamburg*; Janetzko, "Arisierung".

299 See Berghoff and Rauh-Kühne, *Fritz K.*, pp. 87–101 and 119–140.

300 Reichsgruppe Industrie, Gliederung, pp. 17–20. In 1936 Gottfried Dierig (Christian Dierig AG—textile business) succeeded Gustav Krupp von Bohlen und Halbach as chairman of the Reich Group Industry.

301 Munich grocer Franz Hayler headed up the Reichsgruppe Handel and the Fachgruppe Einzelhandel from 1938 onwards. For information on the role played by Cologne family business owner Kurt von Schröder as head of the Fachgruppe Privatbanken in the economic persecution of the Jews, see Köhler, "Arisierung", pp. 67 et seq.

302 See Bean, *Broker*, p. 5.

303 Quote as per ibid., p. 1.

304 See Schefer, *Verbot*, pp. 5–10.

305 Schivelbusch, *Verwandtschaft*.

306 See Kennedy, *Freedom*, pp. 84–85.

307 Patel, *New Deal*, pp. 66–79, quote p. 66.

308 Quote as per Bean, "World War", p. 218.

309 Zeigler, *Politics*, p. 138.

310 See Bean, "World War", p. 218; Zeigler, *Politics*, p. 13.

311 See http://www.sbc.senate.gov/public/index.cfm?p=History (accessed: February 15, 2018).

312 Quote as per Bean, "World War", p. 215.

313 See Hearings before the Special Committee to Study and Survey Problems of Small Business Enterprises, US Senate, 77th Congress, 1st Session, December 15–19, 1941, Washington 1942, https://babel.hathitrust.org/cgi/pt?id=umn.31951d03 587417o;view=1up;seq=1098 (accessed: February 15, 2018).

314 See Jones, "Position", p. 2.

315 Quote as per Bean, "World War", p. 221.

316 See ibid., pp. 222–225 and 230; id., *Broker*, pp. 99–119.

317 Cf. Martin and Moore, "Small Business".

318 Quote as per Bean, *Broker*, p. 144.

319 See ibid., "World War", p. 228.

320 Lilienthal, *Business*, p. 204.

321 See Murphy, Business, p. 281.

322 Quote as per Bean, *Broker*, p. 121.

323 See ibid.

324 Blackford, "Small Business", pp. 5–6.

325 Bunzel, *Small Businessman*, p. 59

326 Quote as per Bean, *Broker*, p. 162.

327 See ibid., pp. 143–156.

328 See ibid., pp. 150–163.

329 See ibid., pp. 156–163.

330 US General Accounting Office/Comptroller General of the US, Report to the Congress, Further Improvement Needed in Administration of the Small Business Investment Company Program B-149685, July 21, 1971, pp. 13 and 20.

331 See Hardach, "Wettbewerbspolitik", pp. 211–212; Ritschl, "Marktwirtschaft", pp. 298–311.

332 Quote in Ritschl, "Marktwirtschaft", p. 307 [our translation].

333 Schmidt, *Ziele*, p. 62.
334 See Ritschl, "Marktwirtschaft", p. 290.
335 Ibid., p. 295 [our translation].
336 See Hagley Library, 1960 Stock, American Chamber of Commerce, Publications Box 39, Big Business Day; ibid., Box 6, 408th Meeting, Board Report, November 15, 1975.
337 Ibid., Box 5, 393rd Meeting, Board Report, February 19–20, 1976, extract from transcript of a hearing before Congress' Committee on Finance dated December 10–12, 1975, Congressional Record, pp. 21589–21589.
338 Quoted from *Der Spiegel*, November 2, 1960.
339 See Grünbacher, *Industrialists*, p. 102.
340 See Pohl, "Symbol", pp. 35–36.
341 Schmidt, *Ziele*, p. 21 [our translation].
342 See ibid., pp. 235–240.
343 See De, *Bestimmungsgründe*, p. 85.
344 See Schmidt, *Ziele*, pp. 227–234.
345 Bundesministerium für Wirtschaft und Finanzen, *Mittelstandsfibel*, pp. 8–9 [our translation].
346 Repayable loans have not been treated as subsidies and not been factored in here. See Schmidt, *Ziele*, pp. 12, 243 and 255.
347 For an explanation of this complicated calculation, see De, *Bestimmungsgründe*, pp. 56–67.
348 For calculation method, see Plagge, "Venture-Capital-Märkte", p. 12.
349 See Weiblen, "Mittelstandspolitik", pp. 176–178.
350 Piore and Sabel, *Production*.
351 *Business Week*, November 22, 1984.
352 See Buder, *Capitalizing*, p. 423.
353 See Bail, "Programs"; Cheav, "Programs"; SBA Press Release, May 2, 2016, http://gtpac.org/2016/05/02/sba-releases-scorecard-on-small-business-partici-pation-in-federal-contracts/ (accessed: April 30, 2018).
354 See Bean, *Broker*, p. 160.
355 See Blackford, "Small Business", p. 7.
356 See Bridging the Capital Formation Gap. The SBA's SBIC Program, 2017, https://www.acg.org/sites/files/SBIC_Overview_12_April_2016.pdf (accessed: April 4, 2018).
357 US General Accounting Office/Comptroller General of the US, Report to the Congress, A Look at how the SBA's Investment Company Program for Assisting Disadvantaged Businessmen in Working, October 8, 1975, p. 12.
358 See Small Business Investor Alliance, undated communication (2015), http://www.sbia.org/?page=sbic_program_ history (accessed: May 4, 2018).
359 See US General Accounting Office/Comptroller General of the US, Report to the Congress, A Look at how the SBA's Investment Company Program for Assisting Disadvantaged Businessmen in Working, October 8, 1975, p. 12.

360 See Buss, *Capital*, p. 84.
361 See Jürgensmann, "EG-Beratungsstellen", p. 96.
362 James, *U.S. Defence R&D Spending*, p. 37.
363 See European Defence Agency, EU and US government's Defence spending, January 25, 2012, https://www.eda.europa.eu/ info-hub/press-centre/latest-news/12–01–25/EU_and_US_government_Defence_spending (accessed: May 9, 2018).
364 See Audretsch and Kettner, "Wandel".
365 See Klein, *Familienunternehmen*, p. 127.
366 See Bührmann and Pongratz, *Unternehmertum*.
367 See *The Economist*, January 21, 1989.
368 Quote as per Reed, Robert, "Once Dismissive of Export-Import-Bank. Bank Could Save 'Bank of Boeing', helping Illinois Businesses", *Chicago Tribune*, April 24, 2017.
369 See *The Hill*, February 24, 2017, http://thehill.com/policy/energy-environ-ment/383802-170-lawmakers-sign-resolution-calling-for-epa-chiefs-resigna-tion (accessed: April 19, 2018).
370 See Euler Hermes AG, *Exportgarantien, Annual Report 2014*, p. 2.
371 See McCartney, *Friends*, and Denton, *Profiteers*.
372 See Schanetzky, *Regierungsunternehmer*, pp. 332–337 and 346–351.
373 See Frei et al, *Flick*, pp. 620–697; Schanetzky, *Regierungsunternehmer*, p. 376.
374 Quoted from Siemens, *Recollections*, p. 16.
375 See Lenger, *Sozialgeschichte*.
376 Reif, "Gewalt", p. 90 [our translation].
377 See Berghoff, "Adel".
378 Quoted from Beckert, *Vermögen*, p. 176 [our translation].
379 See Gorißen, *Handelshaus*, pp. 132–134 and 143; Bosecker, "Rekrutierung", p. 78.
380 Numerous examples in Berghoff, "Adel".
381 See Schumann, *Bayerns Unternehmer*, pp. 75 and 219 as well as *Chronik der Gemeinde Stein*.
382 https://www.faber-castell.de/corporate/historie/familie/ (accessed: February 20, 2020).
383 Tönnies, *Gemeinschaft*.
384 Hegel, *Grundlinien der Philosophie des Rechts*, p. 323 (emphasis as in original) [our translation].
385 See the influential book by Wilhelm Heinrich Riehl (Naturgeschichte des Volkes, Vol. 3: Die Familien) from 1855, for whom the family was the nucleus of society.
386 See Beckert, *Vermögen*, p. 69; Carney, Gedajlovic and Strike, "Dead Money".
387 See Kocka, *Unternehmer*, pp. 35–41.

388 Jefferson, Thomas, *Bill for Abolition of Entails,* August 11, 1776, http://teach-ingamericanhistory.org/library/document/bill-for-abolition-of-entails/ (accessed: September 28, 2018).

389 See Beckert, *Vermögen,* p. 145.

390 See Sawyer, "Entrepreneur", pp. 11 and 20–22.

391 See Mills, "American Business Elite".

392 See Sarachek, "American Entrepreneurs".

393 See Beckert, *Vermögen,* pp. 96–97.

394 See Cochran, *Frontiers,* pp. 11–12 and 20–21.

395 Tocqueville, *Democracy,* p. 106.

396 Ibid., p. 124.

397 Grund, *Americans,* pp. 1–3.

398 See Rose, *Firms,* p. 304.

399 See Cochran, *Challenges,* pp. 6–12 and 33.

400 Cochran, *Frontiers,* p. 12.

401 Cochran, *Challenges,* p. 27.

402 See Atack, Bateman, and Parker, "Farm".

403 See Köhnen, *System Wal-Mart,* p. 19 [our translation].

404 See Bergmann, "Wal-Mart", p. 2.

405 See Köhnen, *System Wal-Mart,* p. 42.

406 See Kreitzberg, "History".

407 Polke-Majewski, Karsten, Wal-Mart gibt auf, *Die Zeit,* July 28, 2006, https://www.zeit.de/online/2006/31/walmart-metro-verkauf (accessed: Aug 15, 2018) [our translation]. See Knorr and Arndt, "How Not to Internationalize", pp. 263–267.

408 See, among others, Berghoff, *Unternehmensgeschichte,* p. 147.

409 See most recently in detail: Tabor, "Heterogeneity", pp. 615 et seq.; Moores, "All the Same", pp. 557 et seq.

410 See Welskopp, "Unternehmenskulturen", p. 280.

411 See Rose, *Firms,* p. 300.

412 Matis, "Unternehmenskultur", p. 1048 [our translation].

413 See Sackmann, *Unternehmenskultur,* p. 173.

414 See Wien et al, "Grundlagen".

415 Berghoff, *Unternehmensgeschichte,* p. 121. See many references in James, *Familienunternehmen,* p. 275.

416 See Berghoff, *Unternehmensgeschichte,* p. 259; Katz, *Margarete Steiff;* Hempe, *100 Jahre Melitta.*

417 Quoted from Hilger, "Paternalismus und Unternehmenskultur", p. 97 [our translation].

418 Quoted from Stremmel, "Familie Selve", p. 25 [our translation].

419 Casson, "Economics", p. 15.

420 See Weber-Kellermann, *Familie,* pp. 75–78.

421 After a difference of opinion, he even applied this rigid "hire and fire" policy to his right-hand man and chief engineer Thomas J. Watson, who after his dismissal went to work for rival firm CTR, from which the technology giant IBM was born. See Dyer, "Culture", p. 41.

422 See, among others, James, *Krupp*, p. 81; for the particularly sociopaternalistic leadership style of Robert Bosch see Bähr and Erker, *Bosch*, p. 26.

423 Rathenau, Walther, "Politische Auslese" (1912), in Walther Rathenau, *Gesammelte Schriften in fünf Bänden*, Berlin 1918, p. 231, quoted here from Scholtyseck, *Freudenberg*, p. 34 [our translation].

424 See ibid.; Kocka, *Unternehmensverwaltung*.

425 Dyer, "Culture", p. 44.

426 See Hettling and Hoffmann, *Wertehimmel*.

427 See Alchian and Demsetz, "Production"; Berghoff, *Unternehmensgeschichte*, p. 47.

428 Hilger, *Sozialpolitik*, p. 363 [our translation].

429 See Crowther, *Patterson*, p. 9, quoted from Dyer, "Culture", pp. 41 et seq.

430 For an overview from the wide range of literature, see Fischer, "Pionierrolle".

431 See James, *Familienunternehmen*, p. 99.

432 See Scholtyseck, *Freudenberg*, p. 35.

433 Stremmel, "Selve", p. 24 [our translation]. See Scholtyseck, *Freudenberg*, p. 35; Bugler, "Mars", p. 29.

434 For instance, Whitney MacMillan also referred to this as a guiding principle of the Cargill family firm: Weinberg, "Going Against", p. 160.

435 Henkoff, "Inside", pp. 83–90.

436 Brenner, *Emperors*, pp. 36 et seq.

437 Lubinski, *Familienunternehmen*, p. 27.

438 Götz, *Unternehmenskultur*, p. 41 [our translation].

439 See Dyer, "Culture", p. 41.

440 See Rothacher, "Mars Inc.", pp. 19 et seq.

441 Whitney MacMillan, quoted from the article "How to Feed the Growing Family", *The Economist*, March 9, 1996, p. 63.

442 MacMillan, "Power of Social Capital", p. 4.

443 See article "How to Feed the Growing Family", *The Economist*, March 9, 1996, pp. 63–64.

444 See Lubinski, *Familienunternehmen*, pp. 153 et seq.

445 Excellent examples can be found in Spitz, *Phänomen*, pp. 35 and 109; also Lubinski, *Familienunternehmen*, p. 126.

446 Dyer, "Culture", p. 41.

447 See for example: Scholtyseck, *Freudenberg*, p. 34; Stremmel, "Selve", p. 21; on Mars: Henkoff, "Inside".

448 See, among others, Stremmel, "Selve", p. 24; Lubinski, *Familienunternehmen*, p. 247.

449 See Berrone, Cruz and Gomez-Mejia, "Family-controlled Firms", p. 187; Gomez-Mejia et al, "Socioemotional Wealth"; Lubinski, *Familienunternehmen*, p. 111.
450 See Lubinski, *Familienunternehmen*, p. 104.
451 See Kocka, "Familie".
452 https://www.muehle-glashuette.de/muehle-glashuette/geschichte/ (accessed: February 20, 2020).
453 Colli and Rose, "Families and Firms", pp. 27–28.
454 See Chandler, *Visible Hand*.
455 Bennedsen, "Governance", p. 379.
456 See Dyer, "Culture", pp. 43–44.
457 Ibid., p. 46.
458 Ibid.
459 Ibid.
460 See Cabrera-Suárez, de la Cruz Déniz–Déniz and Martín-Santana, "Familiness", pp. 34–42; Zellweger, "Building".
461 See DiMaggio and Powell, "Gehäuse".
462 See, among others, Berghoff, "End", p. 274; Stürmer, *Herbst*; Haupt, *Ende*.
463 For continuities in the design of the educational system see Berghoff, Köhler and Wixforth, "Navigation", pp. 455 et seq.
464 See Lubinski, *Familienunternehmen*, pp. 122–167. For the feudalisation thesis of the European mercantile middle classes, see Berghoff, "Aristokratisierung", pp. 178–182.
465 See Köhler and Rossfeld, "Bausteine", p. 20; Schwarzkopf, *Fostering*, pp. 21 and 124 et seq.
466 See Sandage, *Born Losers*.
467 See Stiefel, *Labor*, p. 73.
468 See Hadding and Schneider, *Recht der Kreditsicherheiten*, pp. 185 et seq.
469 See Stiefel, *Labor*, p. 73.
470 See Gratzer, "Introduction", pp. 5–12.
471 See Köhler and Rossfeld, "Bausteine", p. 27.
472 See Stiefel, *Labor*, p. 122.
473 See Köhler and Rossfeld, "Bausteine", pp. 18–19.
474 See Eckhardt, *Restschuldbefreiung*.
475 For international comparisons see Osterkamp, "Insolvenzen".
476 See Stiefel, *Labor*, pp. 84–85.
477 See Kaelble, *Sozialgeschichte Europas*, p. 54.
478 See Inglehart, "Silent Revolution", pp. 991–1017; Rödder, "Materialismus".
479 See Roethlisberger and Dickson, *Management*; also Mayo, *Probleme*.
480 See Dyer, "Culture", p. 46.
481 See Rothacher, "Mars Inc.", p. 31; Kaplan and Adamo, "Inside Mars", p. 72.
482 Bugler, "Mars", p. 29.
483 Habermas, *Theorie*, p. 26; also Herbert, "Liberalisierung" [our translation].

484 See Schelsky, *Wandlungen*, p. 63; Herbert, *Geschichte*, p. 687.

485 See Lubinski, *Familienunternehmen*, p. 219.

486 Stiftung Familienunternehmen, *Familienunternehmen in Ostdeutschland*, pp. 37–76.

487 For details see the company files in the Sächsisches Wirtschaftsarchiv Chemnitz, holdings SWA U44, U55 and U98. The authors thank Ms. Veronique Toepel for her valuable help. See also Steiner, *Plan zu Plan*, p. 175; article "Als die DDR die letzten Familienbetriebe verstaatlichte", in MDR-Zeitreise, October 24, 2017, https://mdr.de/zeitreise/enteignungen-von-familienbetrieben-100.html (accessed: March 3, 2018).

488 See for example the case of the Veltins brewery, where the daughter gave up her veterinary medicine degree in order to take over the management of the business after her brother died; see Plate et al, *Familienunternehmen*, p. 93.

489 See Spoerer, *C&A*, p. 242.

490 See Plate et al, *Familienunternehmen*, pp. 58–59.

491 See Bähr and Erker, *Bosch*, pp. 25–26.

492 See James, *Krupp*, p. 214.

493 See Welskopp, "Unternehmenskulturen", pp. 284 et seq.

494 Vorwerck and Dunkmann, *Werksgemeinschaft*, p. 8 [our translation].

495 See Berghoff, Köhler and Wixforth, "Navigation", pp. 445 et seq.

496 Landes, "French Business", p. 339.

497 Ibid., p. 345.

498 Ibid., p. 343.

499 See the list at https://die-deutsche-wirtschaft.de/die-top-15-branchen-der-groessten-familienunternehmen (accessed: August 25, 2018).

500 See Global Family Business Index (as note 10) and Oxford Economics Information. The figures relate to revenues and employees in the sectors, https://www.ey.com/Publication/vwLUAssets/EY-family-business-in-north-america-facts-and-figures/$FILE/EY-family-business-in-north-america-facts-and-figures.pdf (accessed: September 9, 2018).

501 Quoted from Scholtyseck, *Freudenberg*, p. 35 [our translation].

502 See Kleinschmidt, *Blick*, pp. 173 et seq.

503 See Bahlsen, Hans, "Die Arbeit des Chefs" (1958), quoted from Kleinschmidt, *Blick*, p. 183 [our translation].

504 See, only by way of example for the majority of family entrepreneurs born during the 1920s to 1940s, among others the case of Dürr AG: Plate et al, *Familienunternehmen*, p. 160.

505 See Unternehmerbrief des Deutschen Industrieinstituts, No. 31, August 2, 1956, p. 2.

506 See Plate et al, *Familienunternehmen*, p. 33.

507 See Hartmann, *Unternehmer*.

508 See Köhler, "Havarie", pp. 253 et seq.; for the contemporary situation, see Servan-Schreiber, *Herausforderung*; OECD, *Gaps*.

509 See article "Ziel erkannt und dann drauf los", *Der Spiegel*, November 24, 1975.

510 See the collation of the documentation results in Schwetlick and Lessing, "Bilanz des Versagens", pp. 26–33; Köhler, "Havarie", p. 278.

511 See Kleinschmidt, "1968" [our translation].

512 See generally also Hilger, "Amerikanisierung".

513 Crainer, "Goodness", p. 37.

514 See Rothacher, "Mars", p. 31.

515 See Lubinski, *Familienunternehmen*, pp. 124 et seq.

516 All quotations from Hengstenberg, *Menschen* (unpublished manuscript in the Hengstenberg company archives) [our translations].

517 *Stuttgarter Zeitung*, January 17, 2018; company website: https://www.hengstenberg.de (accessed: September 20, 2018).

518 See the description of the case studies in Plate et al, *Familienunternehmen*.

519 See Lubinski, *Familienunternehmen*, p. 215.

520 See Henkoff, "Inside", p. 87.

521 See James, *Familienunternehmen*, pp. 102–103.

522 See Spoerer, C&A, p. 371, in detail pp. 339 et seq.

523 Ibid., p. 341.

524 See Brenninkmeijer, Alexander, "Ein Verkauf von C&A wäre ein Verkauf unserer Identität", *Focus Money Online*, https://focus.de/finanzen/diverses/unternehmen-mit-familientradition-alexander-brenninkmeijer-ein-verkauf-von-c-a-waere-ein-verkauf-unserer-identitaet_id_8489583.html (accessed: December 14, 2018).

525 See Anderson, Mansi, and Reeb, "Founding Family Ownership", pp. 263–285.

526 See, among others, Feick, *Stiftung*; Berghoff, "Blending", p. 865.

527 See Steingart, Gabor, "Er oder ich", *Der Spiegel*, August 5, 2002, pp. 90–94.

528 See Plate et al, *Familienunternehmen*, p. 84.

529 See Inglehart, "Silent Revolution"; Klages, *Wertorientierungen*; from an HR perspective Rosenberger, "Transformationsstrategie".

530 See Jakobi, *Personalpolitik*; Lubinski, *Familienunternehmen*, p. 279.

531 See Hofstede, *Culture's Consequences*.

532 See Opresnik, *Unternehmenskultur*, p. 133.

533 See Hoffmann, "Unternehmenskultur", pp. 91 et seq.; Trompenaars, *Riding the Waves*.

534 See Brozio, "Instrument", pp. 1–18.

535 The statistics reflect not only consumer wishes, but also old-age poverty. The data are taken from Ben-Shlomo, *Reverse Mortgage*, p. 27.

536 See estimates of IfM Bonn: Kay et al, *Unternehmensnachfolgen in Deutschland 2018 bis 2022*, p. 23; Robert Landgraf and Christian Potthoff, "Mittelstand treibt Bankgeschäft an", *Handelsblatt*, January 3, 2007; K.E.R.N-Studie zur

Unternehmensnachfolge 2017, https://www.die-nachfolgespezialisten.eu/studie-unternehmensnachfolge/ (accessed: August 28, 2018).

537 Quoted from Noon, *Yuengling*, p. 185.

538 See *Westfalenpost*, July 12, 2017 [our translation].

539 See *Pittsburgh Post-Gazette*, May 28, 2007.

540 See https://www.theatlantic.com/business/archive/2012/10/think-were-the-most-entrepreneurial-country-in-the-world-not-so-fast/263102/ (accessed: September 20, 2018).

541 James, "Family Values", p. 79.

List of Tables

List of Figures

Photo Credits

Bibliography

"500 Jahre Unternehmensgeschichte. The Coatinc Company. Das älteste Familienunternehmen Deutschlands", *Stahlreport*, August 7, 2019, pp. 18–20.

Abelshauser, Werner, *Kulturkampf. Der deutsche Weg in die neue Wirtschaft und die amerikanische Herausforderung* (Berlin, 2003).

Abou El Fadil, Yassin, *Erbschaftsteuergesetzgebung und Familienunternehmen im transatlantischen Vergleich – Die USA und Westdeutschland in den 1970er-Jahren*, unpublished MA thesis (Univ. Göttingen, 2016).

Adams, A. Frank, True, Sheb L. and Winsor, Robert D., "Corporate America's Search for the 'Right' Direction: Outlook and Opportunities for Family Firms", *Family Business Review* 15/4, 2002, pp. 269–276.

Albers, Sönke, *Elemente erfolgreicher Unternehmenspolitik in mittelständischen Unternehmen* (Stuttgart, 1989).

Albert, Michel, *Kapitalismus contra Kapitalismus* (Frankfurt a. M./New York, 1992).

Alchian, Armen and Demsetz, Harold, "Production, Information Costs and Economic Organisation", *American Economic Review* 62, 1972, pp. 777–795.

Alcorn, Pat B., *Success and Survival in the Family Owned Business* (New York, 1982).

Almeida, Heitor and Wolfenzon, Daniel, "A Theory of Pyramidal Ownership and Family Business Groups", *Journal of Finance* 61/6, 2006, pp. 2637–2680.

Amit, Raphael and Villalonga, Belen, "Financial Performance of Family Firms", in Leif Melin, Mattias Nordqvist and Pramodita Sharma (eds.), *The Sage Handbook of Family Business* (Los Angeles, CA, 2014), pp. 157–178.

Ampenberger, Markus, *Unternehmenspolitik in börsennotierten Familienunternehmen. Eine Analyse von Investitions-, Diversifikations- und Kapitalstrukturentscheidungen* (Wiesbaden, 2010).

Anderson, Ronald C. and Reeb, David M., "Founding-Family Ownership and Firm Performance. Evidence from the S&P 500", *Journal of Finance* 58/3, 2003, pp. 1301–1327.

Anderson, Ronald C., Duru, Augustine and Reeb, David M., "Founders, Heirs, and Corporate Opacity in the United States", *Journal of Financial Economics* 92, 2009, pp. 205–222.

Anderson, Ronald C., Mansi, Sattar and Reeb, David M., "Founding Family Ownership and the Agency Cost of Debt", *Journal of Financial Economics* 68/3, 2003, pp. 263–285.

Ang, James S., Cole, Rebel A. and Lin, James Wuh, "Agency Costs and Ownership Structure", *The Journal of Finance* 55/1, 2000, pp. 81–106.

Arens, Tobias, *Inter- und intragenerative Umverteilung im deutschen Steuer-Transfer-System. Langfristige Wirkungen im Lebenszyklus* (Frankfurt a. M., 2009).

Arnold, Arnd, "Entschädigung von Mehrstimmrechten bei Übernahmen. Überlegungen zur geplanten Übernahmerichtlinie", *Der Betriebs-Berater* 58/6, 2003, pp. 267–270.

Aronoff, Craig, "Self-Perpetuation Family Organization Built on Values: Necessary Condition for Long-Term Family Business Survival", *Family Business Review* 17/1, 2004, pp. 55–59.

Arp, Agnès, *VEB, Vaters ehemaliger Betrieb. Privatunternehmer in der DDR* (Leipzig, 2005).

Astrachan, Joseph H. and Dean, Kathy Lund, *Arthur Andersen American Family Business Survey* (St. Charles, IL, 1995).

Atack, Jeremy, Bateman, Fred and Parker, William N., "The Farm, the Farmer, and the Market", in Stanley L. Engerman and Robert E. Gallmann (eds.), *The Cambridge Economic History of the United States, Vol. 2. The Long Nineteenth Century* (Cambridge, MA, 2000), pp. 245–284.

Atack, Jeremy, "Firm Size and Industrial Structure in the United States during the Nineteenth Century", *Journal of Economic History* 46/2, 1986, pp. 463–475.

Audretsch, David B. and Kettner, Anja, "Der Wandel von traditioneller Mittelstandspolitik zu 'Entrepreneurship Policy'. Ein Blick auf Deutschland und die USA", *Politische Studien* 53/384, 2002, pp. 81–92.

Aufmkolk, Emmy, *Die gewerbliche Mittelstandspolitik des Reiches – unter besonderer Berücksichtigung der Nachkriegszeit* (Emsdetten, 1930).

Bade, Franz Josef, *Die wachstumspolitische Bedeutung kleinerer und mittlerer Unternehmen* (Berlin, 1985).

Bähr, Johannes and Erker, Paul, *Bosch. Geschichte eines Weltunternehmens* (Munich, 2013).

Bähr, Johannes, *Thyssen in der Adenauerzeit. Konzernbildung und Familienkapitalismus* (Paderborn, 2015).

Bähr, Johannes, "'Corporate Governance' im Dritten Reich. Leitungs- und Kontrollstrukturen deutscher Großunternehmen während der nationalsozialistischen Diktatur", in Werner Abelshauser, Jan Otmar Hesse and Werner Plumpe (eds.), *Wirtschaftsordnung, Staat und Unternehmen. Neuere Forschungen zur Wirtschaftsgeschichte des Nationalsozialismus*. Festschrift for Dietmar Petzina (Essen, 2003), pp. 61–80.

Bähr, Johannes, "Unternehmens- und Kapitalmarktrecht im 'Dritten Reich'. Die Aktienrechtsreform und das Anleihestockgesetz", in Johannes Bähr and Ralf Banken (eds.), *Wirtschaftssteuerung durch Recht im Nationalsozialismus. Studien zur Entwicklung des Wirtschaftsrechts im Interventionsstaat des "Dritten Reichs"* (Frankfurt a. M., 2006), pp. 35–69.

Bähr, Johannes and Banken, Ralf, "Wirtschaftssteuerung durch Recht im 'Dritten Reich'. Einleitung und Forschungsstand", in ibid. (eds.), *Wirtschaftssteuerung durch Recht im Nationalsozialismus. Studien zur Entwicklung des Wirtschaftsrechts im Interventionsstaat des "Dritten Reichs"* (Frankfurt a. M., 2006), pp. 3–32.

Bail, Philip G. Jr., "Federal Small Business Programs and the Small Business Act of 1953", *Contract Management*, Oct. 2009, pp. 24–41.

Bainbridge, Stephen M., *Corporate Governance after the Financial Crisis* (New York, 2012).

Bainbridge, Stephen M., "The Short Life and Resurrection of Sec Rule 19c-4", *Washington University Law Quarterly 69*, 1991, pp. 565–634.

Bajohr, Frank, *"Arisierung" in Hamburg. Die Verdrängung der jüdischen Unternehmer 1933–1945* (Hamburg, 1997).

Bajohr, Frank, *Parvenues und Profiteure. Korruption in der NS-Zeit* (Frankfurt a. M., 2001).

Ballarini, Klaus and Keese, Detlef (eds.), *Die Struktur kleiner Familienunternehmen in Baden-Württemberg* (Heidelberg, 1995).

Barton, S. L. and Matthews, C. H., "Small Firm Financing: Implications from a Strategic Management Perspective", *Journal of Small Business Management 27*, 1989, pp. 1–7.

Bauer, Tim, Nicolai, Alexander T. and Kolbeck, Christoph, *Innovationen in Familienunternehmen. Eine empirische Untersuchung* (Wiesbaden, 2013).

Baus, Kirsten, *Die Familienstrategie. Wie Familien ihr Unternehmen über Generationen sichern* (Wiesbaden, 2003).

Bayer, Walter and Habersack, Mathias (eds.), *Aktienrecht im Wandel der Zeit, Vol. 1: Historische Entwicklung des Aktienrechts, 1807–2007* (Tübingen, 2007).

Bean, Jonathan J., *Big Government and Affirmative Action: The Scandalous History of the Small Business Administration* (Lexington, KY, 2001).

Bean, Jonathan J., *Beyond the Broker State: Federal Policies toward Small Business, 1936–1961* (Chapel Hill, NC, 1996).

Bean, Jonathan J., "World War II and the 'Crisis' of Small Business: The Smaller War Plants Corporation, 1942–1946", *Journal of Policy History 6/3*, 1994, pp. 215–243.

Becht, Marco and De Long, J. Bradford, "Why Has There Been so Little Blockholding in America?", in Randall Morck (ed.), *A History of Corporate Governance around the World. Family Business Groups to Professional Managers* (Chicago/London, 2007), pp. 613–665.

Bechtle, Christine, *Die Sicherung der Führungsnachfolge in der Familienunternehmung* (Esslingen, 1983).

Beckert, Jens, *Unverdientes Vermögen. Soziologie des Erbrechts* (Frankfurt a. M., 2004).

Beck-Gernsheim, Elisabeth, "Auf dem Weg in die postfamiliale Familie. Von der Notgemeinschaft zur Wahlverwandtschaft", in Ulrich Beck and Elisabeth Beck-Gernsheim (eds.), *Riskante Freiheiten. Individualisierung in modernen Gesellschaften* (Frankfurt a. M., 1994), pp. 115–138.

Beier, Joachim, *Zeitraumanalyse. Bindeglied einzel- und gesamtwirtschaftlicher Unternehmensstatistik* (Berlin, 1975).

Bell, Daniel, *The End of Ideology. On the Exhaustion of Political Ideas in the Fifties* (Glencoe, IL, 1988).

Bendel, Daniel, Demary, Markus and Voigtländer, Michael, "Entwicklung der Unternehmensfinanzierung in Deutschland", *Vierteljahresschrift zur empirischen Wirtschaftsforschung 43*, 2016, pp. 37–54.

Bennedsen, Morten, Perez-Gonzalez, Francisco and Wolfenzon, Daniel, "The Governance of Family Firms", in H. Kent Baker and Ronald C. Anderson (eds.), *Corporate Governance. A Synthesis of Theory, Research, and Practice* (Hoboken, NJ, 2010), pp. 371–390.

Bennett, Robert J., *Entrepreneurship, Small Business and Public Policy Evolution and Revolution* (London, 2014).

Ben-Shlomo, Jonathan, *Reverse Mortgage. Ein integrativer Ansatz zur Erklärung der Nachfrage nach Umkehrhypotheken*, Ph.D. diss. (Freiburg University, 2015).

Berg, Christian, *Heinz Nixdorf. Eine Biographie* (Paderborn, 2016).

Berger, Johannes (ed.), *Kleinbetriebe im wirtschaftlichen Wandel* (Frankfurt a. M., 1990).

Bergeron, Louis, "Familienstruktur und Industrieunternehmen in Frankreich (18. bis 20. Jahrhundert)", in Neidthard Bulst, Joseph Goy and Jochen Hoock (eds.), *Familie zwischen Tradition und Moderne. Studien zur Geschichte der Familie in Deutschland und Frankreich vom 16. bis zum 20. Jahrhundert* (Göttingen, 1981), pp. 225–245.

Berghoff, Hartmut and Rauh-Kühne, Cornelia, *Fritz K. Ein deutsches Leben im zwanzigsten Jahrhundert* (Stuttgart, 2000).

Berghoff, Hartmut, *Moderne Unternehmensgeschichte. Eine themen- und theorieorientierte Einführung* (Paderborn, 2004).

Berghoff, Hartmut, "Aristokratisierung des Bürgertums? Zur Sozialgeschichte der Nobilitierung von Unternehmern in Preußen und Großbritannien 1870–1918", *Vierteljahrsschrift für Sozial- und Wirtschaftsgeschichte 81*, 1994, pp. 178–182.

Berghoff, Hartmut, "Unternehmenskultur und Herrschaftstechnik. Industrieller Paternalismus: Hohner von 1857 bis 1918", *Geschichte und Gesellschaft 23*, 1997, pp. 167–204.

Berghoff, Hartmut, "Adel und Industriekapitalismus im Deutschen Kaiserreich. Abstoßungskräfte und Annäherungstendenzen zweier Lebenswelten", in Heinz Reif (ed.), *Adel und Bürgertum, Vol. 1: Entwicklungslinien und Wendepunkte im 19. Jahrhundert* (Berlin, 2000), pp. 233–271.

Berghoff, Hartmut, "Historisches Relikt oder Zukunftsmodell? Kleine und mittelgroße Unternehmen in der Wirtschafts- und Sozialgeschichte der Bundesrepublik Deutschland", in Dieter Ziegler (ed.), *Großbürger und Unternehmer. Die deutsche Wirtschaftselite im 20. Jahrhundert* (Göttingen, 2000), pp. 249–282.

Berghoff, Hartmut, "Abschied vom klassischen Mittelstand. Kleine und mittlere Unternehmen in der bundesdeutschen Wirtschaft des späten 20. Jahrhunderts", in Volker R. Berghahn, Stefan Unger and Dieter Ziegler (eds.), *Die deutsche Wirtschaftselite im 20. Jahrhundert. Kontinuität und Mentalität* (Essen, 2003), pp. 93–113.

Berghoff, Hartmut, "The End of Family Business? The Mittelstand and German Capitalism in Transition, 1949–2000", *Business History Review* 80, 2006, pp. 263–295.

Berghoff, Hartmut, "Blending Personal and Managerial Capitalism. Bertelsmann's Rise from a Medium-sized Publisher to a Global Media Corporation, 1950–2002", *Business History* 45/6, 2013, pp. 855–874.

Berghoff, Hartmut, "The Immigrant Entrepreneurship Project: Rationale, Design and Outcome", in Hartmut Berghoff and Uwe Spiekermann (eds.), *Immigrant Entrepreneurship: The German-American Experience since 1700* (Washington, D.C., 2016), pp. 53–68.

Berghoff, Hartmut, "Familienunternehmen. Stärken und Schwächen einer besonderen Unternehmensverfassung", in Maria Spitz et al. (eds.), *Phänomen Familienunternehmen. Überblicke* (Mettingen, 2016), pp. 15–23.

Berghoff, Hartmut, "Varieties of Financialization? Evidence from German Industry in the 1990s", *Business History Review* 90, 2016, pp. 81–108.

Berghoff, Hartmut, Köhler, Ingo and Wixforth, Harald, "Navigation im Meer der Interessen. Binnenwirtschaftliche Steuerungsinitiativen des Reichswirtschaftsministeriums", in Carl-Ludwig Holtfrerich (ed.), *Das Reichswirtschaftsministerium der Weimarer Republik und seine Vorläufer. Strukturen, Akteure, Handlungsfelder – Wirtschaftspolitik in Deutschland 1917–1990, Vol. 1* (Berlin, 2016), pp. 421–516.

Berghoff, Hartmut, "Die 1990er-Jahre als Epochenschwelle? Der Umbau der Deutschland AG zwischen Traditionsbruch und Kontinuitätswahrung", *Historische Zeitschrift* 308, 2019, pp. 364–400.

Bergmann, Jens, "Wal-Mart in Deutschland. Augen zu und durch", in *Brandeins* 2/6, 2000.

Berle, Adolf A. and Means, Gardiner C., *The Modern Corporation and Private Property*, rev. new edition of the 1932 original edition (New York, 1968).

Berrone, Pascual, Cruz, Cristina and Gomez-Mejia, Luis R., "Family-controlled Firms and Stakeholder Management. A Socioemotional Wealth Preservation Perspective", in Leif Melin, Mattias Nordqvist and Pramodita Sharma (eds.), *The Sage Handbook of Family Business* (Los Angeles, CA, 2014), pp. 179–195.

Berthold, Florian, *Familienunternehmen im Spannungsfeld zwischen Wachstum und Finanzierung*, Lohmar 2010.

Bianchini-Hartmann, Maren and Richter, Andreas, "Die Besteuerung von Familienstiftungen", in Dieter Birk (ed.), *Transaktionen. Vermögen. Pro Bono. Festschrift zum 10jährigen Bestehen von P+P Pöllath und Partners* (Munich, 2008), pp. 337–362.

Biggeleben, Christof, *Das "Bollwerk des Bürgertums". Die Berliner Kaufmannschaft 1870–1920* (Munich, 2006).

Bjuggren, Per-Olof and Sund, Lars-Göran, "Strategic Decision Making in Intergenerational Successions of Small- and Medium-Size Family-Owned Businesses", *Family Business Review* 14/1, 2001, pp. 11–24.

Blackbourn, David, "Mittelstandspolitik im Kaiserreich", in David Blackbourn (ed.), *Landschaften der deutschen Geschichte. Aufsätze zum 19. und 20. Jahrhundert* (Göttingen, 2016), pp. 112–132.

Blackford, Mansel G., *The Rise of Modern Business: Great Britain, the United States, Germany, Japan, and China*, 3rd edition (Chapel Hill, NC, 2008).

Blackford, Mansel G., "Small Business in America. A Historiographic Survey", *Business History Review* 65, 1991, pp. 1–26.

Blair, Margaret M., *Ownership and Control. Rethinking Corporate Governance for the Twenty-First Century* (Washington, D.C., 1995).

Bloom, Nick and Van Reenen, John, "Measuring and Explaining Management Practices Across Firms and Countries", *National Bureau of Economic Research (NBER) Working Paper* 12216, 2006.

Boelcke, Willi A., *"Glück für das Land". Die Erfolgsgeschichte der Wirtschaftsförderung von Steinbeis bis heute* (Stuttgart, 1992).

Böhm, Franz, "Das Reichsgericht und die Kartelle. Eine wirtschaftsverfassungsrechtliche Kritik an dem Urteil des Reichsgerichts vom 4.2.1897, Entscheidungen des Reichsgerichts in Zivilsachen (RGZ) 38/155", *Ordo* 1, 1948, pp. 197–213.

Böllhoff, Christian G. (ed.), *Management von industriellen Familienunternehmen. Von der Gründung bis zum Generationsübergang* (Stuttgart, 2004).

Börstler, Burkhard and Steiner, Joachim, *Zur Personalsituation in mittelständischen Betrieben des produzierenden Gewerbes. Ergebnisse einer empirischen Untersuchung* (Göttingen, 1982).

Bosecker, Kai, "Rekrutierung und Nachfolge", in Maria Spitz et al. (eds.), *Phänomen Familienunternehmen. Überblicke* (Mettingen, 2016), pp. 75–81.

Brenner, Joel Glenn, *The Emperors of Chocolate. Inside the Secret World of Hershey and Mars* (New York, 1999).

Brozio, Tim, "Das Instrument der Umkehrhypothek als Altersvorsorge. Ein Praxismodell", *Recklinghäuser Beiträge zu Recht und Wirtschaft* 10, 2012, pp. 1–18.

Bruchey, Stuart (ed.), *Small Business in American Life* (New York, Guildford, 1980).

Buchheim, Christoph and Scherner, Jonas, "The Role of Private Property in the Nazi Economy: The Case of Industry", *Journal of Economic History* 66, 2006, pp. 390–416.

Buder, Stanley, *Capitalizing on Change. A Social History of American Business* (Chapel Hill, NC, 2009).

Bugler, Jeremy, "Mars. Bringer of Peace. The American Way of Business", *The Times* May 27, 1968, p. 29.

Bührmann, Andrea Dorothea and Pongratz, Hans J., *Prekäres Unternehmertum. Unsicherheiten von selbstständiger Erwerbstätigkeit und Unternehmensgründung* (Wiesbaden, 2010).

Bundesverband der Deutschen Industrie and Ernst & Young (eds.), *Der industrielle Mittelstand. Ein Erfolgsmodell* (Berlin, 2003).

Bunzel, John H., *The American Small Businessman* (New York, 1962).

Burch, Philip H., *The Managerial Revolution Reassessed. Family Control in America's Large Corporations* (Lexington, MA, 1972).

Burghof, Hans-Peter and Hunger, Adrian, "Access to Stock Markets for Small and Medium Sized Growth Firms: The Temporary Success and Ultimate Failure of Germany's Neuer Markt", working paper, 2005, https://papers.ssrn.com/sol3/papers.cfm?abstract_id=497404.

Burmistrova, Marina A., *Corporate Governance and Corporate Finance. A Cross-Country Analysis* (Bremen, 2005).

Burnham, James, *The Managerial Revolution, or, What is happening in the world now* (London, 1942).

Buss, Terry F., *Capital, Emerging High-growth Firms and Public Policy. The Case against Federal Intervention* (Westport, Conn., 2001).

Cabrera-Suárez, M. Katiuska, de la Cruz Déniz-Déniz, Maria and Martin-Santana, Josefa D., "Familiness and Market Orientation: A Stakeholder Approach", *Journal of Family Business Strategy* 2/1, 2011, pp. 34–42.

Cadbury, Adrian, *Family Firms and their Governance. Creating Tomorrow's Company from Today* (Zurich, 2000).

Carnegie, Andrew, "Wealth", *The North American Review* 148/391, 1889, pp. 653–664.

Carnevali, Francesca, *Europe's Advantage. Banks and Small Firms in Europe and Britain* (Oxford, 2005).

Carnevali, Francesca, "Social Capital and Trade Associations in America, 1860–1914: A Microhistory Approach", *Economic History Review* 64/3, 2010, pp. 905–928.

Carney, M., Gedajlovic, E. and Strike, V. M., "Dead Money: Inheritance Law and the Longevity of Family Firms", *Entrepreneurship Theory and Practice* 38, 2014, pp. 1261–1283.

Carosso, Vincent P. and Bruchey, Stuart Weems, *The Survival of Small Business* (New York, 1979).

Casson, Mark, "The Economics of the Family Firm", *Scandinavian Economic History Review* 47/1, 1999, pp. 10–23.

Chandler, Alfred D., *The Visible Hand. The Managerial Revolution in American Business* (Cambridge, MA, 1977).

Chandler, Alfred D., *Scale and Scope. The Dynamics of Industrial Capitalism* (Cambridge, MA, 1990).

Cheav, Votey, "Programs of Parity: Current and Historical Understandings of the Small Business Act's Section 8(a) and HUBZone Programs", *DePaul Business & Commercial Law Journal* 12/4, 2014, pp. 477–505.

Chernow, Ron, *The House of Morgan. An American Banking Dynasty and the Rise of Modern Finance* (New York, 1996).

Chester, Ronald, "Inheritance in American Legal Thought", in Robert K. Miller and Stephen J. McNamee (eds.), *Inheritance and Wealth in America* (New York, 1998), pp. 23–43.

Chronicle of the Stein family, donated by Johann Faber on his silver wedding anniversary on February 20, 1873, Stadtarchiv Stein, B 58.

Clignet, Remi, *Death, Deeds, and Descendants: Inheritance in Modern America* (New York, 1992).

Cochran, Thomas C., *Frontiers of Change: Early Industrialism in America* (Oxford, 1981).

Cochran, Thomas C., *Challenges to American Values: Society, Business, and Religion* (New York/Oxford, 1985).

Coffee, John C., "The Rise of Dispersed Ownership: The Roles of Law and the State in the Separation of Ownership and Control", *The Yale Law Journal: Symposium on World Organization* 111/1, 2001, pp. 1–82.

Colli, Andrea, *The History of Family Business, 1850–2000* (Cambridge, UK, 2003).

Colli, Andrea and Fernandez Perez, Paloma, "Business History and Family Firms", in Leif Melin, Mattias Nordqvist and Pramodita Sharma (eds.), *The Sage Handbook of Family Business* (Los Angeles, CA, 2014), pp. 269–292.

Colli, Andrea and Rose, Mary B., "Families and Firms. The Culture and Evolution of Family Firms in Britain and Italy in the Nineteenth and Twentieth Centuries", *Scandinavian Economic History Review* 47/1, 1999, pp. 24–47.

Colli, Andrea and Rose, Mary B., "Family Business", in Geoffrey Jones and Jonathan Zeitlin (eds.), *The Oxford Handbook of Business History* (Oxford, 2008), pp. 194–218.

Commander, Jennifer L., "Using Different Classes of Stock in Family", https://www.familybusinessadvocates.com/2017/11/using-different-classes-stock-family-owned-business/ (accessed: February 7, 2020).

Conze, Werner, "Mittelstand", in Otto Brunner, Werner Conze and Reinhart Koselleck (eds.), *Geschichtliche Grundbegriffe, historisches Lexikon zur politisch-sozialen Sprache in Deutschland, Vol. 4* (Stuttgart, 1978), pp. 49–92.

Crainer, Stuart, "Goodness, Greatness, Mars", *Business Strategy Review* 1, 2014, pp. 34–37.

Crowther, S., *John. H. Patterson: Pioneer in Industrial Welfare* (New York, 1923).

Dana, Leo Paul and Ramadani, Veland, *Family Businesses in Transition Economies Management, Succession and Internationalization* (Cham, 2015).

Davidoff, Leonore and Hall, Catherine, *Family Fortunes. Men and Women of the English Middle Class, 1780–1850* (Chicago, IL, 1987).

De, Dennis, *Bestimmungsgründe für die Zunahme der Mittelstandsförderung als Beispiel für Staatseingriffe*, Ph.D. (Cologne University, 1996).

Denton, Sally, *Profiteers. Bechtel and the Men who Built the World* (New York, 2016).

Derix, Simone, *Die Thyssens. Familie und Vermögen* (Paderborn, 2016).

Desens, Marc and Hey, Johanna, "Dokumentation zur Körperschaftssteuer in der Bundesrepublik Deutschland", in Carl Herrmann, Gerhard Heuer and Arndt

Raupach (eds.), *Einkommensteuer- und Körperschaftsteuergesetz. Kommentar*, Looseleaf, update 249 (Cologne, 2011), pp. 1–50.

Deutsches Industrieinstitut, *Unternehmerbrief*, No. 31, August 2, 1956.

Di Fabio, Udo, *Die Reform der Erbschaftsteuer. Verfassungsrechtliches Gutachten zu den Vorschlägen des Bundesfinanzministeriums und der Stiftung Familienunternehmen* (Munich, 2015).

DiMaggio, Paul J. and Powell, Walter W., "Das 'stahlharte Gehäuse' neu betrachtet. Institutioneller Isomorphismus und kollektive Rationalität in organisationalen Feldern", in Hans-Peter Müller and Steffen Sigmund (eds.), *Zeitgenössische amerikanische Soziologie* (Opladen, 2000), pp. 147–173.

Dinkel, Jürgen, "Erben und Vererben in der Moderne. Erkundungen eines Forschungsfeldes", *Archiv für Sozialgeschichte* 56, 2016, pp. 81–108.

Dobkin Hall, Peter and Marcus, George E., "Why Should Men Leave Great Fortunes to Their Children?", in Robert K. Miller and Stephen J. McNamee (eds.), *Inheritance and Wealth in America* (New York, 1998), pp. 139–171.

Dodd, Sarah Drakopoulou and Dyck, Bruno, "Agency, Stewardship, and the Universal-Family Firm: A Qualitative Historical Analysis", *Family Business Review* 28/4, 2015, pp. 312–331.

Dorn, Franz, "Das Erbrecht des Code Civil und seine Auswirkungen auf den bäuerlichen Grundbesitz in den Gebieten des 'Rheinischen Rechts'", in Werner Schubert and Mathias Schmoeckel (eds.), *200 Jahre Code Civil. Die napoleonische Kodifikation in Deutschland und Europa* (Cologne, 2006), pp. 17–45.

Dukeminier, Jesse and Krier, James E., "The Rise of the Perpetual Trust", *University of California Law Review* 50/6, 2003, pp. 1303–1343.

Dumas, Colette, "Understanding of Father-Daughter and Father-Son Dyads in Family-owned Businesses", in Joseph H. Astrachan, (ed.), *Family Business* (Cheltenham, 2008), pp. 475–490.

Dunlavy, Colleen A., "From Partners to Plutocrats: Nineteenth-Century Shareholder Voting Rights and Theories of the Corporation", in Kenneth Lipartito and David B. Sicilia (eds.), *Constructing Corporate America: History, Politics, Culture* (Oxford, 2004), pp. 66–93.

Dunlavy, Colleen A., "Why Did Some American Businesses Get So Big?", in Regina Lee Blaszczyk and Philip Scranton (eds.), *Major Problems in American Business History* (New York, 2006), pp. 257–263.

Dunlavy, Colleen A. and Welskopp, Thomas, "Myths and Peculiarities: Comparing U.S. and German Capitalism", *Bulletin of the German Historical Institute* 41/2, 2007, pp. 33–64.

Dunn, Barbara, "The Family Factor: The Impact of Family Relationship Dynamics on Business-Owning Families during Transitions", *Family Business Review* 12/1, 1999, pp. 41–57.

Dyer, W. Gibb, *Cultural Change in Family Firms. Anticipating and Managing Business and Family Transitions* (San Francisco, CA/London, 1986).

Dyer, W. Gibb, "Culture and Continuity in Family Firms", *Family Business Review* 1/1, 1988, pp. 37–50.

Eckhardt, Alexander, *Die Restschuldbefreiung. Probleme der Voraussetzungen und Rechtsfolgen der Restschuldbefreiung unter vergleichender Berücksichtigung des US-amerikanischen Rechts*, Ph.D. diss. (Cologne University, 2005).

"Economic Impact of Family Businesses – A Compilation of Facts", *Tharawat Magazine. The Publication for Family Businesses,* May/June 2014.

Ehrhardt, Olaf, Nowak, Horst and Weber, Felix-Michael, "'Running in the Family'. The Evolution of Ownership, Control, and Performance in German Family-owned Firms, 1903–2003", *Swiss Finance Institute Research Paper Series* 6–13, 2006.

Eifert, Christiane, "Succession Patterns in German Family Firms in the 20th Century", *International Economic History Conference* (Helsinki, 2006).

Engenendt-Papesch, Renate, *Die Funktionen der Klein- und Mittelbetriebe in der wettbewerblichen Marktwirtschaft* (Cologne, 1962).

Evans, Heberton George, *Business Incorporations in the United States, 1800–1943* (New York, 1948).

Faccio, Mara and Lang, Larry H.P., "The Ultimate Ownership of Western European Corporations", *Journal of Financial Economics* 65/3, 2001, pp. 365–395.

Fairlie, Robert W. and Robb, Alicia M., "Families, Human Capital, and Small Business: Evidence from the Characteristics of Business Owners Survey", *Institute for the Study of Labor Discussion Paper* 1296, 2004.

Fear, Jeffrey R., *Organizing Control. August Thyssen and the Construction of German Corporate Management* (Cambridge, MA/London, 2005).

Fear, Jeffrey R., "Straight outta Oberberg. Transforming Mid-Sized Family Firms into Global Champions 1970–2010", *Jahrbuch für Wirtschaftsgeschichte* 53/1, 2012, pp. 125–169.

Feddersen, Dieter, "Die Vorzugsaktie ohne Stimmrecht: Viel geschmähtes Relikt aus vergangenen Zeiten oder nützliches Finanzierungsinstrument", in Mathias Habersack et al. (eds.), *Festschrift für Peter Ulmer zum 70. Geburtstag am 2. Januar 2003* (Berlin, 2003), pp. 105–118.

Feick, Martin (ed.), *Stiftung als Nachfolgeinstrument. Zivilrecht, Steuerrecht und internationales Recht* (Munich, 2015).

Fernández Pérez, Paloma and Colli, Andrea (eds.), *The Endurance of Family Businesses. A Global Overview* (New York, 2014).

Fernández Moya, Maria; Fernández Pérez, Paloma and Lubinski, Christina, "Standing the Test of Time. External Factors Influencing Family Firm Longevity in Germany and Spain during Twentieth Century", *Journal of Evolutionary Studies in Business* 5/1, 2020, pp. 221–264.

Ferreira, M., "Risk Seeker or Risk Averse? Cross-Country Differences in Risk Attitudes towards Financial Investment", *The Behavioral Economics Guide 2018*, pp. 86–95.

Fey, Gerrit, *Unternehmenskontrolle und Kapitalmarkt. Die Aktienrechtsreformen von 1965 und 1998 im Vergleich* (Stuttgart, 2000).

Fiedler, Martin, "Netzwerke des Vertrauens. Zwei Fallbeispiele aus der deutschen Wirtschaftselite", in Dieter Ziegler (ed.), *Großbürger und Unternehmer. Die deutsche Wirtschaftselite im 20. Jahrhundert* (Göttingen, 2000), pp. 93–115.

Finger, Jürgen, Keller, Sven and Wirsching, Andreas, *Dr. Oetker und der Nationalsozialismus. Geschichte eines Familienunternehmens 1933–1945* (Munich, 2013).

Fischer, Wolfram, "Die Pionierrolle der betrieblichen Sozialpolitik im 19. und beginnenden 20. Jahrhundert", in Hans Pohl (ed.), *Betriebliche Sozialpolitik deutscher Unternehmen seit dem 19 Jahrhundert* (Wiesbaden, 1978), pp. 34–51.

Fleschutz, Karin, *Die Stiftung als Nachfolgeinstrument für Familienunternehmen. Handlungsempfehlungen für die Ausgestaltung und Überführung* (Wiesbaden, 2008).

Fletcher, Denise E. (ed.), *Understanding the Small Family Business* (London, 2007).

Fligstein, Neil, *The Transformation of Corporate Control* (Cambridge, MA, 1990).

Fligstein, Neil, "Bank Control, Owner Control, or Organizational Dynamics: Who Controls the Modern Corporation", *American Journal of Sociology* 98/2, 1992, pp. 280–307.

Fohlin, Caroline, *Finance Capitalism and Germany's Rise to Industrial Power* (New York, 2007).

Fohlin, Caroline, "The Rise of Interlocking Directorates in Imperial Germany", *Economic History Review* 52/2, 1999, pp. 307–333.

Fohlin, Caroline, "The History of Corporate Ownership and Control in Germany", in Randall K. Morck (ed.), *A History of Corporate Governance around the World. Family Business Groups to Professional Managers (NBER Series)* (Chicago, IL, 2005), pp. 223–281.

Fohlin, Caroline, "A Brief History of Investment Banking from Medieval Times to the Present", in Youssef Cassis and Richard Grossman (eds.), *Oxford Handbook of Banking and Financial History* (Oxford, 2016), pp. 1–39.

Frank, Dieter, *Erbschaftsteuer und Unternehmung. Eine steuerrechtliche und betriebswirtschaftliche Untersuchung unter Berücksichtigung des britischen, französischen und schweizerischen Rechts* (Berlin, 1969).

Frantzke, Stefanie, Grohs, Stefanie and Laux, Christian, *Initial Public Offerings and Venture Capital in Germany*, CFS Working Paper 26 (Frankfurt a. M., 2003).

Frei, Norbert et al., *Flick. Der Konzern, die Familie, die Macht* (Munich, 2009).

Freund, Werner, Kayser, Gunter and Schröer, Evelyn, *Generationswechsel im Mittelstand. Unternehmensübertragungen und -übernahmen 1995 bis 2000*, ifm-Materialien No. 109 (Bonn 1995).

Freund, Werner, *Familieninterne Unternehmensnachfolge. Erfolgs- und Risikofaktoren* (Wiesbaden, 2000).

Friedman, Lawrence M., *American Law in the Twentieth Century* (New Haven, CT/ London, 2002).

Frugier, Florian, *Die Einrichtung moderner interner Kontrollsysteme in Unternehmen mit US-amerikanischem Listing. Politische und betriebliche Rahmenbedingungen und Besonderheiten der Umsetzung des Sarbanes Oxley Act in Deutschland* (Hamburg, 2009).

Funk, Walther, *Befreiung von Kriegstributen durch wirtschaftliche und soziale Erneuerung*, Vortrag von Chefredakteur Walther Funk von der "Berliner Börsen-Zeitung" vor dem Hochschulring deutscher Art in Tübingen am 12. Juli 1929 (Berlin, 1929).

Gall, Lothar et al., *Die Deutsche Bank 1870–1995* (Munich, 1995).

Garretson, John, "Supplementary Statement", in United States Senate (ed.), *Industrial Relations. Final Report and Testimony Submitted to Congress by the Commission on Industrial Relations* (Washington, D.C., 1915), pp. 291–295.

Gehlen, Boris, "Aktienrecht und Unternehmenskontrolle. Normative Vorgaben und unternehmerische Praxis in der Hochphase der Deutschland AG", in Ralf Ahrens, Boris Gehlen and Alfred Reckendrees (eds.), *Die "Deutschland AG". Historische Annäherungen an den bundesdeutschen Kapitalismus* (Essen, 2013), pp. 165–194.

Geiger, Theodor, "Panik im Mittelstand", *Die Arbeit* 10, 1930, pp. 638–654.

Geisst, Charles R., *Die Geschichte der Wall St. Von den Anfängen der Finanzmeile bis zum Untergang Enrons* (Munich, 2007).

Gersick, Kelin E., *Generation to Generation. Life Cycles of the Family Business* (Boston, MA, 1997).

Gersick, Kelin E., *Generations of Giving. Leadership and Continuity in Family Foundations* (Washington, D.C., 2004).

Gersick, Kelin E. and Feliu, Neus, "Governing the Family Enterprise: Practices, Performance and Research", in Leif Melin, Mattias Nordqvist and Pramodita Sharma (eds.), *The Sage Handbook of Family Business* (Los Angeles, CA, 2014), pp. 196–225.

Gestrich, Andreas, *Geschichte der Familie im 19. und 20. Jahrhundert* (Munich, 1999).

Gewandt, Heinrich (ed.), *Die Zukunft des Mittelstands. Strukturpolitik in einer dynamischen Wirtschaft* (Düsseldorf, 1969).

Gischer, Horst et al., *Geld, Kredit und Banken*, 3rd edition (Berlin, 2012).

Goebel, Lutz, *Deutschlands Familienunternehmen. Wo sie herkommen, was sie stark macht* (Frankfurt a. M., 2014).

Gomez-Mejia, L. R. et al., "Socioemotional Wealth and Business Risks in Family-controlled Firms. Evidence from Spanish Olive Oil Mills", *Administrative Science Quarterly* 52, 2007, pp. 106–137.

Gömmel, Rainer, "Die Entstehung und Entwicklung der Effektenbörsen im 19. Jahrhundert bis 1914", in Rainer Gömmel and Hans Pohl (eds.), Deutsche Börsengeschichte (Frankfurt a. M., 1992), pp. 133–207.

Gorißen, Stefan, *Vom Handelshaus zum Unternehmen. Sozialgeschichte der Firma Harkort im Zeitalter der Protoindustrie 1720–1820* (Göttingen, 2002).

Gothein, Georg, *Mittelstand und Fleischnot.* Nach einem am 20. Oktober 1905 in Greifswald gehaltenen öffentlichen Vortrage (Berlin, 1906).

Götz, Irene, *Unternehmenskultur. Die Arbeitswelt einer Großbäckerei aus kulturwissenschaftlicher Sicht* (Münster, 1997).

Gratzer, Karl, "Introduction", in Karl Gratzer and Dieter Stiefel (eds.), *History of Insolvency and Bankruptcy from an International Perspective* (Huddinge, 2008), pp. 5–12.

Graves, Chris and Thomas, Jill, "Determinants of the Internationalization Pathways of Family Firms: An Examination of Family Influence", *Family Business Review* 21/2, 2008, pp. 151–167.

Griffin, Clyde and Griffen, Sally, "Family and Business in a Small City: Poughkeepsie, New York, 1850–1880", *Journal of Urban History* 1/3, 1975, pp. 316–338.

Groppe, Carola, *Der Geist des Unternehmertums. Eine Bildungs- und Sozialgeschichte der Seidenfabrikantenfamilie Colsman, 1649–1840* (Cologne, 2004).

Grosser, Alfred, "Familie und Firma als gesellschaftlicher und wirtschaftlicher Funktionsverbund. Geschichte und Entwicklung der Familie und Firma B. Metzler seel. Sohn & Co. 1674-1974", in ibid. et al. (eds.), *Wirtschaft, Gesellschaft, Geschichte* (Stuttgart, 1974), pp. 264–290.

Groth, Torsten and Simon, Fritz B., "100 Jahre und älter. Die Leistung und Entwicklungsschritte von Mehrgenerationen-Familienunternehmen", in Markus Plate et al. (eds.), *Große deutsche Familienunternehmen: Generationenfolge, Familienstrategie und Unternehmensentwicklung* (Göttingen, 2011), pp. 18–42.

Grühler, Wolfram, *Wirtschaftsfaktor Mittelstand. Zu Wesen und Bedeutung kleinerer und mittlerer Unternehmen in der Bundesrepublik Deutschland* (Cologne, 1984).

Grünbacher, Armin, *West German Industrialists and the Making of the Economic Miracle. A History of Mentality and Recovery* (London/New York, 2017).

Grunberg, Emile, "The Mobilization of Capacity and Resources of Small-Scale Enterprises in Germany", *Journal of Business of the University of Chicago* 14/4, 1941, pp. 319–344.

Grunberg, Emile, "The Mobilization of Capacity and Resources of Small-Scale Enterprises in Germany (concluded)", in *Journal of Business of the University of Chicago* 15/1, 1942, pp. 56–89.

Grund, Francis J., *The Americans in their Moral, Social, and Political Relations* Vol. 2 (London, 1837).

Gudmundson, Donald, Hartman, E. Alan and Tower, C. Burk, "Strategic Orientation: Differences between Family and Nonfamily Firms", *Family Business Review* 12/1, 1999, pp. 27–39.

Guinnane, Timothy et al., "Ownership and Control in the Entrepreneurial Firm: An International History of Private Limited Companies", *Yale University Center Discussion Paper* 959, 2007.

Gurland, Arcadius et al., *The Fate of Small Business in Nazi Germany* (Washington, D.C., 1943).

Habermas, Jürgen, *Theorie des kommunikativen Handelns* (Frankfurt a. M., 1981).

Habersack, Mathias, "Der Abschlussprüfer", in Mathias Habersack and Walter Bayer, *Aktienrecht im Wandel*, Vol. 2 (Tübingen, 2007), pp. 681–707.

Hadding, Walther and Schneider, Uwe, *Recht der Kreditsicherheiten in den Vereinigten Staaten von Amerika, Teil 1: Kreditsicherheiten an beweglichen Sachen nach Art. 9 UCC* (Berlin, 1983).

Hall, Peter A. and Soskice, David, *Varieties of Capitalism. The Institutional Foundations of Comparative Advantage* (Oxford, 2001).

Hannah, Leslie, "Mergers, Cartels and Concentration. Legal Factors in the U.S. and European Experience", in Norbert Horn and Jürgen Kocka (eds.), *Law and the Formation of the Big Enterprises in the 19th and early 20th Centuries* (Göttingen, 1979), pp. 306–316.

Hannah, Leslie, "From Family Firm to Professional Management. Structure and Performance of Business Enterprise", *Zeitschrift für Unternehmensgeschichte* 28/2, 1983, pp. 120–125.

Hannah, Leslie, "The 'Divorce' of Ownership from Control from 1900 onwards: Recalibrating Imagined Global Trends", *Business History* 49/4, 2007, pp. 404–438.

Hardach, Gerd, "Wettbewerbspolitik in der Sozialen Marktwirtschaft", in Werner Abelshauser (ed.), *Das Bundeswirtschaftsministerium in der Ära der Sozialen Marktwirtschaft. Der deutsche Weg der Wirtschaftspolitik* (Berlin/Boston, MA, 2016), pp. 193–264.

Hartmann, Heinz, *Der deutsche Unternehmer: Autorität und Organisation* (Frankfurt a. M., 1968).

Haßenpflug, Maximilian, *Der deutsche Mittelstand als gesellschaftliches Projekt. Eine institutionenökonomische Analyse staatlicher Förderungsinstrumente am Beispiel Niedersachsens der 1970er und 1980er-Jahre,* unpublished master's thesis (Univ. Göttingen, 2016).

Hau, Michel, "Traditions Comportamentales et Capitalisme Dynastique: Le Cas des 'Grandes Familles'", *Entreprises et Histoire* 9, 1995, pp. 43–59.

Haupt, Heinz-Gerhard, *Das Ende der Zünfte. Ein europäischer Vergleich* (Göttingen, 2002).

Hawkins, David F., "The Development of Modern Financial Reporting Practices among American Manufacturing Corporations", in Richard S. Tedlow and Richard R. John Jr. (eds.), *Managing Big Business. Essays from the Business History Review* (Boston, MA, 1986), pp. 166–199.

Hegel, Georg Wilhelm Friedrich, *Grundlinien der Philosophie des Rechts (Naturrecht und Staatswissenschaft im Grundrisse). Zum Gebrauch für seine Vorlesungen)*, Werke, Vol. 7, first edition: Berlin (Nicolai) 1820, forward dated to 1821 (Frankfurt a. M., 1979).

Hein, Jan von, *Die Rezeption US-amerikanischen Gesellschaftsrechts in Deutschland* (Tübingen, 2008).

Hempe, Mechthild, *100 Jahre Melitta. Geschichte eines Markenunternehmens* (Cologne, 2008).

Hengstenberg, Richard, *Menschen unserer Zeit. Persönlichkeiten des öffentlichen Lebens, der Kirche, Wirtschaft und der Politik*, published by Akademie "Kontakte der Kontinente", unpublished manuscript (Bonn, 1972).

Henkoff, Ronald, "Inside America's Biggest Private Company", *Fortune*, July 13, 1992, pp. 83–90.

Hennerkes, Brun-Hagen, *Die Familie und ihr Unternehmen. Strategie, Liquidität, Kontrolle* (Frankfurt a. M./New York, 2004).

Herbert, Ulrich, *Geschichte Deutschlands im 20. Jahrhundert* (Munich, 2014).

Herbert, Ulrich, "Liberalisierung als Lernprozeß. Die Bundesrepublik in der deutschen Geschichte. Eine Skizze", in Ulrich Herbert (ed.), *Wandlungsprozesse in Westdeutschland. Belastung, Integration, Liberalisierung 1945–1980* (Göttingen, 2002), pp. 7–49

Hersh, Burton, *The Mellon Family. A Fortune in History* (New York, 1978).

Hettling, Manfred and Hoffmann, Stefan L. (eds.), *Der bürgerliche Wertehimmel. Innenansichten des Jahrhunderts* (Göttingen, 2000).

Hilger, Susanne, *Sozialpolitik und Organisation. Formen betrieblicher Sozialpolitik in der rheinisch-westfälischen Eisen- und Stahlindustrie seit der Mitte des 19. Jahrhunderts bis 1933* (Stuttgart, 1996).

Hilger, Susanne, *'Amerikanisierung' deutscher Unternehmen. Wettbewerbsstrategien und Unternehmenspolitik bei Henkel, Siemens und Daimler-Benz (1945/49–1975)* (Stuttgart, 2004).

Hilger, Susanne and Soenius, Ulrich S., *Familienunternehmen im Rheinland im 19. und 20. Jahrhundert. Netzwerke – Nachfolge – soziales Kapital* (Cologne, 2009).

Hilger, Susanne, "Vom Netzwerk zum Cluster. Düsseldorf als Industriestandort im 19. Jahrhundert", in Wilfried Feldenkirchen, Susanne Hilger and Kornelia Rennert (eds.), *Geschichte. Unternehmen. Archive* (Essen, 2008), pp. 259–272.

Hilger, Susanne, "Paternalismus und Unternehmenskultur", in Maria Spitz et al. (eds.), *Phänomen Familienunternehmen. Überblicke* (Mettingen, 2016), pp. 95–104.

Hirsch, Adam J., "Inheritance: United States Law", in Stanley N. Katz (ed.), *Oxford International Encyclopedia of Legal History, Vol. 3* (Oxford, 2009), pp. 235–240.

Hoffmann, Friedrich, "Unternehmenskultur in Amerika und Deutschland", *Harvard Manager* 1, 1989, pp. 91–97.

Hoffmann, Heinz, *Als privater Unternehmer in der DDR. Eine Dresdner Firmengeschichte* (Beucha, 2003).

Hoffmann, Walther G., *Das Wachstum der Deutschen Wirtschaft seit der Mitte des 19. Jahrhunderts* (Berlin, 1965).

Hofstede, Geert, *Culture's Consequences. International Differences in Work-Related Values* (Beverly Hills, 1980).

Howorth, Carole, Rose, Mary B. and Hamilton, Eleanor, "Definitions, Diversity and Development. Key Debates in Family Business Research", in Mark Casson et al. (eds.), *The Oxford Handbook of Entrepreneurship* (Oxford, 2006), pp. 225–247.

Huber, Ernst Rudolf, *Dokumente zur deutschen Verfassungsgeschichte, Vol. 3: Dokumente der Novemberrevolution und der Weimarer Republik 1918–1933* (Stuttgart, 1992).

Hüller, Jasmin and Ley, Michael, *Durch Erfindergeist zum Weltmarktführer. Die hundertjährige Geschichte des Familienunternehmens Haas* (Vienna, 2005).

Inglehart, Ronald, "The Silent Revolution in Europe. Intergenerational Change in Post-Industrial Societies", *The American Political Science Review* 65, 1971, pp. 991–1017.

Institut für Mittelstandsforschung (ed.), *Generationswechsel im Mittelstand. Unternehmensübertragungen und -übernahmen 1995–2000* (Bonn, 1995).

Institut für Mittelstandsforschung (ed.), *Die internationale Wirtschaftstätigkeit kleiner und mittlerer Unternehmen im Lichte der amtlichen und nicht-amtlichen Statistik* (Bonn, 2001).

Jacobson, Darien B., Raub, Brian G. and Johnson, Barry W., "The Estate Tax. 90 Years and Counting", *Internal Revenue Service*, 2007, pp. 118–128.

Jacobi, F., *Personalpolitik heute und morgen* (Düsseldorf/Vienna, 1963).

James, Andrew D., *U.S. Defence R&D Spending: An Analysis of the Impacts. Rapporteur's Report for the EURAB Working Group ERA Scope and Vision* (Manchester, 2004).

James, Harold, *Familienunternehmen in Europa. Haniel, Wendel und Falck* (Munich, 2005).

James, Harold, *Krupp: Deutsche Legende und globales Unternehmen* (Munich, 2011).

James, Harold, "Family Values or Crony Capitalism?", in Paloma Fernandez Pérez and Andrea Colli (eds.), *The Endurance of Family Businesses. A Global Overview* (Cambridge, UK, 2013), pp. 57–84.

James, John A., "Structural Change in American Manufacturing, 1850–1890", *Journal of Economic History* 43/2, 1983, pp. 433–459.

Janetzko, Maren, "Die 'Arisierung' von Textileinzelhandelsgeschäften in Augsburg am Beispiel der Firmen Heinrich Kuhn und Leeser Damenbekleidung GmbH", in Andreas Wirsching (ed.), *Nationalsozialismus in Bayerisch-Schwaben. Herrschaft – Verwaltung – Kultur* (Ostfildern, 2004), pp. 153–183.

Johnson, Barry W. and Britton Eller, Martha, "Federal Taxation of Inheritance and Wealth Transfers", in Robert K. Miller and Stephen J. McNamee (eds.), *Inheritance and Wealth in America* (New York, 1998), pp. 61–90.

Joly, Hervé, *Großunternehmer in Deutschland. Soziologie einer industriellen Elite, 1933–1989* (Leipzig, 1998).

Joly, Hervé, "Ende des Familienkapitalismus? Das Überleben der Unternehmerfamilien in den deutschen Wirtschaftseliten des 20. Jahrhunderts", in Volker R. Berghahn, Stefan Unger and Dieter Ziegler (eds.), *Die deutsche Wirtschaftselite im 20. Jahrhundert. Kontinuität und Mentalität* (Essen, 2003), pp. 75–91.

Jones, Geoffrey and Rose, Mary B. (eds.), *Family Capitalism* (London, 1993).

Jones, Geoffrey, "Globalization", in Geoffrey Jones and Jonathan Zeitlin (eds.), *The Oxford Handbook of Business History* (Oxford, 2008), pp. 141–170.

Jones, Rudolph, "The Relative Position of Small Business in the American Economy since 1930", in Vincent P. Carosso and Stuart Weems Bruchey (eds.), *The Survival of Small Business. Small Business Enterprise in America* (New York, 1979), pp. 1–35.

Jürgensmann, Hans-Herrmann, "EG-Beratungsstellen. Hilfen für die Suche von Kooperationspartnern für den Mittelstand", in Jürgen Berthel and Fred Becker (eds.), *Unternehmerische Herausforderungen durch den europäischen Binnenmarkt 1992* (Wiesbaden, 1990), pp. 95–105.

Kaelble, Hartmut, *Sozialgeschichte Europas 1945 bis zur Gegenwart* (Munich, 2007).

Kaiser, Monika, *1972 – Knockout für den Mittelstand. Zum Wirken von SED, CDU, LPD und NDPD für die Verstaatlichung der Klein- und Mittelbetriebe* (Berlin, 1991).

Kaltenbach, Annette (ed.), *Verbinden und Bewegen. 150 Jahre Emil Kaltenbach* (Ennepetal, 2004).

Kampmann, Tobias, *Vom Werkzeughandel zum Maschinenbau. Der Aufstieg des Familienunternehmens W. Ferd. Klingelnberg Söhne 1900–1950* (Stuttgart, 1994).

Kaplan, Abraham David Hannath, *Small Business. Its Place and Problems* (New York, 1948).

Kaplan, David A. and Adamo, Marilyn, "Inside Mars", *Fortune*, April 2, 2013, Vol. 167/2, p. 72.

Karofsky, Paul et al., "Work-Family Conflict and Emotional Well-Being in American Family Businesses", *Family Business Review* 14/4, 2001, pp. 313–324.

Karras, Neri, Tracey, Paul and Phillips, Nelson, "Altruism and Agency in the Family Firm. Exploring the Role of Family, Kinship, and Ethnicity", *Entrepreneurship. Theory and Practice* 30/6, 2006, pp. 861–877.

Katz, Gabriele, *Margarete Steiff. Die Biografie* (Karlsruhe 2015).

Katz, Jonathan G., "Securities Exchange Act of 1934. Release No. 34–27034/July 14, 1989", *SEC Docket* 44/1, 1989, pp. 2–9.

Kay, Rosemarie, Suprinovi, Olga, Schlömer-Laufen, Nadine and Rauch, Andreas, *Unternehmensnachfolgen in Deutschland 2018 bis 2022*, IfM Bonn: Daten und Fakten 18 (Bonn, 2018).

Kayser, Gunter and Wallau, Frank, "Industrial Family Businesses in Germany – Situation and Future", *Family Business Review* 15/2, 2002, pp. 111–115.

Kennedy, David M., *Freedom from Fear. The American People in Depression and War, 1929–1945* (Oxford, 2004).

Kieser, Alfred, "Organizational, Institutional, and Societal Evolution: Medieval Craft Guilds and the Genesis of Formal Organizations", *Administrative Science Quarterly* 34/4, 1989, pp. 540–564.

Kirchbach, Judith Maria von, *Publizitätspflichten börsennotierter Gesellschaften in Deutschland und den USA*, Ph.D. diss. (Cologne University, 2007).

Kirchdörfer, Rainer et al., *Familienunternehmen in Recht, Wirtschaft, Politik und Gesellschaft. Festschrift für Brun-Hagen Hennerkes zum 70. Geburtstag* (Munich, 2009).

Klages, Helmut, *Wertorientierungen im Wandel. Rückblick, Gegenwartsanalyse, Prognosen* (Frankfurt a. M., 1984).

Klein, Sabine B., *Familienunternehmen. Theoretische und empirische Grundlagen* (Wiesbaden, 2000).

Klein, Sabine B., "Family Businesses in Germany: Significance and Structure", *Family Business Review* 13/3, 2000, pp. 157–181.

Klein, Sabine B. and Blondel, Christine, "Ownership Structure of the 250 Largest Listed Companies in Germany", *IIFE Working Paper Series* 123, 2002.

Klein, Sabine B., "Family Business Research in German Publications 1990–2000", *IIFE Working Paper Series* 05, 2003.

Klein, Sabine B., "KMU und Familienunternehmen", *Zeitschrift für KMU und Entrepreneurship* 52/3, 2004, pp. 153–173.

Klein, Sabine B., "Beiräte in Familienunternehmen. Zwischen Beratung und Kontrolle", *Zeitschrift für KMU und Entrepreneurship* 53/3, 2005, pp. 185–207.

Kleinschmidt, Christian, *Der produktive Blick. Wahrnehmung amerikanischer und japanischer Management- und Produktionsmethoden durch deutsche Unternehmer 1950–1985* (Berlin, 2002).

Kleinschmidt, Christian, "Das '1968' der Manager. Fremdwahrnehmung und Selbstreflexion einer sozialen Elite in den 1960er-Jahren", in Christian Kleinschmidt, Jan-Otmar Hesse and Karl Lauschke (eds.), *Kulturalismus, Neue Institutionenökonomie oder Theorienvielfalt. Eine Zwischenbilanz der Unternehmensgeschichte* (Essen, 2002), pp. 19–31.

Knorr, Andreas and Arndt, Andreas, "How Not to Internationalize in Retailing. The Case of Wal-Mart in Germany", in Alexandr N. Krylow and Tobias Schauf, (eds.), *Internationales Management* (Berlin, 2008), pp. 263–267.

Koch, Eckart, *Globalisierung: Wirtschaft und Politik: Chancen – Risiken – Antworten* (Wiesbaden, 2014).

Kocka, Jürgen, *Unternehmensverwaltung und Angestelltenschaft am Beispiel Siemens 1847–1914. Zum Verhältnis von Kapitalismus und Bürokratie in der deutschen Industrialisierung* (Stuttgart, 1969).

Kocka, Jürgen, *Unternehmer in der deutschen Industrialisierung* (Göttingen, 1975).

Kocka, Jürgen, "Familie, Unternehmer und Kapitalismus. An Beispielen aus der frühen deutschen Industrialisierung", *Zeitschrift für Unternehmensgeschichte* 24, 1979, pp. 99–135.

Köhler, Ingo, *Die "Arisierung" der Privatbanken im Dritten Reich. Verdrängung, Ausschaltung und die Frage der Wiedergutmachung*, 2nd edition (Munich, 2008).

Köhler, Ingo, "Wirtschaftsbürger und Unternehmer. Zum Heiratsverhalten deutscher Privatbankiers im Übergang zum 20. Jahrhundert", in Dieter Ziegler (ed.), *Die wirtschaftsbürgerliche Elite im 20. Jahrhundert* (Göttingen, 2000), pp. 116–143.

Köhler, Ingo and Rossfeld, Roman, "Bausteine des Misserfolgs. Zur Strukturierung eines Forschungsfeldes", in Ingo Köhler and Roman Rossfeld (eds.), *Pleitiers und Bankrotteure. Geschichte des ökonomischen Scheiterns vom 18. bis 20. Jahrhundert* (Frankfurt a. M./New York, 2012), pp. 9–34.

Köhler, Ingo, "Havarie der 'Schönwetterkapitäne'? Die Wirtschaftswunder-Unternehmer in den 1970er-Jahren", in Ingo Köhler and Roman Rossfeld (eds.),

Pleitiers und Bankrotteure. Geschichte des ökonomischen Scheiterns vom 18. bis 20. Jahrhundert (Frankfurt a. M./New York, 2012), pp. 251–283.

Köhnen, Heiner, *Das System Wal-Mart. Strategien, Personalpolitik und Unternehmenskultur eines Einzelhandelsgiganten*, Arbeitspapier 20 der Hans Böckler-Stiftung (Düsseldorf, 2000).

Kollmer-von Oheimb-Loup, Gert and Wischermann, Clemens (eds.), *Unternehmernachfolge in Geschichte und Gegenwart* (Ostfildern, 2008).

Koropp, Christian, *Financial Behavior in Family Firms*, Ph.D. diss. (WHU Vallendar, 2010).

Kreitzberg, M., "Wal-Mart's History in Germany", in Patrick Siegfried (ed.), *International Management in Practice. Vol. 2: VW, Google, H&M, Wal-Mart, IKEA, Inditex, Nike, Red Bull* (Munich, 2015), pp. 77–100.

Kreutzmüller, Christoph, *Ausverkauf. Die Vernichtung der jüdischen Gewerbetätigkeit in Berlin 1930–1945*, 2nd edition (Berlin, 2013).

La Porta, Rafael et al., "Law and Finance", *Journal of Political Economy* 106/6, 1998, pp. 1113–1155.

La Porta, Rafael, López De Silanes, Florencio and Shleifer, Anrei, "Corporate Ownership around the World", *Journal of Finance* 54/2, 1999, pp. 471–517.

Lamoreaux, Naomi R., "Partnerships, Corporations, and the Theory of the Firm", *American Economic Review* 88/2, 1998, pp. 66–71.

Lamoreaux, Naomi R., "Partnerships, Corporations, and the Limits on Contractual Freedom in U.S. History: An Essay in Economics, Law, and Culture", in Ken Lipartito and David B. Sicilia (eds.), *Constructing Corporate America: History, Politics, Culture* (Oxford/New York, 2004), pp. 29–65.

Lamoreaux, Naomi R., "The Shape of the Firm. Partnerships and Corporations", in Regina Lee Blaszczyk and Philip Scranton (eds.), *Major Problems in American Business History* (New York, 2006), pp. 120–125.

Lamsfuß, Christoph and Wallau, Frank, *Die größten Familienunternehmen in Deutschland. Daten, Fakten, Potenziale – Ergebnisse der Frühjahrsbefragung 2012, Untersuchung im Auftrag des BDI e. V. und der Deutsche Bank AG* (Berlin/Frankfurt a. M., 2012).

Landes, David S., *Die Macht der Familie. Wirtschaftsdynastien in der Weltgeschichte* (Munich, 2006).

Landes, David S., *Dynasties: Fortunes and Misfortunes of the World's Great Family Businesses* (New York, 2006).

Landes, David S., "French Business and the Businessman. A Social and Cultural Analysis", in Edward Mead Earle (ed.), *Modern France. Problems of the Third and Fourth Republics* (Princeton, NJ, 1951), pp. 334–353.

Lange, Heinrich, Erwerb, *Sicherung und Abwicklung der Erbschaft. 4. Denkschrift des Erbrechtsausschusses der Akademie für Deutsches Recht* (Tübingen, 1940).

Langenscheidt, Florian and Venohr, Bernd, *Lexikon der deutschen Weltmarktführer. Die Königsklasse deutscher Unternehmen in Wort und Bild* (Cologne, 2010).

Langenscheidt, Florian and Venohr, Bernd, *The Best of German Mittelstand. The World Market Leaders* (Cologne, 2015).

Lantelme, Maximilian, *The Rise and Downfall of Germany's Largest Family and Non-Family Businesses: A Historical Study and Strategic Analysis from 1971 to 2011* (Wiesbaden, 2017).

Larner, Robert J., *Management Control and the Large Corporation* (New York, 1970).

Larner, Robert, "Ownership and Control in the 200 Largest Non-Financial Corporations, 1929 and 1963", *American Economic Review* 56/3, 1967, pp. 777–787.

Leendertse, Julia, "Stiftungen boomen wie nie zuvor", *Die Zeit*, January 20, 2010.

Lemelsen, Joachim, "Zur Gründung der ersten niedersächsischen Wirtschaftsförderungsgesellschaft", *Neues Archiv für Niedersachsen. Landeskunde Landesentwicklung*, 18/1–4, 1969, pp. 71–71.

Lenger, Friedrich, *Sozialgeschichte der deutschen Handwerker seit 1800* (Frankfurt a. M., 1988).

Lilienthal, David Eli, *Big Business. A New Era* (New York, 1973).

Lipartito, Kenneth and Sicilia, David B. (eds.), *Constructing Corporate America: History, Politics, Culture* (Oxford, 2004).

Löffelholz, Josef, *Repetitorium der Betriebswirtschaftslehre*, 2nd edition (Wiesbaden, 1966).

Lohr-Kapfer, Gudrun, *Franz Lohr 125 Jahre, 1879–2004* (Ravensburg, 2004).

Loveman, Gary and Sengenberger, Werner, "The Re-emergence of Small-Scale Production: An International Comparison", *Small Business Economics* 3, 1991, pp. 1–37.

Löwe, Christian von (ed.), *Familienstiftungen: Gründung und Gestaltung – ein Leitfaden für Stifter und Berater* (Berlin, 2010).

Lubinski, Christina, *Familienunternehmen in Westdeutschland. Corporate Governance und Gesellschafterkultur seit den 1960er-Jahren* (Munich, 2010).

Lubinski, Christina, "Path Dependencies and the Choice of Governance in German Family Firms, 1850–2008", *Business History Review* 85/4, 2011, pp. 699–724.

Lundgreen, Peter, *Techniker in Preußen während der frühen Industrialisierung. Ausbildung und Berufsfeld einer entstehenden sozialen Gruppe* (Berlin, 1975).

Luttermann, Claus, *Unternehmen, Kapital und Genußrechte. Eine Studie über Grundlagen der Unternehmensfinanzierung und zum internationalen Kapitalmarktrecht* (Tübingen, 1998).

MacMillan, Whitney, "Power of Social Capital", *Harvard Management Update*, June 2006, pp. 3–6.

Mahr, Werner and Eisen, Roland, *Allgemeine Volkswirtschaftslehre. Grundlagen für die Versicherungswirtschaft*, 3rd edition (Wiesbaden, 1986).

Manly, Basil M., "Final Report of the Commission on Industrial Relations", in United States Senate (ed.), *Industrial Relations. Final Report and Testimony Submitted to Congress by the Commission on Industrial Relations* (Washington, D.C., 1915), pp. 1–252.

Marcus, George E. and Hall, Peter Dobkin, *Lives in Trust: The Fortunes of Dynastic Families in Late Twentieth-Century America* (Boulder, CO/Oxford, 1992).

Marcus, George E., "Law in the Development of Dynastic Families Among American Business Elites: The Domestication of Capital and the Capitalization of the Family", *Law and Society Review* 14/14, 1980, pp. 859–903.

Martin, Willian John and Moore, Ralph J., "The Small Business Investment Act of 1958", *California Law Review* 47/1, 1959, pp. 144–169.

Matis, Herbert, "Unternehmenskultur und Geschichte", in Wilfried Feldenkirchen (ed.), *Wirtschaft, Gesellschaft, Unternehmen. Festschrift für Hans Pohl zum 60. Geburtstag* (Stuttgart, 1995), pp. 1028–1053.

Mayo, Elton, *Probleme industrieller Arbeitsbedingungen* (Frankfurt a. M., 1949).

McCartney, Laton, *Friends in High Places: The Bechtel Story: The Most Secret Corporation and How It Engineered the World* (New York, 1988).

McCraw, Thomas K., *Prophets of Regulation* (Cambridge, MA, 1984).

McDonald, Forrest, *Insull. The Rise and Fall of a Billionaire Utility Tycoon*, (Chicago, IL, 1962).

McLane, Louis, *Documents Relative to the Manufactures in the United States, House of Representative Doc. 3008*, 2 vols (Washington, D.C., 1833).

Means, Gardiner C., "The Diffusion of Stock Ownership in the United States", in *The Quarterly Journal of Economics* 44/4, 1930, pp. 561–600.

Means, Gardiner C., "The Separation of Ownership and Control in American Industry", *The Quarterly Journal of Economics* 46/1, 1931, pp. 68–100.

Metzger, Ulrike and Weingarten, Joe, *Einkommensteuer und Einkommensteuerverwaltung in Deutschland. Ein historischer und verwaltungswissenschaftlicher Überblick* (Opladen, 1989).

Meyer zu Hörste, Gerhard, *Die Familienstiftung als Technik der Vermögensverewigung* (Göttingen, 1976).

Meyer-Stamer, Jörg and Wältring, Frank, *Behind the Myth of the Mittelstand Economy: The Institutional Environment Supporting Small and Medium-Sized Enterprises in Germany*, INEF-Report 46 (Duisburg, 2000).

Miller, Robert K. and McNamee, Stephen J. (eds.), *Inheritance and Wealth in America* (New York, 1998).

Miller, Robert K. and McNamee, Stephen J., "The Inheritance of Wealth in America", in Robert K. Miller and Stephen J. McNamee (eds.), *Inheritance and Wealth in America* (New York, 1998), pp. 1–22.

Mills, C. Wright, "The American Business Elite: A Collective Portrait", *Journal of Economic History* 5/S1, 1945, pp. 20–44.

Mitterauer, Michael, "Zur familienbetrieblichen Struktur im zünftischen Handwerk", in Michael Mitterauer (ed.), *Grundtypen alteuropäischer Sozialformen* (Stuttgart, 1980), pp. 98–122.

Mohnhaupt, Heinz, *Zur Geschichte des Familien- und Erbrechts. Politische Implikationen und Perspektiven* (Frankfurt a. M., 1987).

Moores, Ken, "Paradigms and Theory Building in the Domain of Business Families", *Family Business Review* 22/2, 2009, pp. 167–180.

Moores, Ken et al., "All the Same but Different: Understanding Family Enterprise Heterogeneity", in Esra Memil and Clay Dibrell (eds), *The Palgrave Handbook of Heterogeneity among Family Firms* (Cham, 2019), pp. 557–587.

Morck, Randall, "Why Some Double Taxation Might Make Sense: The Special Case of Intercorporate Dividends", *NBER Working Paper* 9651, 2003.

Morck, Randall and Yeung, Bernard, "Family Control and the Rent-Seeking Society", *Entrepreneurship Theory and Practice* 28/4, 2004, pp. 391–409.

Morck, Randall (ed.), *A History of Corporate Governance Around the World. Family Business Groups to Professional Managers* (Chicago, IL/London, 2007).

Morck, Randall and Steier, Lloyd, "The Global History of Corporate Governance: An Introduction", in Randall Morck (ed.), *A History of Corporate Governance around the World. Family Business Groups to Professional Managers* (Chicago, IL/London, 2007), pp. 1–64.

Moritz, Katja and Gesse, Marko, *Die Auswirkung des Sarbanes-Oxley Act auf deutsche Unternehmen*, Beiträge zum transnationalen Wirtschaftsrecht 49 (Halle, Saale 2005).

Mugler, Josef and Schmidt, Karl Heinz (eds.), *Klein- und Mittelunternehmen in einer dynamischen Wirtschaft. Ausgewählte Schriften von Hans Jobst Pleitner* (Munich, 1995).

Müller, Armin, "Von Familien- zu Parteibetrieben. Unternehmernachfolge und Elitenkontinuitäten in den beiden Leipziger Unternehmen Karl Krause und Gebrüder Brehmer (1945–1959)", in Gert Kollmer-von Oheimb-Loup and Clemens Wischermann (eds.), *Unternehmernachfolge in Geschichte und Gegenwart* (Ostfildern, 2008), pp. 181–208.

Müller, Margit (ed.), *Structure and Strategy of Small and Medium-Size Enterprises since the Industrial Revolution* (Stuttgart, 1994).

Murphy, Ralph William, *Small Business Ideology: An in-Depth Study*, Ph.D. diss (University of Washington, 1978).

Myers, Stewart C. and Majluf, Nicholas S., "Corporate Financing and Investment Decisions. When Firms Have Information That Investors Do Not Have", *Journal of Financial Economics* 13, 1984, pp. 187–221.

Naujoks, Wilfried, *Unternehmensgrößenbezogene Strukturpolitik und gewerblicher Mittelstand* (Göttingen, 1975).

Naujoks, Wilfried, *Mittelstand 1983. Lage im Wettbewerb und betriebswirtschaftliche Praxis* (Göttingen, 1983).

Nenova, Tatiana, "The Value of Corporate Voting Rights and Control: A Cross-Country Analysis", *Journal of Financial Economics* 68, 2003, pp. 325–351.

Neubauer, Fred and Lank, Alden G., *The Family Business: Its Governance for Sustainability* (New York, 1998).

Neubauer, Herbert, "The Dynamics of Succession in Family Businesses in Western European Countries", *Family Business Review* 16/4, 2003, pp. 269–281.

Noon, Mark A., *Yuengling. A History of America's Oldest Brewery* (Jefferson, NC, 2007).

Nowak, Eric, Ehrhardt, Olaf and Weber, Felix Michael, "Running in the Family. The Evolution of Ownership, Control, and Performance in German Family-Owned Firms, 1903–2003", *Swiss Finance Institute Research Paper* 06–13, 2006.

O'Brian, Anthony Patrick, "Factory Size, Economics of Scale, and the Great Merger Wave of 1898–1902", *Journal of Economic History* 48/3, 1988, pp. 639–649.

Odaka, Konosuke and Minoru, Sawai (eds.), *Small Business, Large Concerns. The Development of Small Business in Comparative Perspective* (Oxford/New York, 1999).

Oetker, Arend, *Wachstumssicherung von Familienunternehmen* (Munich, 1969).

Okoroafo, Sam C., "Internationalization of Family Businesses: Evidence from Northwest Ohio, U.S.A", *Family Business Review* 12/2, 1999, pp. 147–158.

Opresnik, Marc Oliver, *Unternehmenskultur in den USA und Deutschland: ein landeskundlicher Vergleich unter dem Gesichtspunkt der Anpassungsfähigkeit*, Ph.D. diss. (Hamburg Univ, 1999).

Osterkamp, Rigmar, "Insolvenzen in ausgewählten OECD-Ländern. Umfang, Tendenzen, Gesetze", *ifo Schnelldienst* 59/9, 2006, pp. 22–29.

O'Sullivan, Mary, *Contests for Corporate Control: Corporate Governance and Economic Performance in the United States and Germany* (Oxford, 2000).

Owens, Alastair, "Inheritance and the Life-Cycle of Family Firms in the Early Industrial Revolution", *Business History* 44/1, 2002, pp. 21–46.

Passow, Richard, *Die Aktiengesellschaft. Eine wirtschaftswissenschaftliche Studie*, 2nd edition (Jena, 1922).

Pellens, Bernhard and Füllbier, Rolf Uwe, "Anforderungen an die Rechnungslegung und Publizität internationaler Unternehmen", in Ulrich Krystek and Eberhard Zur (eds.), *Internationalisierung. Eine Herausforderung für die Unternehmensführung* (Berlin, 1997), pp. 423–443.

Patel, Kiran Klaus, *The New Deal. A Global History* (Princeton, 2016).

Perry, Mark J., "Fortune 500 firms in 1955 vs. 2014. 88% are gone, and we're all better off because of that dynamic 'creative destruction'", in *Aeladeas. A Public Policy Blog from AEI*, August 18, 2014, http://www.aei.org/publication/fortune-500-firms-in-1955-vs-2014–89-are-gone-and-were-all-better-off-because-of-that-dynamic-creative-destruction/ (accessed: August 24, 2018).

Pfannenschwarz, Armin, *Nachfolge und Nicht-Nachfolge im Familienunternehmen* (Heidelberg, 2005).

Pieper, Christian, "Dauerbrenner. Tücken der Erbschaftsteuer", *Unternehmermagazin* 58/4, 2010, pp. 42–43.

Piore, Michael J. and Sabel, Charles F., *Das Ende der Massenproduktion. Studie über die Requalifizierung der Arbeit und die Rückkehr der Ökonomie in die Gesellschaft* (Berlin, 1985).

Plagge, Arnd, "Die Venture-Capital-Märkte der USA und der Bundesrepublik Deutschland. Eine Gegenüberstellung", Working Paper Series (FU Berlin, 2001), unpublished.

Plate, Markus et al., *Große deutsche Familienunternehmen. Generationenfolge, Familienstrategie und Unternehmensentwicklung* (Göttingen, 2011).

Plate, Markus and Groth, Stefan, "Streben nach Resilienz. Unternehmensstrategien über Generationen", *Unternehmermagazin* 58/7, 2010, pp. 42–43.

Pohl, Manfred, "Das Symbol für Freiheit und Stabilität. Die D-Mark", in Carl Ludwig Holtfrerich, Harold James and Manfred Pohl (eds.), *Requiem auf eine Währung. Die Mark 1873–2001* (Stuttgart, 2001), pp. 7–59.

Polke-Majewski, Karsten, "Wal-Mart gibt auf", *Die Zeit*, July 28, 2006.

Potthast, Thilo, *Die Entwicklung der Körperschaftsteuer von den Vorformen bis zur Unternehmenssteuerreform 2001. Eine Untersuchung körperschaftsteuerlicher Entwicklungstendenzen in Steuergesetzgebung und Steuergestaltung* (Frankfurt a. M., 2008).

Prinz, Gustav Adolf, *Die mittelständische Erbunternehmung* (Cologne, 1966).

Pross, Helge, *Manager und Aktionäre in Deutschland. Untersuchungen zum Verhältnis von Eigentum und Verfügungsmacht* (Frankfurt a. M., 1965).

Rajan, Raghuram G. and Zingales, Luigi, "The Great Reversals: The Politics of Financial Development in the Twentieth Century", *Journal of Financial Economics* 69, 2003, no. 1, pp. 5–50.

Rau, Sabine B., *Familienunternehmen. Theoretische und empirische Grundlagen*, 3rd edition (Lohmar, 2010).

Rauh-Kühne, Cornelia, "Zwischen 'verantwortlichem Wirkungskreis' und 'häuslichem Glanz'. Zur Innenansicht wirtschaftsbürgerlicher Familien im 20. Jahrhundert", in Dieter Ziegler (ed.), *Großbürger und Unternehmer. Die deutsche Wirtschaftselite im 20. Jahrhundert* (Göttingen, 2000), pp. 215–248.

Reckendrees, Alfred, "Historische Wurzeln der Deutschland AG", in Ralf Ahrens, Boris Gehlen and Alfred Reckendrees (eds.), *Die "Deutschland AG". Historische Annäherungen an den bundesdeutschen Kapitalismus* (Essen, 2013), pp. 57–84.

Reichsgruppe Industrie (ed.), *Gliederung der Reichsgruppe Industrie. Der Aufbau der gewerblichen Wirtschaft in Einzeldarstellungen* (Leipzig, 1941).

Reif, Heinz, *Die Familie in der Geschichte* (Göttingen, 1982).

Reif, Heinz, "Väterliche Gewalt und 'kindliche Narrheit'. Familienkonflikte im katholischen Adel Westfalens vor der Französischen Revolution", in Heinz Reif (ed.), *Die Familie in der Geschichte* (Göttingen, 1982), pp. 82–113.

Reith, Reinhold and Schmidt, Dorothea (eds.), *Kleine Betriebe, angepasste Technologie? Hoffnungen, Erfahrungen und Ernüchterungen aus sozial- und technikhistorischer Sicht* (Münster, 2002).

Reitmayer, Morten, *Bankiers im Kaiserreich. Sozialprofil und Habitus der deutschen Hochfinanz* (Göttingen, 1999).

Rey-Garcia, Marta and Puig Raposo, Nuria, "Globalization and the Organisation of Family Philanthropy. A Case of Isomorphism?", *Business History* 55/2, 2013, pp. 1–28.

Richter, Klaus W., *Die Wirkungsgeschichte des deutschen Kartellrechts vor 1914. Eine rechtshistorisch-analytische Untersuchung* (Tübingen, 2007).

Richter, Ralf, "'Is Friendly Co-operation Worth While?' Die Netzwerke der Werkzeugmaschinenbauer von Chemnitz (Deutschland) und Cincinnati (USA), 1890er bis 1930er Jahre", in Hartmut Berghoff and Jörg Sydow (eds.), *Unternehmerische Netzwerke. Eine historische Organisationsform mit Zukunft?* (Stuttgart, 2007), pp. 143–173.

Riehl, Wilhelm Heinrich, *Die Naturgeschichte des Volkes als Grundlage einer deutschen Social-Politik (Vol. 3: Die Familie)*, 3rd edition (Stuttgart/Augsburg, 1855).

Ritschl, Albrecht, "Soziale Marktwirtschaft in der Praxis", in Werner Abelshauser (ed.), *Das Bundeswirtschaftsministerium in der Ära der Sozialen Marktwirtschaft. Der deutsche Weg der Wirtschaftspolitik* (Berlin/Boston, MA, 2016), pp. 265–389.

Roberge, Michael W. et al., "Lengthening the Investment Time Horizon", *White Paper Series,* July 2016.

Rödder, Andreas, "Vom Materialismus zum Postmaterialismus? Ronald Ingleharts Diagnosen des Wertewandels, ihre Grenzen und Perspektiven", *Zeithistorische Forschungen/Studies in Contemporary History* 3/3, 2006, pp. 480–485.

Rödiger, Werner, Schumacher, Herbert and Demel, Wilfried (eds.), *Wachsen und Werden. Biographie der Unternehmerfamilie Knauf* (Iphofen, 2003).

Roethlisberger, Fritz Jules and Dickson, Walter J., *Management and the Worker* (Cambridge, MA, 1939).

Rommel, Gunter, *Simplicity Wins: How Germany's Mid-sized Industrial Companies Succeed* (Boston, MA, 1995).

Rose, Mary B., *Firms, Networks and Business Values: The British and American Cotton Industry since 1750* (Cambridge, MA, 2000).

Rosenbaum, Heidi, *Formen der Familie. Untersuchungen zum Zusammenhang von Familienverhältnissen, Sozialstruktur und sozialem Wandel in der deutschen Gesellschaft des 19. Jahrhunderts* (Frankfurt a. M., 1990).

Rosenberg, Charles E. (ed.), *The Family in History* (Philadelphia, PA, 1975).

Rosenberger, Ruth, "Von der sozialpolitischen zur personalpolitischen Transformationsstrategie. Zur Verwissenschaftlichung betrieblicher Personalpolitik in westdeutschen Unternehmen 1945–1980", *Zeitschrift für Unternehmensgeschichte* 50, 2005, pp. 63–82.

Rothacher, Albrecht, "Mars Inc.: More than Candies and Cat Food", in Albrecht Rothacher (ed.), *Corporate Cultures and Global Brands* (Singapore, 2004), pp. 19–39.

Rüsen, Tom A., Schlippe, Arist von and Groth, Torsten, *Familienunternehmen. Exploration einer Unternehmensform* (Lohmar, 2009).

Rutterford, Janette and Sotiropoulos, Dimitris P., "The Rise of the Small Investor in the US and the UK, 1895 to 1970", *Enterprise & Society* 18, 2017, pp. 485–535.

Sachse, Wieland, "Familienunternehmen in Wirtschaft und Gesellschaft bis zur Mitte des 20. Jahrhunderts. Ein historischer Überblick", *Zeitschrift für Unternehmensgeschichte* 36, 1991, pp. 9–25.

Sackmann, Sonja A., *Unternehmenskultur. Erkennen – Entwickeln – Verändern* (Wiesbaden, 2017).

Sandage, Scott A., *Born Losers. A History of Failure in America* (Cambridge, MA, 2005).

Sarachek, Bernard, "American Entrepreneurs and the Horatio Alger Myth", *Journal of Economic History* 38, 1978, pp. 439–456.

Sawyer, John, "The Entrepreneur and the Social Order. France and the United States", in William Miller (ed.), *Men in Business. Essays in the History of Entrepreneurship* (Cambridge, MA, 1952), pp. 7–22.

Schader, Norwin, *Staatliche Steuerungsfähigkeit unter den Bedingungen der Globalisierung* (Münster, 2006).

Schanetzky, Tim, *Regierungsunternehmer. Henry J. Kaiser, Friedrich Flick und die Staatskonjunkturen in den USA und Deutschland* (Göttingen, 2015).

Schardt, Anne and Weiler, Heinrich, *Aspekte der Erbschaftsbesteuerung* (Göttingen, 1980).

Schefer, Benjamin C., *Das Verbot der vertikalen Preisbindung. Eine betriebswirtschaftliche Analyse am Beispiel der Lebensmittelbranche* (Wiesbaden, 2013).

Schelsky, Helmut, *Wandlungen der deutschen Familie in der Gegenwart. Darstellungen und Deutung einer empirisch-soziologischen Tatbestandsaufnahme* (Dortmund, 1953).

Scherer, Stephan, *Familienunternehmen. Erfolgsstrategien zur Unternehmenssicherung* (Frankfurt a. M., 2005).

Scheybani, Abdolreza, *Handwerk und Kleinhandel in der Bundesrepublik Deutschland. Sozialökonomischer Wandel und Mittelstandspolitik 1949–1961* (Munich, 1996).

Schielke, Joachim E., "Vertrauen durch Kontinuität. Unternehmensnachfolge bei mittelständischen Familienunternehmen aus Sicht einer Bank", in Gert Kollmer-von Oheimb-Loup and Clemens Wischermann (eds.), *Unternehmernachfolge in Geschichte und Gegenwart* (Ostfildern, 2008), pp. 85–104.

Schivelbusch, Wolfgang, *Entfernte Verwandtschaft. Faschismus, Nationalsozialismus und New Deal 1933–1939* (Munich, 2005).

Schlippe, Arist von, Groth, Torsten and Plate, Markus, "Entscheidungsfähigkeit sicherstellen. Familienstrategie und Familienmanagement in Familienunternehmen", in Markus Plate et al. (eds.), *Große deutsche Familienunternehmen. Generationenfolge, Familienstrategie und Unternehmensentwicklung* (Göttingen, 2011), pp. 522–560.

Schmidt, Matthias, *Ziele und Instrumente der Mittelstandspolitik in der Bundesrepublik Deutschland* (Cologne, 1988).

Schmidt, Reinhard H., "Corporate Governance in Germany. An Economic Perspective", in Reinhard H. Schmidt and Jan P. Krahnen (eds.), *The German Financial System* (Oxford, 2004), pp. 386–424.

Schneider, Annette, *Unternehmensstiftungen. Formen, Rechnungslegung, steuerliche Gestaltungsmöglichkeiten* (Berlin, 2004).

Scholtyseck, Joachim, *Freudenberg. Ein Familienunternehmen in Kaiserreich, Demokratie und Diktatur* (Munich, 2016).

Schönherr, Karlheinz, *Nach oben geschraubt. Reinhold Würth. Die Karriere eines Unternehmers* (Künzelsau, 2001).

Schröder, Susanne, *Steuerlastgestaltung der Aktiengesellschaften und Veranlagung zur Körperschaftsteuer im Deutschen Reich und den USA von 1918 bis 1936. Ein Beitrag zum Problem der Besteuerung in der Demokratie* (Berlin, 1996).

Schumann, Dirk, *Bayerns Unternehmer in Gesellschaft und Staat, 1834–1914* (Göttingen, 1992).

Schwarz, Thomas V., "Industrial Family Businesses in Germany. Continuity in Change by Gunter Kayser, Frank Wallau", *Family Business Review* 15/2, 2002, pp. 116–118.

Schwarzkopf, Christian, *Fostering Innovation and Entrepreneurship: Entrepreneurial Ecosystem and Entrepreneurial Fundamentals in the USA and Germany* (Wiesbaden, 2016).

Schwetlick, Wolfgang B. and Lessing, Rainer, "Bilanz des Versagens", *manager magazin*, March 3, 1977, pp. 26–33.

Scranton, Philip, *Proprietary Capitalism. The Textile Manufacture in Philadelphia 1800–1885* (Cambridge, MA, 1983).

Scranton, Philip, *Endless Novelty. Specialty Production and American Industrialisation, 1865–1925* (Princeton, NJ, 1998).

Scranton, Philip, "Diversity in Diversity", *Business History Review* 65, 1991, pp. 27–90.

Scranton, Philip, "Small Business, Family Firms, and Batch Production: Three Axes for Development in American Business History", *Business and Economic History* 20, 1991, pp. 99–106.

Scranton, Philip, "Understanding the Strategy and Dynamics of Long-Lived Family Firms", *Business and Economic History* 21 (2nd Series), 1992, pp. 219–227.

Scranton, Philip, "Build a Firm, Start Another: The Bromleys and Family Firm Entrepreneurship in the Philadelphia Region", *Business History* 35/4, 1993, pp. 115–151.

Scranton, Philip, "Manufacturing Diversity. Production Systems, Markets, and an American Consumer Society, 1870–1930", *Technology and Culture* 35, 1994, pp. 476–505.

Seer, Roman, "Das Betriebsvermögen im Erbschaftsteuerrecht, 23. Jahrestagung der DStJG e.V. in Münster im Sept. 1998", in Dieter Birk (ed.), *Steuern auf Erbschaft und Vermögen*, Vol. 22 (Cologne, 1999), pp. 191–216.

Servan-Schreiber, Jean-Jacques, *Die amerikanische Herausforderung*, 5th edition (Hamburg, 1968).

Sethe, Rolf, "Historische Entwicklung der Vermögensverwaltung", in Frank A. Schäfer, Rolf Sethe and Volker Lang (eds.), *Handbuch der Vermögensverwaltung* (Munich, 2012), pp. 20–33.

Shanker, Melissa C. and Astrachan, Joseph H., "Myths and Realities: Family Businesses' Contribution to the US Economy—A Framework for Assessing Family Business Statistics", *Family Business Review* 9/2, 1996, pp. 107–123.

Siegrist, Hannes, "Die Propertisierung von Gesellschaft und Kultur. Konstruktion und Institutionalisierung des Eigentums in der Moderne", *Comparativ.*

Zeitschrift für Globalgeschichte und Vergleichende Gesellschaftsforschung 16/5–6, 2006, pp. 9–52.

Siemens, Werner von, *Lebenserinnerungen* (Munich/Zurich, 2008).

Siemens, Werner von, *Recollections* (Munich, 2008).

Simon, Hermann, "'Hidden Champions': Speerspitze der deutschen Wirtschaft", *Zeitschrift für Betriebswirtschaft* 60, 1990, pp. 875–890.

Simon, Hermann, *Die heimlichen Gewinner (Hidden Champions). Die Erfolgsstrategien unbekannter Weltmarktführer* (Frankfurt a. M., 1996).

Simon, Hermann, *Hidden Champions des 21. Jahrhunderts. Die Erfolgsstrategien unbekannter Weltmarktführer* (Frankfurt a. M., 2007).

Simon, Hermann, *Hidden Champions. Aufbruch nach Globalia. Die Erfolgsstrategien unbekannter Weltmarktführer* 2nd edition (Frankfurt a. M., 2012).

Simon, Hermann, "Gespräch 'Die Faszination für Hidden Champions ist in China stark'", *FuS – Zeitschrift für Familienunternehmen und Strategie* 8/5, 2018, pp. 145–147.

Sklar, Martin J., *The Corporate Reconstruction of American Capitalism, 1890–1916. The Market, the Law, and Politics* (Cambridge, MA, 1988).

Soltow, James H., "Origins of Small Business Metal Fabricators and Machinery Makers in New England, 1890–1957", *Transactions of the American Philosophical Society* 5/December, 1965, pp. 1–58.

Spiekermann, Uwe, *Basis der Konsumgesellschaft. Entstehung und Entwicklung des modernen Kleinhandels in Deutschland 1850–1914* (Munich, 1999).

Spindler, Gerald, *Recht und Konzern. Interdependenzen der Rechts- und Unternehmensentwicklung in Deutschland und den USA zwischen 1870 und 1933* (Tübingen, 1993).

Spitz, Maria et al. (eds.), *Phänomen Familienunternehmen. Überblicke* (Mettingen, 2016).

Spoerer, Mark, *Vom Scheingewinn zum Rüstungsboom. Die Eigenkapitalrendite der deutschen Industrieaktiengesellschaften 1925–1941.* Vierteljahrschrift für Sozial- und Wirtschaftsgeschichte, Beiheft 123 (Stuttgart, 1996).

Spoerer, Mark, *C&A. Ein Familienunternehmen in Deutschland, den Niederlanden und Großbritannien 1911–1961* (Munich, 2016).

Stamm, Friedrich H., *Die Bundesfinanzen der Vereinigten Staaten von Amerika. Entwicklung und gegenwärtiger Stand* (Stuttgart, 1969).

Stamm, Isabell, *Unternehmerfamilien. Der Einfluss des Unternehmens auf Lebenslauf, Generationenbeziehungen und soziale Identität* (Berlin, 2013).

Stamm, Isabell and Lubinski, Christina, "Crossroads of Family Business Research and Firm Demography. A Critical Assessment of Family Business Survival Rates", *Journal of Family Business Strategy* 2/3, 2011, pp. 117–127.

Stamm, Isabell, Breitschmid, Peter and Kohli, Martin (eds.), *Doing Succession in Europe. Generational Transfers in Family Businesses in Comparative Perspective* (Zurich, 2011).

Steier, Lloyd, "Family Firms, Plural Forms of Governance, and the Evolving Role of Trust", *Family Business Review* 14, 2001, pp. 353–367.

Steindl, Joseph, *Small and Big Business. Economic Problems of the Size of Firms* (Oxford, 1947).

Steindl, Joseph, "Some Evidence of Concentration", in Vincent P. Carosso and Stuart Weems Bruchey (eds.), *The Survival of Small Business* (New York, 1979), pp. 48–62.

Steiner, André, *Von Plan zu Plan. Eine Wirtschaftsgeschichte der DDR* (Berlin, 2007).

Steingart, Gabor, "Er oder ich", *Der Spiegel*, August 5, 2002, pp. 90–94.

Stiefel, Dieter, *Im Labor der Niederlagen. Konkurspolitik im internationalen Vergleich* (Vienna, 2008).

Stiftung Familienunternehmen (ed.), *Die Kapitalmarktfähigkeit von Familienunternehmen. Unternehmensfinanzierung über Schuldschein, Anleihe und Börsengang* (Munich, 2011).

Stiftung Familienunternehmen (ed.), *Das neue Erbschaft- und Schenkungsteuerrecht. Was ändert sich für Familienunternehmen?* (Munich, 2016).

Stiftung Familienunternehmen (ed.), *Country Index for Family Businesses*, 6th edition (Munich, 2016).

Stiftung Familienunternehmen (ed.), *Länderindex Familienunternehmen. Erbschaftsteuer im internationalen Vergleich* (Munich, 2017).

Stiftung Familienunternehmen (ed.), *Die volkswirtschaftliche Bedeutung der Familienunternehmen* (Munich, 2017).

Stiftung Familienunternehmen (ed.), *Länderindex Familienunternehmen*, 7th edition (Munich, 2019).

Stiftung Familienunternehmen (ed.), *Industrielle Familienunternehmen in Ostdeutschland. Von der Jahrhundertwende bis zur Gegenwart* (Munich, 2019).

Stremmel, Ralf, "Die Familie Selve und ihr Unternehmen (1861–1977). Möglichkeiten und Grenzen einer historischen Analyse von Familienunternehmen", in Karl-Peter Ellerbrock, Nancy Bodden and Margrit Schulte Beerbühl (eds.), *Kultur, Strategien und Netzwerke. Familienunternehmen in Westfalen im 19. und 20. Jahrhundert* (Münster, 2014), pp. 13–44.

Stupp, Matthias, *GmbH-Recht im Nationalsozialismus. Anschauungen des Nationalsozialismus zur Haftungsbeschränkung, juristischen Person, Kapitalgesellschaft und Treupflicht. Untersuchungen zum Referentenentwurf 1939 zu einem neuen GmbH-Gesetz* (Berlin, 2002).

Stürmer, Michael, *Herbst des Alten Handwerks* (Munich, 1979).

Tabor, William et al., "The Heterogeneity of Family Firm Ethical Cultures: Current Insights and Future Directions", in Esra Memiland Clay Dibrell (eds), *The Palgrave Handbook of Heterogeneity among Family Firms* (Cham, 2019), pp. 615–642.

Tagiuri, Renato and Davis, John, "Bivalent Attributes of the Family Firm", in *Family Business Review* 9/2, 1996, pp. 199–208.

Tatzkow, Monika, "Privatindustrie ohne Perspektive. Der 'Versuch zur Liquidierung der mittleren privaten Warenproduzenten'", in Jochen Cernij (ed.), *Brüche,*

Krisen und Wendepunkte. Neubefragung von DDR-Geschichte (Berlin, 1990), pp. 97–103.

Tocqueville, Alexis de, *Democracy in America*, translated by Henry Reeve (New York, 1899) [1835].

Tönnies, Ferdinand, *Gemeinschaft und Gesellschaft. Abhandlung des Communismus und des Socialismus als empirischer Culturformen* (Leipzig, 1887).

Tooze, Adam J., *Ökonomie der Zerstörung. Die Geschichte der Wirtschaft im National-sozialismus* (Bonn, 2007).

Trompenaars, Fons, *Riding the Waves of Culture. Understanding Cultural Diversity in Business* (London, 1993).

Tuckman, Howard P., *The Economics of the Rich* (New York, 1973).

Uhlaner, Lorraine M., "Family Business and Corporate Governance", in Mike Wright et al. (eds.), *The Oxford Handbook of Corporate Governance* (Oxford, 2013), pp. 389–420.

Ulin, Robert C., "Work as Cultural Production. Labour and Self-Identity Among Southwest French Wine-Growers", *Royal Anthropological Institute News* 8, 2002, pp. 691–712.

Ullmann, Hans Peter, *Interessenverbände in Deutschland* (Frankfurt a. M., 1988).

Ullmann, Hans Peter, *Der deutsche Steuerstaat. Geschichte der öffentlichen Finanzen vom 18. Jahrhundert bis heute* (Munich, 2005).

Veblen, Thorstein, *The Theory of Business Enterprise* (New Brunswick, NJ, 1978, re-print of the first edition 1904).

Venohr, Bernd, *Wachsen wie Würth. Das Geheimnis des Welterfolgs* (Frankfurt a. M./New York, 2006).

Venohr, Bernd, "Das Erfolgsmodell der deutschen Weltmarktführer", in Bernd Venohr and Florian Langenscheid (eds.), *Lexikon der deutschen Weltmarktführer* (Cologne, 2015).

Venohr, Bernd, Fear, Jeffrey and Witt, Alessa, "Best of German Mittelstand. The World Market Leaders", in Florian Langenscheid and Bernd Venohr (eds.), *The Best of German Mittelstand. The World Market Leaders* (Cologne, 2015), pp. 5–22.

Villalonga, Belen and Amit, Raphael, "How do Family Ownership, Control and Management Affect Firm Value", *Journal of Financial Economics* 80, 2006, pp. 385–417.

Villalonga, Belen and Amit, Raphael, "How Are U.S. Family Firms Controlled?", *Review of Financial Studies* 22/8, 2009, pp. 3047–3091.

Vorwerck, Karl and Dunkmann, D. Karl, *Die Werksgemeinschaft in historischer und soziologischer Beleuchtung* (Berlin, 1928).

Ward, John L., "The Active Board with Outside Directors and the Family Firm", *Family Business Review* 1/3, 1988, pp. 223–229.

Ward, John L., *Perpetuating the Family Business. 50 Lessons Learned from Long-lasting, Successful Families in Business* (Basingstoke, 2004).

Ward, John L., *Keeping the Family Business Healthy. How to Plan for Continuing Growth, Profitability, and Family Leadership* (New York, 2011).

Weber, Felix Michael, "Monetäre und nicht-monetäre Werttreiber von Unternehmensdynastien. Dimensionen der Performance in Deutschlands Mehrgenerationen-Familienunternehmen", in Gert Kollmer-von Oheimb-Loup and Clemens Wischermann (eds.), *Unternehmernachfolge in Geschichte und Gegenwart* (Ostfildern, 2008), pp. 153–163.

Weber-Kellermann, Ingeborg, *Die deutsche Familie. Versuch einer Sozialgeschichte*, 4th edition (Frankfurt a. M., 1996).

Weiblen, Willi, "Mittelstandspolitik vor der Herausforderung einer drohenden Nachfolgerlücke", in Gert Kollmer-von Oheimb-Loup and Clemens Wischermann (eds.), *Unternehmernachfolge in Geschichte und Gegenwart* (Ostfildern, 2008), pp. 173–179.

Weinberg, Neil, "Going Against the Grain", *Forbes*, November 25, 2002, pp. 158–168.

Welskopp, Thomas, "Unternehmenskulturen im internationalen Vergleich – oder integrale Unternehmensgeschichte in typisierender Absicht?", in Hartmut Berghoff and Jakob Vogel (eds.), *Wirtschaftsgeschichte als Kulturgeschichte. Dimensionen eines Perspektivenwechsels* (Frankfurt a. M., 2004), pp. 265–294.

Wernicke, Johannes, *Kapitalismus und Mittelstandspolitik*, 2nd edition (Jena, 1922).

Whittington, Richard and Mayer, Michael, *The European Corporation. Strategy, Structure and Social Science* (Oxford, 2000).

Wiechers, Ralph, *Familienmanagement zwischen Unternehmen und Familien. Zur Handhabung typischer Eigenarten von Unternehmensfamilien und Familienunternehmen* (Heidelberg, 2005).

Wien, Andreas et al., "Grundlagen der Unternehmenskultur", in Andreas Wien and Normen Franzke (eds.), Unternehmenskultur, Wiesbaden 2014, pp. 29–45.

Will, Martin, *Selbstverwaltung der Wirtschaft. Recht und Geschichte der Selbstverwaltung in den Industrie- und Handelskammern, Handwerksinnungen, Kreishandwerkerschaften, Handwerkskammern und Landwirtschaftskammern* (Tübingen, 2010).

Wimmer, Rudolf, Groth, Torsten and Simon, Fritz B., *Erfolgsmuster von Mehrgenerationen-Familienunternehmen* (Witten, 2004).

Wimmer, Rudolf et al., *Familienunternehmen. Auslaufmodell oder Erfolgstyp?*, 2nd edition (Wiesbaden, 2005).

Winkler, Heinrich August, "Vom Protest zur Panik. Der gewerbliche Mittelstand in der Weimarer Republik", in Hans Mommsen, Dietmar Petzina and Bernd Weisbrod (eds.), *Industrielles System und politische Entwicklung in der Weimarer Republik* (Kronberg, 1974), pp. 778–791.

Winkler, Heinrich August, "Der entbehrliche Stand. Zur Mittelstandspolitik im 'Dritten Reich'", *Archiv für Sozialgeschichte* 17, 1977, pp. 1–40.

Winkler, Heinrich August, "Stabilisierung durch Schrumpfung. Der gewerbliche Mittelstand in der Bundesrepublik", in Werner Conze and Mario Rainer Lepsius (eds.), *Sozialgeschichte der Bundesrepublik Deutschland. Beiträge zum Kontinuitätsproblem* (Stuttgart, 1983), pp. 187–219.

Wischermann, Clemens, "Die Erbschaftsteuer im Kaiserreich und in der Weimarer Republik. Finanzprinzip versus Familienprinzip", in Eckart Schremmer (ed.), *Steuern, Abgaben und Dienste vom Mittelalter bis zur Gegenwart* (Stuttgart, 1994), pp. 171–196.

Wischermann, Clemens, "'Mein Erbe ist das Vaterland'". Sozialreform und Staatserbrecht im Kaiserreich und in der Weimarer Republik", in Frank Lettke (ed.), *Erben und Vererben. Gestaltung und Regulation von Generationenbeziehungen* (Konstanz, 2003), pp. 31–58.

Wittgens, Jonas, *Das Spruchverfahrensgesetz*, Berlin 2005.

Wixforth, Harald and Ziegler, Dieter, "'Bankenmacht'. Universal Banking and German Industry in Historical Perspective", in Youssef Cassis, Gerald D. Feldman and Ulf Olsson (eds.), *The Evolution of Financial Institutions and Markets in Twentieth-Century Europe* (Aldershot, 1995), pp. 249–272.

Zachary, Ramona K., "The Importance of the Family System in Family Business", *Journal of Family Business Management* 1/1, 2011, pp. 26–36.

Zahra, Shaker A., "International Expansion of U.S. Manufacturing Family Businesses. The Effect of Ownership and Involvement", *Journal of Business Venturing* 18/4, 2003, pp. 495–512.

Zeigler, Luther Harmon, *The Politics of Small Business* (Washington, D.C., 1961).

Zeitel, Gerhard, "Die Familienunternehmen in der Bundesrepublik Deutschland", *Zeitschrift für Unternehmensgeschichte* 36, 1991, pp. 27–35.

Zeitlin, Maurice, "Corporate Ownership and Control: The Large Corporation and the Capitalist Class", *American Journal of Sociology* 79/5, 1974, pp. 1073–1119.

Zellweger, Thomas M., *Managing the Family Business. Theory and Practice* (Cheltenham/Northhampton, 2017).

Zellweger, Thomas and Kammerlander, Nadine, *Family Business Groups in Deutschland. Generationenübergreifendes Unternehmertum in großen deutschen Unternehmerdynastien* (St. Gallen, 2014).

Zellweger, Thomas M. et al., "Building a Family Firm Image: How Family Firms Capitalize on their Family Ties", *Journal of Family Business Strategy* 3, 2012, pp. 239–250.

Zeumer, Sandra, *Die Nachfolge in Familienunternehmen. Drei Fallbeispiele aus dem Bergischen Land im 19. und 20. Jahrhundert* (Stuttgart 2012).

Zeumer, Sandra, "Nachfolgefinanzierung in Familienunternehmen. Der Nutzen sparsamer Vorfahren", in Susanne Hilger and Ulrich S. Soenius (eds.), *Familienunternehmen im Rheinland im 19. und 20. Jahrhundert. Netzwerke – Nachfolge – soziales Kapital* (Cologne, 2009), pp. 188–211.

Ziegler, Dieter, "Das Zeitalter der Industrialisierung", in Michael North (ed.), *Deutsche Wirtschaftsgeschichte. Ein Jahrtausend im Überblick* (Munich, 2000), pp. 192–281.

Ziegler, Dieter, "Die wirtschaftsbürgerliche Elite im 20. Jahrhundert: Eine Bilanz", in Dieter Ziegler (ed.), *Großbürger und Unternehmer. Die deutsche Wirtschaftselite im 20. Jahrhundert* (Göttingen, 2000), pp. 7–29.

Ziegler, Dieter, "Kontinuität und Diskontinuität der deutschen Wirtschaftselite 1900–1938", in Dieter Ziegler (ed.), *Großbürger und Unternehmer. Die deutsche Wirtschaftselite im 20. Jahrhundert* (Göttingen, 2000), pp. 31–53.

Ziegler, Dieter, "Das deutsche Modell bankorientierter Finanzsysteme (1848–1957)", in Paul Windolf (ed.), *Finanzmarkt-Kapitalismus* (Wiesbaden, 2005), pp. 276–294.

Zwack, Mirko, *Die Macht der Geschichten. Erzählungen als Form der Wertevermittlung in Familienunternehmen* (Heidelberg, 2011).

Statistical Collections

American Bankruptcy Institute (ed.), *Annual Business and Non-Business Filings by Year (1980–2017): Statistics from the Administrative Office of the US Courts*, https://s3.amazonaws.com/abi-org/Newsroom/Bankruptcy_Statistics/Total-Business-Consumer1980-Present.pdf (accessed: October 4, 2018).

Besser, Christoph, *Grunddaten der Bevölkerungsstatistik Deutschlands von 1871 bis 1939*, https://histat.gesis.org/histat/table/details/98A1BFDCBF8E69DAC7F4C FC5EBED536F (accessed: November 20, 2018).

Bundesministerium für Wirtschaft (ed.), *ERP-Hilfe zur Wirtschaftsförderung 1965* (Bonn 1965).

Bundesministerium für Wirtschaft (ed.), *ERP Programm, various years* (Bonn, 1972–1995).

Bundesministerium für Wirtschaft (ed.), *Mittelstandsfibel* (Bonn 1972).

Bundesministerium für Wirtschaft und Energie (ed.), *German Mittelstand: Motor der deutschen Wirtschaft, Zahlen und Fakten zu deutschen mittelständischen Unternehmen* (Berlin 2014).

Bundesverband Deutscher Stiftungen (ed.), *Zahlen, Daten, Fakten zum deutschen Stiftungswesen* (Berlin, 2014).

Bundeszentrale für politische Bildung (ed.) *Finanzierungsstruktur G-7-Staaten*, http://www.bpb.de/nachschlagen/zahlen-und-fakten/globalisierung/52587/finanzierungsstruktur-g-7 (accessed: November 15, 2018).

Center for Family Business, University of St. Gallen (ed.), *Global Family Business Index*, http://familybusinessindex.com/ (accessed: July 20, 2016).

Deutsche Ausgleichsbank, *Geschäftsberichte, various years* (Bonn, 1995–2000).

Deutsche Bundesbank (ed.), *Deutsches Geld- und Bankwesen in Zahlen 1876–1975* (Frankfurt a.M., 1976).

Deutsches Aktieninstitut (DAI), *Factbook 2013. Statistiken, Analysen und Graphiken zu Aktionären, Aktiengesellschaften und Börsen* (Frankfurt a. M., 2013).

Die Welt (ed.), *Top 500 Unternehmen*, http://top500.welt.de/list/2014/U/?i=10&p=1 (accessed: July 20, 2016).

Euler Hermes AG, *Exportgarantien der Bundesrepublik Deutschland. Jahresbericht 2014* (Hamburg, 2015).

Family Firm Institute (ed.), *Global Data Points*, https://archive.org/details/perma_cc_CF89-K2JB (accessed: December 13, 2018).

Fiedler, Martin and Gospel, Howard, "The Top 100 Largest Employers in UK and Germany in the Twentieth Century", *Cologne Economic History Paper* 3, 2010.

Forbes Magazine (ed.), *America's Largest Private Companies 2016*, https://www.forbes.com/largest-private-companies/list (accessed: September 2, 2018).

Fortune Magazine (ed.), *Fortune 500*, http://beta.fortune.com/fortune500/ (accessed: July 20, 2016).

KfW Bankengruppe, *Annual Reports* (Frankfurt a. M., various years).

OECD, *Gaps in Technology: General Report* (Paris, 1968).

Small Business Administration (ed.), *Agency Financial Report* (Washington, D.C., various years).

Small Business Administration (ed.), *Annual Reports* (Washington, D.C., various years).

Small Business Administration (ed.), *The State of Small Business. A Report of the President* (Washington, D.C., various years).

Statistisches Bundesamt (ed.), *Anzahl der Privatinsolvenzen in Deutschland von 2000 bis 2017*, https://de.statista.com/statistik/daten/studie/150565/umfrage/privatinsolvenzen-in-deutschland-seit-2000/ (accessed: October 4, 2018).

Statistisches Bundesamt (ed.), *Ehescheidungen im Zeitverlauf*, https://www.destatis.de/DE/ZahlenFakten/GesellschaftStaat/Bevoelkerung/Ehescheidungen/ (accessed: November 20, 2018).

Statistisches Bundesamt (ed.), *Sonderauswertung des Unternehmensregisters im Auftrag des IfM Bonn* (Wiesbaden, various years).

Statistisches Bundesamt (ed.), *Statistisches Jahrbuch für die Bundesrepublik Deutschland* (Stuttgart/Mainz, various years).

Statistisches Bundesamt (ed.), *Unternehmen und Arbeitsstätten, Series 2, No. 11, Arbeitsstätten, Unternehmen und Beschäftigte 1987, 1970, 1961, 1950* (Stuttgart, 1990).

Statistisches Bundesamt (ed.), *Wirtschaft und Statistik* (Stuttgart/Mainz, various years).

Statistisches Reichsamt (ed.), *Statistisches Jahrbuch für das Deutsche Reich* (Berlin, various years).

US Census Bureau (ed.), *Population Estimates*, http://www.census.gov/popest/estimates.html (accessed: November 20, 2018).

US Department of Commerce (ed.), *Company Summary: Survey of Business Owners 2002, Company Statistics Series* (Washington, D.C., 2006).

US Department of Commerce (ed.), *Company Summary: Survey of Business Owners 2012, Company Statistics Series* (Washington, D.C., 2016).

US Department of Commerce (ed.), *Enterprise Statistics, Part 1: General Report* (Washington, D.C., various years).

Index

This register lists only the personal or family names and *companies* mentioned in the text (not the footnotes).

About the Editor:
The Foundation for Family Businesses

More than 90 percent of all companies in Germany are family-owned. The purpose of the Foundation for Family Businesses, a non-profit organization, is to preserve the country's family-business landscape. The foundation is the most important sponsor of scientific research in this field, regularly commissioning studies into topics of relevance to family businesses. It supports the establishment and operation of related teaching and research institutions, and functions as a point of contact for media representatives and political decision-makers when it comes to the legal, tax and economic interests of family-owned businesses. The Foundation for Family Businesses is supported by more than 500 companies that are among the largest family enterprises in Germany.

This book is an extended and updated version of the study *Family Businesses in Germany and the USA since Industrialisation. A Long-Term Historical Study* by Prof. Hartmut Berghoff and Dr. Ingo Köhler, published in 2019 by the Foundation for Family Businesses (ISBN 978-3-942467-73-5).

Foundation for Family Businesses
Stiftung Familienunternehmen
Prinzregentenstraße 50
80538 Munich
Germany
Phone: +49 89 / 12 76 400 02
Fax: + 49 89 / 12 76 400 09
Email: info@familienunternehmen.de
www.familienunternehmen.de/en

Foundation for
Family Businesses